MIMESIS
INTERNATIONAL

PHILOSOPHY
n. 68

MICHAEL UEBEL

SEEDS OF EQUANIMITY
Knowing and Being

© 2025—MIMESIS INTERNATIONAL
www.mimesisinternational.com
e-mail: info@mimesisinternational.com

Isbn: 9788869774904
Book series: *Philosophy*, n. 68

© MIM Edizioni Srl
P.I. C.F. 02419370305

Cover Image: Unidentified artist, *Man Juggling His Own Head*, ca. 1880, published by Alain de Torbéchet et Cie.

CONTENTS

ILLUSTRATIONS	9
ACKNOWLEDGEMENTS	11

I.
FRAMING EQUANIMITY

1 CASTING SEEDS	15
Just Looking	17
Defining Equanimity	23
Equanimity Exempt from Curing	30
Pomegranate Seeds	34
In the Middle of All This	37
Opening Seeds	43
The Wise Old Men	49
2 THE VALUE OF TENDING	55
Growing a Human	57
Traversing Binaries	61
Levels of Magnification	68
Respect	71
The Unthinkable	74
The Mustard Seed	77
Tending	83
Tending the Garden	84

II.
EQUANIMITY AND KNOWLEDGE

3 SEEDS OF EQUANIMOUS KNOWING:	
GOETHEAN SOFT EMPIRICISM TO THE WAY OF TEA	91
Duke Mu's Horse	94
Goethe's Delicate Empiricism	97

Seeds of Consciousness	103
The Question of Knowledge	108
The Answer in Your Hands: Interlude on the Question of Knowledge	114
Pathways of Knowing	118

4 SEEDS OF EQUANIMOUS AWARENESS: MULTIPLYING PERSPECTIVES — 127
- Above All of This — 127
- "Where it Seems Best": Perspectivism and Greater Knowledge — 140
- The Necessity of Others — 146
- Thinking Aside — 150
- Of One Mind: Visions of Integration — 159

5 NATURALLY EQUANIMOUS: CONTEMPLATING A TREE — 185
- Ways of Perceiving a Tree — 185
- The Crooked Tree — 191
- Throwing Stones at a Tree — 205
- Contemplating a Tree — 216
- Attempting to Murder a Tree — 220

III.
EQUANIMITY AND IDENTITY

6 SUBJECTS OF EQUANIMITY: IN MOTION — 233
- Free and Easy Rambling — 236
- *Ukiyo* Existence — 249
- Middle Beings — 256
- Generative Being — 260

7 SUBJECTS OF EQUANIMITY: WITH THE POSSIBLE — 271
- The Priest without Borders — 272
- The Person with Belly — 279
- The Alert Hunter — 289
- Homo Ludens — 300

FUTURE DIRECTIONS — 317

REFERENCES — 325

For Louisa

ILLUSTRATIONS

Figure 1 (chapter 5, p. 225): Treaty Oak, Austin, Texas, U.S.A (Author photo)

Figure 2 (chapter 7, p. 315): Robert Delaunay, *Windows*, Paris, 1912

ACKNOWLEDGEMENTS

Legei pou Herakleitos hoti panta chorei kai ouden menei.

Though I did not write anything toward this book for several years after, in 2014 I wrote to my wife that I wanted to write a book for our teenage daughter. In heartfelt language, I said that "I feel it's the most important thing I could write, do, ever. I want to call it *For My Daughter, Some Seeds*." "I want to bring to bear every scrap of humanistic seeing I can," I continued, for "showing that some things matter more than others in this world, that people are just people, and they do things that exceed understanding, understanding by themselves and others, and if we don't make the attempt to really see them as such, then we have just remained comfortable, our hearts not bare and not broken when maybe they must be, given the pain in this world, or as [Jack] Kornfield would say, in this incarnation." Equanimity, I became confident, is the way to that kind of flexible human seeing that never turns away from the sufferings and joys of existence in all their unremitting disclosures. The mission was now clearer: to think through how equanimity allows us to entertain the world on its own terms.

Once the writing was underway, I recalled the famous Walter Benjamin quote from "Unpacking my Library": "Writers are really people who write books not because they are poor, but because they are dissatisfied with the books which they could buy but do not like." Recasting the quote into something a bit more equanimous, we might say that we write the books we ourselves would wish to find. So, wishing to discover something like the present book, I ended up writing it less because sustained philosophical treatment of important aspects of equanimity has been missing than because it felt like all that I had been teaching weekly for years in mindfulness groups was in fact equanimity, and so I had a solid impression that there were some things, something more, that needed to be said about the kinds of seeing and being in this world equanimity invites and allows.

To a host of very reflective and wise people, whose fields and expertises span philosophy, psychology, literature, film, social work, neonatology, psychiatry, medieval history, Buddhism, and political science, I owe a tremendous amount. I can only try to meet your generosity with my gratefulness: Sarath Jakka, Jonathan Flatley, Oswais Tirmizi, Mark Adams, Trent Schmiedehaus, Susana Kugeares, Dina Smith, Gwenn Afton, Erin Labbie, Casey Durham, Mackenzie Steiner, Debra Morris, Christen Mullane, Whitney McCray, Maurice Apprey, Clayton Shorkey, Simon Michael, Ethan Knapp, Thomas M. Ferguson, Niall Gildea, Jeremy Russell, Bilal Hamamra, and Vance Smith. And it is from my patients, and the veterans whom I try to help, that what I have to say now or in the future draws its active inspiration.

I.
FRAMING EQUANIMITY

CHAPTER 1
CASTING SEEDS

> The vegetable life does not content itself with casting from the flower or the tree a single seed, but it fills the air and earth with a prodigality of seeds, that, if thousands perish, thousands may plant themselves, that hundreds may come up, that tens may live to maturity; that, at least one may replace the parent.
> —Ralph Waldo Emerson, "Nature"

As a metaphor, the distributing or sowing of seeds has described elements of so many human enterprises. From fields as diverse as sports, religion, art, economics, politics, education and parenting, sexuality and reproduction, computer networking, psychotherapy, and ethics emerges the general notion that if favorable results of some kind are going to appear then they will likely issue from a plenitude of seeds, a multiplicity of beginnings. With more seeds cast, more is potentially—which is also to say, spontaneously—generated. Seeds represent nothing less than the genesis of things, and their natural power is change and evolution of the living. The real mystery of seeds, though, resides in never knowing in advance which ones will flourish, thereby surpassing their source. Seeding is always in prospect. It involves an ongoing act of faith, accepting its accidental power of surprise and so appreciating there always being something unintended in its progress. In the spirit of prodigality, this book is offered as a kind of seeding—across wide-ranging fields of inquiry, from multiple directions and perspectives—where ideas about equanimity as a way of seeing flexibly and generously, a way of being and thinking, may begin to settle and take root. Through teaching stories drawn from multiple traditions, and by the philosophies illuminating and constellating around them, come generative inquiries into identity (who we are), thinking (how we understand what is), ethics (how we live with others and the world), and adversity (how we deal with suffering).

This book sets out mindful of my successes and failures as a teacher and psychotherapist—and, at once most deeply challengingly and rewardingly, as a father—who has long been inspired to offer to my students, patients, and daughter meditations on pertinent ideas and readings of traditional stories involving seeds and growth, all related to an attitude that I take to be central to living fully or vitally. A vital existence, it will be shown, is one that is lived in the amplest awareness, with an evenly-hovering alertness and sensitivity to what is, in all actions and relations as they appear, beginning right now. Such a life is one lived with equanimity. This book proposes an experiment in being and thinking summed up by the equanimity necessary for nurturing any outcome whatsoever. Equanimity, we will see, never aims at a specific result. It is not so much a feeling state as an attitude, a way of being present through opening to what is. As a relationship to the world, it dances, floating over all things present to us. It has been observed that no one dances with the intention of being at one specific place on the dance floor when the song ends. In just moving to the music, going with what the body and senses in the moment receive, choreography drops into the background as that which keeps the whole thing moving, doing so without end purpose. In dance, direction and distance lose the primary roles they otherwise have in goal-directed movements. Instead, the expressive features of dance movements override any measuring or delimiting of the space we move in. Unlike goal-oriented movements, like walking to one's car, expressive motility never aims at realizing practical goals. Dance remains in this way vital, never becoming work but a form of play. Engaged in non-directed movement, we do not move so much *through* space as simply *within* it, a distinction the phenomenologist and neurologist Erwin Straus (1891-1975) made in describing the expansive spatial quality of dance ("Forms of Spatiality," p. 23). Equanimity offers the space for mobile awareness within life liberated from telos. Only that which has space can move.

Just Looking

> Don't think—Look!
> —Ludwig Wittgenstein, *Philosophical Investigations*

Equanimity is the mode of smooth awareness that may be best described as "choiceless," operating without interference, within rather than against the world. Although it may appear in what follows that equanimity is being implicitly prescribed at times as a kind of method, it will be instead explicitly argued that it is not a technique with steps or rules that one must follow in order to end up somewhere else. Methods, because they are for producing things that do not yet exist, are, within the scope of equanimity, finally irrelevant for the simple reason that our concern is only with what already exists—the present in its shifting plenitude. There can be no step-by-step guide or manual ensuring the production or engineering of equanimity. The mechanical use of equanimity as a method necessarily fails since it turns out, in the end, that what this "method" does is simply free us from all methods. Or, putting it another way, imposing a method on our world or our behaviors must give way to an intimacy with the world and its mysteries as they unfold. In the deepest moments of intimacy, methods are not welcome or useful. Technical mastery of equanimity would only put it at odds with the world, and thus, minimally, narrow it, and maximally, ruin it by disenchanting it completely. To face the wonder of the world, the phenomenologist Maurice Merleau-Ponty (1908-61) reminds us, is only possible when reflection "steps back to watch," and "slackens the intentional threads which attach us to the world" (*Phenomenology of Perception*, p. xiii). Furthermore, if equanimity were strictly a special method, carried out without fault, then it would cease to be interesting since there would be no surprises, no amazement, left. The very openness or spaciousness of equanimity allows us to experience the enchantment of the unexpected, the uncalculated. Take away the element of surprise, and the impetus to look and marvel at this world is extinguished. It was the teacher and philosopher Alan Watts (1915-73), who wrote and taught outside prescribed methods, who put it quite pithily: "There is no rule but 'Look!'" (*The Wisdom of Insecurity*, p. 99). There is no rule. Look.

When looking becomes merely a matter of consuming, with screens exerting an increasing gravitational pull on our attention, we risk disenchanting the world. It is difficult to engage the world broadly with equanimity when screen images are forever competing for center stage. Better than any preceding one, my daughter's generation (Gen Z) knows just how image-laden the world can present itself to be, just how much there is simply to look at—and to judge, sift through and evaluate. Smartphones, always at hand, serve up an infinitude of images, with apps and platforms like X (formerly Twitter), TikTok, Instagram, Snapchat, Twitch, Tumblr, YouTube, and so on, designed mainly for the purpose of circulating and recirculating images. The world is nothing, it can seem, other than something to be consumed as a whirl of effigies. Critiques of such a chimeric universe of obsessional picturing have been made many times along the general lines of arguing that contemporary society is increasingly replacing reality and meaning with phantasms and signs, or that, if reality is graspable at all, it is only as a hollow parade of images, a glossy double standing in, like a fetish, for something else. Reality becomes harder to grasp cognitively the more it is mediated by screens and devices. To highlight just one fascinating study from 2017 by Ward and colleagues at the University of Texas at Austin: it showed that even when we are not interacting with our smartphones, their mere presence imposes a "brain drain" by reducing available cognitive capacity. This happens in part because the attentional resources that are otherwise available for moment-to-moment awareness are recruited for the narrow purpose of hypervigilance, one symptom of which is the feeling that a phone is vibrating nearby when in fact it isn't.

Equanimity then does not seem much encouraged by the evolutions of postmodern living. What is striking, however, from a historical perspective broadly concerned with the workings of human awareness and consciousness, is that the way we consume images has itself remained basically unchanged since our first use of imagery to represent that which the eye's retina has captured. (This was around 50,000 years ago, as a result of what archeologists refer to as the "cultural big bang.") To be late-modern human beings, as opposed to our Paleolithic ancestors, means in part that the sights we inexhaustibly reproduce result from choices in looking that far transcend the immediately perceptible world. We have never been as capable of consciously immersing ourselves in alternative and repeatable sensorial "worlds." Nonetheless, we see only what we look at, and so the very act of looking is taken to involve an act of choice situating us in relation to whatever objects we pick out at a particular moment. As art critic John Berger (1926-2017) reminds us, "we never look at just one thing; we are always looking at the relation between things and ourselves. Our vision is continually active, continually moving, continually holding things in a circle around itself, constituting what is present to us as we are" (*Ways of Seeing*, p. 9). This "as we are" conditions to a great extent how we see and thus what comes into view. Seeing is, then, inextricably a matter of identity (as explored in chapters 6 and 7).

One crucial aspect of our identity as active perceivers hinges on how the emergence of objects of attention against a neutral or plain background is handled. "All life is figure and ground," says a character in Samuel Beckett's novel *Murphy* (p. 4), an insight that points to the idea that the two together constitute the experience of what we call awareness since it is not possible to have one without the other. If there were no ground, there would be no objects, and if there were no objects, it would be impossible to identify the ground. In general, in normal awareness, a higher degree of reality is attributed to figures than to their backgrounds. Given a strong tendency to ignore constant stimuli, we can easily become focused on troublesome things that puncture the constancy of our lives or on things that stand out based upon our judgments, and we often and consistently discount the rest. A clear illustration of bias toward the negative is the difference between, on one side, a myopic fear-based view of the world that screens out from attention that which is not immediately important to a scanning system interested only in what is dangerous and, on the other side, a holistic perception of the phenomenal world that allows the figure and the ground to switch places, to oscillate as the whole field is apprehended fluently and evenly. Though our perception produces only one interpretation of figure or of ground at a given moment—as in the famous Rubin vase/profile illusion—our capacity actively to switch back and forth between them defines an essential quality of equanimity. Holding the entire picture with an undivided, undifferentiated view, we are never caught in the illusion that our ego somehow depends on something being one way as opposed to another. Equanimity, in these terms, is a form of noncoercive relatedness to what is. Always seeing with scope, it allows for any individual contrasts, however stark, in the name of an active balancing between focus and field.

Equanimity is the preeminent function of a flexible perceptual system. It ranges over whatever may appear, fluidly noticing, for example, both the pleasant and the unpleasant with the awareness that one depends on the other for its meaning. It is through an orientation toward the fullness of what is, always operating without imposing itself, that equanimity is best recognized. It is marked above all by deference. It sets aside egoistic identification with its singular perspective-taking. One of the precepts of the Hindu sage Patañjali (2nd-4th century CE) describes the ignorance of egoism as resting in "the identification of the seer with the instruments of seeing" (*Yoga Sutra*, §2.6). Our instruments of sensing, as wonderfully sophisticated as they are, are limited given that they operate only from a single perspective (in a given moment). Looking up at the summer night sky from anywhere in the continental United States, we easily spy the Big Dipper since from our angle on the constellation Ursa Major seven of its brightest stars form a dipper, a pattern that from other angles in the universe, or even on our own planet, simply does not exist. To identify with our particular vision of the Big Dipper would be both egoistic, through force of valorizing a single perspective or focus ("mine"), and ignore-ant, in the sense of discounting the possibility of other perceptual and cognitive relationships or fields ("mine is the correct view"). There can be no static place where the stars actually are. Throughout our examination of equanimity, we will be framing seeing in terms of a kind of thinking: mobile perceptual relations that are, for example, at once ethical perspective-takings. Equanimity is never inert description or merely subjective impression. Nor is it explicitly non-evaluative. As I will argue in chapter 2 and in the chapters on knowledge, it includes a flexible, mimetic quality. Here resonates a memorable sentence from Hugo von Hofmannsthal's *Book of Friends*: "Plasticity develops not through observation, but through identification" with the objects of our knowledge (p. 371). Equanimity, then, is put forward in this book less as a feeling or even disposition than an intimate understanding of the full interdependence of our human sensibilities and the environment-world of which we are a dynamic aspect.

To frame it one way, our instruments of sensing only exist as processes, relations to their objects, and, as such, identifying with these media makes no sense as they are constantly shifting, mirroring the flux of reality around them. Usually our sense organs operate transparently, as if the presumed boundary between subject (perceiver) and object were seamless and untroubled. Generally speaking, an organ's environmental receptivity and flexible functioning are hallmarks of its vitality. Yet, for instance, when our sense organs get in their own way—as they sometimes do with tinnitus, neuropathy, glaucoma, or other diseases—then they may at that moment appear as something with which to identify intensely, albeit often from the unfortunate point of view of dis-ease, which is fundamentally a sign of difference and separateness. Things that function well are not alienated from themselves; they do not impair themselves. A Rinzai Zen capping phrase puts it like this: "Like the sword that cuts well but still does not cut itself, / Like the eye that sees well but still does not see itself" (Hori, *Zen Sand*, p. 559). Marcus Aurelius coupled the functioning of healthy organs with the operations of a mind that, through its openness and even attention, remains immune to dis-ease:

> The healthy eye sees whatever is visible and does not say, like someone suffering from ophthalmia, "I want only to see what is green." Having a healthy sense of hearing and smell means being alert to every sound and scent. The healthy stomach can digest all kinds of food, like the molar that is prepared to grind whatever we put in our mouths. Just so, the healthy mind should be open to whatever happens. The mind protesting, "Keep my children from dying!" and "May all men praise every little thing I do!" is an eye looking only for what is green and a tooth wanting only what is easy to chew. (*Meditations*, 10.35)

Flourishing existence depends upon a mind-body that functions fluidly and flexibly, interacting with its surroundings in ways unhampered by partiality and hyperfocus. Here, equanimity is measured by the organism's range of response to an environment from which it cannot be separated. The interdependent status of mind-body and environment renders it free from the ego lures of aversion, exemplified here as the wishful escape from death, and of desire, here the hunger for acclaim.

Our "seeing" can interfere with our "being" in another sense as well, that is, when our purpose in questioning the world is only to probe it for answers to satisfy a self that seemingly stands apart from it. Zen teacher Joshu Sasaki (1907-2014) saw the futility of such willful interrogating: "There is no need to understand what the world is. If human consciousness is perfect and this world is perfect, then there is no need to observe the world as object. If your consciousness works perfectly, you know that the world is you and you are the world" (*Buddha is the Center of Gravity*, p. 21). The world taken as a *separate* object of observation makes sense only if the observing consciousness is not moving with it. Perfection, in Sasaki's terms, does not mean a collapsing into inert oneness but rather a working movement of consciousness that aligns itself with the world with the immediacy of a shadow adjusting itself to a moving body. To presuppose that our awareness can only be understood in the rigid framework of the Cartesian divorce of subject from object, the separation of consciousness from world, conceals from us universal and flexible modes of seeing and thinking. The founder of quantum mechanics, Erwin Schrödinger (1887-1961), saw the power of the new physical sciences as residing in the special insight that "the barrier between [subject and object] cannot be said to have broken down...for this barrier does not exist" in the first place (*What is Life? and Mind and Matter*, p. 137). Equanimous consciousness always moves toward the Heraclitan *panta rhei*: everything flows; the only reality is the process by which perceiver and objects form a seamless whole. The dynamic interdependence and inter-being of self and world, as appreciated by the equanimous mind, is a subject to which I will return in chapters 3-5, and, in relation to subjectivity, in chapters 6-7.

Equanimity, we might say, is consciousness working perfectly. The appeal, indeed, the quiet joy of equanimity lies in its ability to help us see the world with spacious awareness. Within this spacious awareness resides a world more open to holistic understanding and a spirit of trust in what is. Here is a world less divided or, more acutely, a world from which we feel less divided. The times when we feel most separated from the world are those in which we experience most profoundly all the limiting conditions from which we seek relief—anxiety, depression, anger, loneliness, boredom, and meaninglessness. Equanimity offers a path through these states not by correcting, arresting, negating, or skirting them but by absorbing them into a larger, diverse fabric of vibrancy and expansiveness. At the same moment, for example, when we become exquisitely aware of the pointlessness of living, we also have the capacity to become more sensitive to the meaning of life, its essence. Meaning and meaninglessness are not opposed qualities of the same thing—life—as if life is broken into some battle between meaning and its opposite, but opposed qualities of *the relationship we may have to the flux of life*. If our focus locks on what will win the battle—meaning must triumph!—then we are mired in an agonizing struggle to pin down something that is constantly changing, and thus likely unmindful of the force of our imposing one reading—*this* has meaning!—over against another. Equanimity affords us the space to resist interpretation through recognizing that our quest for meaning can only be satisfied partially, momentarily. Our intensely interpretative and evaluative relationship to the world is one that, as Susan Sontag (1933-2004) famously stressed, impoverishes and depletes it. "It is," she writes, "to turn *the* world into *this* world. . . the world, our world is depleted, impoverished enough. Away with all duplicates of it, until we again experience more immediately what we have" (*Against Interpretation and Other Essays*, pp. 4-5; emph. in orig.).

Defining Equanimity

> Mind here, mind there are not different.
> —*Rinzai-roku*, §18

Surprisingly, extended examinations of equanimity rarely appear in the Western mindfulness literature, whether scientific (psychological, psychiatric, and neurobiological), specific to a tradition of contemplative practice (e.g., insight meditation or Zen Buddhism), or therapeutic (the proliferating library of self-help books for lay persons and guides for clinicians). By comparison, compassion/self-compassion (Skt. *karuṇā*) and loving-kindness/benevolence (*maitrī*)—two of the four Buddhist "sublime attitudes" (*brahmavihāras*), along with appreciative joy (*muditā*) and equanimity (*upekṣā*)—receive by far the most attention. Synoptic philosophical study of equanimity has not been undertaken, and this book offers a vocabulary for such an undertaking. Of the limited scientific literature on equanimity, it may be helpful to briefly examine three rather recent and important papers that attempt to define the concept. The first two undertake an explicit integration of traditional Buddhist thought and psychological science, and both underscore that equanimity as a separate concept, worthy of its own investigation, has not been much discussed in Western psychological theory. The third builds on the work of the first two, and tests a hypothesis concerning the extent to which equanimity may attenuate approach/avoidance tendencies.

The first, published in 2015, by Gaëlle Desbordes and colleagues, looks at the psychological state of equanimity from the perspectives of how it might be best defined as a concept distinct from mindfulness. Equanimity, they suggest, is recognized as "an even-minded mental state or dispositional tendency toward all experiences or objects, regardless of their affective valence (pleasant, unpleasant or neutral) or source" (p. 357). Their definition turns on the state of even-mindedness—a sense of calmness, stability, and composure that is linked to an attitude of impartiality where the experience of unpleasant thoughts and emotions occurs without efforts to avoid them through repression, denial, judgment, or aversion and, similarly, pleasant or rewarding experiences occur without over-excitation or artificial prolongation. As they rather tidily summarize it, "equanimity enables a skillful emotional response to the full range of feeling tones" (p. 359). Skillfully maintaining a balanced or even-minded response to provocative stimuli, whether internal or external, negative or positive, helps us to regulate emotionally and thereby be less likely to rely upon habitual coping behaviors that are unhelpful or harmful (e.g., drug use as avoidance or anger as aggression). For the authors, equanimity is a special form of contemplative practice to be distinguished from mindfulness more generally, even though the terms used in discussions of both, such as acceptance, letting-go, and non-judgment, markedly overlap. Mindfulness, they suggest, following Buddhist psychological conceptualization, is conscious awareness of what is happening in the experiential field, while equanimity "allows awareness to be even and unbiased by facilitating an attitude of non-attachment and non-resistance" (p. 358).

A more capacious definition of mindfulness makes this distinction seem overstated. As I understand it and teach it, if one could be fully mindful—that is, openly, which is to say fluidly, and consciously aware—of what is happening, then that person is by the same process evenly and unbiasedly aware. This is because in order to maintain open awareness, consciousness must sweep or move over the experiential field, whether it is as relatively delimited or focused as a cycle of the in-breath and out-breath or as expansive and complex as a sports game viewed from box-seats. Roving over the field of our experience, mindful equanimity operates free of all but the most momentary of stops (attachments) and detours (resistances). In other words, if one is mindful, in the sense of using both open and focal awareness and fluidly shifting between them, one is always already equanimous. The special qualities of equanimity, such as its evenness of attention and its fluidity, belong equally to mindfulness, and in fact animate it. Equanimity, we might say, serves as a gateway to the attitudinal state of mindful awareness. While clearly for the purposes of future research, such as the development of better scientific measures of equanimity, dissociating it from mindfulness, as the latter is currently measured, may be indispensable, the case can also be made that restricting the definition of mindfulness to received scientific definitions and ways of measuring is itself unnecessarily limiting. The more radical approach, pursued in this volume, is to essentially resist some of the limiting contemporary language of mindfulness, while at times implicitly recasting it fully in terms of equanimity.

Viewing equanimity as both practice and concept, the second essay, published a year later (2016) by Yuval Hadash and colleagues, specifies a new model for conceptualizing equanimity. In their view, it is best understood in terms of what they call "the decoupling model," where desire is detached both from wanting to have or prolong a pleasant experience only because it is pleasant and from avoiding or stopping an unpleasant experience only because it is unpleasant. In other words, in the state of equanimity, the pleasantness or unpleasantness of any current or anticipated experience does not affect desire, and instead such things as values, goals, and prosocial intentions determine our wanting or not wanting the experience. It follows then that equanimity manifests as both "an intentional attitude of acceptance" toward any experience regardless of its agreeable or disagreeable tonality and a "reduced automatic reactivity" to such tonality (p. 1215). They suggest that habitual psychological and behavioral reactions to both kinds of hedonic tone are suspended in a state of equanimity. Current research, as well as their own study, supports the efficacy of this suspension, especially when it comes to negative experiences like pain, anxiety, and sad mood. Weaker reactions of wanting to stop or avoid an unpleasant experience, it appears, indicate a higher level of equanimity.

Both of these treatments of equanimity approach it as an intentional skill, and one synonymous with acceptance rooted in a negation or suppression of attachment to pleasant, or of resistance to unpleasant, experience. Acceptance, as it is practiced in equanimity, does not mean merely delaying or denying our desire to attach to what is pleasant or resist what is unpleasant for the simple reason that equanimity, as I will be emphasizing, allows for something more profound: namely, the acceptance of an intimate coupling or *co-existence*, in this case, of pleasure and unpleasure. Under the equanimous eye, there are no opposed conditions; rather, in their mutual entailment, they flow together. So, the approach this book takes to equanimity is more expansive since it views equanimity as an integrated way of relating to all experiences, beyond those that may be dichotomously categorized as pleasant or unpleasant (as if, except in laboratory conditions, any experience actually has a purity of tone), and, more crucially, it suggests that it is inherently unintentional, untechnical. Of course, equanimity *can be* intentional; it can be taught as a skill or practiced as a technique, cultivated in the context of mindfulness training or contemplative practice, for example. Yet as a natural way of seeing inner and outer worlds, equanimity is like opening and then moving your eyes, not out of a sense of pointed interest but simply because you are awake. (*Natural* is to be distinguished from our *customary* or ordinary ways of seeing.) In the midst of our reality now, equanimity orients us to a condition in which there is nothing to try to isolate for any purpose such as keeping it around or turning away from it as if compelled to do something else. A key feature of equanimity, as we will see recurrently, is its purposelessness.

The third paper by Catherine Juneau and colleagues (2021) accepts the findings of previous research examining the application of mindful attention to both negative and positive objects, findings that highlight the familiar roles of non-judgment and acceptance in reducing, or de-automatizing, cognitive reactivity to internal and external stimuli. The authors go on to posit that equanimity attenuates approach/avoidance bias or motivation, that is, the direction of behavior toward positive stimuli and away from negative ones. One of their experiments involved exposing test subjects to randomly ordered negative and positively valenced words, to which they could indicate either approach or avoidance by pressing a button. Subjects' approach and avoidance motivation turned out to be significantly moderated by their measured level of equanimity such that those with lower equanimity scores needed more time to approach negative words and to avoid positive ones than to avoid negative words and approach positive ones. Persons with higher equanimity avoided this classical compatibility effect. For this group, it was shown that their subjective evaluations of the arousal generated by positively and negatively valenced words were weaker. Their automatic motivational reactivity to positive and negative stimuli showed a smaller difference at the same time that they tended to evaluate these stimuli as more neutral. The authors do not question the received correlation of equanimity with both non-judgment and acceptance, and they rightfully urge more research into how equanimity modifies the evaluation of positive and negative stimuli, how it in the process reduces the intensity of emotional reactivity and behaviors of approach and avoidance.

To uncouple equanimity from the exclusive mechanisms of acceptance and non-judgment requires a creative inquiry into the philosophical history of the concept, where it can be shown that equanimity is a matter of continual (re)balancing, an essential mobility in everyday life—in short, an agility that is unintentional. Acceptance and non-judgment can be thought more broadly in terms of flexible, non-teleological modes of relating and perceiving. Equanimity is not merely a matter of weaker evaluative responses to things normally producing stronger ones. Thus, in the ideal state of equanimity, for example, any word—positive, negative, or neutral in valence—is experienced evenly as no more than a collection of lines and figures that we allow ourselves to see without trying first to understand or interpret them (our brains take care of that automatically if the language is known to us). It is like how we might experience words in a totally unfamiliar language—as merely visible forms, inviting, like ink blots, a multiplicity of interpretations. In equanimous seeing, form and content are equally of interest, with form balancing out the usual primacy of content or meaning. Words are perceived just as we might stand back and look at a painting or an oriental rug—as occurrences of shapes, representations, colors, geometries. The lines and curves that stand out on a page, like the figures on a rug, are complementary with their backgrounds or surroundings. Indeed, they cannot be created apart from each other, as in the weaving of a rug where attention paid to the background is equal to that paid to figures. In giving existence to each other, figure and ground have an interdependence that erases the usual division between "significant" articulated elements and "insignificant" vague backgrounds. Equanimity becomes recognizable, for example, when scanning attention over single letters and patterns of them (words, lines of text) while also attending to the shifting "blank" background. The positive figure that a line encloses is of equal perceptual status as the negative shape that the figure cuts out from the ground. At this point, simply looking at the general panorama of sensory experience, we are released from making choices based upon the often fraught division of that which we label negative or positive. We are also released from the imperative of distinguishing whether this object stimulates us one way or another. Equanimity is that unbidden multi-dimensional perception embracing both figures and ground, the provocative and the inconsequential.

Not inconsistent with some of the conclusions of current research on equanimity, this book builds a more capacious understanding of equanimity, unconstrained for the time being by the specifying of variables and their requisite measurement in quantitative research projects. Ranging freely over the history of philosophy—itself an equanimous gesture of sorts—should help us conceptualize in new ways the place of equanimity in thinking (epistemology) and identity (ontology). Psychotherapy is one realm where mentation and selfhood are the primary objects of careful and caring inquiry. As a clinician, I began to recognize clearly, and unfortunately too often, equanimity collapsing in the vain effort to grasp a piece of reality in the name of either fusing with or rejecting it. The evidence that disequanimity increases suffering is striking, as in the case of posttraumatic stress disorder (PTSD), where there is an imperative to scan the world continually for those specific pieces of reality that may be perceived as threats. And so, when teaching mindfulness to military combat veterans, I will hear their hesitation based on an insistence that they are already mindful, already aware of everything going on around them. What can open, ranging awareness teach them, they legitimately wonder, when their attention is already sharp, persistent? Encountering a new space, they know where the exits and windows are, whose hands are where, who may pose a threat in a crowd, where the best places for cover are, and so on. On one level, they are in no way resisting the potentially unpleasant. Indeed, quite the opposite; they are deeply engaging with it, nourishing a state of readiness that is beyond wanting or not wanting it. Yet, on another level, such fused awareness is limiting, narrowly based as it is upon survival and rooted in exhausting fear. Equanimity, I wish to suggest, offers *a release from the imperative to be aware*. It adjusts the lens of survival by evening out our negativity bias, so that dangerous things appear no more salient at first than neutral and benign ones. It loosens around, decentering with a more agile awareness, these strictly focused and charged posttraumatic ways of seeing, without ever deeming them pathological or, finally, dispensable. Equanimity is thus additive, never strictly corrective, having no stake in converting "maladaptive" behaviors into adaptive ones. Instead, it affords the detachment to run awareness over any kind of behavior, sign, or event, all from the cool vantage point of a flexible and present mind. With respect to PTSD, for example, it allows for an easing into an awareness that does not sacrifice its acuity with respect to threat, but sheds its tense imperativeness.

Equanimity Exempt from Curing

Let's look at this idea that equanimity is not corrective, since it relates to the earlier assertion that it is unintentional in nature. A comparison to water may be helpful. Water, essential as it is to sustaining life, is not intrinsically curative. Water becomes curative only when the organism in need of it has reached a level of dehydration or another biological imbalance. Hydration, when curative, can restore energy, reduce toxin levels, regulate body temperature, induce regularity, boost the immune system, and so on, but an adequately hydrated organism will never experience water as a corrective to any deficient condition. Instead, the experience of water will be completely in tune with what water intrinsically is: *the* medium of life. Every organism known to us, it turns out, needs water to survive, to be. Water is not therefore a corrective to death, but the blood of vitality. Like water when it is consumed, equanimity can go unnoticed and at the same time, without argument, be the most precious commodity in the world. Equanimity shares with water this essentialness and this "bland" universality, and one may describe it as *the* medium of awareness.

Demanding of equanimity that it function as a corrective to other kinds or degrees of awareness has the unfortunate consequence of separating it out, externalizing it, when instead it operates from the place of experiencing that is all inclusive. Equanimity approximates an aerial view of things in which focusing or refocusing on objects below gives way entirely to the marvelous range of perspective itself. Looking out the window of a plane, our eyes are captured by nothing so much as the wondrous perspective of vastness itself. The sky above and the ground below are not noticed because of any desire, or any need, to see them. The sense of equanimity is not a product of our will, and though it may be suppressed by the will, it is not strictly generated by it. Such perspective-taking, a kind of perspective on perspective, reminds us of what we always already have available to us, and accounts for the feeling of lightness and naturalness in which equanimity rests. Daoist writers often compared such vision to that of a baby who, without motivation and self-consciousness, embodies harmony and equanimity: "The baby stares all day without blinking its eyes—it has no preferences in the world of externals. To move without knowing where you are going, to sit at home without knowing what you are doing, traipsing and trailing about with other things, riding along with them on the same wave" comprise "the virtue of the Perfect Man" (Zhuangzi, *Complete Works*, pp. 192-93; cf. *Dao de jing*, p. 163).

There is, then, something absolutely unforced about true equanimity. Undertaken as an exercise, a deliberate practice by which a desired attitude such as non-resistance or acceptance is cultivated, equanimity forfeits the fluidity and mobility that are its supremely inexhaustible elements. By this I mean that the effectiveness of equanimity is an effect in perpetual operation, in motion, and is therefore never completely realizable in a directed, delimited practice. The ways in which we carve up our world—through our desires (even our desires not to desire, our desires to accept)—arrest the open flow of equanimity. Equanimity, like its natural objects, refuses to be measured in terms circumscribed by desires that orient us in one direction at the exclusion of another. Nature, Ralph Waldo Emerson (1803-82) reminds us, is inexhaustible, the secret of its manifold perfection remaining safe at the same time that it remains radically open to human curiosity. "Nature," he declares, "never became a toy to a wise spirit." What Emerson describes as the "poetical sense" of our world harmonizes with an equanimous, wise vision:

> all natural objects make a kindred impression, when the mind is open to their influence.... It is this [poetical sense] which distinguishes the stick of timber of the wood-cutter from the tree of the poet. The charming landscape which I saw this morning is indubitably made up of some twenty or thirty farms. Miller owns this field, Locke that, and Manning

the woodland beyond. But none of them owns the landscape. There is a property in the horizon which no man has but he whose eye can integrate all the parts, that is, the poet. This is the best part of these men's farms, yet to this their warranty-deeds give no title. (*Nature*, p. 23)

Gaining a poetical sense of the world is predicated upon having an equanimous one. The "kindred impression" that reality makes is one beyond our initial divisions and distinctions, encompassing continuities between the utilitarian and the lyrical, the man-made and the natural, the private and the universal. Integrating alternative perspectives, equanimity offers a tree that is no less impressive because it yields lumber and a landscape no less majestic because it contains built farms or property lines. The poetical sense of equanimity derives from its appreciation that what is explicitly different or separate is implicitly continuous or united.

Equanimity is the mode of consciousness that best appreciates that the world is in an endless state of becoming, and is therefore most aptly approached "on the go" by our integrative sense of its complexity and variability. Reality, which is always changing, can only be "seen" from the vantage point of a process that is itself forever unfolding. Outlining the Chinese concept of efficacy, the French sinologist François Jullien describes the central notion of "processivity" in terms that resonate with how we may think of equanimity: "All reality is a process, so, at the level of things coming about, only that which is the object of a process—that is to say, only that to which a process leads—becomes real" (*A Treatise on Efficacy*, p. 121). Equanimity is a process that *leads to* reality as it is, and therefore it cannot be sought as a unitary goal but is better understood as emerging as a consequence of the very way reality is (i.e., changing, mobile, and, on that account, never manifestly complete). If the envisaged goal of an equanimity practice is, for example, to let go of an attachment to pleasure, then the only way that will happen is indirectly since to effectively let go means to go through a process that is its very precondition. This is why, as we will see repeatedly, equanimity is like a seed, changing imperceptibly and eventually growing in multiple directions; it is not some calculated or in any way singularly noble gesture designed to impose itself on, or come to grips with, reality. One cannot, as it were, see reality by surprising it, somehow catching it unawares. Setting aside for now the idea that this is impossible because we are already part of the reality we are trying to see in a new way—that is, the classic Eastern notion of the universe regarding itself through us—it is enough to recognize that equanimity is an allowing of reality to unfold for the reason that this unfolding is the precondition for its deployment. One does not pull on a seedling to make it grow; it must be allowed to grow by itself—naturally—at the same time that one does not neglect it but instead allows for its potential growth by co-creating favorable conditions.

In the natural course of aging, our organs work effectively until they stop doing so, sometimes dramatically as, for example, in the case of type 2 diabetes wherein the pancreas eventually cannot regularly produce or efficiently use the insulin the body needs to adjust blood glucose levels. If, however, one's pancreas is working effectively, then there is nothing to "try to do"; the use and storage of sugar just happens, outside of any intentional awareness. By not aiming for any specific effect—in this case, stable blood glucose levels—the true effectiveness of the pancreas passes unnoticed. For it to remain unnoticed, it must be liberated from whatever might damage its efficacy (e.g., poor diet). And so it is with equanimity, which, like a perfectly functioning organ, goes unnoticed, unintentionally exercised but at the same time involving the use of awareness in such a way that the action of evenly and fluidly seeing things comes to merge with the spontaneous course and distribution of things themselves. All the objects, internal and external, that *could be* objects of my awareness are instead *allowed to be* objects of my awareness, and in this way the frontier between seeing and what is seen is effaced. It becomes impossible to trace the effect of being aware in this way back to anyone or anything. Equanimity does not produce dramatic effects like an injection of insulin since it cannot be identified with any corrective to dysregulated functioning. As a consequence of being aware rather than a means of being so, equanimity reveals "results" only in a way that is unforced, indirect, and independent of the aim of achieving some end. It requires time for unfolding, and it is realized through transformation.

This indirect, unforced way of acting in the context of healing transformation is well illustrated in the Sufi tale of the pomegranate seeds, as collected by Idries Shah (1924-96), and so we turn now to the story before commenting on it.

Pomegranate Seeds

Once upon a time, a Sufi physician received a young man who urgently knocked at his door and asked to become an apprentice in the art of medicine. "You appear impatient," remarked the physician, "and so you will fail to observe things that you will need to learn." The young disciple pleaded, and so eventually the Sufi agreed to accept him. After a few years, the young man felt he was ready to practice some of the skills he had acquired. And so one day the doctor saw a man walking toward the house, and, after looking at him from a distance, said, "That man is ill; he needs pomegranate seeds." The young student replied, "Given that you've made the diagnosis, allow me to do the prescribing, and that way I will have done half of the work." "Splendid," said the teacher, "provided that you remember that any action is also to be viewed as an illustration." As soon as he met the patient at the door, the student declared, "You are ill; you need pomegranate seeds." "Pomegranate seeds! Phooey!" cried the patient. "I've never heard of such nonsense," he shouted, as he went away. Surprised and dismayed, the apprentice asked his master what had gone wrong, and how best to understand this interchange. The Sufi simply said, "I will show you the next time we receive a similar case." After a short time, the two were sitting outside the house and the master saw a man approaching in the distance. "That man needs pomegranate seeds," he said. After welcoming the patient, the doctor began his treatment: "You are a challenging and complex case—that I can see. You will require a special diet. This must be made of something round, with small sacs inside, something like an orange. Let's see...that's the wrong color. Hmmm...a lemon? No, no, that's too acidic. I've got it! Pomegranates!" The patient left, pleased and grateful. The student was impressed, if slightly confused. "Why didn't you just come straight to the point, and definitively prescribe pomegranate seeds?" "Because," said the Sufi, "he needed time as well as seeds." (The Dermis Probe, pp. 92-93)

In this parable, the training physician practices a kind of medicine whose power of healing rests upon key elements of equanimity. From the outset of the tale, the Sufi doctor uses the power of natural observation founded upon making space for seeing what is present to him. As he practices it, the art of medicine necessitates a slowing down so that space for observation can emerge. Observing patients from a distance, as the doctor does both times in this story, allows him to range over possibilities before making what otherwise might seem to be a rather snap assessment. Impatience, he reminds his student, can interfere with the learning process. The acquisition of knowledge is less about the progress one makes than the attention one is willing to give in each instance—as modelled by working with patients or teaching students. In this tale, time and attention replace progress and knowledge. With every action to be viewed as an illustration, a generalizable example or "case" whose final meaning is suspended, the teacher demonstrates that the art of medicine demands an equanimity that produces outcomes only in an indirect and unforced manner. Equanimity ensures the openness and flexibility that healing needs in order to be fully sufficient to the individual "case." The practice of medicine as a specialization places before us the necessity of genuine mental *de*specialization, the requiring of a mind whose spaciousness frees it from all fixed points of privilege, preference, or valuation.

This tale suggests that the moment that an effect—the cure—is taken as the object of the healing arts, singled out and rushed toward as the goal, doctoring may be reduced to the act of prescribing. From the patient's point of view, this is invariably disappointing. The student's blunt prescription of pomegranate seeds to the first patient triggers an ardent rejection of the recommended treatment. Perhaps what the initial patient rejected was less the seeds themselves than their manner of introduction. When a similar patient, who would also benefit from the seeds, presents to the doctor, the treatment approach is markedly different, this time demonstrating that there is no such thing as a straight line from diagnosis to prescription. The doctor's treatment approach dramatizes for the student how one might arrive at a curative effect, coming to a definitive prescription only after presenting alternatives according to a process in which the patient himself might engage. It is fair to assume that the patient's compliance with the medication regime is only enhanced by his participation in the process. The physician leads the patient to the seeds as if it were a naturally unfolding process, a "how" rather than a calculated exercise in heuristic reasoning focused on delivering a singular "what." By giving the patient time as well as seeds, as he puts it, the doctor practices an art of equanimity by which satisfaction—the cure—becomes bearable for the simple reason that grasping it would have destroyed its value as an end still capable of inspiring the patient's desire to achieve well-being.

Equanimity must work in this way: its efficacy depends upon the distance and perspective required to appreciate the "whole field" while all the while participating in a natural process of movement that reflects the nature of individual things in constant flux. This is not merely abstracting what is general, but is rather a way of perceiving—thinking—that consists in just opening to the movement of diverse and connected things. It *allows for* rather than forces with intention the ability to focus on any goal, and by this very process permitting one to be carried along by ceaseless effect as opposed to ceaseless effort. Such an attitude belongs, as the Daoist philosopher Zhuangzi attributes it, to that of the Chinese sage, the person who embodies calm, equipoise, effortless action, and harmony with what is, and so is said to live a floating life in simplicity: "In life he floats; at death he rests" (*The Book of Chuang Tzu*, p. 131; cf. Graham, *The Inner Chapters*, p. 266). *Floating* expresses better than any other word the purposeless action of the equanimous observer of the world. I will return to the ways in which floating is an essential embodiment of equanimous identity in chapter 6. For now, it suffices to say that to float conveys freedom from the requirements of destination or final meaning. It means tending in no particular direction, yet always remaining in motion, riding over the rhythmical ebb and flow of the life course. To float in equanimity evades the tension that comes from having any goal, and not least the desperation that often accompanies the compulsion to be happy. Floating, in this sense, is not a state of indifference or disengaged neutrality but a dynamic response of balancing as the evolving moment requires. The involvement of the equanimous floating observer entails a poised welcoming of all changes as they unfold without end. Equanimity, imitating the motion of the transitory world, floats unfettered by the drama of beginnings and endings. It ceaselessly traverses the middle.

In the Middle of All This

There is a wonderful synonym for *upekṣā* (Sanskrit)—or *upekkha* (Pali)—the Buddhist term most commonly translated as equanimity. The word is *tatramajjhattatā*, a compound of three simple Pali elements: *tatra*, meaning "there," or sometimes "all these things"; *majjha* meaning "middle"; plus *tata*, meaning "to stand." (Pali is the language of the *Tipiṭaka*, the sacred canon of Theravāda Buddhism.) This position "there in the middle" is the place where we always reside, only sometimes we live as if that were not true, as if, for example, all that matters is what maximizes pleasure or decreases pain. Splitting experience into the categories of pleasant or unpleasant risks reducing experience to immersion or avoidance, respectively, and consists of life lived on one of the sides, as though the middle were valueless. For a consciousness concerned with either hoarding pleasure or avoiding displeasure, the middle is a kind of ghost, lifeless and dismal. The most dramatic loss of vitality occurs when the middle—the now—is evacuated in favor of either the past or the future. Trying to flee the certainties of an unhappy past or the uncertainties of an anxious future means that the opportunities that equanimity holds out for clearly seeing the middle as it is, the present with its fluid integration of "all these things"— positive, negative, and neutral—are lost. Because the only moment we are alive is in fact this middle instant, conventionally figured between past and future, one of the most adaptive things we can do is recognize our interposing responses in relation to whatever is in the course of presenting itself. These responses usually comprise our conditioned reactions of mind and body. Equanimity encourages us to generate a lively vocabulary for identifying our shifting conditioned responses—those masking our naturally unmediated and uncontrived ones—in the midst of any state, the good, the bad, and the ugly, in which we may find ourselves. In *Experience and Education*, John Dewey (1859-1952) captured some of the urgency of this for living a rich life: "We always live at the time we live and not at some other time, and only by extracting at each present time the full meaning of each present experience are we prepared for doing the same thing in the future" (p. 51).

So, with equanimity, both the conventionally beneficial side of human experience (e.g., compassion, trust, connectedness) and its dark side that we tend to shun and judge as corruptive are brought into an integrated awareness, manifesting a fluidity characterized by, as I have suggested, a kind of hovering or floating. Ajahn Chah (1919-92), the influential Thai Forest monk, once pointed out that genuine awareness does not necessarily arise from sitting still for hours and hours meditating, but from being attentive no matter what you are doing. "Wisdom," he said, "comes from being mindful in all postures," and, we may add, all dispositions. When you "let things take their natural course," Ajahn Chah continued, "then your mind will become still in any surroundings, like a clear forest pool. All kinds of wonderful, rare animals will come to drink at the pool, and you will clearly see the nature of all things. You will see many strange and wonderful things come and go, but you will be still. Problems will arise, and you will see through them immediately" (*A Still Forest Pool*, p. 162; *Modern Buddhist Masters*, p. 42). This exemplifies the unmistakable kind of wise satisfaction and ease of the person who perceives with equanimity. Equanimity makes no appeal to a static or singular vision of things or to a mind that passively, inertly mirrors them. It rather taps indeterminate aspects of our experience to call into being a novel world—replete with the comings and goings of "many strange and wonderful things." A mind open and attuned, in equanimity, to spontaneously emerging novelty works to revitalize the world.

A clear pool reflects images of the unfamiliar and wondrous world passing around it, yet the reflections do not stick. There, in the middle, the equanimous mind is imperturbable, taking it all in, tempering whatever has moved to an extreme. No single moment, no matter how undue, has the power to claim our reality when we realize that everything is a passing experience, a temporary visitor reclaimed by the clear pool of the mind. Through this radical stance of being fluidly present with any experience—ranging across the perfectly normal human attitudes of anticipation, anger, fear, shame, guilt, sorrow, regret, and so on—we gain a freedom from being defined or fixed by their putative negativity. Being in the middle of all this liberates us from ever having to force a swing from one side of experience to the other, from the negative to the positive, as if a person can compel herself to be happy in the midst of sorrow or unguarded in the midst of shame. The truly unbearable part of sorrow or shame is less the emotion itself than the sense that one is stuck in that particular emotional reality. Mired in such a world, our narrowed subjective experience at a given time can so easily become an emblem for the entire lived or imagined world—past, present, and future. And so, for example, what is temporary can be mistaken for what is permanent. Confusing in this way a transitory event for the unchanging totality reinforces the feeling of being stuck since any reflective space around the emotion has been forfeited. Recovery of the perceptual space necessary to see the whole field, the interplay of the inner and outer, depends upon a willingness to reappraise our emotions from the perspective of an equanimity affirming that there is, finally, no reality to find other than the (im)mediate one. When we find ourselves in the middle, realizing that we have never lived anywhere else, the wisdom of equanimity becomes fully available to us.

Disequanimity is perhaps best recognizable when a dramatic shift has taken place whereby a *particular* way of relating becomes the form or style of *all relationships*. Being-in-the-middle, by contrast, means that the *content* of any emotional or cognitive relationship to self, others, or the world is not generalizable as *context*. The pitfall of content becoming context, which is the work of the ego, is that in the shame or sorrow, for example, that a person might be feeling, she sees there the deepest truth, the most radical misfortune, of her existence. And the temptation to normalize such a truth by referring it to the whole of one's life is especially strong. Here, a deeper meaning of equanimity emerges. Equanimity can be understood as the dispensing with any univocal "point of view" or unitary relationship with what constitutes one's existence *in order to* grasp its common core, its essence. Inviting paradox, it can be stated like this: equanimity reveals that what is "specific" to living is precisely its ability to elude its own grasp. One inspiration for such a contradiction is found in the Gospel of John (12:24): "Unless a kernel of wheat falls to the ground and dies, it remains only a single seed. But if it dies, it produces many seeds." A well-known allegory in Christian vernacular of the resurrection and the way to salvation, the generative dying seed points also to the antithetical power of equanimity, the realization that only through the decay of singular understanding is real growth possible. Attachment to life through singular understanding negates it, and opening up affirms it. As the next verse (12:25) apprehends it: "He who loves his life will lose it, and he who hates his life in this world will keep it for eternal life." Considering the equanimous mind, interpretation that holds narrowly to "life in this world"—which in Greek is the worldly soul (*psuche*)—through either attachment (love) or aversion (hate) marks the ending of the possibility of inner renewal. Ego-centered states such as these signify the likelihood of spiritual regression, a retreat from the natural and vital middle to the more tense edges of existence. Out on the edge, the risk of remaining open can be met with the perspective of either calm, even acceptance or, as is more often the case, impatient, selective defensiveness.

To be "on edge" commonly describes a feeling of tension or nervousness, the kind of uncomfortable self-involvement in which we are anxiously sensitive to any signs of change the future may bring. On the excitable edges of our being, we inhabit this uneasy state of expectancy, with frantic readiness to act hastily with little or no consideration of the "big picture." Put simply, it is hard to respect the middleness, the rich embeddedness, of our present existence when the edge becomes our predominant vantage point. From the perspective of the edge, the world forfeits its multidimensionality, and with that loss, as Edwin A. Abbott's novel *Flatland* (1884) illustrates, comes a relinquishing of imaginative freedom. More dimensions equate to greater mobility and flexibility of vision, as when the two-dimensional protagonist, A. Square, considers himself intellectually superior to the inhabitants of universities with fewer dimensions than his own, yet struggles when an unexpected guru, a sphere, confronts him with "the deeper mysteries of Spaceland" (p. 65). Once exposed to the panoptical vision of three-dimensionality, A. Square feels god-like, surveying Flatland from above: "For the wise men in our country say that to see all things, or as they express it, *omnividence*, is the attribute of God alone" (p. 66). With the unveiling of the dimensional fullness of Euclidean geometry, A. Square, having left the edge for the middle of all things, can never really be at home again in his native Flatland, a plane of realities that for him now appears, as he composes his memoirs in prison, "no better than the offspring of a diseased imagination, or the baseless fabric of a dream" (p. 82).

Here again is a paradoxical aspect of equanimity: in the very quest for the mysteries of life, it is discovered that the lack, or absence, initiating the quest is a central quality of the mysteries (to be) discovered. When mysteries become part of an expanded reality, a sense of lack necessarily remains that keeps the whole process moving, evolving. A wisdom flowing in equanimity consists in forever expanding the range of things where distinctions between certain and uncertain, mysterious and ordinary, or adequate and inadequate do not apply. The French poet Paul Valéry (1871-1945) went so far as to suggest that true vision—we might say true wisdom—involves the absence of mediating conventions like nouns: "To see is to forget the name of the thing one sees" (qtd. in Weschler, *Seeing is Forgetting*, p. 207). This equanimous approach to things, where lack is perpetually recognized, is taken one step further in the Zen phrase, "Mind and things are both forgotten" (Hori, *Zen Sand*, p. 136).

When distinctions between mystery and mundanity dissolve in the state of equanimity, we come to see that the analysis of objects, pointing them out and forming ideas of them, never brings us nearer to them but, on the contrary, separates us from them, keeping them in some sense "other." Thus, as philosopher Walter Benjamin (1892-1940) observes, "we penetrate mystery only to the degree that we recognize it in the everyday world ("Surrealism," p. 216). Or, as the Daoist sage Lieh-tzu also paradoxically frames it: "Without concepts, your mind is the same as it; / Without pointing, you reach everything; / Whoever exhausts the object exists forever" (*The Book of Lieh-tzu*, p. 88). While I will take up related aspects of equanimity and knowledge in chapter 2, it suffices now to observe that, from the perspective of the equanimous mind, mystery occurs simultaneously with the everyday, and that what we call mystery does not underlie or emerge out of the everyday. No trace remains of some other world behind or beyond this one, and, in the vast operation of things, equanimity imitates the motion of transitions without beginning or end. Sustained change means that clinging and resisting, desiring and avoiding, are less opposed ways of being than merely the tragic limits or poles of a life that is otherwise inescapably in the middle of all this. The middle is the reservation in which the rational mind no longer has to labor making the obvious inaccessible or the everyday mysterious. Here, the basic equation of desire, which demands that it be directed toward what is not, is suspended in the recognition that the real mystery of life is not what it is (where it began or will end) but rather what it does (how it is going on). One can easily imagine that Eastern philosophical insights on transience and interdependent causality inspired reflections like this from Marcus Aurelius: "All things are continually born of change.... Whatever is, is in some sense the seed of what is to emerge from it" (*Meditations*, 4.36).

Emergence happens from the middle, the very site where we always discover the seed whose role as and in the center ensures that both things and consciousness remain open, untethered to the privileging of one way or one view over another. Seeds offer models for human living and thinking. For philosopher Michael Marder, the seed and, by extension, the plant, are the exemplary media for making a start unrestricted by origin:

> One of the most compelling reasons for wishing to be in the place of the seed is, it seems to me, that germination commences in the middle, in the space of the in-between. That is to say: it begins without originating and turns the root and the flower alike into variegated extensions of the middle, in marked contrast to the idealist insistence on the spirituality of the blossom and the materialist privileging of the root. Like sentient and conscious subjects who always find themselves in the midst of

something that has already begun outside the sphere of their memory and control, the plant is an elaboration on and from the midsection devoid of a clear origin. (*Plant-Thinking*, p. 63)

To understand a plant seed is to grasp existence *in medias res* and, ultimately, to appreciate the freedom of beginnings there.

We turn now to thinking more about seeds themselves, whose inceptive relation to the world opens up possibilities for remodeling human perception and invigorating human ecology. Ecology describes a condition of being in its relationality through which our state of existence is most fully realized, a point I will also take up in chapter 2 discussing creativity and the equanimous mind.

Opening Seeds

> A seed, which is a plant or tree in embryo, which has the principle of growth, of life, in it, is more important in my eyes, and in the economy of Nature, than the diamond of Kohinoor.
> —Henry David Thoreau, *Journal*, 22 March 1861

Seeds are emblems of process, flexibility, interrelation, and patience that bring before us some of the essential qualities of equanimity. A seed is such a precious and vital thing that there are twenty-one major banks worldwide, and as many as 1,700 smaller gene banks, forming a global network for the collecting, conserving, and sharing of seeds. The most famous of these is the Svalbard Global Seed Vault, the so-called doomsday vault, located deep within an icy mountain on an island above the Arctic Circle between Norway and the North Pole. Holding the world's largest collection of agricultural diversity, some 930,000 varieties of food crops comprising around thirteen millennia of agricultural history, this vault, on the edge of civilization, safeguards the future of global food sources. As a repository, recalling the Sufi physician's words, of "time as well as seeds," this vault functions to preserve the global balance of genetic material increasingly threatened by natural forces (disease, climactic change) and the destruction of regional wars. While the loss of a seed bank in war-torn Syria recently triggered the opening of the vault, other human-made doomsday scenarios have emerged more gradually. With agricultural practices changing dramatically over the past 50 years, fueled by advanced technologies for large-scale crop production, the increase in crop yields has meant an alarming decrease in biodiversity to the point that now only about 30 crops provide 95% of human food-energy needs. In China, merely 10% of the rice varieties used in the 1950s are still used today, while in the U.S. over 90% of fruit and vegetable varieties have disappeared, with crops like lettuce dropping from 500 varieties to just 36. Most alarmingly, we have already lost 75% of the planet's seed diversity. When the balance of *agri*culture is disturbed by the imposition of *mono*culture, food supplies are left unusually susceptible to the threats of diseases and drought. Another consequence is the erosion of cultural diversity, some of which, for example, is based upon ancient heirloom recipes that have enriched lives individually and collectively.

Seed vaults, as well as local seed-sharing programs, like those flourishing in over 500 public libraries across the U.S., are registers of the vital importance of seeing with equanimity, in this case, the vision necessary to conserve biodiversity through interchange and ecological balance. With the fostering of regional reproduction and exchange of multiple species, for example, new plant generations can develop adaptations to changing environmental conditions, resulting in diverse heirloom varieties. In part, preserving regional differences redresses the increasing control of food production and seed distribution by large companies invested in relentlessly streamlining and homogenizing agriculture. And, with the effect of climate change on the environment, cultivating more diverse seed varieties becomes especially vital for food growers at both micro and macro levels to cope with extreme conditions. While we usually think of seeds as beginnings—metaphorical and literal—they are also, it seems, precisely what orient us, now, to an inclusive awareness that holds a feeling for the past and the future. As in the title of this book: seeds that are the *genesis of* equanimity, but also seeds *composed of* equanimity, of ways of seeing and being that make possible the processual experience of the immediate as itself reflecting continuity between the inconsequential and the urgent.

Seeds cannot be thought of apart from processes that are nothing less than the signs of their *becoming* as distinct from their *being*. The becoming of a seed is another way of describing its transactional relationships with the environment. All natural growth processes, inseparable from the context in which they occur, are accompanied by regulated processes of death and decay. In fact, understanding growth necessitates understanding death. The seed, as it germinates under conditions that vary across species, changes from an independent, encapsulated object— like an acorn carried by a mouse to be stored for food—into an interactive, vital, and complex organism. As the seed's casing becomes porous to the moisture of the environment, the tissue swells, breaking open the casing, and the solidity of nutrient starch begins to transform into the fluidity of sugar sap. The most evident transformation is of course the growing of roots out and down into the soil simultaneously with the upward growth of the shoot and leaves. The opening of a seed is nothing less than the birth of its self-orientation to, and inseparability from, the fullness of its environment. As an interdependent entity, the developing plant changes its environment—for example, acid-secreting roots alter the soil—at the same time that the environment supports its growth. The French botanist Charles-François Brisseau de Mirbel (1776-1854), one of the earliest investigators of plants at the microscopic level, concluded that the plant, given its multiplicity of "living individuals," that is, the transforming cells comprising it, is nothing but a "collective being" (Kirsch, p. 68). As a heterogenous entity, the plant troubles dichotomies like part and whole and any one-way causal frameworks that might explain them. The resultant beauty or usefulness of the plant, flower, and tree is not the point of the seed, however much we might be captured by their splendor or dependent upon the sustenance they offer. The fact that seeds cannot be understood apart from the processes they both inaugurate and arrange means that any form of human attending to them must be a mark of patient balance and care (an idea explored momentarily in our discussion of a Romanian folktale about seeds).

The transformation of a seed is a time-intensive process, and, in this respect, it nullifies instant gratification. It is an ineluctable performance complete with its own cadence, continuities, and pauses. In his museful study of the life of thale-cress plants, biologist Nicholas Harberd marks time from "Seed to seed to seed, the ticking clock of the years" (*Seed to Seed*, p. 231). The ecology of the seed dramatizes the impermanence of existence, with its constantly changing forms reminding us of the wave-like structure of the world and our wave-like relation to it. To separate the crest and trough of any wave into opposites, into distinct events or "things" carrying the value of "high" and "low," ignores their irreducibly reciprocal existence. Our lived experience is nothing other than the circumstances at play according to Ajahn Chah's famous formulation: "Everything arises, everything falls away." Such a maxim at once accounts for the rhythms of daily living and for the context in which all novelty, surprise, and poignancy are made possible. Equanimity appeals then to the full breadth of experience as it unfolds, at the same time plumbing the indeterminate elements that lie on the boundaries of what is known, and that lend experience its inexhaustible novelty and mysterious depth.

One cannot design and plan the future of a seed, construct its potential shape, or assemble its eventual living forms from parts. It must unfold as a process, emerge into being organically. As the architect Christopher Alexander (1936-2022) casts it:

> if you want to make a living flower, you don't build it physically, with tweezers, cell by cell. You grow it from the seed. Suppose you are trying to create a flower—a new kind of flower. . . . You know that any attempt to build such a complex and delicate thing directly would lead to nothing. The only flowers which men have built directly, piece by piece, are plastic flowers. If you want to make a living flower, there is only one way to do it—you will have to build a seed for the flower and let *it*, the seed, generate the flower. . . . [T]he great complexity of an organic system, which is essential to its life, cannot be created from above directly; it can only be generated indirectly. (*The Timeless Way of Building*, p. 162)

This organic process of indirect generation is free from the stress that often accompanies the top-down labor of designing, creating, building. The Danish physician Petrus Severinus (1542–1602) described seeds (L. *semina*) in these striking terms:

> Nor have they gotten a laborious lot in life: without anxiety, exhaustion, ratiocination, or doubt, they make up their minds, with a knowledge of their life that is inborn and in the end becomes itself essence/being. Those who have no common feeling or awareness of this kind of knowledge are said not to know what they are doing, even though they seem to know: for, in fact, they employ in their works proofs of a divinely revealed knowledge (*Idea medicinae philosophicae*, p. 91; trans. mine)

A seed, untroubled by anxiety and doubt, and unhampered by fatigue or the method of reasoning, does not get in its own way, for the seed is itself a way of acting in the world, one whose progress is measured outside usual forms of purposeful knowledge. The seed effortlessly reveals the way, illuminating a process that leads from knowledge to vital becoming.

Seeds, like all natural things, generate from the inside (or center) out, and their evolving is indirect, autopoietic, spontaneous. This organic growth model operates inversely to the mechanical or artificial one, where parts are put together, assembled, linearly, from the outside in, working from a plan or schema. It is unfortunate that in early schooling, at least in the U.S., most learning about plants and seeds involves colored diagrams with individually labeled parts rather than the patient observation of them changing and interacting with their natural environment. To give narrow referential attention to something as a rule sacrifices the kind of holistic attention enacted by equanimous observation. An inert pictorial diagram will rarely encourage an appreciation of the fully reciprocal nature of organism and environment, where each is an emerging product of the other at the same time. It is hard, for example, to capture only with static pictures the reality that seedlings serve as the environment of the soil, and what they are always in the process of becoming is an expression of their dynamic environment. Such representations also ignore the complex bio-attention of plants, their ability to respond to changing environmental circumstances through multiple local adjustments. As plant biologist Anthony Trewavas has pointed out, plants pay open and active attention to at least fifteen environmental factors acting simultaneously, chief among them are resource availability and the presence or absence of competitors ("Aspects of Plant Intelligence," p. 9; 12). Plants' multifocal attunement to variable environmental signals—presence of primary minerals, light, temperature, wind, gravity gradients, and so on—has been described as a kind of "objectless attention," that is, a form of knowing the world that translates stimuli not into images but instructions for growth and reproduction dispersed throughout the sentient organism (Marder, "Plant Intelligence and Attention," p. e23902-2). Plants demonstrate focal as well as peripheral attention, in addition to both selective and sustained attention. In their sophisticated attentional flexibility plants may be said to embody a natural equanimity.

"A plant," writes nature scientist Craig Holdrege, "does not simply unfold its forms; it forms itself through its environment. A plant does not exist without an environment. It brings this context to expression in its own form and substance" (*Thinking Like a Plant*, p. 173). To see a plant in this way entails transitioning from seeing the individual elements (plant organs, soil elements, etc.) to seeing the formative movement or becoming that is the plant itself. "The first [...] meaning of plant life," Michael Marder contends, must be "a certain pace and rhythm of movement, which we customarily disregard, since it is too subtle for our cognitive and perceptual apparatuses to register in an everyday setting, and with which the tempo of our own lives is usually out of sync" (*Plant-Thinking*, p. 21). Appreciating the process of becoming, equanimity then allows us to see the living field, engaging always with a recognition that the universe as we experience it is dynamic. Equanimity offers us nothing less than the capacity to be more in tune with its movements. The consequences of not seeing living things in this way, of not being in sync, is well illustrated in the Romanian folktale "The Wise Old Men," to which we now turn.

The Wise Old Men

Once upon a time in a village in Romania, a group of young people gathered together. As the evening went on, with everyone laughing and joking, one of them suddenly asked, "Why do we need the old men?" At first the others gasped, but then they began to talk about their fathers, who forever were giving unwanted advice, and they complained about their grandfathers' sagas, their uncles' tales, and their neighbors' old-fashioned ideas. They all came to agreement: The old men had lived their lives, and so no one really needed to hear what they had to say. Surely, the young people believed, we have ideas that make more sense in these modern times.

So they decided to go to the palace to tell the young king their idea—that it was time to get rid of all the old men. The king agreed this was a fine plan. The next day, he ordered his soldiers to gather all the old men in the whole country and to lock them away, so no one would have to listen to their stories, their advice, or their ideas anymore. The soldiers carried out the orders. But there was one young person named Felix who resented this new law. He loved his father and considered him the wisest man in the world. But Felix and his father were fearful of what would happen if they disobeyed. So they agreed that the old man would hide in the cellar, and they would visit each other only at night, and no one would know.

That spring, while the old men were being imprisoned, flowers bloomed, and succulent grapes grew on every vine. Every tree bore fruit, and the young people started to celebrate their new freedom from the old. By summer, though, a hard drought had hit the land, killing crops, withering trees, and causing much suffering among the wildlife. A severe winter followed the summer of drought. They had never felt such bitter cold. The fields were covered in snow and ice, and, when at long last winter ended and spring came again, nothing grew. The people were hungry, and they were fearful. None of the seeds grew because drought and frost had killed them all, and the people were so distraught that they could not think what to do.

The young king urgently gathered his group of young wise men, but they were too burdened by worry to offer any wisdom. One night, Felix visited his father as he always did but this time his father looked at him and said, "I know something is wrong. I've never seen you looking so sad. What's wrong? Has somebody died?" "Oh father!" Felix exclaimed, "Our land is dying. Our seeds have all died, and there is nothing to do but wait and starve." The father reached out and gently touched his son's hand. "Do not be afraid," he calmly said. "Take our plow and go to the city. Plow up the roads that lead into the city and the roads leading out. Don't answer anyone's questions. Just do as I say."

Felix trusted his father. So the next morning, he harnessed his horse to the plow and set off. As he plowed up the main roads, he saw the earth that he turned over was thick and moist, and, to his astonishment, he saw the seeds beneath this soil were not dried up or frozen or dead. The weather was warm, the sun bright, and in just a few days, these seeds began to sprout and grow up from the tilled land. Quickly they grew tall—corn and wheat and other crops. When people saw this, they began to ask questions: "What happened? What have you done? Is there some magic here?" Recalling his father's words, Felix answered no questions. He just smiled and simply said, "We are growing food."

The neighbors ran to the palace to report this to the young king, who soon sent for Felix. "I have no doubt that your father is with you still," the young king said. "I suspect it was he who advised you to plow up our roads. Speak the truth and I promise your life will be spared. Lie to me, and you shall die." Felix looked down. "It's true, your majesty," he said. "My father lives in my cellar. I could not bear to give him up. And it was he who advised me to plow up the main roads." "Bring your father to me," the king commanded. So Felix returned home, and the next day he and his father traveled together to the palace. People gasped at the sight of an old man freely traveling in a carriage, and the whispering began. What could this mean?

When Felix and his father arrived at the palace, the young king looked the old man in the eye. "What is the meaning of the advice you gave your son?" he demanded. "Why have you destroyed our main roads?" "Your majesty," the old man began, "carts filled with seeds and corn pass through our village all year-round. Some of those seeds fall from their carriages to the ground, and the carts and plows and *people tread over them. But those seeds that are left behind may grow if given a chance. That is why I told my son to dig up the dirt—to give them a chance." The king understood at once that the old man was wise indeed, and understood the folly of his ways. That very day he ordered all the old men to be set free. After that, with people old and young talking and giving advice, sharing wisdom, meeting together and listening to each other, life was much richer and more nourishing.* (cf. Gaster, "Roumanian Tales," pp. 213-15)

This tale turns on the implications of dividing natural reality into parts, separating what was once integral—society, family—into fragments. The young people's initially playful, subjective opinions and judgments quickly became firm expressions of how the world ought to be—a static vision that unwittingly stifled creative possibilities and ultimately led to deprivation. It is remarkable that the calamity in this tale begins with an open question leading rather quickly to consensus. Moving from open to closed off, with the freedom of laughter and joking turning into fixed judgments and moral conclusions, the way is paved to unconcealed claims for power and control that would make the world as the young people wanted it to be. But, in singling out and isolating through imprisonment one part of the world, they ignored something absolutely crucial regarding the living whole: that they themselves will become old someday, and have thereby in effect sentenced themselves to future imprisonment! We may summarize their fundamental mistake as seeing and acting upon the world from the outside, at once dispassionately and moralistically, as if they were standing apart from it. Such a view is undoubtedly about separation at the expense of perspective, whereby the world is easily approached as something to dominate rather than understand intimately and holistically.

By the end of the tale, the young/old dichotomy cannot hold, and society is regenerated by acts of mutuality and intimacy. Seeds serve as the central image in the tale, and their apparent loss, due to the inclement weather, symbolizes the dis-integration of wisdom, the dysregulation of an ethos based on opening to the natural environment as a totality. To lock away the wise old men means not only silencing their contributions to their lived world but precluding the total environment itself from supplying the people in return. In short, reciprocity was disrupted; the land(scape)—human and non-human—was imperiled. The threat of starvation caused such a level of confounding anxiety that even the young king's counselors were unable to solve the crisis of the inert seeds. Felix's father, compassionately attuned to the suffering of others as embodied in his son, calmly offers a solution rooted in an understanding of the importance of mutuality and of how the environment functions as a field of processes. His instructions to plow up the roads, those manmade markers of civilization, could not at first be grasped by others, including the young king. They were unable to see the connection between a road, used for commerce, and a field, rich with seeds, for growing. Plowing up both entry and exit ways to the city symbolizes the mental flexibility necessary to solve problems by erasing traditional avenues of received thinking. The narrow line gives way to the open field, marking a new kind of awareness involving equanimity attuned to systems of relations in which everything is happening simultaneously. What was once the epitome of utility, the road is deemed no longer beneficial when viewed through conventional eyes. Felix's father, however, grasps the multiple ways by which the environment functions co-creatively, interdependently. He recognizes that roads are surfaces for moving seeds at the same time that they are fields for their unsuspected planting. In this, he proves exquisitely sensitive to the rhythms of existence, as they are lived through the mutual implication of self and other.

Insight into the cadence of life, into its indirect and simultaneous workings, reflects a wisdom that is not about finding solutions so much as letting solutions unfold, "giving them a chance," as Felix's father says of the forgotten seeds thereby justifying his reason for refashioning the roads. In this tale, the replenishing of the world came about because, in an important sense, the world was allowed to replenish itself. Equanimity equates to the recognition of potential, to seeing more than what is only superficially present (or absent). Philosopher G. W. F. Hegel (1770-1831) once remarked that "This fostering of the grain of seed in the earth is therefore a mystical, magical action. It shows that the seed contains secret powers which are still dormant, and that in reality it is something other than what it is as it lies there" (*Hegel's Philosophy of Nature*, vol. 3, p. 68). By allowing the world to unfold spontaneously while at the same time indirectly participating in it, Felix's father, and all the "wise old men" he stands for, offers a conception of the natural order that reveals the perils of dividing it into fragments. The world is best managed or governed when it is recognized that any disrupting or arresting of the transactional nature of part and whole, any separating out of what is naturally and mutually entailed, threatens the vitality of the cosmos. The complexity of nature, Watts once observed, consists in "a dance with no destination other than the figures now in performance, figures improvised not in response to an over-ruling law but mutually to each other" (*Nature, Man and Woman*, p. 124). A vision of reality's dance that sees it as mutual, improvisational, and without destination rests in the kind of replenishing that equanimity brings to life. It is nothing less than the vital art of tending.

CHAPTER 2
THE VALUE OF TENDING

Though I do not believe that a plant will spring up where no seed has been, I have great faith in a seed.... Convince me that you have a seed there, and I am prepared to expect wonders.

—Henry David Thoreau,
"The Succession of Forest Trees"

Equanimity is here presented as more than a salutary affective state associated with, or subordinated to, the practice of mindfulness, as it is often presented in Western Buddhist-informed teachings. In the context of Western psychotherapy, teaching mindfulness has meant for me, among other things, folding it largely *into equanimity*, noting that the two share a description of the flexibility of mind and the attitudes required to hold multiple, often contradictory, perspectives at once. Whereas mindfulness emphasizes conscious attention to inner and outer experience, equanimity underscores the freely ranging aspect of that attention, its deference and the active balancing producing moments of impartiality. Equanimity is a dynamic approach to self, others, and the world that avoids the stickiness of judgment, the fixity of needing to be right or in the know, and the violence of dogmatic conviction. As a mode of perception, equanimity is supremely mobile, on the move, looking over things (internal and external) with an evenly-hovering attention. Equanimity is not about calmly settling. It is never averse to the presence of judgments, just to their rigidifying. It is never indifferent to the objects of its awareness. It reminds us, for instance, that there is no advance without sacrifice, no light without the darkness out from which it shines, and no knowledge without the initial condition of not-knowing. From taking and retaking positions of equipoise, the attitude of equanimity encompasses the totality of what is, respecting the fact that any single object, like any point on the surface of a sphere, is the center of everything else. In this way, equanimity tends categorically in the direction of intellectual humility since all unique foci are experienced as inseparable from the fields in which they are embedded. And, in this manner of appreciating the correlativity of every seemingly opposed side, they create and nurture new ways of experiencing the world.

This book recurrently dedicates itself to redefining equanimity—and, to a lesser extent and by implication, mindfulness—in fresh terms, often transplanting the concepts into languages pointing to what is left unspoken or has been lost in current discussions. Considered in terms of its Buddhist origins, mindfulness and the equanimity it can nurture may be broadly grasped as ways of seeing oneself, others, and the world that are unadulterated by our usual inattention to, and defenses against, our deep interrelatedness with what is. The art of tending that underpins both mindfulness and equanimity rests upon seeing and relating to—being with—what is, with full openness, active balancing, and poised understanding. This art is inseparable from ethics, orienting us to the moral project of recognizing and tending to that which we would otherwise wish to screen out, dodge, or even degrade. Doubtless the most poignant example of that which we are eager to escape is our own suffering and the suffering we too often encounter in the world. This is especially so if we ourselves have knowingly caused the suffering. We can go to rather extraordinary lengths to evade our pain and suffering: passively, like putting off a visit to the dentist or, in the case of the military veterans I treat, avoiding reminders of war trauma by not watching certain movies or the news; or, actively, like using substances to dull or blot out unbearable memories. The deeper ethics of equanimity rests upon the insight that whatever we do to elude our fears, sufferings, and confusions, not only feeds them but blocks us from connecting to the most responsive parts of ourselves and others. Without equanimity in particular, we are only partial, isolated, stunted selves, condemned to live in a universe in which others are seen to be just as fragmented, alienated, and arrested.

Growing a Human

Over 50 years ago, an important theory of how human beings most meaningfully change appeared in American Gestalt psychology, a discipline owing a great deal to Buddhist insights. Introduced by psychiatrist Arnold Beisser (1925-91), "the paradoxical theory of change" states that authentic change occurs when persons become more fully what they are, as opposed to becoming, or being compelled to become, what they are not. It is a process of change whereby person X does not become person Y, but becomes X prime (X^1) or, we might say, more completely and interdependently X. As a model of change, it recognizes that there is always a sort of developmental continuity, or potentiality, entailed in the unfolding of all living activities. Working as a psychotherapist with traumatized military veterans and others with chronic mental health issues has convinced me that the formula of X becoming Y is not only impossible, but potentially adverse. To realize one's original potential means growing or reaching beyond the personal, the level at which change is usually measured, to engage openly with the interpersonal and the collective or environmental. Change gestures beyond itself. The most profound change occurs *without*—in the double sense of "lacking" and "outside of, beyond"—the compulsion of "you must be this" or "you really should be that." The forcing of personal change, internally or externally, reinforces the very structures that inhibited change or growth in the first place. It is rather like the title of a popular 1930s self-help book that reached its fifth edition in 1978, *You Must Relax*, whose subtitle "A Practical Method of Reducing the Strains of Modern Living" begs the question of how much of the stress of modern living can be tied to *obligatory* relaxation.

The paradoxical theory of change also emphasizes that what humans become is conditioned by their dynamic relation to the changing environment. We grow and flourish, just like plants and everything else natural, as a result of multiplex transactions with our environment, and to that extent it does not make sense to speak only of organisms, but rather *organism-environments*. It was thinkers like Herbert Spencer and John Dewey who, in the nineteenth century, put forward novel understandings of the interactions between humans and their environments that ultimately swept aside the delusion that we are merely autonomous bags of skin, or "skin-encapsulated egos" as Alan Watts called them, acting unilaterally upon the universe. Inclining the universe toward the desires or fears of our egos assumes that one somehow has a vantage point outside it or against it. Humans of course have nothing of the sort, and are immersed in the changing material world, navigating a complex mixture of not entirely reconcilable influences. The Russian philosopher and literary critic Mikhail Bakhtin (1895-1975) described the compound world as necessarily involving both "centripetal" tendencies toward order and unity at the center and "centrifugal" ones toward diversity and difference on the borders or margins (*The Dialogic Imagination*, pp. 270-72). One of the keynotes of equanimity-based awareness is realizing that the constant state of flux is inescapable, and, being always in the middle of things, the best we can do is stay moving with them. This is not a surrendering to rushing currents but rather the apprehension that setting an existential course means staying attuned to both centripetal and centrifugal forces. Within the space between idealism and materialism, the interstice where flexible perspectives and holistic approaches may be cultivated, cravings for permanence, certainty, or a coherent life-narrative are recognized as operating in the midst of forces whose dynamism means that contingency, perplexity, and the incalculably fragile are inexorable.

We resist change to the extent we equate permanence with security and predictability. If things remain formally the same, if they follow the same sequence, then that means, so the logic goes, that we cannot be taken unawares, truly surprised, or shocked. This is why young children gleefully listen to the same bedtime story or watch the same movie over and over, and why the predictable rhythms of rocking, swinging, or bouncing are comforting to many, not only infants. At best, regularity offers us, as Robert Frost (1874-1963) put it when he described the effect of poetry, "a momentary stay against confusion" (*Complete Poems*, p. vi). Our own mental and emotional "momentary stays" reveal just how provisional our relation to what we take or wish to be unchanging indeed is. We can observe that such a relation is actually based on probabilities rather than certainties. Zen masters used to equate our yearning for the unchanging to the failed attempt to nail a peg into the sky. Our own minds are the best models of uncertainty and impermanence, if we choose to observe the ever-flowing stream of thoughts and feelings. One of the first lessons about the mind that meditators appreciate is: *at any given moment*, you cannot control your thoughts, feelings, or sensations. And: *there is no need to*. It is the nature of the mind to elude control at any point, despite our efforts to master it or subject it to the compulsions of certain kinds of psychotherapy, like cognitive therapy, in efforts to reform and regulate it. The mind is a kind of internal, intimate escape artist whom we can, as witnesses, come to respect in a spirit of ease.

Co-existing peacefully with our own fugitive minds is one of the most profound, and certainly the most challenging, models of psychological development. A unique process of *discovering peace* may serve then as a working definition of equanimity: equanimity does not change reality by making it, including ourselves, necessarily more peaceful; instead, it deeply alters our relationship with ourselves, others, and the world so that peace may emerge. Equanimity is a process without guaranteed outcomes. While there is no doubt that equanimity has far-reaching capacities for changing how we live, think, and feel, it works in part by refamiliarizing us with aspects of existing that were always already there. The image is that of a journey recirculating us to and past the point of departure, a kind of existential re-membering. Some teachers and gurus frame this as a return to our genuine nature, comparing it to the possession of a diamond that we already possess, right in one's own pocket, but that one is trying desperately to acquire elsewhere. In one famous teaching story, a diamond merchant boards a train with a master thief who spends his time during the long rail journey trying to pick the merchant's pocket. Exasperated by the effort of having used all his thievery skills to no avail, the thief stops the merchant as they exit the train together, and says, "I am the greatest of thieves, so tell me, now that the journey is over and you have nothing to fear, where you hid the diamond I was trying to steal." The merchant calmly replies, "Well, I saw you board the train and thought you might try to steal it, so I hid it in the one place I wagered you would not look…right here." And, as the merchant said this, he reached into the thief's own jacket pocket and held out the large diamond. And so, in a similar way, equanimity returns us to a state of ease free from the pressure to guard ourselves against the losses that we associate with negative change and, at the same time, from the relentless pressure to improve ourselves.

The existential condition of the person in a state of equanimity was beautifully, if rather enigmatically, captured in a haiku collected by the English writer R. H. Blyth (1898-1964): "Above, not a piece of tile to cover the head; / Beneath, not an inch of earth to put one's foot on" (*Haiku*, p. 31). Like her attention, hovering lightly over the multitude of reality between the sky and the ground, the equanimous person floats without a fixed abode since she is not imprisoned by stories that inevitably rest upon desires or aversions, wishes or judgments. In the true state of equanimity, one does not cling to ideas of what is supposed to protect one (tiles above) or where one is supposed to go (ground below). Equanimity means instead that one has continual freedom to inquire about what existence would be like without the certainties of fixed destinations or well-worn dependencies. Having no tile and no earth means there is no place to hide, and no solid place to hang existence. One is no longer findable by, subject to, dogmas guiding, channeling, and ruling existence. One is free, instead, to wander and wonder, a phonologically minimal pair that comes together in the inspiration of the 12th-century Zen Master Hongzhi: "wander into the center of the circle of wonder" (*Cultivating the Empty Field*, p. 30). When we are actively wondering, we are always at the center of things; there is no tile above or ground below to inhibit the ranging or wandering of the equanimous and questioning mind. This is precisely what wonder involves: it includes, yet goes beyond, our senses (touching the ground, for example) and our knowledge about the world (tile offering protection against the elements), to incorporate a crucial third way of seeing things in their present mystery and absolute novelty. As a third and complementary way of seeing, it is both mediated *and* pure, cognitive *and* experiential, intellectual *and* intuitive. Wandering in the midst of wonder, one of the most descriptive metaphors for equanimity, brings before us a way of seeing not driven by a need to control or use. It embodies values opposite those associated with the utilitarian. Equanimity allows the world to become ever more mysterious, affording the pursuit of what the literary polymath George Steiner (1929-2020) calls "the sovereignly useless," the object of a uniquely human drive "to be interested in something for its own enigmatic sake," which, he claims, "may be the best excuse there is for man" (*Has Truth a Future?*, pp. 16–17).

Traversing Binaries

> But the living all make the same mistake: they distinguish too sharply.
> —Rainer Maria Rilke, The First Elegy,
> *The Duino Elegies*

Equanimity does not submit to binaries as they appear frozen in either/or reasoning. It does not move beyond dualisms but inhabits them, lives and moves with them, yet in a singular way. Equanimity works according to a process whose apprehension of the world resembles that of Hegel's *Aufhebung*, a word that means a "lifting up" of something. *Aufhebung* refers to the way in which the earlier stages of an organic process are superseded rather than repudiated by later ones. Earlier stages, even if incompatible with later ones, are "lifted up," or subsumed into the succeeding stages. The process recapitulates a story about growth, and it is not surprising that Hegel used the metaphor of a developing plant to clarify the activity of *aufheben*:

> The bud disappears when the blossom breaks through, and we might say that the former is refuted by the latter; in the same way when the fruit comes, the blossom may be explained to be a false form of the plant's existence, for the fruit appears as its true nature in place of the blossom. These stages are not merely differentiated; they supplant one another as being incompatible with one another. But the ceaseless activity of their own inherent nature makes them at the same time moments of an organic unity, where they not merely do not contradict one another, but where one is as necessary as the other; and this equal necessity of all moments constitutes alone and thereby the life of the whole. (*The Phenomenology of Mind*, p. 68)

There are several problems with binaries that equanimity remedies. First, equanimity transcends the dogmatic valuing of conflict inherent in the logic of "it must be this as opposed to that." Declarations such as these strive for a settled, rigid view of reality where, for example, one interpretation of a situation is deemed "correct" and others "wrong." To be stuck in this kind of thinking means to reside in a universe in constant need of correction, and the point is simply that this is an embattled and exhausting place to live. It is also a narrow place where growth, resulting from new discovery and ongoing refinement of beliefs and hypotheses, is sorely limited, as we saw in our discussion of the folktale "The Wise Old Men." This may also be described as the place where the potentially explosive rigidity of fundamentalisms takes root in the social organism. Dichotomies where "X conflicts with Y, and X is right so therefore Y must be ignored, suppressed, and so on" ignore the productive possibilities of paradox in favor of static views of reality.

Scientific discovery, as is well known, often depends on the initial acceptance of a paradox in order to initiate lines of inquiry aimed at some future resolution. Working with a paradox is rarely a matter of felicitous compromise, but a realization that paradox is part of a larger process, which, if placated by compromise, loses the energy of creativity. In his book *The Marriage of Heaven and Hell*, the poet William Blake (1757-1827) celebrated the generative energy from tension inherent in paradox, declaring that "without Contraries is no progression" (*Complete Writings*, p. 149). A fine example of this is the current reworking of the models of how stars burn, which began when the Hubble Space Telescope provided evidence suggesting that the universe is not as old (younger than 12 billion years) as current theories of how stars burn suggested (with some stars dated as old as 18 billion years). Of course, a star cannot be older than the universe that contains it, and so this apparent paradox triggered a massive revision of cosmology models, for example, those pertaining to whether stars are structurally stable with defined layers or more dynamically structured with mixing layers. The newer dynamic modelling has required calculations so complicated that the fastest supercomputers are taking many years to run them.

Equanimity, ranging over the universe as a phenomenal field, values the open-ended and the not-easily-resolved. It sees questions as being equal to, even more important than, answers or solutions (a notion explored in chapter 3). The attitude here involves that which in Sanskrit is called *ehipasyika*, an invitation to "come and see for oneself." As an orientation toward knowledge, *ehipasyika* rests upon actively experimenting with your conclusions, rather than unreflectively accepting or dogmatically asserting them. It was a word the Buddha frequently used to describe his own teachings (Skt. *dharma*). Equanimity similarly proposes that any answer you can arrive at is inherently provisional, merely the product of the moment when questioning ceased or experimenting stopped. Equanimity is thus inherently unfinished business. It is a mobile, continually evolving questioning rather than a conclusive answering, and so it will always operate with perspectives exceeding the neat hierarchical categories and sequential orderings that normally structure our ways of knowing and learning. One way to think of equanimity is that it permits a shift of focus from a static body of knowledge, rigidified by dualisms and categories, to the dynamic process of knowing itself, where the latter has far-reaching implications for knowing/seeing as a radically generative practice. Each insight that equanimity offers is only one more point of departure for further inquiry. In chapter 3, I will reapproach this crucial feature of equanimity as a way or process rather than a destination. If equanimity means something like "not going anywhere," it is only because it understands that, in the most fundamental sense, there is really nowhere "special" to go. "If there's nowhere to rest at the end," asks the fifteenth-century Zen priest Ikkyū Sōjun, "how can I get lost on the way?" (*Crow with No Mouth*, p. 17). Equanimity releases one from the pressure of finding *the* answer, and perhaps even from censure for not finding it, for the simple reason that, as the philosopher O. F. Bollnow (1903-91) puts it, "anyone who has no particular destination cannot take the wrong path" (*Human Space*, p. 111).

The ongoing practice of equanimity eschews the relatively subjective and arbitrary work of choosing or elevating one thing over another. This then is the second way that equanimity addresses a problem in the meaning of binaries as they are formally used: it troubles hierarchy. Binaries, as they appear in cultural conventions such as Health/Illness, Reason/Unreason, Reality/Appearance, Mind/Matter, Subject/Object, or Presence/Absence, and so on, reflect not only the human affinity for thinking in oppositional terms but the culturally- and historically-determined tendency to privilege one term over the other. No conventional binary escapes becoming a hierarchy, thereby ensuring its cultural stability to some degree. Yet the durability of such binaries, over time and across different contexts, is anything but certain. In contemporary Western psychiatry, for example, psychosis, as a form of disordered thinking and sensation, is firmly pathologized, devalued in relation to what is called sanity and the "normal" experiencing of reality. At the same time, to claim that all psychosis is pathological is untenable. The point here, from the perspective of equanimity, is not to romanticize psychosis, but to recognize that the dualistic relationship of psychosis to "normal" experience is imprecise at best, that it eludes clear hierarchical ordering. What is "normal" in examples of religious and mystical experience, for instance, may be typical also of psychotic experience. The breakdown of ego boundaries in both experiences is often pointed to as a commonality where differences between self and other (typically, ego and cosmos) momentarily collapse. While the model of reality shared by mystics and psychotics has marked differences from a model of mundane reality, it is also clear that mystical experience is compatible with psychological adjustment. In a famous study from 1991, A. Y. Tien calculated that 10-15% of the normal population has had some kind of hallucinatory or altered "peak" (non-drug-induced) experience over the course of their lives. Remarkably, in a U.S. Gallup Poll from 2001, 70% answered "yes" to the following question: "Have you ever been aware of, or influenced by, a presence or a power—whether you call it God or not—which is different from your everyday self?" (Gallup, 2002). Furthermore, given that in some non-Western cultures experiences such as auditory hallucinations appear as forms of divine communication, to construe psychosis as categorically negative amounts to Eurocentrism. Data and observations such as these point to the historically- and culturally-determined privileging of Reason over Unreason—behind which nest other binaries reinforcing its meaning, such as Science/Religion, Health/Illness, and Normal/Abnormal. Acceptance of their hierarchical thrust is inversely proportional to the wide-angle and mobile view of reality that equanimity calls and recalls into existence. In sum, equanimity does not allow the easy slippage of binaries into hierarchies, and instead grasps the fluidity and complementarity of any two conventionally opposing elements. It holds the power to draw them back into complementarity, escaping alienation in the process.

Over against a fluid and complementary world, binaries furnish the appearance of stability, clear division, and predictability. So, the third way that equanimity undoes the logic of dualism is through its even attention to differences in perspective and, specifically, to the messiness of chance and change. Binaries such as Life/Death and Order/Randomness test the very limits of human comprehensibility, and historically we have gone to extravagant lengths, psychologically and cognitively, to master such dichotomies so that a semblance of legibility can be preserved. The problem of the existence of luck or fortune serves as a fine example of our endeavoring to make sense of our universe. If there is such a thing as good or bad fortune, then that means the universe operates according to chance, the random distribution of positive and negative outcomes. Notably, however, the idea that luck operates like an invisible force has been rejected by Muslims, traditional Jews and Christians, and Buddhists. Instead of luck, it is the will of Allah; instead of the randomness of events, it is the result of God determining the course of history (e.g., Calvinistic belief in divine predestination); and instead of a transcendental power called "fortune," life is subject to *karma*. Until only about 500 years ago, with the exception of persisting strands of Greek and Buddhist philosophy, the prevailing worldview was that everything is determined by God, gods, or ancestors. Then the mechanistic sciences of Newton, Galileo, and Copernicus revolutionized such religious conceptions by positing the universe as a completely predictable machine that evolved out of randomness and chance. Darwin's science of biological evolution similarly demonstrated how minute chance mutations, as the origin of new species, are ultimately tempered by natural selection, a process of adaptation that is non-random. So, it can be appreciated how, historically, both religion and science have worked from patently different perspectives to tame chance in favor of some kind of Order, providential or natural.

Equanimity helps us see through this assertion of order and legibility that, to whatever degree illusory, furnishes us with a sense of control or stability. This does not necessarily mean that we conclude, with the Nobel-prize-winning biochemist Jacques Monod (1910-76), that chance alone is the source of all innovation and of life itself, but equanimity gives us pause to consider that when something happens in the universe its prior chance of happening *exactly* that way was infinitesimal. Monod believed that we humans exist only because "our number came up in the Monte Carlo game," and what he goes on to say is very interesting: "Is it surprising that, like the person who just made a million at the casino, we should feel strange and a little unreal?" (*Chance and Necessity*, p. 137). This sense of strangeness and unreality may be likened to the sense of wonder that equanimity opens up. Our intimacy with the fundamental question of how things turn out the way they do means that we are open to seeing each moment as absolutely novel, in the sense that any moment in our lives is one that we have never lived before and will never live again. Nothing is fully predictable or absolutely repeatable, a fact that emerges the more completely we look at our lived world. Equanimity reveals to us that any single moment is both familiar and unfamiliar, that any given moment, however insignificant or neutral, carries with it, as the novelist Joseph Conrad put it, "the seeds of further incalculable chances" (*Chance: A Tale in Two Parts*, p. 106). Indeed, a *moment* really comes from *movement* (L. *momentum* from *movimentum*). Holding both familiarity and unfamiliarity in a provisional balancing with respect to the moments of our lives is another way to describe a key aspect of equanimity. In resonating with the sheer reality of the world, the known and the unknown, our attitude relates to what Stendhal called an awareness of *l'imprévu*, or the unforeseen, in all events (*Mémoires d'un Touriste*, p. 46). He believed that without such understanding one could not act spontaneously, let alone ever discover joy in the inexhaustibility of existence. To resonate with the unforeseen means that one can never be bored.

Occasionally, when illustrating for my patients how equanimity welcomes the uncalculated, I refer to "the attitude of one-in-a-trillion," which simply involves asking yourself if you can name any activity, however extraordinary or mundane, that, in the act of doing it today, was done in such a way that there were not an infinitude of other ways it could have been done. A mundane example: I routinely drive my car to work in the morning. The exact path, to the precise micrometer, that my car's tires took will never be replicated, just as the road itself, altered through constant imperceptible wear and tear, will not be the same road taken tomorrow. Nothing will ever be the same again: obstacles (bumps, pebbles, patches of moisture or ice, debris, etc.) go unrepeated; my speed at any given point on the trip will never be precisely matched; and the cars around me will never be the same ones or in the same pattern again, and so on. Indeed, everything, every element, of what is summarily called "my drive to work" is utterly unique or, in shorthand, "one-in-a-trillion" or, to use a famous Zen expression, "once in a lifetime." The "strange and unreal" aspect of this is that everything—every event, act, thought, emotion, and so on—that constitutes one's lived day, indeed one's very existence, is unique, which is to say that every lived moment is like hitting the jackpot at the casino. A shift in perspective is entailed here, from an external orientation to static Being to one engaged within ongoing Becoming where each moment in time is unique. What is knowable, then, are only positions in a complex of unfolding interrelations comprising a dynamic field of "once-occurrent events of Being," as Bakhtin called them (*Toward a Philosophy of the Act*, p. 2). Equanimity, then, allows us the freedom of never being shockingly surprised. It affords us the space *to expect* infinite surprise. "Man," the psychologist Amos Tversky (1937-96) once noted, "is a deterministic device thrown into a probabilistic Universe / In this match, surprises are expected" (Lewis, *The Undoing Project*, p. 145).

Equanimity offers the insight that only to the extent that aspects of existence are seen as unique, which is also to say outside of our full control, do we then have the capacity to avoid feeling that our experiences are doomed to repeat, that we are locked in some particular reality from which it seems imperative to escape. States of depression or chronic pain, for example, readily condition sufferers to believe that the predominant feature of such states is precisely the grip of their unbroken persistence. Such belief only compounds and prolongs suffering. Equanimity can prove such conditioning unsoundly partial by encouraging a fuller, present-centered examination of any suffering state through an open appreciation of its flux and rhythm, the reciprocal relation of appearance and disappearance, as one unpredictably becomes the other. The effects of depression, for example, are then no longer subject to, or wedded to, predicting their persistence. Predicting and expecting that a state will endure means that, in effect, we have *already had it*, when of course we have not yet. Unfortunately, this kind of foreknowing, the contemporary psychoanalyst Michael Eigen remarks, "has a way of spreading through our mental field and acting like an anesthetic" ("Omniscience," p. 245). A life lived as if we have already experienced parts of it condemns us to a deadening monotony, and so equanimity liberates us from the grip of repetition by placing us in an emergent state, aware, unencumbered, less agitated. In the fluidity of equanimity, the apparent morbid eternity of our condition is nowhere to be found.

Levels of Magnification

> A hair swallows the great ocean, a mustard seed contains Mount Sumeru.
> —Shibayama Zenkei, *Zenrin kushū*, verse 237

Equanimity is thus a matter of perspective-taking that sees order and randomness not as an opposed duality but as just two different levels of magnification of the same experience or event. Returning to our earlier example: on one level of magnification, my drive to work was essentially like any other. I got to work on time, there were no accidents (mine or others'), I managed not to get a ticket (knock on wood), etc. Now if any of those things went differently—I was late because I was held up by an accident or I got pulled over given my penchant for speed—then I would be impressed by the striking difference from the typical, and conclude something like "that was odd" or "I didn't see that coming," and probably tack on a negative judgment of myself or others. Being caught up in a perception of the violation of order, I am prone to blaming thoughts and to self-centeredness. Yet, at another (lower) level of magnification, the drive to work went just as it always does, consistent with the Zen saying, "Each time you bring it up it is new" (Hori, *Zen Sand*, p. 259). At this level of magnification, nothing is anomalous; therefore, the novelty of it all eludes the fixity of judgment (crucially, not judgment itself) and serves as a reminder that resistance to the inevitability of difference and change is always fruitless. Available, as we zoom out, is relief from the burden of behaving as if control over chance or the unexpected was a belief that must be preserved. Equanimity is like never calling "misdeal" in a game of poker because one understands that the distribution of a winning hand is ultimately beyond anyone's control. Equanimity is thus wisdom in the midst of variables whose sheer number means they exceed our strenuous efforts to govern them.

From the point of view of equanimity, thinking in binaries is merely one manner of interpreting the world, which is also to say controlling the world. Binaries provide (often all-too-convenient) shortcuts. Part of the difficulty of embracing equanimity has to do with the feeling that if we abandon our accustomed dualistic explanations then we will be lost in what William James (1842-1910) once called "a big blooming buzzing confusion, as free from contradiction in its 'much-at-oneness' as it is all alive and evidently there" (*Some Problems of Philosophy*, p. 32). James is importantly suggesting that when oneness displaces contradiction—when *and* replaces *or*—the world comes fully alive in its presentness. Equanimity is the seed of this bloom, which we can watch unfold only when we relax our tendency to interfere, to divide by classifying and categorizing. The fear of *confusion*—a word that comes from the Latin verb for mingling or mixing—not infrequently leads to the wish for a universe in which everything is neatly separated, cut up into discrete categories and things. Of course, much of this separating takes place through language, by firmly distinguishing, for example, between nouns and verbs, taking nouns to exist in nature and verbs to be what nouns or things do. But all of this is grammar, not reality (or Reality). In other words, the grammatical rule that states that verbs (processes) must have subjects (nouns) is a curious notion because things cannot put processes into action. What we call things are already processes. Take the example of lightning when we say, redundantly, that "the lightning flashes." Notice that there is no lightning to be found that does the flashing—there is just the flashing. The philosopher Alfred North Whitehead (1861-1947) termed this conceptual trap "the fallacy of misplaced concreteness," that is, when human beings mistake conventions, like grammatical forms, for Reality itself, or when they confuse social rules with the actualities of the concrete, valuing the former as more fundamental than the latter. At the moment we forget that the realness of the world has nothing to do with our processes of reifying, our practices of projecting abstract forms of knowing onto the world, we succumb to the fallacy of misplaced concreteness. There are times when being reminded—or reminding ourselves—of this opens us more fully to Reality, more directly to what is: "Though you say 'fire,' you don't burn your mouth; / Though you say 'water,' you don't drown your body" (Hori, *Zen Sand*, p. 433).

Equanimity relieves us from this fallacy by reminding us constantly that our conventional efforts to pin down the flow of reality or experience only serve to get between us and the plenitude and messiness of everyday experience. What is true only relative to us is not taken to be true independently of our customary ways of seeing. Equanimity rests upon the insight that map is not territory, and offers us adjustable points of perspectival balance between the two. When, for example, we are too attached to, or persuaded by, our "maps"—our words, symbols, analyses, ideologies, and so on—we may fine-tune that with the realization of the immediate present in its plenitude. And, should we become too detached from convention, too unanchored in the flux and flow of experience, we may then reacquaint ourselves with "the rules of the game," even as we may resist them. A wonderful Zen phrase captures the lure of convention, using the image of a set of scales: "The graduations are on the balance arm, not in the balance pan" (Hori, *Zen Sand*, p. 304). To mark units of measure, while useful, is no substitute for handling reality. Flexibly moving between the neat parsing of reality and messy immersion in it, equanimity, however momentarily, allows for balance in our lives. Smashing clocks in an attempt to stop disciplining the flow of experience into coherence and predictability, or switching to a barter system because money only slices reality up into conventional bits by assigning arbitrary value, is hardly a sensible solution. It amounts much more to a finer and delicate balancing act, as when, walking a narrow line suddenly feeling yourself falling to one side, naturally and momentarily you lean into that direction in order to reestablish equilibrium. Equanimity may be described then as the virtually concurrent movement of attachment and detachment. It may be formulated like this: equanimity engages a perspective of balance not for the sake of balance but because mobile perspectivism affords engagements with the whole.

Respect

To entertain the possibility that opposites can be respected at the same time is at the core of equanimity. The standard definition of mindfulness—non-judgmental awareness of the present moment—ostensibly excludes our judgmental awareness. But, since such an exclusion, as actually practiced by humans, is impossible (or, we could say simply, unnatural), the prefix *non-*, by setting up a negation, is more than a little misleading. Preferable to the prefix *non-* would be something like *poly-* or *multi-*, in order to convey the fully shifting and simultaneous states of consciousness as they mirror the eternal flow and flux of reality. This harmonious relation of fluid mind to fluid reality means the mind is never stuck or blocked. So, one may have as many judgments as the moment elicits—that is how minds naturally operate—and at the same time recognize that any individual judgment is just one among many possible ones, and as such is always subject to revision, expansion, or reversal. Judgments are not, however, as the prefix *non-* otherwise implies, subject to negation. Judgment, in moments of equanimous awareness, does not have to somehow become non-judgment, as if judgments are intrinsically negative and need to be resolutely abandoned. Indeed, in its encouragement of a kind of finality, having no judgments would be the equivalent of having only dogmatic ones. In other words, the very suspension of my judgment is itself a judgment. When, however, we just let them flow, from one to another, there is no problem whatsoever with judgments. Observed from the fluid points of view of equanimity, negative judgments tend to exhaust themselves so quickly that they often leave little or no emotional trace (sometimes becoming their opposites). Yet if we choose to keep them around longer, with justifications and self-righteousness, then judgments can indeed turn into rather "ugly" problems. So, then, a less elegant, though more precise, way of defining this trope of mindfulness in terms of how judgments are equanimously employed would be something like awareness of the present moment by means of "non-sticking judgments." Judgments glide across the expansive non-stick surfaces of consciousness, with room always for more. The 5th-century Theravāda Buddhist commentator Buddhaghosa wonderfully compared mental stuck points such as judgments to meat sticking to a hot frying pan (*The Path of Purification*, xiv.162). Reframing mindfulness then in terms of equanimity, we understand it not as a *kind of* awareness but rather as an *attitude toward* awareness of any kind. Judgments are no more than instants or kinds of awareness, and thus from the perspective I am endorsing, they represent less problems to be corrected or views to be suspended than opportunities for actively observing them with total flexibility. In the process, we may approach them with a wise detachment, balancing and rebalancing any attachments and dissociations through spacious and changing perspectives. Such an approach may be described as one of profound respect.

Respect is predicated upon this continual balancing act of attaching and defusing. From the Latin verb meaning "to look at" (*specere*) plus the element *re-*, meaning "again, anew, once more," respect is a perpetual looping back to the object (e.g., idea, emotion, or person), where it is seen, considered, appreciated, then distanced from just enough to allow the process to begin again. Distancing, as a feature of respect, affords the space for grasping otherness through acknowledging its sheer variety and manifold modes of being. It involves accepting these as setting limits on our action, an aspect of *being at a distance* that Immanuel Kant (1724-1804) saw as characteristic of respect between persons as opposed to the compelling proximity of love (*Metaphysics of Morals*, p. 244). To respect is to look over or again, to take up perspectives. True respect for a person involves, then, the dual capacities of attaching to, engaging with, that person when it is perhaps adaptive or even pleasant to do so, and then of detaching, giving space to the person, who is now seen with the objectivity of contemplation or imagination. Only when having been given space can the other person be in a sense who she truly is, and thus be apprehended as who she truly is. So, in this way, in a moment of respect, one is aware of the object of one's emotion (e.g., affection) and also aware of one's own experiencing and relating, without which respect would become mere obsequiousness or a kind of hypnotic absorption. If we recall that *upekṣā*, the Sanskrit term most commonly translated as equanimity, also carries this association of looking and, more precisely, *over looking/looking over*, then the deep connection between equanimity and respect emerges quite clearly. (*Upa* means "over" and *iksha* "to look.") To look with engaged detachment *and* detached engagement is sometimes a matter of emotional survival, as when we are witnesses to events beyond our normal comprehension.

One such witness is pioneering documentary photographer Margaret Bourke-White (1904-71), the first female correspondent accredited by the American military to cover war zones, who arrived in Germany as World War II was drawing to a close. Her assignments included photographically documenting the concentration camps as they were first being liberated. In her memoir, she writes about being deeply absorbed in her photography and then stepping back to process it later given the sheer enormity of the atrocities she recorded which otherwise might have been completely overwhelming. She discovered, out of emotional necessity really, a way to balance engagement and disengagement as mediated by the camera lens. "Using the camera," she wrote, "was almost a relief. It interposed a slight barrier between myself and the horror in front of me." Notably, the words "almost" and "slight" signal the inherent fragility of this engaged relationship to the terrible scenes she encountered.

Operating with what she called a "veil over [her] mind," she conveyed the respect allowing her to recognize the historical importance of her photographic subjects and to continue to do so without being choked by disgust or indignation (*Portrait of Myself*, p. 259).

The Unthinkable

Equanimity offers a path through events that are "generally outside the range of usual human experience"—which is how the DSM-III once defined traumatic stressors for the purpose of diagnosing PTSD (American Psychiatric Association, p. 236). This definition is not a statement about trauma's infrequency, how statistically uncommon the experience of such events is (which, it turns out, it is not), but rather about its real impact upon persons, its disruption of personhood itself. Experiences of dehumanization, violence, and death are sometimes described as "unthinkable" or "unspeakable" precisely because they defy efforts to rationalize them, to express or contain them in language that could in any way capture their enormity in terms of the pain and horror associated with them. Certain transgressions of the social compact are too horrible to summon with words or mental images, and so are often banished, however imperfectly, from consciousness. Imperfectly, because what we think is expelled always returns home, like folk-story ghosts that return to expose the murderer. The site of this repression or banishment is precisely where equanimity can enter to restore a movement of balancing. This can happen through recognizing and actively tolerating the contradictions inhabited by the traumatized person who is caught between taboo, a will to disavow the story or deny the memory, and revelation, an imperative to tell the truth of the experience. What is deeply apparent from two decades of working with traumatized civilians and military veterans is that their symptoms are ways of telling a horrible story without words consciously chosen (in nightmares, self-destructive behaviors, isolation and avoidance, flashbacks, intrusive memories, hyperarousal, and so on). A story is being offered up, indirectly, fragmentarily, sometimes metaphorically or symbolically, but it is being told. Genuine healing,

I have found, begins when the unthinkable or unspeakable story is told to others *and*, often more importantly, the stories of others are listened to, reminding all of us that we are not alone, and that the truly horrific has a place *within* the bounds of the human condition. For us, there is, after all, no standing outside human experience and looking in, no clean vantage point from which we can divide human experience into the human/the inhuman. Often the best we can do is to "look over," with equanimity, the place where we stand now, letting the fullness of reality speak its words no matter its effect on belief in our immunity or separateness.

Equanimity is thus an awareness of action happening in a unified field, unbound by the contradictions of "my story" over against "your story" or "our actions" versus "their actions." Such distinctions clearly lead in the direction of moral judgments, exclusions, -isms, and conflict (internal and external). Alan Watts once very brilliantly pointed out that, while we can observe the conventional differences between what I do or say and what you do or say because they happen at different places in the same field, it would only

> mean something to say that I, the ego agent, make choices, perform actions, or think thoughts if it could make any demonstrable difference to what choices and actions occur. But it is *never* demonstrable either that what is done *could* have been done otherwise, or that what is done *must* be done—except by confining one's attention to very small fields, by cutting out variables, or, in other words, taking events out of the context in which they happened. Only by ignoring the full context of an action can it be said either that I did it freely or that I could not help it. I can try the same action again; if it comes out differently, I say that I could have done it otherwise, but if the same, that I could not. But in the meantime the context has of course changed. Because of this the same action can never be repeated. (*Psychotherapy East & West*, p. 67)

Equanimity attends to changing contexts in their fullness, allowing us to see, as described earlier, that every action is unrepeatable. Ignorance or, as Watts often parsed it, *ignore-ance*, equates to the Buddhist mental "poison" *avidyā*, a word used to describe the unwisdom of seeing the world as disunified, of mistaking our ideas about the world for reality itself (a process called reification, or the fallacy of misplaced concreteness described above), which explains a good bit of human suffering. *Avidyā* militates against holistic knowing. The word itself is a compound of the prefix *a-*, meaning "not X," and *vidya*, the Proto-Indo-European root of which means "to see" and is a cognate of Latin *videre/video* (again, to see). We are returned then to two alternate ways of viewing the world: *upekṣā*, looking over the whole field with shifting attention to details, a comprehensive and diffuse experiencing, and *avidyā*, not seeing the totality in the sense of hyperfocusing so that a part of the world or a sign (e.g., a word or image), being separated out, is mistaken for the whole or reality itself or construed as something that demonstrably could have happened otherwise. For dealing with extreme events outside the range of usual human experience, the implications of this difference between *upekṣā* and *avidyā* are profound. Equanimity, while respecting that some things in their full horror are beyond full representation in words or thought, resists taking them independent of their context, not because this could excuse or justify them, but because it relocates us within the space of what is. The process of contextualizing (re)humanizes us— even our persecutors. With the fearless presence marking equanimity, we turn into our suffering to find not only pain and transgression but *what else* is there.

The courage necessary for this turning toward suffering cannot be exaggerated. One of the most powerful *human* (and I wholeheartedly underscore this word) documents of equanimity was discovered when the Ravensbrück concentration camp, which was the only one of its kind designed exclusively for women and children prisoners, was liberated in April 1945. On a piece of wrapping paper, found near the body of a dead child, an anonymous prayer was recorded:

> O Lord, remember not only the men and women of goodwill, but also those of ill will. But do not remember all the suffering they have inflicted upon us; remember the fruits we brought thanks to this suffering, our comradeship, our loyalty, our humility, the courage, the generosity, the greatness of heart which has grown out of this; and when they come to judgement, let all the fruits that we have borne be their forgiveness. (Appleton, *Oxford Book of Prayer*, p. 112)

Every time I read this temperate plea, an oscillation happens, between what I can only imagine as immense sorrow, pain, and fury, which ultimately must defy full description, and "the greatness of heart" that is expressed so beautifully but, still, given its terrible context, pushes the limit of human mercy. The extraordinary power of this prayer is that somewhere in the space between suffering and a plea for forgiveness, the author found comfort in being part of a universe that contains both great malevolence and great virtue. It is a prayer of incredible presence and fearlessness that, with unmired and unmarred spirit, finds a place beyond binaries like good and evil wherein the fullest of what humans are capable of resides.

Sometimes, ways to equanimity depend upon venturing into the heart of precisely that which we terribly dread, that which has profoundly wounded us, as the famous Buddhist story of the mustard seed exemplifies.

The Mustard Seed

A woman, who had just lost her only infant son, was out of her mind with intense grief. Carrying the lifeless body in her arms throughout the village, wailing, she implored all those she met for help. Everyone wanted to assist her, but they were unsure of how precisely to do so, until one villager suggested that she visit a wise teacher who was camped at the edge of town. Heartened, the woman thought that perhaps this wise man would know a way to bring her son back to life. There must be a medicine, she thought, that would work this way. When she found the Buddha, she explained that her only wish was to have her son back. The Buddha carefully listened to her plea, and then said only, "I think I know a way." Fixated upon a way out of her desperate situation, she readily agreed to do anything he suggested. "All you have to do," said the Buddha, "is return to the village and ask the residents for a mustard seed, and bring it back to me." The woman was pleased since she knew mustard seeds were so common a culinary ingredient that any household would have some on hand to give her. As she was about to set off, the Buddha said to her, "One more thing: make sure the house you stop at has not known death." The woman knocked at the first door she came upon, told her story, and asked for a mustard seed which she was promptly given. Before leaving the house, she remembered to ask if this house had not also been touched by death. The man frowned and explained that a close relative had been tragically killed in an accident. The woman thanked him, and went to the next home. There she was given another mustard seed but finally heard a story about a mother who died in childbirth. After thanking this neighbor, she moved on, visiting all the houses in the village, and while she first received many mustard seeds, she also heard a story about loss connected to each seed. With no seeds collected, she returned to the Buddha, and said, "Thank you. I am healed." The woman devoted herself to being a disciple of Buddhism and eventually a teacher in her own right.

In the Buddhist scriptural version of this story, after the woman completes her search, the Buddha gives a rather lengthy teaching concerning the inevitability of death, pain, and suffering, reminding her that all are subject to death, that dying is everywhere a presence in this changing world. He emphasizes that wise people do not grieve because they know the terms of the world, and they discern that grief only increases the suffering related to loss. He points out that the injurious arrow of lamentation, complaint, and grief must be drawn out in order to find peace. The Buddha's metaphor of the arrow is one that has a privileged place in his teachings regarding suffering and dis-ease, the Sanskrit word for which is *duhkha*. "Life is *duhkha*," declares the Buddha in his first Noble Truth, a statement that was meant not as a pessimistic pronouncement, but as a reminder that suffering in the widest sense, whether physical, psychological, or spiritual, is simply a fact, a mark of human existence. The problem is therefore not *duhkha* itself, since it is inescapable, but the *duhkha* that we might add to the already existing *duhkha*, in other words, our responses to suffering that serve to mire us in more suffering. Think of *duhkha*, to use the famous Buddhist metaphor, as the first arrow that strikes: it hurts, and, understandably, one wants the agony to go away. But rather than attend to this wound in its bare state, we often generate narratives and questions about it that only compound the pain. In times of suffering, thoughts like these are familiar to us all: Why did this happen to me? This should never have happened. I can't believe it did. This other outcome would have been preferable.

Why does this always happen to me? This proves that my life has been a failure. And so on. Carrying on with self-referential thoughts, questions that utterly lack satisfactory answers, and wishes for alternate realities merely serves to distract from the first arrow's agony. Yet, these distractions only compound suffering—as if being struck by more arrows—until we, like the woman in the story, are momentarily disconnected from the world, isolated from the broader reality of our essential human existence.

Before returning to the story in its own terms, and the way through suffering that it proposes, I want to point out one way that equanimity affords us the opportunity to tend to the pain of the subsequent arrows of suffering. Equanimity is a constant folding of everything back into even attention. It looks over thoughts/stories, feelings, and sensations, with an attitude of "Notice this…what's going on now… notice that too." Rather than playing out a full story of what should or should not have happened, equanimity attends to every partial story, noting for example, "this is what distraction is like…that is what getting pulled into a story is like…this is what grief is like…." When we observe "this is what it's like…that's what's going on," we realize—and this observation is only ever a process—that, from the points of view of equanimous perception, there is nothing that does not need to happen. Rather, whatever happens is just one more thing to which we pay attention. By paying attention evenly, immense freedom is discovered: no longer is one caught, pressed, influenced, or driven by what is going on inside or outside one's life. Equanimity allows attention to function in this capacious way, tending toward and tending to our self-generated wounds.

The brilliance of the mustard seed story transcends its message about the acceptance of death and transience. The usual interpretations of the story focus on the significance of recognizing our shared mortality, and the finding of comfort through connection with others who, just like us, search for ways to escape the vulnerability of loss. When the woman comes to realize that she is not alone, that she has not been singled out by fate or fortune, she is able to see herself as part of something larger—the web of life and death. While there is no doubt these themes are immensely valuable, the story also teaches why and how exactly these lessons can be so difficult to grasp.

At the beginning of the story, the woman is immersed in a state of grief in such a way that her vision of what might bring her relief is so restricted that she can imagine only one solution—restoring her son's life. The villagers are unable to help her, not because they feel no empathy or fail to see the enormity of her grief, but because the woman herself has foreclosed the possibility of being helped due to her single focus on what is, admittedly, the obvious solution. If her son were brought back to life, her problem would vanish, so she imagines. The Buddha recognizes that even if her son were resurrected, her orientation to loss in general would not change. So, the Buddha plays along with her when he asks her to bring him a mustard seed, knowing that she would take this as a sign that he can in fact do what is impossible. The Buddha reveals himself as a consummate physician, a healer of the soul, who meets his patient along the grain of her symptoms rather than confront her with what, while true—he cannot raise the dead—would only send her into deeper despair, likely extinguishing her will to recover. By sending her back to the village to ask for mustard seeds, he in effect returns her to the site of her grief and pain. She must turn back into what for her was the unthinkable and was initially expressible only with inarticulate wailing. She must also keep moving. The Buddha returns her to the fullness of the present, to what is, in all its sorrow and enormity. He does this with a stroke of therapeutic genius when he requires that she collect seeds only from those households that have been untouched by death. He in effect administers a medicine that is inherently impotent. The Buddha prescribes a remedy that works by not working in the way that the patient expects.

By restricting her in this way, the Buddha places the woman in the position of someone who must ask questions ("do you have a mustard seed...has this home experienced death?") and then listen to the stories of others. She is not explicitly instructed to tell her singular story, though she may do so, but rather to open herself to others and, through the field of their different personally painful histories, encounter the suffering that has always existed around her. Through listening, she emerges from the cocoon of her self-centered pain, and eventually comes to see her own suffering as only a part of the larger human condition. While, on one level, her healing is the crucial result of her connection to others, on a deeper level, she is healed by transcending the very binaries that locked her into profound grief, namely, life/death and patient/healer. The language of grief is just that—words, sounds, reifications—while the essence of loss is something other. Loss, in its power to take root and emotionally flourish, may be compared to a mustard seed, which, though very tiny, produces a towering plant (black mustard plants, cultivated for spice, approach a height of nine feet, and grow prodigiously, like weeds). The first-century Roman naturalist Pliny the Elder observed that when mustard "has once been sown it is scarcely possible to get the place free of it, as the seed, when it falls, germinates at once" (*Natural History*, Bk. 19, ch. 56). The Buddha, as it were, sends the woman back to the seed of her anguish, a sort of return to origins from which she can generate a new approach to life, death, suffering, and healing. In the monumental collection of legends pertaining to plant life assembled by the early-twentieth-century American myth-collector Charles Skinner, there appears a relevant story about the generative virtue of mustard:

> In India the mustard symbolizes generation, and it is told that a farmer, having plowed over the site of a temple in which the nymph Bakawali had dwelt immovable for twelve years, her body having been transformed to marble, sowed mustard over the freshened earth. This, ripening, was eaten by his wife, who till then had been childless. The pair soon became the parents of a little one, lovely as a nymph, whom they named Bakawali, and who was believed to be no less than the original Bakawali, still in progress through the states of being. (*Myths and Legends*, p. 187)

The dualisms of life/death and patient/healer are central to this story. The dualism of life and death may be said to be what this story is about, especially if we consider that the woman, throughout her quest, is solely focused on bringing her son back to life. Initially for her, death does not—cannot—exist, and, in this state, she is out of balance to the extent she clings to one side of the duality. The anguish of her being alive and her son dead approximates the Buddhist condition of absolute *duhkha*. What the woman must come to understand is that being is relative to non-being and that the possibility of ceasing to be is present at any moment and certain in the end. The lesson she must grasp about death is, however, not merely its inevitability but, more crucially, its inseparability from life. Not to confront one's own existence with the constant possibility of nonexistence means that life is not taken seriously. By returning her to the life, the existences and non-existences, around her—i.e., the villagers and their lost loved ones—the Buddha guides her to a serenity of vision that is rooted in equanimity. Her "cure" results from transcending this dualism of being and non-being. Yet it also results from moving between the subject position of the patient and that of the healer in such a way that it transcends that dichotomy as well. A *patient*, from the Latin verb *patior*, meaning *to suffer*, is simply a person who is or feels trapped in *duhkha*. Certainly, the woman may be viewed as the Buddha's patient, yet she is also installed in the position of a rudimentary healer, listening to the painful stories of others, and the sequel to the mustard seed story is that she becomes a teacher, delivering others from their *duhkha* with the insights of Buddhism. It seems to me that, from the beginning, the Buddha was determined not to view her only as a victim of her loss, but saw that the potential for becoming a guide for others resides in every person.

To this point in our exploration, the story of the mustard seed dramatizes several important aspects of equanimity's potential to offer liberation from suffering. Equanimity offers freedom from the tensions of occupying the center of the universe in our usual ways: egoistically, defensively, dichotomously, and masochistically. When things are perceived to be out of balance in our lives, we will often struggle desperately, like the woman in the story, to regain a sense of equilibrium. The problems in our lives, however, may increase when we fail to recognize that some of the very efforts at balancing send us further out of alignment and attunement with what is. They may produce disequanimity. From the opening of the story, the woman's acute grief state is an example of an unconscious attempt at balance that resulted only in further misalignment with reality when she became fixed on the idea of resurrection. The perspectival and existential equipoise that is the essence of equanimity—a process, not an achievement—escapes the kind of suffering that results from being, like an asymmetrically-weighted wheel, off center when in movement. Interestingly, *duhkha* was a word used colloquially in ancient India to describe a wheel that hopped or wobbled due to imbalance (*kha* means axle hole, and when combined with *dus/duh*, meaning "bad," you get the image of wheels going awry). The opposite of *duhkha*, incidentally, is *sukha*, a stable axle producing level-going wheel movement or, we might say, a smooth ride. Equanimity is this condition of *sukha*, functioning, like a good axle, as the still points (of awareness) anchoring the smooth rotation of the wheel (experiences as they change, revolve, and flow moment to moment). Equanimity in a given moment is the featureless perspective from which a person acts, perceives, and remembers. The natural process of equanimity involves ongoing identifications with this perspective, which incidentally are available from the outset, in order to look over the constantly fluctuating thoughts, feelings, and experiences that comprise existence.

Tending

> Clear away weeds and seek the profound.
> — Shibayama Zenkei, *Zenrin kushū*, verse 60

The practices of tending and attending combine in the fluid process of equanimity. They have at their heart the act of paying attention to something in both active and passive ways. While applying oneself to the care of or managing the smooth cultivation or growth of something may be crucial, so too is allowing things to grow at their own pace and to develop their own forms. This is tantamount to *attending* in the archaic sense of the word—a waiting for. Seeds and gardens often need tending to, whether by human efforts or favorable natural conditions like rain and sunlight, furnishing the conditions conducive to their flourishing, in ways that are prolific at moments and even over time. The vital creativity of our lives also depends on the activities of looking after and caring for (ourselves and other beings), and the passivity of being cared for by others and of waiting and listening (another meaning of attending). Tending, as an important aspect of equanimity, means paying attention in flexible and holistic ways that appreciate the mutual entailment of the active and the passive. Tending is thus always a tending *toward*, a developing capacity to discern when it is best to act and when it is best to simply be or let be. To take a simple example related to a Zen story we will turn to in a moment: tending a garden means tending equally to the sprouting plants and the mature flowers or vegetables and to the weeds and insects that compromise their growth. Focusing only on eliminating the weeds and insect pests will not result in a thriving garden (and might even threaten it). The microcosm of the garden is tended to in its plenitude, involving one's full attention to the cycle of growth and its interdependence with the changing climate, seasons, and so on. There are two important aspects of tending that this brings before us: first, that, as we characterized the work of equanimity earlier, the work of tending can never be said to be completed because a mind in tune with the unfolding of events is itself always unfolding; and, second, that tending is as much a voluntary activity as it is an involuntary one, since the line between what we think we control and what happens to us is fuzzy to the point of nonexistence. Muso Soseki, a master architect of Japanese gardens, observes that "He who distinguishes between the garden and the practice cannot be said to have found the true way" (Berthier, *Reading Zen in Rocks*, p. 3). Let's go into this further with a Zen story.

Tending the Garden

A priest was in charge of the garden within a well-known Zen temple. Because he loved flowers, shrubs, and trees he was given this particular duty. Next to the temple there was another, smaller temple where there lived a very old Zen master. One morning, before the priest was to be visited by some special guests, he devoted extra time and care to tending the garden. He pulled the weeds, trimmed the shrubs, pruned tree branches, combed the moss, and spent a long time meticulously raking up and carefully arranging all the dry autumn leaves in neat piles. As he worked, the old master watched him with interest from across the wall that separated the two temples. When he had finished, the priest stood back to admire his work. "Isn't it beautiful now," he exclaimed to the old master. "Indeed, it is," replied the old master. "But there is something not quite right. If you'll help me over the wall, I'll put it right for you." Slightly taken aback, the priest agreed to help the old man over and set him down. Slowly, the master walked to a tree near the center of the garden, grabbed it by the trunk, and shook it hard. Leaves, orange, yellow, and brown, cascaded down over the garden. "There, that does it" said the old man, "you can put me back now."

The story turns on the old Zen master's "correction" or improvement of the priest's labor. Before I describe some terms of the Zen corrective, let's look at the positive dimensions of the priest's gardening. First, the gardening is clearly a labor of love, borne of the priest's appreciation for natural elements—trees, shrubs, and flowers are specified—whose beauty can be enhanced by care and tending. Second, and relatedly, the priest's actions and his mind appear to be in sync. Indeed, he was given the temple duty of tending to the garden precisely because he loves what gardening produces. He is acting on his desires—to make things beautiful and orderly as well as to impress his impending visitors—and in this he is apparently not blocked by such things as worry or fear; in short, he is not neurotically hampered, even if he is a bit obsessive in his raking. And, third, he is thorough and meticulous in his work. Psychologist Gordon Allport (1897-1967) noted that when Freud was once asked, "What should a normal person be able to do?" the founder of psychoanalysis replied, "He should be able to love and work" (*Personality*, p. 275). Given the priest's industriousness and penchant for gardening, he appears patently normal. Yet the old Zen master, looking over the wall, sees something more in the priest's activities.

Something *more*, rather than something *other* to be replaced: after observing the priest's labor and its conclusion, the master agrees that indeed something beautiful has been produced. The old master has observed another man creating order and beauty by imposing his will on nature with the activities of uprooting, trimming, pruning, combing, and raking. The question is then: what has the priest missed in his creation of beauty? The shaking of the tree, causing multicolored leaves to cover the garden was, on one level, a reminder that nature is beautiful just as it is, in its disorder (leaves do not gather naturally into neat piles), its randomness, and its growth and decay according to its own timetable. More specifically, it is only from a certain point of view that nature appears disordered, random, or untimely. From the point of view of nature, however, everything is just as it is. Indeed, the Chinese word for nature—*zìrán*—means "that which happens of itself," in other words, a spontaneous happening, not subject to any compulsion to be this or that, and thereby reminding us that there is inherently no necessity for things to turn out one way as opposed to another. Nature is perfect precisely because perfection is an ontological notion rather than an evaluative one. As a Zen phrase puts it, "From the start it is naturally so, it does not need any sculpting" (Hori, *Zen Sand*, p. 360). So, on another level, the beauty the priest created was an imposition on nature, perhaps based on ideas that he held concerning perfection or what his imminent guests would consider a perfect garden to be like, and therefore the beauty, from the old master's perspective, was in effect halted or limited by the priest. By shaking the tree, and recovering the garden with leaves, the master demonstrated that efforts to shape the spontaneous growth and change of nature in one direction actually stop the whole process. The Zen master, with a good shake, simply restarted it.

So, in this sense, the priest had not gone far enough in his tending to the garden, that is, in the old master's view, he did not understand that the work of tending is never complete, since there is no final mastery over the vicissitudes of nature. It is a mistake to believe that nature is teleological. The Zen master, looking over the wall to survey the miniature world of the garden, is seeing with the eyes of equanimity, rooted in an understanding that true vision of the world involves keeping pace with life's constant growth. To draw a line and declare that one has "got it all," that one has put it all right, is to oppose the fabric and structure of natural existence itself. Plants remind us that final meaning is illusory. "The plant," writes Elaine P. Miller, "always has one or more open end(s), turned toward metamorphosis and toward unspecified growth" (*The Vegetative Soul*, p. 12). Within equanimity resides an understanding that vitality is maintained by evolving in concert with the world, as seeds, plants, and the seasons do without rehearsals. This then is the most interesting aspect of the story because the Zen master "puts it right" by messing it up, by ruining one image of beauty by creating another. Equanimity accommodates different perspectives toward the same object, and has therefore a certain playfulness and spontaneity that often cuts against the seriousness, the work, that conventionally defines our lives. It avoids a conflict between conceptual consciousness (e.g., ideas about what beauty is) and nature, between the desire for order and the reality of flux. The Zen master in our story sees the futility of these self-created wars since he recognizes that such conflicts are really between two parts of the same thing. A vicious circle results, one that Watts once described quite clearly: "when we fail to see that our life *is* change, we set ourselves against ourselves and become like Ouroboros, the misguided snake, who tries to eat its own tail. Ouroboros is the perennial symbol of all vicious circles, of every attempt to split our being asunder and make one part conquer the other" (*The Wisdom of Insecurity*, p. 43; emph. in orig.).

In its free-floating attending to what is, equanimity never tries to make sense out of life through fixation. Putting leaves into neat piles does not make sense out of change or disorder; rather it merely provides the kind of "momentary stay against confusion" that I described earlier. Liberation from the imperative of "fixing" that equanimity provides allows for the freedom to dive into the pile of leaves, like few children can resist doing. The only way to understand change is to plunge into it, to go with it, to tend in its direction at any given moment. The question is not whether the world is changing but whether the mind is moving with the change. This problem of whether the mind moves was illustrated in the well-known Zen story of the two monks who were watching a flag flapping in the wind. One monk commented that the flag is moving, while the other replied that the wind is moving. Their teacher (none other than The Sixth Patriarch, Ch'an Master Huineng, 638-713) overheard them and intervened, observing that neither the flag nor the wind is moving but the mind is. The teacher transports the monks to a third, more capacious understanding: the mind that is moving is the one that embraces both perspectives—the wind is moving *and* the flag is moving—and a moving mind accommodates the inner reality of knowing without fixing, without declaring it is one thing as opposed to another. When we tend to our changing reality with an equanimous mind, we are free to respond immediately and appropriately rather than in contrived, defensive, discriminatory, or forced ways. Although such responding is never finished, as the master dramatized for the priest when he shook the tree, its roots in humility, naturalness, and spontaneity transform it from something like work into something more like play (a transition I will take up in chapter 7). The 14th-century Sufi poet Hafiz once said that our difference from the saints is simply that we think we still have "a thousand serious moves" (*I Heard God Laughing*, p. 127). The literary scholar and novelist C. S. Lewis (1898-1963) grasped the felicitous imbrication of play and seriousness: "It is one of the difficult and delightful subtleties of life that we must deeply acknowledge certain things to be serious and yet retain the power and will to treat them often as lightly as a game" (*The Four Loves*, p. 127).

II.
EQUANIMITY AND KNOWLEDGE

CHAPTER 3
SEEDS OF EQUANIMOUS KNOWING
Goethean Soft Empiricism to the Way of Tea

> Let mind come forth without fixing it anywhere.
> —*The Diamond Sutra*

> He who sees the Ratio only, sees himself only.
> —William Blake, "There is No Natural Religion"

This chapter expands our view of equanimity by describing more dimensions of it as a distinctive way of knowing. Equanimity, to this point, may be described as a dynamic and holistic way of seeing—knowing—the world. The equanimous mind, never rigidly schizoid (from the ancient Greek σχίζω, "to split"), always moves across and over dualisms. Through a flexible experience of the whole phenomenal field, connections between multiple objects of attention may be apprehended with a directness and freshness that more habitual modes of knowing tend to fracture or ignore. When binary and linear ways of thinking customarily split and channel our experience of the world, we forfeit something of the wholeness that is the essential nature of what can be seen. If naturally by looking over things, we come to understand that we are nothing other than one of the world's ways of revealing itself to itself, then there is also before us the opportunity to grasp how the world in a sense wants to reveal itself. Equanimity is the capacity for, the art of, receiving and making sense of more of the world's unremitting disclosure.

As we will see, some of the thinkers most deeply engaged with the world around them, like Goethe and Thoreau, grasped that, for the world to disclose itself in its fullness, the observer must be attuned to it to the point not just of familiarity or even intimacy, but of resemblance and identity. The basic idea, Neoplatonic in nature, is that only like can know like. Goethe, in a poetic epigram that begins "if the eye were not sun-like, it could not see the sun" (*Selected Verse*, p. 282), alludes to a famous passage from Plotinus's *Enneads* (I.6.9): "To any vision must be brought an eye adapted to what is to be seen, and having some likeness to it. Never did an eye see the sun unless it had first become sun-like." William Blake echoes this imagery in the frontispiece of his poem "The Gates of Paradise": "The Sun's Light / When he unfolds it...Depends on the Organ that beholds it" (*Complete Writings*, p. 760). If what we see crucially depends on what we in a sense mimetically bring to it, then genuine knowledge emerges from the vital harmony between mind and world, a parity, I suggest, exemplified above all by the dynamic ways of relating and resembling engendered by equanimity (L. *aequus*, "equal" + *animus*, "mind" or "soul"). Every object of knowledge, in a single moment, opens up a new possibility for its perception. And to keep pace with objects of knowledge—to "go on" with them, as Ludwig Wittgenstein would say—requires that our minds remain limpid, lithe.

Thinkers like Goethe and Thoreau appreciated that analytical intellect alone is inadequate to full, real, useful inquiry. The analytic mind, while undeniably helpful for breaking down, cutting up and tapering the world, risks allowing these intellectual acts to become primary attitudes toward the world. In the process of division, analysis exchanges living for dead knowledge. This rather grave conclusion, as we will see over the next three chapters, is a thread that winds through epistemologies found in Daoism, Buddhist philosophy and aesthetics (e.g., Mahayana Buddhist philosophers, Japanese Tea Masters), European *Naturphilosophie* and empirical science (Goethe), English Romanticism (Blake, Coleridge, Wordsworth), American transcendentalism (Thoreau, Emerson), Western philosophy (Nietzsche, Dewey, Heidegger, Koestler, Noë), 20th-century American psychology (William James, Maslow, Trigant Burrow), and the philosophy of neuroscience (McGilchrist). These different, and at times incompatible, views of how knowledge works all offer up novel kinds of seeing that bear important relations to the functions of equanimity broadly explored in this book. As I see it, they are united around the signal recognition that the mind only very imperfectly, by narrowly attending to facts or turning out interpretations, adds any kind of wholeness to what it apprehends in the moment. Imperfectly, since the usual process of grasping wholeness is one that tends to be abstract, indirect, or reductionistic. It also tends, as we will see, to be mechanistic.

Yet because things, as we may experience them, already and vitally interanimate, this means that we do not always need a third in order to join two, for example, subsuming things under a general rubric or organizing them according to some methodized theory. There is no requirement to systematize, to vigorously introduce conceptual connections, in order to make phenomena belong, or "hang," together. In fact, to over-rely on methods of order threatens creativity. "Too many apples from the tree of systematized knowledge lead to the fall of progress," as A. N. Whitehead evocatively put it (*Modes of Thought*, p. 79). So, in place of categorically parsing and rubricizing, the equanimous mind allows intrinsic wholeness and unity to emerge through what Wittgenstein—and here he was in fact following Goethe—called the perspicuous representation or synoptic overview (*übersichtliche Darstellung*), which consists in "seeing connections" (*Philosophical Investigations* I, 122). The idea is rather elementary: if knowing is tied to seeing synoptically, then there is no way that the world can offer us *any single way* of cutting things up. A theme of the present chapter is that the world reveals itself, through the lens of equanimity, in its very diversity, flux, and interconnectedness, thereby continuously offering opportunities for reflective, intuitive, and preeminently supple, understandings of our place in and relations to the totality of things. Equanimity can only proceed in such an additive way, where the process of approaching a more complete view of reality is the essence of creativity. "Real thinking," Gertrude Stein (1874-1946) observed, "is conceptions aiming again and again always getting fuller, that is the difference between creative thinking and theorizing" (Katz, "Matisse, Picasso, and Gertrude Stein," p. 60).

One of the remarkable things about equanimous mentation is that, through its comprehensiveness, it engages a higher cognitive function than abstracting what is general. Equanimity, despite its broad and sweeping attention, is not primarily a search for commonality in the form of a shared plan or general order for things. Rather, by looking at the same time for the internal "spirit" or essence of things, it appreciates how parts and wholes intertwine. In this way, it challenges traditional ways of seeing/knowing by overcoming separation but not *at* the level of separation. In other words, if the mind looks for unity by removing differences, then it works abstractly by means of seeing generally. However, the equanimous mind, by not taking abstractions as ends, operates by apprehending things comprehensively, understanding *differences as a unity*. In this way, it is free to travel in the opposite direction to theorizing or thinking abstractly. Equanimity is well suited for attending to the ways by which things are internally related to each other as dynamic elements of an expansive, indivisible totality. As an epistemic approach, equanimity demands more than safely distanced spectatorship, inviting instead involvements sometimes as shambolic as the world itself. Equanimity, as we will see, is never allergic to the messiness and vagaries of life, since to be so is ultimately to opt for a world that has stopped moving, a world devolved from a tremulous organic whole into separate, manageable, non-living bits. Watts once put it succinctly: "If anything that lives and moves is held, it dies just like a plucked flower" (*Become What You Are*, p. 59).

Before we turn to Goethe's view of knowledge and its affinities to equanimity, let's look at a notable story from the Book of Lieh-Tzu, one that highlights the difference between seeing vitally, comprehensively on one hand, and seeing abstractly, partially on the other.

Duke Mu's Horse

Duke Mu of Chin said to Po-lo: "You are getting on in years. Is there anyone in your family whom I can send to find me horses?" [Po-lo responded]: "A good horse can be identified by its shape and look, its bone and muscle. But the great horses of the world might be extinct, vanished, perished, lost; such horses raise no dust and leave no tracks. My sons all have lesser talent; they can pick a good horse but not a great one. But there is a man I know who carries and hauls, and collects firewood for me, Chiu-fang Kao. As a judge of horses, he is my equal. I suggest that you see him." Duke Mu saw the man and sent him away to find horses. After three months, Kao returned and reported to the Duke: "I have got one. It is in Sha-chiu." "What kind of horse?" "A mare, yellow." The Duke sent someone to fetch it; it turned out to be a stallion, and black. The Duke, displeased, summoned Po-lo. "He's no good, the fellow you sent to find me horses. He cannot even tell one color from another or a mare from a stallion. What can he know about horses?" Po-lo breathed a long sigh of wonder. "So now he has risen to this! It is just this that shows that he is worth a thousand, ten thousand, any number of people like me. What such a man as Kao observes is the innermost native impulse behind the horse's movements. He grasps the essence and forgets the dross, goes right inside it and forgets the outside. He looks for and sees what he needs to see, ignores what he does not need to see. In the judgement of horses of a man like Kao, there is something more important than horses." When the horse arrived, it did prove to be a great horse. (pp. 169-70)

We notice in this story that Kao practices a kind of knowing, a way of looking, whose skill transcends the abstract precision that the science of picking a great horse is conventionally taken to require. Kao's principal trade, after all, is gathering and carrying firewood, yet he seems to grasp that traditional equine disciplines, because they might be overly concerned with the "dross" or the "outside," risk obscuring, discounting, or even nullifying what is most precious about natural things. Kao's practice of going "right inside" admits the role of imagination, insight, and intuition into technical inquiry. The seemingly impossible quest for phantom-like horses that "raise no dust and leave no tracks" furnishes a clue to the nature of the special knowledge required for such a formidable task. The finding of such elusive horses—possibly, it is said, "extinct, vanished, perished, lost"—is not imaginable in terms of static images or fixed abstractions only, but more crucially as movements, transience, anticipations, possibilities. What is essential about such horses seems to reside in both their intangible spirit and their "hard" reality, their evanescence as well as their fixity. In Spinoza's terms, the horse embodies both nature actively in flux (*natura naturans*) and nature as finished product for scrutiny (*natura naturata*).

To a mind engaging relationally, imaginatively, and intuitively, the world of conventional qualities and quantities appears less consequential. The assertion that "there is something more important than horses" seems like a contradiction when the ostensible purpose is precisely to judge and select an exceptional horse. Yet such a statement makes sense when it is grasped that the preconceived categories used to describe horses, like color or sex, do not bring us at all closer to the object. Categories exist only as the result of superimposing our own framework upon the phenomena before us. Without recognizing that such a framework is never itself an intrinsic part of natural things, we risk disregarding the already existing internal relations within them, what Po-lo calls "the innermost native impulse" that truly comprises the essence of a great horse. So, becoming aware of what the animal may disclose of itself, the depths of its essential nature, involves being aware simultaneously of imposed concepts and categories themselves and any readiness to apply them in ways that may obscure the very essential phenomena we are seeking.

Equanimity, then, is crucial to knowledges absolutely in tune with the nature of things, since it allows entities to become intelligible within themselves, without relying exclusively upon external explanatory abstractions or forever reducing qualities to quantities. Equanimity allows for flexible shifting back and forth between modes of perception—in the context of this story, between "seeing horses" to "seeing a particular horse." It affords the opportunity to provisionally suspend all conventional classification systems, in order to encounter the entity as it is, not merely in terms of how it might appear identical to others (e.g., as a mare, as yellow). To know a horse strictly via facts about it amounts to no more than a limited form of knowledge that offers a partial account of such multiplex natural phenomena. "The totality of our so-called knowledge or beliefs," W.V.O. Quine (1908-2000) declares, "is a man-made fabric which impinges on reality only along the edges" ("Two Dogmas of Empiricism," p. 42). Kao's way of seeing a prize horse balances the pragmatic and the judgmental by attending to the edges *and*, vitally, to the center, appreciating the inner and outer forms and movements embodying an extraordinary animal.

To look in this way, as John Shotter (1937-2016) puts it so well, is to "win an insight into the inner formative movements responsible for the emergence of such forms into existence by sensing within ourselves—from within our relations to them—the differential responses such movements occasion in us" ("Goethe and the Refiguring of Intellectual Inquiry," p. 136). In these differential responses, and through the relations they open up, resides our capacity to see, as it were, from the inside out. This allowing of forms and meanings to come into existence is a crucial dimension of equanimous understanding. Without this imaginative faculty of cognition, we are liable only to see from the outside in, a kind of looking that imperils its subject, as Wordsworth apprehended when he wrote: "Sweet is the lore which Nature brings; / Our meddling intellect / Mis-shapes the beauteous forms of things:— / We murder to dissect" ("The Tables Turned," ll. 25-28). Any philosophy that substitutes fragmentary abstractions for the organic whole in its approach to the living, Coleridge wrote to Wordsworth, is no more than a "philosophy of mechanism, which…strikes *Death*" (*Letters*, II, p. 649; emph. in orig.).

Goethe's Delicate Empiricism

> Dear friend, all theory is grey
> And green the golden tree of life.
> —Goethe, *Faust*

> In my room, the world is beyond my understanding;
> But when I walk I see that it consists of three or four hills and a cloud.
> —Wallace Stevens, "Of the Surface of Things"

Contrary to the deadliness of intellectual dissection, which must proceed from the outside to the inside, stands Goethe's "delicate empiricism" (*zarte Empirie*), the term he favored to describe a mode of inquiry, of knowledge, that "makes itself utterly identical with the object, thereby becoming true theory," and, he adds, marks an "enhancement of our mental powers belong[ing] to a highly evolved age" (*Scientific Studies*, p. 307). One way to understand the "evolved" nature of this approach to the cognizable world involves appreciating Goethe's departure from any disengaged, abstract theory belonging to traditional scientific inquiry while bearing in mind the central ancient Greek meanings of theory (*theorein*: to look at) as a sort of cognitive apprehending or contemplation of the cosmos. Theory, in this sense, is predicated upon what Goethe called higher contemplation (*höhere Anshauung*). To engage with the world in order to know it depends upon deep mutuality and identity: "Man knows himself only to the extent that he knows the world; he becomes aware of himself only within the world, and aware of the world only within himself. Every new object, well contemplated, opens up a new organ of perception in us" (*Scientific Studies*, p. 39). The emphasis here on the interiority of vision and mimesis suggests that, while primacy is given to perception, such empiricism is "delicate" to the extent that it opens itself anew to each object and, in the process, enhances the observer's direct and mobile awareness. For Goethe, such a dynamic mode of looking is ultimately a kind of humility toward the object, an affirmation of nature as something sacred: "Natural objects should be sought and investigated as they are and not to suit observers, but respectfully *as if* they were divine beings" ("Cautions for the Observer," p. 57; my emph.).

This "as if" mode of study, by suspending our preconceptions, allows for the kind of respect and wonder that characterizes the attitude of equanimity generally, as suggested in chapter 1. Equanimity helps us to become transparent instruments of seeing and knowing, and does so most successfully in the context of preserving the reciprocity inherent in all relationships. Goethe emphasizes the geniality of balancing self and nature: "It is a pleasurable practice to examine nature and self at the same time without doing violence to the spirit of either, but rather to balance them both through a gentle exchange of their reciprocal influence" (*Maxims and Reflections*, #500, p. 434; my trans.). This equanimous perspective, a quintessential balancing act practiced in non-interfering relation to self and other, is a form of active attention that corresponds to Goethe's notion of authentic theorizing. "For simply to look at a thing cannot get us any further," he states. "Rather," he continues, "every act of looking [*Ansehen*] becomes observation [*Betrachten*], every act of observing becomes contemplation [*Sinnen*], every contemplation is an act of connecting [*Verknüpfen*]; therefore, one can say that, with every attentive glance at the world, we are already theorizing" ("Vorwort," *Zur Farbenlehre*, p. 317; my trans.). The progression from looking to observing to contemplating and, finally, to connecting is one of increasing involvement on the part of the observer, one that issues in the essential unity of observer and observed. Subject and object are not two but participate in a wider process joining them in interdependency. When the early German psychiatrist Johann Christian Heinroth (1773-1843) suggested that employing this processual and participatory thinking resulted in a new kind of concrete or "objective thinking [*gegenständliches Denken*]," Goethe was decidedly approving: "Here he means that my thinking is not separate from the objects; that the elements of the object, the perceptions of the object, flow into my thinking and are fully permeated by it; that my perception itself is a way of thinking, and my thinking a perception" ("Significant Help Given by an Ingenious Turn of Phrase," p. 39). To think "objectively" is a continual rediscovery of the object whereby "the manifestation of a phenomenon is not detached from the observer—it is caught up and entangled in his individuality" (*Scientific Studies*, p. 307).

Perception, in Goethean inquiry, flows; it is animated, vital, resonant; it moves with things rather than against them, in a spirit of openness. Its imaginative dynamism distinguishes it from what he called "the gloom of the empirico-mechanico-dogmatic torture chamber" of Baconian and Newtonian science (*Maxims and Reflections*, #430). Goethe's careful studies of architecture, color and light, comparative anatomy, meteorology, geology, and botany are all marked by a kind of equanimity of vision, a balancing between Aristotelian precision and Platonic intuition. For Goethe, equanimity avoids the possibility of two extreme relations to existence, both, he suggests, inimical to inquiry: the collapse of difference into a mystical oneness and the utter fragmentation of existence into isolated monads. "Everything that exists," he exclaims, "is an analogy for the whole of existence; for this reason, being [*das Dasein*] strikes us at one and the same time as separate and interconnected. Pursue the analogy too far, and everything coalesces and becomes identical. Avoid the analogy, and everything degenerates into infinite particulars. In both cases, contemplation falters—on the one hand there is an excess of vitality, on the other a deadness" (*Maxims and Reflections*, #554, my trans.). Equanimity makes an appearance here as a form of contemplation allowing the observer to steer between a holistic imagination devoid of attention to concrete particularities and an attention to individualities without a sense of the whole field.

Whether Goethe was contemplating and studying mineral formations, weather patterns, the plan of the Strasbourg Cathedral, the intermaxillary bones of humans compared to those of animals, the experience of primary color, or the morphology of seeds and plants, he recognized that forms of knowledge exist only in dialectical relation with their objects. So, the typical ways we investigate and describe the inanimate world—counting, weighing, measuring, for example—that require things to be divided into separate, self-contained bits of reality are not alone appropriate for living things whose fragmentation would mean nothing less than their extinction. Understanding the natural world is a process of knowing it from without and from within, where conscious, focused attention dovetails with the wider style of experience that forms its background.

Delicate empiricism thus amounts to a delicate balancing act where, by accepting the perceived object on its own terms, it is allowed to act upon the observer. Though it can be non-interfering, knowledge can never be a strictly passive event in the sense that a dynamic interaction with the world is instated as soon as we appreciate that nothing is ever really at rest. For this reason, our knowledge of the world itself must always be in process. Describing how our knowledge of the world takes shape, Goethe employed two key terms—*Gestalt* and *Bildung*—which he explained as follows:

> The German has the word *Gestalt* for the complex of existence of an actual being. He abstracts with this expression, from the moving, and

assumes a congruous whole to be determined, completed, and fixed in its character. But if we consider *Gestalts* generally, especially organic ones, we find that independence, rest, termination nowhere appear, but everything fluctuates rather in continuous motion. Our speech is accustomed to use, therefore, the word *Bildung* appertaining to both what has been brought forth and the process of bringing-forth. If we would introduce a morphology, we ought not to speak of the *Gestalt* at all, or if we do use the word, should think thereby only of an abstraction — a notion of something held fast in experience but for an instant. What has been formed is immediately transformed again, and if we would succeed, to some degree, to a living view of Nature, we must attempt to remain as active and as plastic as the example she sets for us. ("On Morphology," *Scientific Studies*, pp. 63-64; trans. modified)

Equanimity, as I have suggested, is another way of describing this "living view," this plasticity of knowledge that mimics its mobile objects. However useful *Gestalten* may be for the purposes of explaining or grasping something, we realize that they give way to *Bildungen* that may turn out to be momentary *Gestalten* for the ongoing formation of more *Bildungen*. We are always in the middle of, borrowing Freud's famous phrase, an *unendliche Analyse*, an interminable analysis of the world around us. The operative metaphor here is that of plant morphology: an elementary seed giving rise to a complex living organism. It unfolds from the bottom up, from the inside out or, if you will, it reverses the reductive, analytic gaze to the holistic panorama. Goethe regards nature as a living whole, always in systolic-diastolic movement, exhibiting "life and development from an unknown center toward an unknowable periphery" (*Scientific Studies*, p. 43). This is a botanical conception of the living. Indeed, when Goethe contemplated the meaning of vitality, he inevitably detected, according to Ortega y Gasset, "life under the image of a plant" ("In Search of Goethe from Within," p. 297). Goethe, in reading Kant's *Critique of Judgment* (1790), found philosophical precedent for paralleling art and nature since both are never required to act purposively: "Nature and art are too big to be harnessed to purposes, and they also do not need them since relations [*Bezüge*] are everywhere, and relations are life" (Letter to Zelter, 29 January, 1830, in *Briefe*, p. 370).

For Goethe, the shape and appearance of plants and their seeds offered the finest image of natural transformation and vital relation requiring a plasticity of mind that equals them. Roughly a century before Edmund Husserl (1859-1938) formulated the epistemological principles of a science of immediate appearances, which he would term a "descriptive morphology," Goethe had begun to practice it with his first major work on the problem, his *Metamorphosis of Plants* (1790). Setting out with a simple question—how is it that all plants look like plants?—Goethe started arranging and comparing plants, for example their stem-leaves, using a graded series in an attempt to find the rudimentary plan for all vegetal form. What he discovered was movement, metamorphosis persisting through the whole range of plant organs such that it is impossible to declare where one organ begins and another ceases. Through a careful process of descriptive morphology, it eventually appeared that all surface vegetal forms were nothing but metamorphs of a single underlying form, a transformation of the leaf. In his meticulous study of natural form, Goethe wanted to understand nature in terms of its becoming (*Werden*), and he found that its rich complexity, striking in its singularities, required models of movement and relationality to do it real justice. Equanimity in this context means turning attention from static singularities to the transformations leading to and from them, and further to reflections of the generative field of movement itself.

Equanimity, through special resonance with the experiential world, understands it as pure movement. The germination of a seed and its development into a plant is, from an equanimous perspective, all one movement. Anything taken to be separate is just an instant of a continual process. A seed, as one form a plant takes, harbors the shapes of the protean leaf. Goethe suggests that, attuned to movement and change, "we will not fail to recognize the leaf form in seed vessels—regardless of their manifold formations, their particular purpose and context. Thus, for example, the pod may be viewed as a single folded leaf with its edges grown together, husks as consisting of leaves grown more over one another, and compound capsules may be understood as several leaves united round a central point with their inner sides open toward one another and their edges joined" (*Scientific Studies*, p. 88). A seed cannot be said to be *in movement* since it *is* movement that constitutes the seed that appears to us. It is nothing but movement, and so, we might say, is everything else or, as the *I Ching* puts it: "Nothing is absolutely at rest; rest is merely an intermediate state of movement, or latent movement" (p. 282). Our consonance with the phenomenal world requires that, as the quantum physicist and philosopher David Bohm puts it, we "be sensitive to the eternally changing differences that are actually to be observed within each thing, and to the unceasing emergence of new similarities and relationships across the boundaries of various things" (*On Creativity*, p. 101). Knowledge, as we have seen in the example of Goethean science, is a mode of unceasing attunement, an opening to the emergence of new appearances that would otherwise be foreclosed in the absence of mimesis or the presence of stasis. The *Book of Lieh-Tzu* quotes the sage Kuan-yin: "If nothing within you stays rigid, / Outward things will disclose themselves. / Moving, be like water. / Still, be like a mirror. / Respond like an echo" (p. 90; cf. Graham, p. 281).

Seeds of Consciousness

"Plant a seed in the earth," invites Rudolf Steiner (1861-1925):

It puts forth root and stem; it unfolds into leaves and blossoms. Place the plant before yourself. It connects itself, in your mind, with a definite concept. Why should this concept belong any less to the whole plant than leaf and blossom? You say the leaves and blossoms exist quite apart from a perceiving subject, but the concept appears only when a human being confronts the plant. Quite so. But leaves and blossoms also appear on the plant only if there is soil in which the seed can be planted, and light and air in which the leaves and blossoms can unfold. Just so the concept of a plant arises when a thinking consciousness approaches the plant. (*The Philosophy of Freedom*, pp. 65-66; trans. modified by C. Holdrege)

To contemplate a plant involves, as it does for Goethe, an awareness of the connections it must actively generate in one's consciousness. Just as a seed comes alive in a hospitable natural milieu, it may also, when contemplated, germinate in the soil of human consciousness, where its reality as a total concept (seed-root-stem-leaves-blossom) is then understood in terms of its interdependence with the thinker. In his preface to the 1924 edition of *Goethe's Theory of Knowledge* (1886), Steiner wrote that normally "human beings feel a need to separate seemingly experienced thoughts from the things; in a true experience of knowing, we return thoughts to the things" (p. 3). This "true experience of knowing" begins in a kind of epistemology of equanimity, where, before conceptual thinking is joined with things, "the world appears to our minds as an absolutely flat surface; no part rises above any other; nothing has any distinction. Until the spark of thinking strikes this surface, we do not perceive elevations and depressions; nothing appears above or below the other" (ibid., p. 19). This smooth plane of consciousness is always available to us in our experience of the world, but often it is effaced when thoughts and judgments quickly form and convert steady mental topography into jagged terrain. Steiner is radically suggesting the appropriateness of considering human consciousness as much a crucial part of the environment necessary for a plant's life and growth as the elements of soil, water, light, and so on. The mind, we might say, is what gives the plant—as percept and concept—space to flourish. The plant can then be grasped as something that develops over time and shifts with different "approaches," different perspectives. A plant is never still.

In this section, introducing Mahayana Buddhist philosophy of mind, equanimity will emerge as a primary means by which thoughts may continue to flow in consciousness. Buddhist thinkers remind us that a preeminent sign of mental health is precisely the ongoing circulation of mental formations (Skt. *citta saṃskāra*) whose origins are called seeds (Skt. *bīja*). In the brief framing of Buddhist thought that follows, it is important to acknowledge that Buddhism is not monolithic, that it consists of multiple streams of philosophy and spiritual practice whose cultural, historical, geographical, and linguistic differences can be significant. Exploring those differences, like the nuances of their commonalities, is well beyond the scope of this book, and so the paths of inquiry pursued are necessarily eclectic. My present purpose is only to introduce some common terminology and traditional Buddhist discussions related to one aspect of mind and knowing in order to refine an understanding of the role equanimity plays in ways of seeing.

So, let us begin then with the important Buddhist term *ālaya-vijñāna*, usually translated as "storehouse consciousness." This is the part of the mind, in close analogy with the Western construct of the unconscious, where our habitual ways of seeing/thinking are maintained and also where they may be transformed. In the Yogācāra school of Indian Mahayana Buddhism (3rd–4th century CE to the 9th century CE), practices such as equanimity are taken to offer the possibility of altering habits of awareness, where one actively changes the way habits are conditioned. Thich Nhat Hanh (1926-2022), indebted to this view in his meditation retreat talks, often compared consciousness to a house, where the basement is the "storehouse consciousness" and the living room is "mind consciousness" in which the above-mentioned *citta saṃskāra* (mental formations) manifest themselves. Resting in the *ālaya-vijñāna*, as seeds (*bīja*), are the mental formations that have not yet manifest. These seeds, Thich Nhat Hanh emphasized, are the origins of the full range of human potentials, from compassion and wisdom to anger and despair, and they reside in the "basement" until they sprout as mental formations such as contentment or hatred. To become a mental formation in mind consciousness, a sensory organ or another thought activates the seed—e.g., a particular sight stimulates desire or the memory of one arouses fear. The notion of a *formation* in Buddhist philosophy represents something created by many conditions coming together, and, depending on the system of Buddhist psychology (*Abhidharma*), there are as many as 52 varieties of seeds that can manifest as 52 distinct mental formations.

Thich Nhat Hanh emphasizes that the passage of store-house seeds to mental formations and their flow down to seeds again is a natural, salutary process signifying sound circulation in the mind. In short, the central concern is allowing the seeds space to flow, neither attaching to nor rejecting them. Each Buddhist philosophical school has its own point of emphasis in terms of how important the care and health of the seeds is to human flourishing or to becoming enlightened. For the Yogācārins, the seeds are, ultimately, a way of discussing the karmic relationship between cause and effect, so there is a sort of karmic "storage" whereby the seeds generated by unenlightened actions are housed. Paramount is cultivating healthy roots, nurturing skillful roots for seeds, for, as Asaṅga (300-370 CE) puts it, store-house consciousness is like a "tree that depends upon its roots" (*Mahāyānasaṃgraha*, I.11). The Buddha often used a series of simple vegetative metaphors—seeds especially—to describe the "growth" and operation of consciousness (e.g., *The Connected Discourses of the Buddha*, III.54; *Anguttara-nikaya* I.223; III.76). And, according to the Sautrāntika view (from a school dating to the 3rd century CE), a seed designates whatever—an afflictive emotion, for instance—brings about a fruit through a modification or change in the mental stream (cf. Vasubandhu, *Abhidharmakośabhāṣyam*, II.36d). Liberation is conversely defined as the eradication of the seeds, a process conveyed by the image of seeds rendered sterile in fire.

In Japanese Zen teachings, which are for the most part consistent with other Mahayana philosophies of mind, the *ālaya-vijñāna* of the Yogācārins came to be translated as *zōshiki*, "all-conserving mind." More than a storehouse, the *ālaya* is figured as an impersonal force of nature in which we are subsumed, structuring our perception so completely that every element of conscious experience arises from, subsists in, and returns to it. The functioning of this unconscious force of being and becoming, so habitual and structurally integral to our grasp of the world and ourselves, and which conditions our very being and our experience of the world, essentially goes unnoticed. Zen teacher Dainin Katagiri (1928-90) characterizes *ālaya-vijñāna* as an "aspect of basic consciousness. It is going constantly without ever stopping, like the flow of a waterfall" (*Each Moment is the Universe*, p. 160). According to Katagiri, time is the energy that keeps basic consciousness circulating, as seeds produce more seeds and then return to their source and start the process all over again, which he describes as a kind of maturing. Through the achievement of a "mind of tranquility," without which one "can't see the panoramic picture of how existence is functioning every day" (ibid., p. 163), he urges, one is then able to "become one with *alayavijnana* and experience the stillness of the original nature of existence" (ibid., p. 164). In its tranquility and panoramic perspective, an equanimous mind supports the vital flow of seeds of consciousness within a systolic-diastolic movement oscillating between the relative knowledge of appearances and the absolute knowledge of what Buddhist texts term the suchness of reality (Skt. *tathatā*). Such a movement opens the possibility of momentarily relinquishing subjective experience and turning toward the immediate non-personal essence of things as they are in themselves (Skt. *yathābhūtam*). In Yogācāra philosophy, the term for this movement is in fact a "turning-over" (Skt. *āśraya parāvṛitti*), a revolution of mind transforming the dualism of subject-object thinking into a wisdom resistant to epistemic coagulation.

The metaphor of a seed aptly conveys the growth and metamorphosis of consciousness in its full potentiality. Seeds might be said to represent the kernels of our multiple and multiplying relations to the world. Sometimes they are the troubling origins of customary modes of perceiving and relating that tend to trap understanding in dualities, fragment the mental field, and arrest the flow of thoughts and perspectives toward things. Yet because no seed ceases to circulate at any moment and can always be reawakened in its circulation, seeds of equanimity are available to hybridize with the already circulating mental formations arising in our consciousness. When equanimity is allowed to disseminate, mental formations may begin to mutate. In this way, any and all emotions (positive, neutral, or negative) that, to follow Thich Nhat Hanh's architectural metaphors, have arrived in the living room of consciousness are mixed with seeds of equanimity that have naturally ascended from the basement of store consciousness. Now with multiple mental formations present—equanimity in a kind of even and shadowing awareness of everything else—they may return more quickly, having dissipated, to the store consciousness, and later begin a new cycle. Further features of equanimous knowledge that may be underscored here: seeds of equanimity naturally disperse or disseminate (L. *disseminare*, to scatter seeds); they do not eradicate (L. *eradicare*, to pull up by the roots). Or, as described in another context in chapter 1: they are additive, not corrective. And though they are never at rest and exhaustive, they are never exhausted.

The Question of Knowledge

> Knowledge has no ultimate goals; its progress is merely a greater differentiation in the questions raised.
> —Hermann Hesse, *Reflections*

> Try to love the questions themselves. Live the questions now.
> —Rainer Maria Rilke, *Letters to a Young Poet*

By taking up a sweeping position in relation to them, equanimous knowledge incorporates and at the same time transcends aversion and attachment, the painful and the pleasurable. And so, we might ask, how can we be at all interested in this kind of knowing if it is not rooted in preferences of some kind? What motivates this kind of inquiry, if not a "result" of some kind, a "payoff" in the form of an answer? What sort of desire underpins a genuine love of knowledge, our moments of unsettled epistemophilia? Framed within equanimity, knowledge cannot be motivated solely by ordinary types of love or desire such as enjoyment or the anticipation of a pleasant result. Nor can equanimous knowing *aim for* neutrality or objectivity, attitudes that are sometimes misguidedly equated with it. This section offers a view of equanimity as a set of possible orientations toward internal and external realities motivated by questioning *per se*. Equanimity poses questions from multiple angles of open, ongoing, and, as opposed to neutral, affectively-attuned inquiry. To the questions it poses, answers may or may not have immediate or lasting value, but value is always found in the very asking of questions. Any answers that questioning produces are understood at once to be provisional and their content—the sought-for "outcome"—forever secondary to the questioning itself. Thinking and knowing, in this sense, are built upon inquisitiveness, questions rather than final responses. "Thought," as the literary theorist and philosopher Mikhail Bakhtin incisively put it, "knows only conditional points" ("Toward a Methodology for the Human Sciences," p. 162).

I will offer one quick observation about contemporary Western mindfulness in the context of the provisional and experimental nature of equanimity. Too often, with an overfocus on intentionality, equanimity is described as a practice or technique that aims at the production of something—usually a state of stillness (where this book proposes the opposite, movement, while also altogether discarding the idea of an aim inherent in equanimity). Other proposed aims include a refashioning of the self (e.g., "to disarm the way we define ourselves in terms of achievements, fame, praise, and what we're told should make us happy" [Feldman & Kuyken, *Mindfulness*, p. 177]), or being compassionate and caring instead of discriminatory and judgmental. True equanimity, however, is not predicated upon changing anything. It lacks prescriptive value. It is not a form of resistance against specific forms of conditioning like those of late capitalism. It "disarms" nothing, converts nothing, and does not *necessarily* end in, or even entail, compassion and kindness (attitudes upon which the psychological science of mindfulness to date remains focused). Its basic function is taking up views in relation to anything and everything. It is additive, supplemental, not subtractive or corrective, and it is encompassing, not exclusionary. Equanimity, I have suggested, has a purposeless purpose. It is a practice of seeing, a *dao*, never a doctrine. As sheer process rather than outcome, its interest exists only in what it is doing, how it is moving *at this moment, from time to time*, e.g., questioning for the sake of revising knowledge and not for the sake of some pat answer to be finally gleaned or some ideology to be confirmed. Equanimity is verbal (as opposed to nounal); no sooner are you at one point than an elaboration or revision suggests itself. The real issue is not what it is heading toward, but simply: Is it moving? Foolishness [*la bêtise*], Gustave Flaubert (1821-80) once exclaimed, "consists of wanting to reach conclusions" (4 Sept 1850, *Letters*, p. 128).

Attempting to describe this methodless method is always more challenging than explaining how our minds habitually operate. Tibetan Buddhist teacher Geshe Tashi Tsering neatly depicts the usual kind of mentality that avoids the investigatory awareness marking equanimity. "The mind," he observes, "misconceiving the mode of existence of the object by seeing the object as existing from its own side, instinctively either moves toward the object or away from it, depending on whether the object supports or threatens the mind's own sense of a concrete, unitary self" (*The Four Noble Truths*, p. 64). Disequanimity describes a mechanical, reactive mind inextricably caught in the push and pull of its efforts to persist in its separateness. Knowing the manifold world is severely hampered when restricted to the narrow function of preserving autonomy through separation. As long as knowledge remains tethered to responses (answers of some sort) rather than open acts of questioning, autonomy then appears only in a purely negative way. The French thinker Georges Bataille (1897-1962) put it like this: "No 'response' can offer man the possibility of autonomy. Every 'response' subordinates human existence. The autonomy—the sovereignty—of man is linked to the fact that man is a question without a response" (*Guilty*, p. 121).

The psychologist Abraham Maslow (1908-70) used the term "deficiency cognition" to describe this egoistically-motivated, dichotomizing style of mental relation to the world, this necessity to find a response to every question. He contrasted it with the rarer "cognition of being," or, adopting his shorthands: D-cognition and its alternative, B-cognition. D-cognition amounts to "selfish cognition, in which the world is organized into gratifiers and frustrators of our own needs, with other characteristics being ignored or slurred" (*Psychology of Being*, p. 223). Its cognitive scope is narrow. Tending to see the world in terms of single causes producing single effects, D-cognition produces mechanistic and atomistic understandings given its propensity to objectify and separate in the style of Aristotelian logic. Once an object and its experience are placed into categories and ordered according to them, prefabricated concepts replace spontaneous experience, and the self overrides everything that it confronts as not-self. Recall the epigraph for this chapter where Blake declares that "He who sees the Ratio only, sees himself only." With one's own concepts and abstractions functioning as a vanity mirror with which to catch at most glimpses of the *moving* world, the range of potential cognition is jeopardized, since here "what we call *knowing*," Maslow warns, "cuts off the possibility of full cognizing" (ibid., p. 100; emph. in orig.). The usual forms of knowing upon which D-cognition relies—including causal thinking, mechanistic explanation, and separation into categories whose most fundamental form is X/not-X—ultimately restrict cognizing about the world. They run the risk not only of disenchanting the world with dull taxonomies but also of endangering its future as something that can otherwise be related to with ease or, as we will see, an epistemic love. Maslow, in his distinctive aphoristic style, sums it up this way: "Ultimately, dichotomizing pathologizes, and pathology dichotomizes" (ibid., p. 192).

Against the pathological, as both cause and result of dichotomizing, Maslow offered the salutary alternative of holistic seeing and spontaneous, flexible cognizing known as B-cognition. B-cognition shares key elements with equanimity: an "Olympian point of view" (ibid., p. 92) that allows wholeness to emerge, a "non-interfering awareness of all the simultaneously existing aspects of the concrete" (ibid., p. 46), and a reliance on perception that is "gentle, delicate, unintruding, undemanding, able to fit itself passively [i.e., receptively] to the nature of things as water gently soaks into crevices" (ibid., p. 46). Like equanimity, B-cognition is agile and predicated upon "a perception of all aspects and attributes of the object simultaneously or in quick succession" (ibid., p. 99). Maslow recognized the affinities of this kind of flowing cognition with Daoism, and he would highlight the receptivity of awareness at its center, a kind of cognition "held in abeyance," operating in a "nonvoluntary rather than volitional" manner (ibid., p. 98), and thus "unmotivated, unusing. . .content to let it be itself" while all the while "letting [the percept] be itself, not changing it" (*The Journals of A. H. Maslow*, vol. 1, p. 208). B-cognition, to the extent that it remains "desire-less and fear-less," is "more veridical, in the sense of perceiving the true, or essential or intrinsic whole nature of the object (without splitting it up by abstraction)" (ibid., p. 223). In Maslow's view, it is an effortless dimension of psychological well-being, consisting in being aware of what really is. It allows for interests in and knowledges of the world not driven by compulsion or egoism.

In short, B-cognition, like equanimity, is never an end but a means by which we may locate an object's genuine nature. This epistemology amounts to the exercise of a spirit of kinship with what is. Stanley Cavell has claimed that perception is at its best when it is based upon affinity, an empathic "love of world" he called it (*The Claim of Reason*, p. 431). Without a doubt, Maslow would agree with this, labeling such perception "fusion knowledge" or "love knowledge," and declaring these ways of knowing the most productive for psychology's humanistic mission of understanding people (*The Psychology of Science*, p. 52). Equanimity underscores that this kinship in the service of knowledge is ongoing, a flexible valuing of the world that is finally not achievable in terms of something that can be said to have been completed, like a task that might be crossed off a list. The unfinished business of equanimity is a mode of care that may be generalized as epistemic love. I have in mind here two related aspects of love that bring us closer to the living center of equanimity: first, there is love's power to help apprehend more fully the object of our interest, as it moves in a direction from the more obvious to the less obvious, often coming to value the latter; and, second, there is love's (often) implicit investment in there being forever something more to what we love. Equanimity, as a form of open, affectively-charged knowing, takes one in the direction of full knowledge yet never arrives there. What is revealed to the lover at a given moment is always partial at best for there is, must be, something extravagant about the beloved, something that, by eluding quantification, keeps interest alive. We are reminded that knowing, truly knowing, before loving is delusory, without meaning, since what we love comes into view the more completely we love it.

While I reserve a more thorough exploration of the imbrication of equanimity and love in a future volume treating ethics, here I will accent affective attunement, at the heart of equanimous knowing, as a mode of genuinely engaging with the world. Valuing the objective or impersonal vantage point, equanimity does not finally posit it as any more empirically veridical than the subjective standpoint. As Goethe reminds us, disengaged empiricism carries the danger of lifelessness as well as, we must add, indifference and a sense of irrelevance. Were they to rely upon reductively mechanistic accounts only, scientific investigations of the universe, according to philosopher Matthew Ratcliffe, "could be of no more worth than a comprehensive account of the precise configuration of all the grains of sand in a bucket" ("The Phenomenology of Mood," p. 362). Such neutrality, he continues, means that "there would be no motivation for formulating a scientific theory, no sense of it being of any potential interest or consequence." There would be merely "a series of hollow claims that one might indifferently assent to or deny but which one could not fully *grasp*" (ibid.; emph. in orig.). In order to more fully know or grasp the world and relate something meaningful about it, affective attunement is indispensable. When it comes to investigating and describing living things, Thoreau was quite clear:

> There is no such thing as pure *objective* observation. Your observation, to be interesting, *i.e.*, to be significant, must be *subjective*. The sum of what the writer of whatever class has to report is simply some human experience, whether he be poet or philosopher or man of science. The man of most science is the man most alive, whose life is the greatest event. Senses that take cognizance of outward things merely are of no avail. . . . I look over the report of the doings of a scientific association and am surprised that there is so little life to be reported" (*Journal*, 6 May 1854, vol. 6, pp. 236-38; emph. in orig.)

Thoreau exposes a contradiction in some scientific investigation: that science is not inversely proportional to subjectivity but actually proportional to life itself, despite how it may officially appear. Not surprisingly, Goethe, whose experiential approaches to nature Thoreau emulated, argued similarly for the scientist to "make conscious use of [different] modes of thought and expression to convey his views on natural phenomena in a multifold language. If he could avoid becoming one-sided and give living expression to living thought, it might be possible to communicate much that would be welcome" (*Scientific Studies*, p. 277). He would truly be "the man most alive." The most complete and relevant model of knowledge that scientific investigation might produce will result from a flexibility of vision and an alliance with the living.

Equanimity, through its natural, unforced attunement and flexibility, fosters the creation of a living knowledge, and its openness to reality, as we will see, depends on its propensity to questioning. Before setting out a few remarks on equanimity and its relation to the question, let's listen to a story as told by author Toni Morrison in her 1993 Nobel Laureate address.

The Answer in Your Hands: Interlude on the Question of Knowledge

'Once upon a time there was an old woman. Blind but wise.' Or was it an old man? A guru, perhaps. Or a griot soothing restless children. I have heard this story, or one exactly like it, in the lore of several cultures.

'Once upon a time there was an old woman. Blind. Wise.'

In the version I know the woman is the daughter of slaves, black, American, and lives alone in a small house outside of town. Her reputation for wisdom is without peer and without question. Among her people she is both the law and its transgression. The honor she is paid and the awe in which she is held reach beyond her neighborhood to places far away; to the city where the intelligence of rural prophets is the source of much amusement.

One day the woman is visited by some young people who seem to be bent on disproving her clairvoyance and showing her up for the fraud they believe she is. Their plan is simple: they enter her house and ask the one question the answer to which rides solely on her difference from them, a difference they regard as a profound disability: her blindness. They stand before her, and one of them says, 'Old woman, I hold in my hand a bird. Tell me whether it is living or dead.'

She does not answer, and the question is repeated. 'Is the bird I am holding living or dead?'

Still she doesn't answer. She is blind and cannot see her visitors, let alone what is in their hands. She does not know their color, gender or homeland. She only knows their motive.

The old woman's silence is so long, the young people have trouble holding their laughter.

Finally she speaks and her voice is soft but stern. 'I don't know,' she says. 'I don't know whether the bird you are holding is dead or alive, but what I do know is that it is in your hands. It is in your hands.' ("The Bird is in Your Hands," pp. 182-83)

This remarkable story brings before us the problem of awareness and its relation to truth, the possibilities—and limitations—of questions, and the relative value of questioning to knowing. Like all great parables, this story is polysemous, and one of its main themes is self-reflexive: how to accept the troubling existence of multiple meanings. The old woman's blindness is in part her curse since she can only choose among "facts" for whose truth value as such she has no direct evidence. Yet it is also her blessing for in this blindness to realities pointing toward truths resides her freedom to interpret and intuit, her opportunity for genuine wisdom. She embodies the kind of supremely wise person who, as Hermann Hesse (1877-1962) puts it, "in knowing, always remains unknown" (*Reflections*, p. 94). The meaning of her disability is unsettled ("she is both the law and its transgression"), and perhaps this ambiguity is what is most unsettling for others, like the young people who attempt to discredit her. The real question they wish to pose to her, the question that lies behind "Is the bird living or dead?" may be: What do you really know about life and death, and what might you have to teach us, being that you, an outsider, are not like us? As a visionary, the old woman inhabits the liminal space between the center and the periphery of social and mental existence, and so it is around the question of the known and the unknown that she is tested. Likely, the young people's petition is rigged. One possibility is that it is all a charade, and the interlocutors have nothing in their hand. Another—which I think the story invites us to entertain—is that they have a living bird in their hand, so if the old woman says it is dead, they simply produce the bird or, if she says it is alive, they furtively break its neck and present it to her lifeless. The old woman knows that she cannot play this game according to the young people's terms since both guessing and cognizance are effectively eliminated as strategies by which their challenge might be met, indeed, answered.

The normal direction of the quest for knowledge, from what is more obvious to what is less obvious, is here reversed. The old woman grasps that the end of attaining knowledge not previously known has been rendered impossible because the only thing that is obvious, certain, is that the bird is in someone's hand. In other words, what is in hand is knowledge itself, knowledge about the bird—whether or not it exists, whether it is alive or dead. But the old woman refuses to play this game of strict binaries. Her long-held silence and her repeated declaration of not knowing the answer signal that the only "solution" to an either-or question is in effect to embrace both possibilities as knowable, which replaces the holding of either with a *tertium quid*. This more comprehensive way of seeing or understanding operates in a world of explanation in which there are few if any differences that actually make a difference. The bird is both dead and alive in the sense that the pertinent difference between being dead and being alive is not locatable in a dead bird or in a living bird, nor in the space of obvious divergences between them. A difference is nothing other than an idea, and as such is never delimitable by a single question. For the young people, everything rides on the answer, which in a sense they control and is for them far more important than the question. For the old woman, who in her silence lingers with the question, even to the point of her interrogators' amusement, what is crucial and consequential is questioning itself.

We suffer, a patient once told me, because we think we have the wrong answers. Part of the brilliance of this observation has to do with the realization that answers are, in a manner, always wrong when deference to the questions themselves is neglected. The most important questions we can ask rarely have answers. So, is there a sense in which the question is always alive, where the answer may be dead (or deadly)? I have always been struck by the fact that, according to the account of Jesus's interrogation by Pontius Pilate in the Gospel of John, no answer is provided to the essential question, the one around which all others must urgently circulate, namely, "What is truth?" (John 18:38). Jesus never answers, and Pilate does not wait for a response before summarily declaring that he finds no reason to sentence the prisoner. Despite Pilate's philosophical question likely indicating his cynical dismissal (though some commentators such as Thomas Aquinas saw no irony in the governor's query), it is the inquiring itself that crucially endures, here sustaining a vital link between all potential believers.

Central to the role equanimity plays in the production of knowledge is the ongoing realization that a focus on answering must give way to a persistent state of questioning. From an equanimous perspective, one more answer is far less valuable in vitally experiencing the world than one more question. Brahma, the Hindu creator deity, the philosopher Luce Irigaray reminds us, "asks questions. His genius is not to know everything but to be capable of one more question. Far from being certain, Brahma remains in a questioning state" (*Between East and West*, p. 41). Irigaray looks to Eastern traditions and finds confirmation that genuine teaching and learning happen through the transmission of knowledge, rooted in experience, from one person to another, in reciprocal fashion. At this site of reciprocity, the practice of thinking itself is shaped differently: "It is necessary to learn again to think without centering on the object, for example, to think in a living and free manner, unattached, neither egological nor possessive. This does not mean not thinking but being capable of going beyond the inertias of thought in order to set its energy free" (ibid., p. 67). The question offers a crucial way to set the energy of thinking free.

Thought whose energy has been liberated transcends any unitary or final perspective through its absolute mobility. The dynamism of such object-less thinking is temporal or diachronic. Never aimed at possession of some final meaning, it is propelled by question after question. This condition of always being capable of one more question characterizes what it means to think equanimously. Rudolf Steiner describes such kinetic thinking in connection with Goethe's morphological method: "it must be so inwardly mobile—living in the medium of time and not space—that it elicits one form (Gestalt) out of the other. This thinking differentiates in an organic way; it continually grows" (*Paths to Knowledge*, p. 10). Organic thinking, attuned to metamorphosis, entails that any "answer" to questions designed to gather some knowledge about the world and ourselves not be taken to have final or authoritative sense. Answers are, in this sense, always and already obsolete. And so, with always more questions to ask, knowledge is continually subject to revision. The questions themselves are what matters; answers are, at best, partial, provisional, conjectural. Emerson advises the prospective explorer in these terms: "Do not require a description of the countries toward which you sail. The description does not describe them to you, and tomorrow you arrive there and know them by inhabiting them" ("The Over-Soul," p. 244). Knowledge that rests upon abstract and static representation will always fail to satisfactorily capture its object. Continually in motion, objects of knowledge are always, in a sense, out ahead, exceeding any received depiction of it. They are vibrant territories for continual exploration, not static maps. To keep pace then with its objects, equanimity frames knowing as a process of dynamic questioning, even when—or especially when—the answer, following philosophers Gilles Deleuze and Félix Guattari, might otherwise appear fully satisfactory or rhetorically self-evident: "To the answer already contained in a question...one should respond with questions from another answer" (*A Thousand Plateaus*, p. 110). If everything is in motion, the possibility of a single question, a single viewpoint, is foiled.

The presence of equanimity denies us the sense that the answers we may be inclined to hold, or content to rest in, are anything more than initial paths toward further knowledge. It is only with more *ways* of knowing that something truly worthwhile can be approached, as in the Sufi proverb "I ask about the sky, but the answer is about a rope" (Shah, *Caravan of Dreams*, p. 181). Or, perfectly equanimously, in the Zen phrase: "Asked about east, straightway he answers about west [*Higashi o towaba sunawachi nishi o kotau*]" (Hori, *Zen Sand*, p. 250). Equanimity discloses the pathways, the lines of flight, whose negotiation calls more often for deference rather than conviction, flexibility rather than force, and silence rather than display.

Pathways of Knowing

> Se hace camino al andar. [The way is made by walking it.]
> —Antonio Machado, "Caminante no hay Camino"

I have urged a reading of equanimity as a methodless method by which we may understand that equanimity is not strictly a disciplined technique but instead calls to mind the making of pathways or passages, as in the ancient Chinese tradition of *dao*. Techniques versus pathways: this may sound like an overly subtle distinction, but it is an important one if we bear in mind that a primary function of techniques is the fashioning of meanings and order out of the fluid. Techniques permit us to contain and construe what is spontaneous whereas pathways afford movement beyond the necessity of interpretation or the inexorability of answers. Consider an example of recognizable technique: one can play the piano with the trained ability to cognitively parse and physically play musical notes and chords in a stylized manner, and it is this technique that allows the musician (and her audience) access to the immediacy of the aesthetic experience. Yet when music is appreciated as process rather than product, we depart from an emphasis on technique, as something culturally stipulated or mechanically defined, and enter into a fluid and reflexive sensibility that allows the music its fullest range of novelty and poignancy. In the realm of piano music, one thinks of the creative interpretations of Mozart, Schubert, Schumann, and Beethoven (especially the Diabelli Variations) by Mitsuko Uchida, the jubilant genre-blending of Jon Batiste, or the magic of Brad Mehldau's contrapuntal improvisation. The immediacy and specificity of music as a creative act are as dependent upon the anticipated responses of technique as the novel impulses and bursts of energy that carry it forward and open it to the full range of feelings and meanings, personal and universal, that may be incited. Indeed, without the latter, music's status as an art is jeopardized.

This section looks at a specific art—a way, or *dao* (Jp. *dō*)—whose form and meaning call into existence ways of knowing the world through purposeless activity. Our focus will be on the way of tea, 茶道 (*chadō*, *sadō*), whose fluent framing of the world may be understood within the context of multiple artistic (path)ways and traditional spiritual practices for attaining the realization of the equanimous Buddha-mind. These other so-called *dō* arts include *gadō*, the way of painting; *shodō*, the way of calligraphy; *kadō*, the way of flower arrangement; *kendō*, the way of swordsmanship; *kyudō*, the way of archery; and *judō*, the way of flexibility. As lived experiences, they are not reducible to ideologies. All of them "work" in a negative way. To use a famous Zen comparison, they are like the sudden emptying of a bucket holding all accumulated knowledge, technique, and effort whose bottom has fallen away. Consistent with the spirit of Zen philosophy, an absolute negation is always at the same time an absolute affirmation, and here what is affirmed is a novel way of relating to inner and outer worlds with consummate poise deriving from the wisdom of equanimity.

The way of tea (*chadō*), as we will see, is centrally the exercise of an abiding mind, one preeminently open and flexible. Indeed, following Japanese legend, the origin of the tea plant calls up a story of radical openness to what is. The story is that Daruma (the Buddhist monk Bodhidharma, fl. 6th c. CE) vowed to stay awake for nine years in meditation. In the seventh year, when he awoke after the first night he accidentally fell asleep, in anger he cut off his own eyelids and threw them down, only to notice that where they struck the ground tea plants immediately started to sprout. With a drink made from an infusion of the wondrous leaves, Daruma was invigorated and able to continue his meditation uninterrupted by sleep. Before long, news spread through China and eventually Japan regarding this fragrant and "divine" drink (茶; *cha*). In Japan, a complex and formal art would develop around the preparation and drinking of tea, the tea ceremony (*chanoyu*), and it came to represent nothing less than an alternative way of knowing and relating to the world. Like other *dao*, the way of tea encompasses a total "art of being in the world" (Okakura, *The Book of Tea*, p. 44). A popular tea scroll, based on Case 2 of *The Book of Serenity*, characterizes Daruma's nine years of wall gazing: "quietly sitting in equanimity at Shaolin, silently expounding the true imperative in its entirety" (*Shōyō Roku*, p. 19).

Despite its fabled beginnings, the essence of *chanoyu*, as the greatest Japanese tea master puts it, is no more than "simply to drink tea, knowing that if you just heat the water, your thirst is certain to be quenched. Nothing else is involved" ("The One-Page Testament of Rikyū," in Hirota, *Wind in the Pines*, p. 245). As a complete art or performance (*temae*), however, it involves balancing the mind and focusing its instruments, the hands, through cultivating what is called a "just-this" mentality. Just-this works equanimously, by the symbiosis of attention to the focal and particular ("just") and to the broad view of the present field of experience ("this"). As an epistemic praxis, *chadō* allows a comprehensive view of experience in which particular events are given context through an unfolding peripheral vision. This enactive way of perceiving or knowing allows one to maintain central or foveal attention while simultaneously anticipating and being open to future possibilities. Thich Nhat Hanh puts it this way: "drink your tea slowly and reverently, as if it is the axis on which the whole world revolves—slowly, evenly, without rushing toward the future" (*The Miracle of Mindfulness*, p. 30). "Just" drinking tea with deferential attention and an even, unhurried attitude opens one up to the "this" of the whole world through its unforced equanimity. In the reverence of tea drinking resides a deep awareness and appreciation of the locus of human awareness as the point at which there is no holding onto what is disappearing and through which there is no resistance to what is exigently appearing. The tea master, as the axis around which everything else turns, participates evenly in multiple orders of reality—the everyday, the aesthetic, the spiritual—without experiencing a sense of discontinuity or discrepancy. Indeed, among the Japanese tea masters, experiences commonly segregated as life, art, and religion are unified into a distinct, graceful aesthetic style, such that "the art of the tea adept constitutes a kind of high point of all art. One might even say that it sums up the human condition itself" (Kato, *Form, Style, Tradition*, p. 163).

Embodied in the art of Sen no Rikyū (1522-91), who is generally recognized as having brought *chanoyu* to its acme as an art form in the sixteenth century, and in that of other great tea masters, is the core Buddhist principle that "in the last resort, nothing is gained" (Feng, *A History of Chinese Philosophy*, p. 433). There is no single point or achievement toward which the tea ceremony aims. It highlights embodied action that is at once qualitative and quantitative since both process and product—the means and the end—are inhabited in a single and, most importantly, unrepeatable moment. In the *chanoyu*, even subjective relations are not reiterable, as in the Zen phrase, "host and guest at every instant are new" (Hori, *Zen Sand*, p. 393). No purpose is allowed to be more crucial than the activity itself, and thus movement is the ground from which all knowledge issues and to which it returns. Before we look at the kind of mobile awareness that *chanoyu* calls into being, I would like to highlight the equanimous attitude inspired by the actions peculiar to tea practice, whose fundamentals are: "Harmony, respect, purity, tranquility" (*Zenrin kushū*, verse 74: ibid., p. 178).

The *Rikyū Hyakushu* (Rikyū's *Hundred Verses*) offers advice for tea practitioners in a rhetorical form consonant with the traditional Rinzai Zen kōan curriculum's capping phrases (*jakugo*). Here are a few characteristic *jakugo* serving as tea practice mnemonic aids: "When using your right hand, remember to have your mind on your left hand" (Iguchi Kaisen, *Rikyū's Hundred Verses*, p. 82); "Show a weak touch with the strong and a heavy touch with the light" (ibid., p. 7); and "To speak of 'right' and 'wrong' in a place of learning—how foolish, how foolish" (ibid., p. 2). The emphasis on avoiding extremes through balance, harmony, and grace or purity of movement is also captured in this poignant verse: "Whenever you set anything down as you change its position, withdraw your hand as though it were parting from a loved one" (ibid., p. 9). C*hadō* is a total experience, not achieved by striving: "Dye your heart with chanoyu; it is not anything visible, and there is nothing to be heard by straining your ears" (ibid., p. 91). In the tea ceremony, domains as varied as the social, aesthetic, ethical, and epistemic are approached equanimously from the perspective of corporeal movements.

The great modern tea *sensei* Sobin Koizumi, now in her late 70s, made numerous attempts to retire, only to be repeatedly consulted by medical students from prestigious Kyoto University imploring her for lessons. Significantly, professors observed that those students who were practicing the *temae* possessed physical movements that became increasingly careful and graceful (see Brady, "This Tea Master"). In addition to promoting sensorimotor knowledge that may have practical implications, *chanoyu* fosters an attitude of equanimity that extends to social and ethical existence. Tachibana Jitsuzan (1655-1708), a samurai who purportedly recovered the text of one of the most important writings of the way of tea, the *Nanpōroku* (*The Southern Records*, attributed to Nanbō Sōkei, a legendary Zen priest and disciple of Rikyū), was a renowned tea lover and calligrapher. In his diary, he recorded this short poem: "Those who come / to my abode and those / who do not come / I never say I like or dislike them" (qtd. in Zalewska, "Expressing the Essence," p. 51). Such a balancing of attitude goes beyond a refusal to praise or blame others, to judge or compare them, and reflects an absolute openness to whatever may transpire, mediated by an unperturbed and flowing mind.

This fluidity of mind, which I have underscored as a primary feature of equanimity, appears in tea literature as the "spirit of continuity" (*kizokudate*) informing the physical movements of *chanoyu*. Jakuan Sōtaku's *Zen Tea Record* (1828), for example, characterizes the preparation of tea with *kizokudate* as occasioning a special moment of abiding awareness called tea-*samādhi* (*cha-zanmai*). Such awareness is expressed in instructions such as these: "when, in putting down a utensil, you release it and withdraw your hand, do so without in the slightest dismissing it from your awareness and shift the mind just as it is to the next utensil to be treated" (Hirota, *Winds in the Pine*, p. 265). Sōtaku continues: "prepare tea as the forms (*kata*) prescribe, without relaxing the spirit at any point; this is called 'performing in the continuity of spirit.' It is wholly the functioning of *chanoyu-samādhi*" (ibid., p. 265). This continuity informing movement is the preeminent sign of the equanimous mind that abides positively in its pure flexibility, its continuity of smooth transition from point of attention to point of attention. Sōtaku observes that *samādhi* is the Sanskrit word that Chinese Buddhists have rendered as "correct perception" (*shōjū*) (ibid., p. 267) in recognition of the mirror-like functioning of a clear, unperturbed mind that allows whatever images or sensations to pass before it without seizing hold of them.

Knowledge, tea masters attest, appears as a function of *zanshin* or "lingering mind," a relation to self, others, and world that allows for coping with all affairs employing a pure, straightforward mind that is immune to untruth. To move through the world with an easeful attitude of *zanshin* embraces two epistemic elements traditionally framed in the context of *chado* equanimity: *sei* (purity), referring to a heart-mind free from emotional turbulence, and *jaku* (tranquility), describing the nature of the ensuing untroubled and even mind. *Chadō* comprises then an important way to realize direct knowing, where the tearoom (*chashitsu*) is often construed as a sort of sacred space in this regard. In the tearoom, *zanshin* is informed by *mushin no shin* ("mind without mind," that is, a fluent, unobstructed mind). Indeed, the rhythm of *chanoyu* depends upon, for example, the host's making heavy utensils seem light and light ones seem heavy (Iguchi

Kaisen, *Rikyū's Hundred Verses*, p. 8; 85), while at the same time apparently handling some implements *mushin ni* ("without concern") while positioning others with ample *zanshin* (here, "lingering care"). An exemplary capping phrase in this regard reads: "I put the white moon into a bottomless basket and keep the pure breeze in the bowl of mindlessness" (*Mottei no ranji ni byakugetsu o mori, mushin no wansu ni seifū o tokowau*; Hori, *Zen Sand*, p. 585).

One of the most prevalent Zen expressions brushed in calligraphy is *ichigo ichie*, meaning "one time, one meeting," or, as it is sometimes translated, "the one chance in one's lifetime." This idea of the singular encounter traces back to 16th-century Japanese tea ceremonies, with participants meeting to have tea together, only with the understanding that this exact ceremony cannot reoccur in their lifetime. In light of its unrepeatability, *chanoyu* is delicately approached with attitudes of respect, acceptance, and equanimous attention. It was the controversial 19th-century political figure and tea master Ii Naosuke (1815-60), living constantly under the threat of assassination (indeed, he was murdered by political enemies), who popularized this classic principle in his *Satō Ichie-shū* (*Anthology of One-time Encounters in Tea*). *Ichigo ichie* encapsulates the kind of unfolding consciousness that, operating only in relation to the ceaseless flow of once-in-a-lifetime encounters and opportunities, lets any agitation that arises with the world's "goings on" fade toward zero. With every encounter understood to be unrepeatable, the potential exists to see each one fully in its individual terms, independent of any experiences, for example, of disappointment or shock. So, in this way, the *ichigo ichie* of the tearoom models the kind of frictionless equilibrium with everything appearing in each moment that I take to characterize the equanimous mind. One of the dynamic achievements of equanimity is grasping that the same encounter will never happen twice, or as a famous Ch'an verse captures it, "Each time it's brought up [presented], each time it's new" (Foster & Shoemaker, *The Roaring Stream*, p. 193). Equanimity acknowledges the thought for which there is no preparation. It always faces the novelty of the world with flexible ways of seeing and imagining what is. For the philosopher Jean-François Lyotard (1924-98), the central element of thinking is to be found here: "Being prepared to receive what thought is not prepared to think is what deserves the name of thinking" (*The Inhuman*, p. 73).

Tea aesthetics, framed as a kind of learning (*manabu*) about the world, is directed toward the fostering of a mind able to find artistry in the natural transience, irregularity, and common imperfections of everyday reality. In terms of this orientation known as *wabi-sabi*—ephemeral sensitivity to the latent beauty of the flawed and transient—Rikyū would refine tea aesthetics, applying it to ordinary existence which offers a flush field of experience whose momentary forms resist ultimate, transmundane meanings. Rikyū once explained that "it is enjoyable to have a tea ceremony when it is raining, or when it is extremely cold; the tea ceremony would lose its very meaning if one did not enjoy rain and snow" (qtd. in Ueda, pp. 96-97). In one significant sense, the meaning of the tea ceremony *is* the rain and snow. *Chanoyu* is interdependent with the fluidity and evanescence of climate and season, while its participants—guests and host—are ardent co-performers in, co-creators of, the singular ceremony. There is no understanding *chanoyu* independent of or beyond its local performance. The *wabi-sabi* experience of the tea performance frames an eternal present that offers a context in which claims to knowledge of the immanent are possible.

CHAPTER 4
SEEDS OF EQUANIMOUS AWARENESS
Multiplying Perspectives

Above All of This

> There's nothing you've done that deserves this experience, that earned it. It's not a special thing just for you. And you know very well at that moment, for it comes through to you so powerfully, that you are the sensing element for all of humanity, you as an individual are experiencing this for everyone. . . . It's not for yourself. The eye that doesn't see doesn't do justice to the body. That's why it's there. That's why you are out there. And somehow you recognize that you're a piece of this total life.
> —Russell Schweickart, Apollo 9 astronaut

Knowledge of the immanent is perhaps best facilitated by realizing, as I proposed in the book's introductory chapters, our dynamic position in the middle of all this. A wonderfully apt image for representing this panoramic position is that of floating or hovering above, seeing from what approximates a *bird's-flight view*, that is, a perspective on what is surrounding that "unfold[s] itself to anyone passing over it, as in a balloon" (Hurst, *Oxford Topography*, p. 4). This bird's-flight view is not precisely the same thing as the idiomatic bird's-eye view. The single point of view of the *bird's-eye view*, while also offering an Olympian perspective, is more like the way a photographic consciousness operates than a consciousness whose essential quality is exploration. While the "eye" view is like standing on a tower or peak looking out, the "flight" view is like floating over an expanse, surveying a world that is available insofar as access to it is changing.

We recall that the Sanskrit word *upekṣā*, the term most commonly translated as equanimity, literally means "looking on or over," and the comprehensive epistemology it suggests is only really possible, as I have stressed in different ways and contexts, if perception is mobile—through sensorimotor activity, imagination, or understanding. In the present section, I want to highlight the emblematic dimension of elevation given its central and indeed salutary place, from the ancient Greeks to their modern representative in Nietzsche, in describing the universal, equanimous perspective on things as they are. For what is at stake here are ways of seeing, processes of intellect and imagination that are total, marked by equipoise, fluidity, and freedom from parochialisms. Together, these possibilities for relating differently to the world are connoted in another Sanskrit term, *samyag-drishti* (literally, whole or complete view; often translated as "right [suitable] view," the first component of the Buddhist Noble Eightfold Path). To acquire such a complete or balanced view involves engaging what is sometimes called the Eye of Wisdom (*prajñā*), a general order of vision we will discuss later in this chapter and the next. *Drishti*, the term for view, points to different ways of seeing things: e.g., seeing them wholly, uniformly, or seeing them in their separateness (a type of *satkāya-drishti*). The work of equanimity offers a crucial alternative to intractably inconsistent, afflicted views (*kliṣṭa-drishti*).

The first technologies, it turns out, for achieving something like a complete view, for enabling a moving vision approximating that of the whole field, were balloons. With the eighteenth century inaugurating hot air balloons capable of carrying humans in flight, an aerostat devised by the Montgolfier brothers put the first person above it all in 1783. The second manned ascent that same year attracted a Parisian crowd estimated to be 400,000, or half of the city's population at the time. "Balloonomania," as Horace Walpole in 1785 dubbed the rapidly developing fascination with the new aerial technology, took Europe by storm, fueling fantasy and the creative imagination (e.g., novels, poetry, stage plays), science, and commerce (Walpole, *Correspondence*, 25:596). Most radically, however, balloon flights changed how the world could be experienced—perceptually, cognitively, emotionally, aesthetically.

In the Englishman Thomas Baldwin's *Airopaidia* of 1786 we find a dramatic instance of the attempt to come to terms with the sheer novelty of the aerial view. Flying over the English countryside, Baldwin savored the "Chearful Serenity" arising from a rare perspective in which "the BEAUTIFUL and SUBLIME were seen united" (pp. 47-48). A zenithal perspective afforded him an equanimous state of knowing, a total sensorial experience, in which ineffable sublimity was coextensive with beauty that could be framed in words. For Baldwin, knowledge followed a Lockean empirical trajectory, with the expansion of the known directly proportional to the scope of sensations. The sensations experienced in a balloon in motion allowed for kinesthetic and polymodal ways of thinking about the world, the formation of mobile points of view enlarging the scope of what is imaginable. Baldwin insisted that such points of view, challenging as they were to the senses, given experiences of colors shifting dramatically and refracted light deforming impressions of scale, furnished above all an unbroken sense of tranquility. Through the perception of continual wonders, he testified that "an infinite Variety charms the Imagination. The Spirits are raised by the Purity of the Air, and rest in a chearful Composure" (p. 127). With his vision momentarily obscured by the clouds, Baldwin lost sight of the earth:

> This august central Situation, ALWAYS CHANGING YET STILL THE SAME, had the most striking Effect on the Senses and Imagination. Yet, however pleasing the Recollection of this GLORIOUS APPEARANCE; however strongly impressed, accurately described, or richly painted; it must fall infinitely short of the original SENSATION. Unity and Sameness were there contrasted with perpetual Variety: Beauty of Colouring; Minuteness, and consummate Arrangement;-- with Magnificence and Splendor: actual Immensity;--with apparent Limitation:--all which were distinctly conveyed to the Mind, at the same Instant, throu' the Intervention of the Organs of Sight: and, to complete the Scene, was added the Charm of NOVELTY." (p. 172)

Presented here is a mind that entertains the coincidence of opposites in its ranging equanimity. The identity of change and constancy, sameness and variety, and minuteness and immensity are grasped in the instantaneity of the panoramic view which never fails to lose its freshness or wonder. Fascination appears without the risk of fixation. *Airopaidia* is, at one level, an extended treatise on how the mind can maintain such an even, continuous state of wonder without becoming utterly spellbound. The book delights in a mobility of vision and knowledge reflected in physical flight. To the equanimous mind, in its buoyant state of suspension, everything is both wondrous and recognizable, awestriking and investigable. Equanimity here is a register of Cicero's contention that expansions of our knowledge are always accompanied by aesthetic experiences of pleasure.

In spite of the special status of Baldwin's book as unique among contemporary accounts of balloon travel for combining pictorial representations in the form of lavish engravings with a detailed subjective account of flight, its readership was probably limited to collectors and connoisseurs. On the wider cultural scene, however, balloonomania was in full swing. Images of balloons became ubiquitous in the late-eighteenth century, appearing on household items like cookery, furniture, children's toys and pacifiers, and displaying the height of current fashion, from clothing (e.g., hats, bonnets, garter belts, men's caps) to accessories such as jewelry and snuff boxes, even hairstyle (e.g., balloon side-curls). Having so stirred the imagination, innovative applications emerged for this novel method of transport and its special viewpoint, including land surveying, urban planning, cartography, and military operations. In 1794, at the Battle of Fleurus, General Jourdan was helped to victory by the earliest use of aerial reconnaissance by the French Aerostatic Corps deploying the portentously named balloon *L'Entreprenant* ("Enterprising One"). Not long after the early French photographer Nadar captured his first images from an aerostat in 1858, the strategic advantages of remote views of the lower world led to a rather robust confidence in aerostation by the Union forces in the American Civil War. The view from above, bound up with the dream of flight and employed as a perspective conceit in ancient and early modern texts—including Varro's *Endymiones* (c. 55 BCE), Cicero's *Dream of Scipio* (54-51 BCE), Lucian of Samosata's *Vera Historia* and *Icaromenippus, or The Sky-Man* (2nd c. CE), Rabelais's *Gargantua and Pantagruel* (1564), Cyrano de Bergerac's *Comical History of the*

States and Empires of the Moon (1657), along with its companion, *The States and Empires of the Sun* (1662), Swift's *Gulliver's Travels* (1726), and Voltaire's *Micromégas* (1752)—was now spectacularly realized as a technology of aeromobility.

Aeromobility opened up vision and radically altered epistemic pathways. Not surprisingly, it gave rise to novel epistemologies that were aligned to varying degrees with authority and power. Military surveillance is certainly a striking example of such an alignment. Before assessing whether equanimity itself is fundamentally immune to this alliance, it is important to acknowledge critiques of so-called scopic regimes of power. Doubtless, elevation itself has strong associations with the power to see or to penetrate with detached, clinical vision. It is seemingly an imperialist gesture. Critical studies of scientific modernity have uncovered the linkages of the totalizing view from above with the privileged vantage point of the modern subject or authority (e.g., masculine, abstracted, imperial). To view New York City from the summit of a skyscraper, French philosopher Michel de Certeau (1925-86) observes, makes the city below available as nothing more than a flat text: "it allows one to read it, to be a solar Eye, looking down like a god." For him, the view from above amounts to "the exaltation of a scopic and gnostic drive...this lust to be a viewpoint and nothing more" (*The Practice of Everyday Life*, p. 92). And when philosopher Hannah Arendt (1906-75) responded to cosmonaut Yuri Gagarin's first orbit of Earth in 1961 as part of what was then popularly referred to as "the conquest of space," she pointed out that such views—literal and figurative—risk detachment from spiritual and relational human commitments and values, and that movement into and through space, fueled by an unreflective belief in technocracy, radically decontextualizes humanity itself. Her famous 1963 essay issued the dire warning that, if the trajectory of space science continued without proper humanistic considerations, "the stature of man would not simply be lowered by all standards we know of, but [would] have been destroyed" ("The Conquest of Space and the Stature of Man," p. 280). More recently, Denis Cosgrove, in *Apollo's Eye*, his study of cartography and the Western imagination, characterizes the "Apollonian view"—literalized in the name of NASA's human spaceflight program from 1961-75—as the paradigmatic example of power relations mediated by scopic regimes.

While an epistemology of verticality can justifiably be said to mirror and often structure the imposition of control from the top down, it is also important to underscore that views from above are not intrinsically about power *over* anything or anyone. The ways in which such views are now taken for granted in the process of acquiring knowledge about our cosmos have perhaps obscured their more innocent epistemological functions. Popular technologies like Google Earth or virtual reality headsets, epitomizing the ease of affording elevated and mobile vantage points, install us in the momentary position of a kind of Aristotelian eternal unmoved mover contemplating the sensible world and beyond. And, as Jody Berland keenly observes, "when we check the weather reports to find out what's coming, we now take the viewpoint of the angels: looking down at the earth, rather than up at the sky (*North of Empire*, p. 242). In other words, it is possible that we are so accustomed to such a view from above that it passes below our awareness, signaling, on one side, its epistemological innocence and, on the other, its seamless flow with the will to power/knowledge.

Less than a hundred years ago, however, the aerial was the pre-eminent "new vision," to borrow the title of the seminal work by the Bauhaus painter and professor László Moholy-Nagy (1895-1946), who declared that "most essential for us is the airplane view, the complete space experience" (*The New Vision*, p. 178). From this view, "space," he wrote, "is conceived as flowing; a countless succession of relationships" (ibid.). In its spaciousness, this total experience embraces all that may be folded, through an open and ongoing process, into awareness—for any purpose, involving all objects in the field, and across multiple perspectives. Moholy-Nagy thought that these novel orientations to things from above were the key to linking traditionally static architecture with movement (*Vision in Motion*, p. 245). In this way, the Olympian view can involve a repudiation of tradition and domination and be thus invoked as the gesture of an offer, a gift of the manifold, enigmatic present. The discovery of the co-ordinates of a wider existence is made possible

Seeds of Equanimous Awareness 133

in this floating world, what the Japanese call *ukiyo* (a concept I will explore in chapter 6 in relation to equanimous identity).

Such an equanimous vision from on high may transcend the bare assertion of power in its usual forms, and is in fact sometimes employed precisely to undo them, often by going around them. Returning to aerostats for a moment, consider the contemporary do-it-yourself technology of balloon mapping deployed, in this case, above the overcrowded Lebanese refugee camp Bourj Al Shamali where lack of proper infrastructure and poverty contribute to detrimental living conditions. Hampered by partial and obsolete maps of the camp, an international team, in collaboration with local leaders and involving the camp's youth, set out to generate new ones using aerial photography in order to help visualize potential water sources and diagnose housing issues. The idea of possibly using drones instead to accomplish the task was quickly dismissed given their clear association with military force and the immunity of the remote observer-pilot. The aim of balloon mapping is the opposite: to use a technology of gathering knowledge that is visible, vulnerable, and affiliative. For the youth, who saw the red balloon openly floating over the camp,

> there was great appeal in knowing that they were bypassing governmental and corporate control over geo-spatial information. In a society where young people encounter so many obstacles in their efforts to contribute to their community, they were happy to be helping with producing something useful for the community and to be given space to solve problems by themselves through experimenting. They were also very excited to be changing the community's as well as their own perceptions of being helpless and ineffectual and to see themselves not as beneficiaries of an innovation but as partners and co-creators of the solutions to their problems. (Mansell, Dakhloul, & Ismail, "A View from Above," p. 56)

Affording an empowering episteme, the balloon-mapping project expands vision by transforming not only external and practical socio-spatial knowledges but also internal understandings of personal values and agency. At once communal and private, a new mentality flourishes within and through the space necessary for inquiry and experimentation.

The cognitive shifts in awareness that equanimity allows and engenders are perhaps nowhere more dramatically enacted than in the exclusive experiences of viewing Earth from orbit or the Moon. Having interviewed and collected the accounts of dozens of astronauts and cosmonauts, Frank White found they reported with remarkable consistency that their frameworks for understanding self, other, and the universe were strikingly changed as a result of having viewed this planet from outside its atmosphere. White called this signal shift "the overview effect" in order to describe how our conceptual schemas—literally, our "world views"—are profoundly shaped and reshaped by the specific perspectives we take up in relation to the universe, with vision from above being acutely transformative. In a radio interview from 2007, White described the overview effect in clear terms: "That experience of seeing the Earth from orbit, or from the Moon, and having a realization of the inherent unity and oneness of everything on the planet. It's a realization that we are all one in terms of our place in the universe and our destiny.... It's a shift in consciousness, a shift in awareness, and identity, and a harbinger of many more evolutionary transformations" (Interview, *The Space Show*). While White admits that such a manifold shift, not unlike a kind of spiritual conversion, is the experience of some and not all, he maintains that "going into space is certainly a modern metaphor for the journey to higher awareness" (*The Overview Effect*, 1987, p. 27).

Unsurprisingly, this extraterrestrial perspective has been, since the pioneering work of White over 30 years ago, of significant interest to psychological researchers who have attempted to specify this "higher awareness." David Yaden and colleagues recently proposed an understanding of the overview effect in terms of awe and self-transcendent experience, given the striking number of astronauts who described adaptive shifts in their self-schema and value systems. Emblematic here is Apollo 14 Astronaut Edgar D. Mitchell's description of the overview effect as an "explosion into a more universal awareness" (White, 1987, p. 220). This new form of consciousness, Mitchell explains, is not something sought after or in any way compulsory simply because you are in space, but rather results from "an allowing...allowing your belief system to be open enough so that you accept the information of the experience, and say, 'That's interesting, isn't it?'" (ibid., p. 222). Cosmonaut Anatoly Berezovoy describes the space traveler as one who "begins to think more, and his thoughts become broader and his spirit kinder" (ibid., p. 232). Going to the moon, Mitchell comments in another interview, "gets you closer to a more universal experience because of the distance and the wider view. You identify more with the universe as it is instead of the Earth as it is" (White, 2014, p. 33). Apollo 9 Astronaut Russell "Rusty" Schweickart elaborates upon his own sense of this interconnectedness as a key dimension of seeing from above:

> You identify with Houston and then you identify with Los Angeles and Phoenix and New Orleans . . . and that whole process of what it is you identify with begins to shift. When you go around the Earth in an hour and a half, you begin to recognize that your identity is with that whole thing. . . . You look down and see the surface of that globe you've lived on all this time, and you know all those people down there and they are like you, they are you—and somehow you represent them. You are up there as the sensing element, that point out on the end. . . . It's not for yourself. The eye that doesn't see doesn't do justice to the body. That's why it's there; that's why you are out there. And somehow you recognize that you're a piece of this total life. (White, 1987, pp. 11-13)

Notably, these astronauts' accounts of viewing Earth from above do not convey detachment, individualism, privilege, or decontextualized meanings. Looking over in this way is never an overlooking, in the sense of ignoring or neglecting. Seeing from above all of this does not correspond to a view from nowhere. Rather, the eye that sees does justice to the body, to borrow Schweickart's terms, precisely insofar as it bears the responsibility of being aware of its embedded relationship to the totality, to the whole "body" or cosmos. Becoming "that point out on the end" means taking up an equanimous view where the usual earthbound awareness is meaningful only when folded into an awareness of the world as a whole, a vision approaching everything in the long framework of space and time, *sub species aeternitatis*. As defamiliarizing as the extraterrestrial viewpoint might be, the familiar is lightheartedly rediscovered in its variety and wonder. "The Earth will show different sides of her face," International Space Station Astronaut Akihiko Hoshide relates, "and different expressions in a fast pace. You see oceans, you see deserts, the forests, and cities. And you see different times of the day. You will never be bored" (White, 2014, p. 1). Never being bored, observing (over) everything, means in essence that any fresh knowledge of other/outer space is also a kind of further self-knowledge.

The view from above is arguably the philosophical view *par excellence* since it affords new, shifting perspectives necessary for curiosity, knowledge and, ultimately, wisdom. Marcus Aurelius's famous injunction to "live as if on mountain heights" (*Meditations*, 10.15) captures the essence of a contemplative existence forged in relation to the "Olympian point of view," to echo Maslow's description of B-cognition, that pre-eminently flexible form of knowing and seeing. The French philosopher and historian Ernest Renan (1823-92) would value such a healthy perspective in his consistent proposal of "a point of view from Sirius," as he puts it in a letter of 1886 to his friend the chemist and politician Marcellin Berthelot (*Oeuvres complètes*, II, p. 1037). Sirius, the brightest star in the night sky, had long fascinated poets like Dante, Milton, Whitman, and Tennyson, and to evoke the star, sometimes even with a tinge of critique, is to call to mind the unconventional idealist, the expansive dreamer, or the impartial contemplative whose cosmic perspective on things furnishes a receptivity not otherwise achievable. The person who "looks at everything from the viewpoint of Sirius" (Sertillanges, *Recollection*, p. 16) enacts buoyant, equanimous viewpoints offering an alternative to partial and negatively-biased perspectives. As Aurelius proposed: "Instead of dwelling on [troubles] in such cramped quarters, why not inhabit spacious chambers by taking into your mind the whole wide world, the vast expanse of eternity, the swift succession of change in the smallest parts of everything" (*Meditations*, 9.32). A recurring theme in the *Meditations* (e.g., 7.47-48, 9.30), this enactment of a cosmic viewpoint has multiple sources and resonances in ancient Western thought—from Plato, the Epicureans, Cicero, Philo of Alexandria, and Boethius—where philosophy is promoted as an exercise for achieving tranquility and evenness of mind, an ataractic state in which, as Lucretius phrases it, one is "able to view all things with a mind at peace" (*pacata posse omnia mente tueri*; *De Rerum Natura*, 5.1203).

As I have suggested, a mind at peace is, almost paradoxically, never a static mentality. To be at peace is not ever to be at rest; rather, the equanimous mind eternally circulates and refocuses, as Walt Whitman (1819-92) lyricizes, "Both in and out of the game and watching and wondering at it" ("Song of Myself," l. 79). To move is precisely to possess, in the first place, the full space to do so, and such space may be plumbed emotionally, psychologically, and spiritually. When French philosopher and sociologist Georges Friedmann (1902-77) reflected on, to his mind, the most powerful "spiritual exercise," he advised simply "to take flight every day" (*Puissance et la Sagesse*, p. 359), echoing Aurelius's counsel to "to fly with the stars in their courses" (*Meditations*, 7.47). Fond of citing Friedmann (not to mention Aurelius), Pierre Hadot (1922-2010) is one thinker who, with incredible historical range, has described the project of Western philosophy precisely as spiritual exercise. He was once asked about the centrality of what he called "the look from above" (*le regard d'en haut*) to the training of the intellect:

> This exercise consists in imaginatively traversing the immensity of space, and in accompanying the movement of the stars, but also in looking at the Earth from above, to observe the behavior of humans....These efforts of the imagination and of the intellect are intended above all to place the human being within the vastness of the universe, making him aware of who he is....[It] leads to an expansion of awareness, to a sort of flight of the soul into the infinite. It especially has the effect of allowing an individual to see things in a universal perspective, and to rid himself of his egoistical point of view. This is why this look from above leads to impartiality. (*The Present Alone is Our Happiness*, pp. 167-68)

Here is an expansive knowledge of the self/world through a kind of ecstatic vision—from the ancient Greek *ekstasis* (ἔκστασις), "to be or stand outside, a removal to elsewhere." This position beyond the place where one stands still holds the possibility of appreciating the whole in ever new ways, relieved of the narrow egoism of will.

Looking from above, one becomes a cool Platonic contemplator who resides in relations unburdened by the subject-object tension of the will of the world, to use Schopenhauer's famous phrase.

Equanimity can be said to be the positive character of this state of being free from will, from force. Schopenhauer thought that this is precisely the calm attitude needed for aesthetic contemplation, where the beautiful emerges when we overcome the drive toward isolating "the where, the when, the why, and the whither in things, [in favor of] simply and solely the *what*" (*The World as Will and Representation*, I, p. 178). Seen from the vantage point of space, the outside or beyond, objects become most fully present in their "whatness." Partial understandings and solitary meanings are now less relevant, no longer obtrusive. Philosopher and novelist Colin Wilson (1931-2013) was fond of putting it like this: "close-upness deprives us of meaning" (*G. I. Gurdjieff*, p. 119; *The Philosopher's Stone*, p. 129; cf. *Poetry and Mysticism*, p. 30). Yet we are not compelled to follow Schopenhauer all the way to some kind of Platonic realm, where, he says, "the pure subject of knowledge knows only Ideas" (*The World as Will*, I, p. 179), in order to appreciate just how interesting, how knowable, even wondrous, things become when looked at from above.

Nietzsche, especially in what is known as his middle period (1878-82), put forward a conception of philosophy as an art of living, a therapeutic practice aimed, like the ancient spiritual exercises that so preoccupied Hadot, at the creation of human flourishing or *eudaimonia* (true happiness). Nietzsche's image of the person who finds joy in contemplating the universe recalls the Stoic sage who, "free from emphasis" and passions, is able to contemplate the universe by means of a "free, fearless hovering over" everything (*Human, All Too Human*, p. 30). In *Daybreak*, Nietzsche evokes the ancient sage's Olympian "look from above" as the primary means of finding felicity in the universe through a generous, holistic view as opposed to being caught in moments of suffering through limited reactions such as moral condemnation or pity. Nietzsche's philosophical naturalism in *Daybreak* dismisses pity [*Mitleid*] as inferior to the ideal of the view from above, since it only mires a person in gloom and suffering in an unedified manner. Pity, like other common emotional responses to misfortune such as fear, distress, and melancholy, are antagonistic to the bright "art of the Olympians" (*Daybreak*, p. 91), which offers the freedom to "serve mankind as physician *in any sense whatever*" using the knowledge gained from transcending these partial, not to mention egocentric, affective responses (ibid., p. 86; emph. in orig.).

In turning explicitly to Aurelius, Nietzsche finds the allure of knowledge to be located precisely in the Stoic practice of an epistemophilia transforming all value judgments of the world:

> Does it not thrill through all your senses – this sound of sweet allurement with which science has proclaimed its glad tidings, in a hundred phrases and in the hundred and first and fairest: "Let delusion [*Wahn*] vanish! Then 'woe is me!' will vanish too; and with 'woe is me!' woe itself will be gone." (Marcus Aurelius) (ibid., p. 190)

In Aurelius's view, when we judge something to be repulsive or inimical, we are simply mistaking the putatively inelegant and negative for the unexamined:

> [T]he perceptive man, profoundly curious about the workings of nature, will take a peculiar pleasure in everything, even in the humble or ungainly parts that contribute to the making of the whole. The actual jaws of living beasts will delight him as much as their representations by artists and sculptors. With a discerning eye, he will warm to an old man's strength or an old woman's beauty while admiring with cool detachment the seductive charms of youth. The world is full of wonders like these that will appeal only to those who study nature closely and develop a real affinity for her works (*Meditations*, 3.2)

Blindness to the wonders of the world is overcome with an equanimity of vision that, while appreciating the interdependent whole, allows us to move across a scale of emotional and intellectual distances between ourselves and reality and between ourselves and reality's representations. Writing about the phenomenology of aesthetics, Ortega y Gasset (1883-1955) proposed a scale where at one end "the world—persons, things, situations—is given to us in the aspect of 'lived' reality; at the other end we see everything in the aspect of 'observed' reality" (*The Dehumanization of Art*, p. 17). Of course, to be fully human, we need both ends or, more precisely, we require the freedom to shuttle between them, to calibrate them in a given moment.

For Nietzsche, the supreme act of courage in thinking derives from a zenithal view of both ends: a cosmic consciousness whose morality amounts to submission to the fate of the worldly. He distills the essence of such a morality of radical acceptance in terms consistent with those of the Stoics: "Whatever is necessary—as seen from the heights and in the sense of an economy of the whole—is also the useful par excellence: one should not only bear it, one should *love* it. *Amor fati*: that is my inmost nature" (*Nietzsche contra Wagner*, p. 680). The real utility of "whatever is necessary" emerges only when seen from above, and it is equanimity, I am suggesting, that defines the attitude necessary to support such an empyrean view. Lucian (c. 120-200 CE), in his advice to the historian, is quite clear about this: knowledge can only be gathered and then ideally conveyed with what he calls "easy transitions" if the historian first takes up the exact "position...of Zeus in Homer" surveying, for example, a Greco-Persian skirmish with "a bird's-eye view." Like Zeus, the historian attends to the whole battlefield, avoiding over-focus or "neglect of proportion" while all the time "pass[ing] swiftly" over geopolitical expanses ("The Way to Write History," pp. 131-32). The purview of Lucian's historiographer brings before us a way of knowing that, as the next section suggests, involves granting that knowledge is conditioned by perspectives, while crucially holding that the fullest knowledge of the world is obtained by actively expanding these perspectives in a salutary manner.

"Where it Seems Best": Perspectivism and Greater Knowledge

> I am animate seeing. I see – consciousness – I see my own seeing – a conscious seeing.
>
> —Johann Gottlieb Fichte,
> *Die Bestimmung des Menschen*

The ways in which we think are often quite limiting. Consider what happens when we think in negations, a common enough way to avoid an unpleasant event or thing by putting something pleasant, or even nothing, in its place. Its simple form is: Try not to think of X. As a boy, Leo Tolstoy (1828-1910) was told by his older brother Nikolai about a mysterious hill and the secret to a life of bliss about which only the older boy knew. But the trick was that Leo and his other younger brothers could only learn the secret of this utopia if they were able to master some preliminary tasks, among them standing in a corner and not thinking of a white bear (Birukoff, *The Life of Tolstoy*, p. 15). Being directed not to think of a white bear, young Tolstoy discovered it was impossible, much in the same way, as psychologists have noted, jurors are in fact swayed by information they have been instructed to disregard and media audiences are unduly influenced by news they are informed is untrue.

Conscious thought suppression, it turns out, is not only an activity that people perform poorly but also one that potentially leads to obsessional thinking and addictive preoccupation. Psychologist Daniel Wegner and colleagues discovered exactly this irony when, inspired by Tolstoy, they employed an image of a white bear that test subjects were instructed to avoid thinking about. In this classic experiment from 1987, participants would verbalize their stream of consciousness for five minutes, while trying not to think of the bear. They were to ring a bell if a white bear came to mind, which it turns out they did, on average, more than once per minute. When participants were then asked to do the same exercise, only this time trying to think of a white bear, they thought of the animal even more often than a different group of participants who had been told from the outset to think of white bears. Suppressing the thought for the first five minutes, it appears, caused a more forceful cognitive "rebound" later, effectively narrowing the scope of further thought. Wegner eventually developed a theory of "ironic processes" where, in the act of thought suppression, one part of the mind successfully avoids the forbidden thought while another part "checks in" periodically to make sure the thought is not arising—thereby, ironically, bringing it to mind. And so, it would indeed appear that, as Jean-Paul Sartre (1905-80) mused, "consciousness cannot produce a negation except in the form of consciousness of negation" (*Being and Nothingness*, p. 11). In short, pure negation fails because it is an inescapably self-reflexive process. The object of negation always reappears, as if it were doomed to be the focus of some sort of perverse mindfulness in which the mind is painfully aware of itself.

What I am tempted to suggest here is that the occasion of equanimity is the fulcrum upon which the relation of our acceptance and rejection resolves itself in the pursuit of a more complete understanding of the world. To engage equanimously with the world means that there can be no total theory or final understanding of it. There can be no grasping of reality solely by means of negation. A single true description of a completely independent reality—of the kind, for example, the metaphysical realist posits—cannot exist since the world does not determine unitary answers to basic ontological questions independently of our mobile conceptual assumptions. The flexibility of our assumptions is reflected by the implicit, practical understandings we generate about the world in which we are moving around and viewing from shifting angles. The preconditions of our theoretical practices in general are, as Goethe knew, tied to the unceasing activities of skillful looking that may give us a more complete access to the world. The contemporary philosopher Alva Noë, as we will see, contends that we find out how things are by exploring how they appear such that the seemingly repeatable experience of an object contains within it the possibility of multiple readings. This exploration forms the ground of our equanimity. But, again, our ways of exploring are often narrow, canalized, for example, by our socially conditioned values. A telling illustration of this emerged as the result of a 1947 study in which psychologists Brunner and Goodman found that value-laden conceptual schemes exert a profound influence on the way we see things. They discovered that children of lower socioeconomic status (SES) households overestimate the size of coins to a greater degree than children from higher-SES households, with the degree of overestimation varying with the value (not the physical size) of the coin (except between the quarter and the half dollar, which the authors describe as "almost too valuable [to a child of ten] to be real!" ("Value and Need," p. 39). They inferred that the visual experience of money, at least in the dimension of size perception, is significantly influenced by its importance within the system of values ordering a child's life.

Aesthetic values also clearly contribute to the shape of our representations of the world. Alberti's seminal treatise *Della Pittura* (1435), in outlining a process for the most effective painting through the use of one-point perspective, emphasizes the arbitrariness of the point itself, around which the perspectival construction is generated. Alberti's instruction to the painter is deceptively straightforward: locate the centric point of the work just "where it seems best" (*On Painting*, p. 56; *Dove a mi paia, fermo uno punto* [Where it suits me, I make a point]). There are no criteria for choosing one point as opposed to another except those of aesthetic value and proportionality. Nietzsche, to whom we will return in a moment, similarly notes that we choose among an array of cognitive perspectives only on the basis of our values and affective attunements. Furthermore, such pragmatic criteria are never sufficiently robust to *require* the enactment of any one point of view over alternatives. Equanimity affords, in an entirely holistic manner, the provisional locating of the "where it seems best." Perspectives actually possess relative value—and this is Alberti's point (as well as Nietzsche's)—and thus some really are "better" than others, yet none are final. There is nothing other than a range, and to this perspectival range equanimity attends.

Without an equanimous manner of knowing/seeing, there could be no appreciation of the manifold conditions we may be in as knowers and how these shape and unshape the choice of one perspective arbitrarily drawn from the variety of potential ones. Knowing is like seeing since both depend upon active perspective-taking. Nietzsche recommended the employment of a variety of perspectives in the service of knowledge. A famous passage from *On the Genealogy of Morals* insists that "There is *only* a perspective seeing, *only* a perspective 'knowing'; and the *more* affects we allow to speak about one thing, the *more* eyes, different eyes, we can use to observe one thing, the more complete will our 'concept' of the thing, our 'objectivity,' be" (p. 119; emph. in orig.). Nietzsche's notebook of 1881 puts it succinctly: "The task: to see things as they are! The means: to be able to see with a hundred eyes, from many persons!" (*Nachgelassene Fragmente*, 11[65]). The idea here is that, since multiple affective attunements disclose different aspects of things, pursuing objectivity amounts to forever broadening our perspective, endlessly multiplying our attunements. Objects of knowledge emerge most fully when our interests in them remain multiple and flexible. Indeed, in the Nietzschean view, the essence of things is to reveal themselves according to an infinity of viewpoints.

To cultivate flexible perspectives allows us to overcome the obvious limitation that we can occupy only one perspective at a time. No single perspective can exhaust the richness of reality. Approaching objectivity demands that we be capable of one more inquiry, one more view—in short, that we keep perspectivally moving. Such mobility produces new knowledge beyond the idiosyncrasy of our current perspective, revealing its parochialism, certainly, and, yet most crucially, marking the way toward better, that is, more complete, ones. Perspectivism, like the equanimity that enables it, is nothing other than a practice equal to attaining a more comprehensive picture of the world around us and through which we move. Here wandering succeeds where dogmatism fails, and so Nietzschean "free spirits" are modeled after Don Quixote rather than Odysseus: "He who has attained only to some degree of freedom of mind cannot feel other than a wanderer on the earth—though not as a traveler *to* a final destination: for this destination does not exist" (*Human, All Too Human*, p. 203). Final destinations mark the cessation of (further) knowledge since shifts in perspective are no longer necessary.

Zhuangzi was one philosopher who profoundly valued perspectival shifting, or wandering (*you* 遊, a word that appears nearly 100 times in the text attributed to him), as the key to achieving what he called "greater knowledge" (*da zhi* 大知). To illustrate the relation of perspectivism to *da zhi*, the Chinese thinker tells of the fabled Peng bird, so imposing an animal that it rises 90,000 *li* (approximately 30,000 miles) in the air and gazes down upon the vast sky below it. Such a view from above is inconceivable to some. So, based upon their own experiences with flight, the cicada and the dove contend that the Peng bird's feat is not possible, and they mock the very idea. Zhuangzi demonstrates a way beyond this conflict of perspectives:

What do these two little creatures know? A small consciousness [*xiao zhi*] cannot keep up with a vast consciousness [*da zhi*]; short duration cannot keep up with long duration. How do we know? The morning mushroom knows nothing of the noontide; the winter cicada knows nothing of the spring and autumn. This is what is meant by short duration. In southern Chu there is a tree called Mingling, for which five hundred years is as a single spring, and another five hundred years is as a single autumn. In ancient times, there was even one massive tree whose spring and autumn were each eight thousand years long. And yet nowadays, Pengzu alone has a special reputation for longevity, and everyone tries to match him. Pathetic, isn't it? (Ziporyn, *Zhuangzi: The Essential Writings*, p. 4; cf. Graham, *The Inner Chapters*, p. 44)

Like mocking the Peng bird, imitating the legendary Pengzu is absurd precisely because it fails to account for the fact that duration (or height) is only a matter of perspective and therefore must be understood contextually. In other words, one long-lived being is short lived in relation to other longer-lived beings. Similarly, the difference between smaller and greater knowledge means that consciousness can always be shown to be narrow or lacking from some further perspective. It is for this reason—and this is one of the great teachings of Daoism that harmonizes with the equanimous view—that we are always (somewhere) in the middle. Indeed, our occupation of the mobile middle becomes a marker of human presence, and here we may recur to Nietzsche, who refers to the fundamental "perspectival character of existence" (*The Gay Science*, p. 336). We know we are present to the extent that we know the places from which we view and the vantage points they furnish us. If all views are perspectival, then the view that "sees" that all views are perspectival is *da zhi*, or, as I am putting it forward, equanimity. By being multiply and fluently attuned to the world, with an equanimous mind, we better grasp the world's multiplicity and appreciate its seeming contradictions, the diverging perspectives it calls forth. Blake, in a memorable verse, offers a felicitous summary of the power of equanimity: "To see a world in a Grain of Sand / And a Heaven in a Wild Flower / Hold Infinity in the palm of your hand / And Eternity in an hour" ("Auguries of Innocence," *Complete Writings*, p. 431).

The Necessity of Others

Writing about Nietzsche's perspectivism, Alexander Nehamas observes that perspectival approaches, even when they are adaptive and encompassing, can never be totalizing. They are, like equanimity as a way of knowing the world, processual:

> Each perspectival approach is capable of correcting itself, and many can incorporate newmaterial and even combine with others to form broader systems of practices and inquiries. What is not possible is that at some point we can incorporate "all" the material there is into a single approach or that we can occupy "every" possible point of view. (*Nietzsche*, p. 51)

Mutually implicated, self-adjusting perspectives are by their very nature unfinished. They are "open works," structurally open-ended, and homologous to the multifaceted and unstillable world we inhabit. To return to Zhuangzi for a moment: in contrast to the fixed perspectives of the cicada and dove, creatures whose narrow-mindedness is a function of their limited domains, stands that of Peng, an animal who owes its very existence to change, since the gigantic bird is, we are told, actually a transmutation of a colossal fish called Kun. Since we cannot achieve the *da zhi* of Peng's perspective by magically morphing into different beings, we rely upon both our movement through the world and the viewpoints of others as exemplars of the way perspectives may transform into other perspectives. While knowledge is never independent of perspective, multiple attunements to the world lead to perception of a fuller account of its ever-shifting aspects. Equanimity lays the ground for multiple responses to the world across different moments of knowing. Grasping the world's multiplicity through "more eyes, different eyes," as Nietzsche phrases it, gestures toward a kind of collectivity whose various viewpoints approach objectivity yet need never yield a single unified picture.

Equanimity of vision and of knowing is one way that we "use" others to take account of aspects of the world obscured by our own singular accounts. Put simply, others condition our world through our dynamic relation to their perspectives. We may come to know a simple object like a cube as a total object—since we can see at most three of its sides in a single glance—by positing its unseen sides as potentially visible to others, which is one way we perceive the environment based on exploring it relationally. "The world," observes Noë, "outstrips what we can take in at a glance; but we are not confined to what is available in a glance" ("Précis," p. 660). We are indeed able to experience, and come to know, what is hidden to the extent we, in a sense, have access to it; and so, we perceptually and dynamically interact with the scenes of our very perception. The world, by being *available* to perception, invites phenomenological interaction. Such interaction takes place in at least two fundamental ways: through our sensorimotor skills, allowing us to perceive by actively exploring things (e.g., visually or tactilely), thereby building an understanding that our movements change our sensory relations to things, and through our imagined relations to others, other perceivers. Knowledge is "enactive," to use Noë's term, in this sense: it is predicated upon the exploratory reach of our minds and bodies, and crucially, I suggest, upon our capacity to attune with other perceiving minds.

Indeed, our sensitivity to other minds, other points of view, is one hallmark of equanimous knowledge. In no small part we depend upon others providing us with a sense of how things look, and our openness to this situation allows us to refine our perspectives when necessary and, generally, move through the world a bit more gracefully. The equanimous mind works at balancing and rebalancing how things look to me and how they look to you. Without a dynamic sense of how things *look*, we forfeit the knowledge of how they *are*. The perspectival nature of knowledge, Noë observes, means that "the world can show up in perceptual consciousness thanks to our sensitivity to the ways how things look inform[ing] of us how they really are" (ibid., p. 665). Knowledge is revealed as a function of the dynamic ways we sense the world. "The art of seeing," Aldous Huxley (1894-1963) points out, "is like the other fundamental or primary psycho-physical skills, such as talking, walking and using the hands" (*The Art of Seeing*, p. 8). And with Noë one more time: "The process of perceiving, of finding out how things are, is a process of meeting the world; it is an activity of skillful exploration" (*Action in Perception*, p. 164).

But how *are* things, *really*? They may just be unbearable if encountered alone, from a singular perspective. Indeed, philosopher Gilles Deleuze (1925-95) has suggested that, without others, the world would be inherently insufferable. A world without Others would be harsh, threatening, abstract and implacable because it forfeits the interdependence—of your view of things and mine, of what you perceive and what I perceive—necessary for negotiating foreground and background, subject and object. Consider Deleuze's description of a familiar situation:

> As for the objects behind my back, I sense them coming together and forming a world, precisely because they are visible to, and are seen by, Others. And what is *depth*, for me, in accordance with which objects encroach upon one another and hide behind one another, I also live through being *possible width* for Others, a width upon which they are aligned and pacified (from the point of view of another depth). (*The Logic of Sense*, p. 305; emph. in orig.)

The coherence of the world depends upon the multiplicity of alternating views, which amounts to a tacit exchange of knowledges about the world. In the midst of the possible worlds that Others call into being, we find a sense of security. Deleuze's lyrical description is worth quoting:

> In short, the Other assures the margins and transitions in the world. He is the sweetness of contiguities and resemblances. He regulates the transformation of form and background and the variations of depth. He prevents assaults from behind. He fills the world with a benevolent murmuring. He makes things incline toward one another and find their natural complements in one another. When one complains about the meanness of Others, one forgets this other and even more frightening meanness—namely, the meanness of things were there no Other. (ibid., pp. 305-6)

To hear the "benevolent murmuring" of the cognizable world is to be reassured that our knowledge of things, while always perspectival, is subject to the comforting refinements of other perspectives. Closed-mindedness, the refusal of other perspectives, carries with it the risk of being subject to the greater "meanness" of existence where natural contiguity and resemblance give way to repulsion and difference. "The absence of the Other," Deleuze notes, "is felt when we bang against things, and when the stupefying swiftness of our actions is revealed to us" (ibid., p. 306). If Others are necessary, they are so to the extent that we may expect, thanks to their presence, not to bang, literally and figuratively, against everything. Perhaps this hope for a softer, smoother world accounts, in part, for the origin of animism as a sensibility or style of engaging with the cosmos. We trust that what we grasp does not bite back.

Kōshō Uchiyama (1912-99), who taught at Antaiji Temple in Kyoto, favored the phrase *atamano tebanashi,* "opening the hand of thought," to describe just this hope. Opening the hand of thought allows us to transcend granting force or effect to the incessant instrumentality of thought in terms of grasper or grasped: "When we think of something, we grasp it with our minds. If we open the hand of thought, it drops away" (*Opening the Hand of Thought*, p. 141). Such a metaphor echoes the words of the Tang dynasty Zen Master Xuefeng Yicun (Hsueh-Feng, 822-908) who once told a monk, "empty handed I leave home, and empty handed I return" (Kusumoto, *Zengo Nyumon*, p. 422). This open- or empty-handedness involves the genuine recognition that, as Emerson famously put it, "the evanescence and lubricity of all objects, which lets them slip through our fingers then when we clutch hardest, [is] the most unhandsome part of our condition" ("Experience," p. 309). Grappling with reality, struggling to pin it down, we lack the broad consciousness to accept what we cannot see. The more intensely we clutch reality, the more it slips away. Equanimity offers a model that recalibrates, in the moment—or, better, on the fly—a balancing between, on one hand, accepting or acknowledging and, on the other, knowing or "grasping" reality. With the presence of others, we may recover the easeful, lighthearted state of suspension characteristic of equanimity, and understand that it affords the optimal way to move smoothly, even handsomely, with reality as it appears and as it actually is.

Equanimity means never getting stuck in our own heads, whose solitary discursive and analytical ways of knowing are inclined to abstract from experience. Instead, it takes its cue from the cadences of nature itself as the preeminent resource for refining, recalibrating, our sensibilities. It recognizes that, without the dynamism of balancing views, any model of knowing the world risks being ossified into a technical epistemology dislocated from the changing world itself. Rabindranath Tagore (1861-1941) speaks of persons "whose idea of life is static," and who

> forget that the true meaning of living is outliving, it is ever growing out of itself. The fruit clings to its stem, its skin clings to the pulp and the pulp to the seed so long as the fruit is immature, so long as it is not ready for its course of further life. Its outer covering and its inner core are not yet differentiated, and it only proves its life by its strength of tenacity. But when the seed is ripe its hold upon its surrounding is loosened, its pulp attains fragrance, sweetness and detachment, and is dedicated to all who need it. Birds peck at it and it is not hurt, the storm plucks it and flings it to the dust, and it is not destroyed. It proves its immortality by its renunciation. (*Thought Relics*, p. 40)

Only when the seed and its shell, through a complex set of natural and unforced transformative processes, loosen their holds upon each other, does the seed enter into full reciprocity with the world—with "all who need it." Knowing, and the desire to know, are also predicated upon the readiness and ability to "let go," as the most appropriate response to a world that is "ever growing out of itself." The metaphor of organic growth here puts before us the essence of equanimity as a way of knowing, at once reciprocal and accretive, spinning out of itself as a spiral galaxy might, triggering bursts of star formation, without implying that what exists before is in any way incomplete.

Thinking Aside

> The knowledge imposes a pattern, and falsifies,
> For the pattern is new in every moment
> —T. S. Eliot, "East Coker"

When we approach the world charitably, with the "open hand of thought," we grant ourselves a certain flexibility of mind that, in the Zen tradition, is called "non-abiding." Zen Master Takuan Sōhō (1573-1645), in *The Mysterious Record of Immovable Wisdom*, offers one of the clearest descriptions of the non-abiding mind by contrasting it with our habitual, "stopping minds":

> One should engender the mind without a place for it to stop. If the mind is not engendered, the hand will not move forward. Those who when moving engender the mind that ordinarily stops in that movement, but do not stop at all in the course of the action—these are called the accomplished men of all Ways. The mind of attachment arises from the stopping mind.... This stopping becomes the bonds of life and death" (p. 25).

Freedom from "the bonds of life and death," captured in the image of the "immortal" seed that Tagore describes, arises through the continuous action of accommodating the objects to which one is responding and interacting intellectually. Here is a kind of relational thinking that, by staying mobile, can always meet the other on its own terms, eschewing reductive and static forms of imitation in favor of ongoing complementarity and coordination.

As the discussions of Goethe's science of participatory observation, Japanese tea literature, and astronauts' extraterrestrial viewing have suggested, knowledge, like aesthetic and creative experience, is intimately tied to attentional flexibility, conditioned partly by the objects being examined or shaped and partly by the investigator/artist herself. Traditional dualisms such as subject and object, art and science, perceiver and performer, do not hold firmly, and instead are interanimating polarities where each element flows into the other in the ongoing transformations we call experience and knowledge. In the co-creative relationality of knower and known, what is "brought forth"—in the sense of the ancient Greek ποίησις (*poiesis*)—is never reducible through causal analysis. Emerson formulated the essence of poiesis in an emphatically contemporary idiom: "How can we speak of the actions of the mind under any divisions, as of its knowledge, of its ethics, of its works, and so forth, since it melts will into perception, knowledge into act? Each becomes the other. Itself alone is. Its vision is not like the vision of the eye, but is union with the things known" ("Intellect," p. 263). We cannot speak of divisions in mental activity since, in the movement of existence, there are no "things" existing as discrete elements, as our senses try to re-present them. Knowable phenomena are, as David Bohm has stressed, "abstracted out of the movement in our perception and thought, and any such abstraction fits the real movement only up to a point, and within limits. Some 'things' may last for a very long time and be fairly stable, while others are as ephemeral as the shapes abstracted in perceptions of clouds" (*Creativity*, p. 78).

Equanimous vision takes into account both the movement of our perception and thought and that of their objects, the things whose duration in consciousness always varies. Equanimity, as a way of knowing, is unperturbed by the inevitable mismatch of our fixed abstractions and fleeting reality. It offers nonetheless ways to see clearly and without attachments. In the Zen School, having neither deluded thoughts nor a fixated mind is described as the state of no-mind, or the mind without mind (*mushin no shin*) often referred to as "without leaving a trace" (i.e., "trackless," as in the expression *mosshōseki* or "leaving no trace"). What makes the equanimous "way" impossible to track is its dynamism reflected in constant "shifts of attention," as Arthur Koestler (1905-83) terms those aspects of experience "which make familiar phenomena appear in a new, revealing light, seen through spectacles of a different colour" (*The Act of Creation*, p. 233).

The more deeply we engage with the cognizable world, the more it may be given new meanings borne out of ever more questions and reframings. As I have emphasized, there can be no method for this process. William James, commenting on Walt Whitman's rapturous engagement with the sensible world, categorically states that this "feeling of the vital significance of an experience" is not something one can acquire with any method: "there is no receipt which one can follow" ("On a Certain Blindness in Human Beings," p. 33). Indeed, the feeling often comes unexpectedly, he adds, "blossom[ing] sometimes from out of the very grave wherein we imagined that our happiness was buried" (ibid., p. 34). This organic process, whose improbable seed may be the satisfaction from thinking we've got it all sussed out, depends upon the energy of a Janus-faced attitude toward conservation and innovation. Janusian thinking, a paradigmatic type of equanimous understanding, finds improbable solutions to problems by attending to unexpected syntheses of traditional and revolutionary ways of seeing. Koestler frames such thinking as "bisociative" processes, the engine, he argues, of creative acts, including humor, art, and science. Novel approaches to problems, he suggests, crucially involve both destruction and construction, habit and originality, the familiar and the unexpected. To manage the mutual entailing of opposites requires a mind marked by "super-flexibility" and guided by the maxim *reculer pour mieux sauter* (literally, to step back in order to leap better, implying a temporary regression allowing forward movement) (*The Act*, p. 660). For Koestler, creativity involves progress—the leap forward— universally escorted and informed by "feedback from the past" (ibid., p. 466). Creativity, while recursive in structure, loops back precisely in order to spiral ever forward. The original often emerges within the context and security of the familiar, where the seed of the unexpected can be found in the shell of the ordinary and rational. Without a mind tending to multiple, even diverging, channels of inquiry, to ideas held lightly, and to cross-fertilizing paradigms, the seed may never germinate.

In his engrossing book about the Wright brothers, historian David McCullough shows that the pair, who accomplished one of the greatest technical achievements in history, were able to do so precisely because their analytic skills were inseparable from, and made possible by, their thorough education in the liberal arts. Developing their sense of imagination with prodigious reading, the Wright brothers learned how to think creatively. Indeed, McCullough's inspiration for the book was discovering, while researching his previous book on 19th-century Americans in Paris, that Wilbur Wright went to the Louvre to look at paintings every opportunity he could (some 15 or more times), and that he was moved by the Flemish master Van Dyck as well as a range of nineteenth-century French painters, from the romantic Delacroix to the realist Courbet, and especially Corot, in ways far exceeding those of an ordinary sightseer. With the synthesis of the imaginative and the logical as a launch pad, the Wright brothers inventiveness was marked by the super-flexible mental attitude of *reculer pour mieux sauter*, rather literally, with the aviation pioneers' repeated failures to sustain flight being legendary.

A lesser-known example of bisociative thinking issued in a revolution of another sort, this one pushing back the limits of knowledge about the past rather than winging into the future. I am thinking of the decryption of Minoan Linear B, an ancient script discovered on vases, tablets, and seal impressions, and first found at a palace at Knossos in 1900. Linear B was undecipherable until 1952, when the British architect and amateur linguist Michael Ventris (1922-56) unlocked large parts of the extant texts, determining that it was an archaic form of Greek. His finding contradicted academic views of the time, including those to which Ventris himself once subscribed. Andrew Robinson's recent biography shows how the disciplinary interplay of Ventris's architectural knowledge and skills—the construction of a globally collaborative work group with whom he shared notes (often dead-ends) plus the use of an architecturally precise grid—with his innate abilities as a linguist radically refigured and expanded knowledge about the ancient world.

Equanimous thinking, negotiating, for example, two (or more) different fields of inquiry, entails an openness to seeing things obliquely, to coming at them from their sides, as it were, as the way to appreciate fully just how the fluctuating relation between the investigator and her object is itself a crucial aspect of knowledge. Walking past ferns, Thoreau observed that

> Sometimes I would rather get a transient glimpse or side view of a thing than stand fronting to it,—as these polypodies. The object I caught a glimpse of as I went by haunts my thoughts a long time, is infinitely suggestive, and I do not care to front it and scrutinize it, for I know that the thing that really concerns me is not there, but in my relation to that. That is a mere reflecting surface.... the point of interest is somewhere between me and them (i.e. the objects). (*Journal*, 5 Nov 1857, vol. 10, pp. 164-65)

Thoreau's "side view," achieved by shifts in attention afforded by movement, opens up the possibility of diving below "mere" surfaces, to find a richer, holistic appreciation of the objects of inquiry in their full relatedness. The side view also generates an understanding that, despite its origin in indirectness and transience, is ultimately more resonant and enduring. To discover the changing "point of interest somewhere between," indirect pathways of knowledge offer alternatives to habitual ways of seeing by embodying the imbrication of objectivity and subjectivity, logicality and the irrational or poetic. Thoreau realized that, as far as mental processes of discovery go,

> Both a conscious and an unconscious life are good. Neither is good exclusively, for both have the same source. The wisely conscious life springs out of an unconscious suggestion.... Indeed, it is by obeying the suggestions of a higher light within you that you escape from yourself and, in the transit, as it were see with the unworn sides of your eye, travel totally new paths. What is that pretended life that does not take up a claim, that does not occupy ground, that cannot build a causeway to its objects, that sits on a bank looking over a bog, singing its desires? (ibid., 30 Aug 1856, vol. 9, pp. 37-38)

Seeing with the eyes' "unworn sides" is a fitting image for equanimity, marking the transition from a narrow consciousness to an expansive one resisting both doctrine and method, and engaged in nothing more than "looking over" the world with deep affinity. Thoreau offers us another image for indirect, mobile looking that is perhaps even more apt, certainly more famous: approaching the world with "a true sauntering of the eye" (ibid., 13 Sept 1852, vol. 4, p. 351). He introduces this wonderful verbal construction by declaring that "what I need is not to look at all," signaling his departure from the kind of looking that is cold, analytical, purely intellectual. The Baconian ideal of putting Nature on the rack is categorically rejected in favor of a meandering observation rooted in an effortless and easeful absorption of impressions from the external world. "You must walk sometimes perfectly free," Thoreau advised, "not prying or inquisitive, not bent upon seeing things," but rather with full openness to what is (ibid., 21 Aug 1851, vol. 2, p. 416).

All of this, I think, brings an ethical imagination to bear on the very conditions of possibility for knowing ourselves and our world. We, and the universe we find ourselves in, are already perfect—a perennial theme of Buddhist philosophy—and so imposing upon them with judgments, categorizations, and discriminations only debases what Thoreau, along with Emerson and Whitman, felt—or, better, deeply "knew"—as the inherent divinity and equilibrium of the cosmos. The deferential activity of equanimity sensitizes us to the importance of non-interfering forms of knowledge that encounter the universe as multiple and veridical rather than as cardinally allegorical. Any concrete "truths" of the world exceed the allegories and conceptual schemes intended to contain them. In multiple ways, existence naturally shows itself in its "inherent excellence," as sensed by Wallace Stevens (1879-1955) in "Notes toward a Supreme Fiction":

> Perhaps there are times of inherent excellence,
> As when the cock crows on the left and all
> Is well, incalculable balances,
> At which a kind of Swiss perfection comes
> And a familiar music of the machine
> Sets up its Schwärmerei, not balances
> That we achieve, but balances that happen (*Collected Poems*, p. 386)

The tentative "perhaps" here encapsulates the deference essential for appreciating elemental "balances that happen" in contrast to those imposed strictly by human technology. The "perfect" Swiss watch can only be understood in the context of another time-keeper, the rooster whose auspicious crowing brings about a humane, almost moral balancing. Similarly, machinic regulation cannot be understood independent of the emotional swarming it sets up. Indeed, the sense accorded to music usually depends upon the order—e.g., rhythm—given to intrinsically meaningless noises. Balancing, everywhere and eternally, is underway; for us, in the middle of things, it's a process of finding it, seeing it, losing it, refinding it. The literary critic Bill Bevis observed with exquisite insight that, in the main, "Stevens was writing a poetry of mind in the act of finding, losing, looking, finding, and losing the sufficient. The process is endless and essentially goal-less" (*Mind of Winter*, p. 255). The excellence of the world may be precisely the endless and goal-less activities it calls into being.

Taking a side-view of things, which I have suggested is one way equanimity proceeds as a way of knowing, fuels the sort of oblique relationality necessary for novel investigation, opening up new paths along which further inquiry can travel. The Wright brothers and Thoreau are exemplary here since part of their genius is to have intuitively realized that approaching their subjects straight on would have in fact limited their originality. The fields they unintentionally founded, for example, aeronautical engineering and environmental sciences, continue to flourish. Koestler has insisted that genuine creativity depends upon "thinking aside," an expression he borrowed from the philosopher Étienne Souriau's dictum *Pour inventer il faut penser à côté* (in order to invent, one must think aside; *Act of Creation*, p. 145). "Thinking aside" is thinking skewed relative to its object. The expression could, plausibly, also be construed as referring to the gesture of putting aside thinking, that is to say, avoiding traditional logic and its self-referentiality. In either meaning, the phrase puts before us an oblique approach to things that refuses a single perspective in order to be open to the unexpected. Koestler felt that to appreciate the "large chunks of irrationality embedded in the creative process," one must grasp the apparent paradox by which the scientific method, with its credo of objectivity, logicality, and verifiability, is underpinned by mental processes that are wholly subjective, irrational, and intuitive (ibid., p. 146). To this end, Koestler turned his attention to the progenitors of Freud's theory of the unconscious and its function in shaping our conscious vision: thinkers such as Socrates, Paracelsus, Leibniz, Goethe, Wordsworth, Nietzsche, and William James (curiously absent is Thoreau). The intervention of unconscious processes in the creative act means that, despite (or along with) technical mastery and skilled technique, our attention, and therefore our discoveries, are steered in such a way that "arrivals at unexpected destinations, and arrivals at the right destination by the wrong boat" are the rule rather than the exception (ibid., p. 145).

Equanimity accommodates the unexpected, the deviating, the unintended, the inexhaustible. It remodels the human ecology of thought and creativity by mobilizing and opening up perception and, in the process, freeing it from morose stuck points such as our tendency to think in terms of finished things, to reason in the vocabulary of inert objects. Less comfortable for us are ways for thinking about the unfinished, the protean, the processual. Henri Bergson (1859-1941) once identified "the natural obstinacy with which we treat the living like the lifeless and think all reality, however fluid, under the form of the sharply defined solid." Over against a vision of world as becoming, he continued, "we are at ease only in the discontinuous, in the immobile, in the dead" (*Creative Evolution*, p. 174). We do not readily rid ourselves of the idea that a world of solids and smooth surfaces, reduced to some type of mechanical causality, is more intellectually hospitable than a world of swirling depths and permeability. For someone like Thoreau, the world exists primarily in its fluidity—from living things held together, he says, by an "invisible fluid" (*Journal*, 31 Aug 1853, vol. 2, p. 63) to the earth itself and what lies below its surface "fluid to the influence of its spirit" (ibid., 31 Dec. 1851, vol. 3, p. 165). Thoreau's project to re-sense the world as dynamic, flowing, to experience the vital order of things, is inseparable from his experimentations with indirect observation. When he would stand on his head, or bend over and view the landscape through his legs (ibid., 1850, vol. 2, p. 51; 4 Mar 1852, vol. 3, p. 333), a posture Emerson also recommended (*Journals*, 19 Nov. 1848, p. 56), Thoreau expands a repertoire of vantage points, thereby demonstrating that the sensible world is never "finished" since it is spontaneously approachable from yet one more angle. To the extent that we are capable of one more view, the world can never devolve into stereotype.

In the same way, equanimity, accommodating variable attitudes, reenchants a cosmos that otherwise, and only, apparently suffices unto itself. Zen master Dōgen (1200-53) had once prescribed a way of refashioning attitudes to the known through the use of stories, kōans, and phrases, "presenting [them] sideways and using [them] upside down" (*Shōbōgenzō*, p. 6). A Zen capping phrase puts it like this: "Play with it sideways, use it upside down" (Hori, *Zen Sand*, p. 107). Realizing our existence in full ecological relationality means, as Dōgen put it, that the "nest of cliché" is to be dismantled. To be intellectually thrown off guard, to abandon the comfortable nest of cliché that is both symptom and cause of mental regression, becomes one key to exchanging dead for living knowledge. The poet Robert Graves (1895-1985) once described his own "embarrassing gift" of immediate intuition, which offered him "the key of truth" that he "could use to open any lock of any door." "Mine," he elaborates, "was no religious or philosophical theory, but a simple method of looking sideways at disorderly facts so as to make perfect sense of them" (*Poetic Craft and Principle*, p. 137). Equanimity follows Emily Dickinson's admonition to tell the truth, "but tell it slant" (*Final Harvest*, p. 248).

Of One Mind: Visions of Integration

> It is a secret which every intellectual [person] quickly learns, that, beyond the energy of his possessed and conscious intellect, he is capable of a new energy (as of an intellect doubled on itself), by abandonment to the nature of things.
>
> —Emerson, "The Poet"

> In order to obtain adequate notions of any truth, we must intellectually separate its distinguishable parts; and this is the technical *process* of philosophy. But having done so, we must then restore them in our conceptions to the unity in which they actually co-exist; and this is the *result* of philosophy.
>
> —Coleridge, *Biographia Literaria*

Two rare neurological conditions, simultagnosia and akinetopsia, bring before us instructive counterexamples to equanimity's agile perspectivism and amplified insight. Equanimity works in a direction opposite to that in patients who suffer from specific visuoperceptual disorders such as agnosias involving acute distortions in the sensory field. The disorder known as simultagnosia is recognizable due to its piecemeal perception, where subjects cannot take in the whole scene at once. Akinetopsia is the inability to detect motion despite having the acuity to see things at rest, and so a moving car might appear to "jump" from one location to another. Simultagnosic patients are unable to grasp the full scope of a visual array, and, for example, will see only one flower at a time while gazing at a lush flower bed. Essentially a defect in spatial processing, it manifests as a general failure to sustain a macro mode of attention—what Goethe calls *Bildung*—where points of interest and the differential play of forces normally self-organize and integrate as associative threads.

What such patients cannot do, we do involuntarily and instantly, at levels below intentional awareness, where these threads compose rich tapestries of discrete elements woven into one meaningfully interrelated whole. Equanimity, I am arguing, may be the most expansive form that this effortless normal functioning takes. Equanimous vision, as intelligential process, ceaselessly encounters a world arrayed such that it cannot offer us just one way of seeing it. Seeing, in the Goethean formulation, is never a mere *experience* (*Erfahrung*) but an *event* (*Ereignis*), which, as I have suggested, bears resemblance to ancient *contemplatio* (*theoria*) and animates knowledge as the mediation of life itself, which is all the time interrelated and moving. Equanimous contemplation necessarily means taking up multiple perspectives from our place in the middle of things. In the ancient world, that place of seeing in the middle of things was conceived of as the temple. Heidegger, citing a dictionary of Latin etymology, highlights that "*Contemplari* is derived from *templum*, i.e., from [the name of] the *place which can be seen* from any point, and from which any *point can be seen*. The ancients called this place a *templum*" ("Science and Reflection," p. 166; emph. in orig.). What, then, does it mean to be precluded from being *with* (prefix *con-/com-*), unable to occupy the central place of observation due to neurologic pathology?

Let's consider a famous case of simultagnosia from the medical literature, recalling that, historically, knowledge about the brain and perception has been acquired in large measure by studying brain damaged patients. Neurologist Alexandra Adler examined a 22-year-old woman who suffered from carbon monoxide poisoning as a survivor of the Cocoanut Grove nightclub fire in Boston that killed nearly 500 people during the Second World War. After her injury, the young woman could only describe her experiences in piecemeal terms. When presented with a complex scene, she described only individual isolated features and was unable to give an overview of the interaction between components. She was, for instance, unable to follow the action of a scene in a movie if too many characters appeared. When shown a four-inch green toy battleship, she mistook it first for a fountain pen, then for a green knife, before finally identifying it as "a boat." She offered this explanation:

> At first I saw the front part. It looked like a fountain pen because it was shaped like a fountain pen. Then it looked like a knife because it was so sharp, but I thought it could not be a knife because it was green. Then I saw the spokes and that it was shaped like a boat, like in a movie where I had seen boats. It had too many spokes to be a knife or a fountain pen. ("Disintegration and Restoration," p. 252)

Clearly, there is a deficit in assimilating what normally would be considered, or taken in, as the whole object. Taking her about three seconds to get from pen to boat, the patient identified a conspicuous feature of the object, then generated serial hypotheses, checking to see if the rest of the picture fits with a given hypothesis. Patients with simultanagnosia view the world in a rather chaotic fashion, unable to assemble elements in a way that creates an immediate sense of the world as coherent. Seeing only one object at a time, and sometimes only pieces of objects, they are unaware that they are fastened on to just one constituent of a larger composite form.

Simultagnosic patients lack precisely the type of perceptual intelligence animating the equanimous process of smoothly responding to the object as appearance by which one obtains access to multiple perspectives. The kinds of perspectivism we have discussed, from Goethe to Noë, through Nietzsche, share a general drive toward narrative by connecting diverse things, and even their hidden aspects, as so many virtual points of reference structuring the flow of the perceiving consciousness. For Goethe, we recall, the changing appearances of organic life, as it grows out from the center, is mirrored in the kind of consciousness whose gentle empiricism builds knowledge only by flowing, changing, attuning to its objects. As equanimity frames it, building knowledge through the attunements of observer and the cognizable world happens only as an event in which "the synthesis which constitutes the unity of the perceived objects and which gives meaning to the perceptual data is," Merleau-Ponty rightly insists, "not an intellectual synthesis." It cannot embody a purely rational integration because it does not, as it does for some simultagnosic patients, result from merely "grasp[ing] the object either as possible or as necessary... [rather] in perception it is 'real'; it is given as the infinite sum of an indefinite series of perspectival views in each of which it is given but in none of which it is given exhaustively" ("The Primacy of Perception," p. 15). The "real" object appears in equanimous seeing as the superordinate sum of fragmentary (as opposed to fragmented) perspectives conditioning the object's very mode of appearance. Pathology, in contrast, veers always toward the fragmented, the uneven, the univocal, as when a *particular* style of existing in and structuring one's world becomes the idiom of *all* relationality. This forfeiture of flexibility describes a spectrum, ranging from relatively benign forms of closed-mindedness to rare disorders such as paranoid psychosis and the visuoperceptual disorders I am describing presently. What is important here is that equanimity mobilizes knowledge as an event that flows over the material and phenomenal world, appreciating the continuities that its interrelatedness affords.

What is the experience of broken continuities like? Akinetopsia, or motion blindness, is a syndrome following brain damage, specifically to the motion center in the cerebral cortex, where smooth successions of the phenomenal world are imperceptible. In 1978, a 43-year-old woman was admitted into hospital suffering from a visual disorder characterized by a loss of movement vision in all three dimensions. She had trouble, for example,

> pouring tea or coffee into a cup because the fluid appeared to be frozen, like a glacier. In addition, she could not stop pouring at the right time since she was unable to perceive the movement in the cup (or a pot) when the fluid rose.... In a room where more than two other people were walking she felt very insecure and unwell, and usually left the room immediately, because "people were suddenly here or there but I have not seen them moving".... She could not cross the street because of her inability to judge the speed of a car, but she could identify the car itself without difficulty. "When I'm looking at the car first, it seems far away. But then, when I want to cross the road, suddenly the car is very near." She gradually learned to "estimate" the distance of moving

vehicles by means of the sound becoming louder. (Zihl, von Cramon, & Mai, "Selective Disturbance," p. 315)

Her rare syndrome, likely caused by bilateral brain lesions, illustrates, by contrast at any rate, the way in which the undamaged brain functions to create a seamless flow out of the still-images that the world presents from moment-to-moment. Under normal conditions, the right hemisphere processes flow as a single unified motion across time, and, unsurprisingly, the understanding of narrative is a right-hemisphere skill. Perceiving moving objects as a progressive series of still snapshots—like viewing a flipbook animation one page at a time—can obviously be very hazardous, as it is for this patient when she crosses a street, plainly able to see cars but never capable of visually confirming if they are actually coming at her. When the world appears de-animated like this, it becomes less comprehensible in context, less intuitive, and consequently more threatening. The patient, for example, found it very troubling to meet friends and chat with them because, unable to respond in time to their handshake, she found their moving hands disturbing. Furthermore, the experience of talking to them was quite distressing since she avoided watching their varying facial expressions while speaking since their lips seemed to jump rapidly up and down. The akinetopsic world, replacing the flow of time with static scenes and dislocated sequences, tends to disrupt meaningful action and the linkages ensuring the smoothness of contexts crucial for interpreting and feeling at ease. Such a world is perhaps best described with the patient's own term: "restless" (Zihl & Heywood, p. 4).

Like simultagnosia, akinetopsia is a symptom of missing the stabilizing, synthesis-generating, context-constructing role that, in normal persons, the right hemisphere effortlessly performs. What I want to suggest here is simply that these, and other, visuoperceptual disorders correspond, at a phenomenological level, to states of total disequanimity of the kind one would expect if the left hemisphere dominated and, essentially, acted independently of the right. No one has offered a more extended analysis of what the cultural, psychological, and epistemological consequences of the left hemisphere's phenomenological suppression of the right have been and will be than Iain McGilchrist. Using the brain's bihemispheric structure as an explanatory tool for the ways the brain has been put to use over the course of Western history, McGilchrist shows that, currently, we are in thrall to a left-hemispheric vision of the lived world. Of course, this is not the only moment of thralldom, and there have been historical resurgences of the right hemisphere such as the Romantic period. One of the clear and present dangers of the left-hemispheric view is precisely to what I have been suggesting equanimity offers an antidote—namely, a devitalized consciousness oblivious to more integrative modes of attention and relationality. In short, the antinomy of equanimous vision is a world predicated upon turning vital flow into depersonalized bits and pieces, holistic and original thinking into bureaucratic rationalities recognizable by their relentless consistency and reduplication. As McGilchrist sees it, a world dominated by a left-hemispheric vision resonates eerily with the skewed visions of certain neurological patients:

> Experiences or things that we would normally see as having a natural, organically evolving, flowing, structure, would come to see composed of a succession of frames, a sum of an infinite series of "pieces." This would include the passage of historical or cultural, as well as personal, time, and organically flowing shapes or forms, and ultimately the development, growth and decay of all things that are alive. This corresponds to the *Zeitraffer* phenomenon. It is coupled with the loss of the sense of uniqueness. Repeatability would lead to an over-familiarity through endless reproduction. (*The Master and his Emissary*, p. 433).

In the left hemisphere's world of mechanical reproduction, the natural fluidity of things across time as gradual, seamless motion is substituted by a succession of moments of stasis grasped according to the logic of the *Zeitraffer* phenomenon, where the altered perception of the speed of moving objects predominates, and the world is experienced as a time-lapsed series of static moments, such as some schizophrenics report (see the classic 1939 paper by Hoff & Pötzl). Even though it is true that, in our most attentive moments, we fail to grasp some of the synchronic implications of the contents of which we are holistically conscious, equanimous seeing involves a very high degree of integration across the multiple dimensions of space and time. Evidence from pathological cases involving the failure of such integration provides important insights into the nature and basis of consciousness and the construction of knowledge. What a harmoniously functioning mind might look like is the real question. Fortunately, there are some clues, in both Western and Eastern philosophy.

At least since Immanuel Kant's articulation of the structure of knowledge in *Critique of Pure Reason* (1781, 1787), the phenomenon whereby the various objects of experience are tied together into a single unified conscious experience of the world has been called the unity of consciousness. Generally, it describes consciousness not of object A and, separately, of B and, separately, of C, but of A-and-B-and-C together, as the contents of a unitary conscious state. Philosopher Tim Bayne proposes the existence of a kind of conscious harmony that he terms "phenomenal unity," capturing a strong intuition about the nature of consciousness, namely, that there is a substantial sense in which all of a person's experiences—perceptual, bodily, emotional, and cognitive—can be unified. This means that, although these experiences are distinct from each other (e.g., I hear a song, read the lyrics, and feel sad even all at once), and the fact is that, while I could experience any of them individually, the experiences, at the same time, seem to be tied together in a profound way. They appear to be unified, by comprising elements of a single encompassing state of consciousness. For Bayne, phenomenal unity is both a universal feature of human consciousness, where this total state is not merely a conjunction of conscious states, and a conscious state in its own right. He suggests that such an encompassing conscious state can serve as the "singularity behind the multiplicity," that is, the single state of consciousness in which all of a subject's states of consciousness are subsumed (Bayne & Chalmers, p. 27). For multiple experiences to be phenomenally co-conscious in this way, it is not necessary to forge an array of intricate representational connections between them or their contents, nor to identify a kind of Gestalt experience whose singular novel content has emerged from the mutual transformation of deeply related experiences and their different objects. Instead, it appears that we normally, simply, are co-conscious, and we can be aware of being so.

Subsumptively unified states possess a conjoint phenomenology, that is, a phenomenology of having multiple states at once that subsumes the phenomenology of each individual state. As Bayne puts it, "there is something it is like for the subject to be in [multiple conscious] states simultaneously" (*Unity of Consciousness*, p. 32). This something-that-it-is-like could be called equanimity. What Bayne is describing yields a distinctive phenomenology that the equanimous processing of reality affords in the form of always attending to the context of shifting phenomenological relations between observer and observed and between the things observed. In this sense, equanimity functions as the never-static singularity *above* the multiplicity. This then is one way in which the kinds of phenomenology we have been describing—from Goethe to Bayne—and equanimous knowledge approach each other: the world becomes intelligible to the extent that we appreciate that we will never succeed in understanding the things of the world independent of the dynamic context in which they are embedded. To start only with isolates pushes thought in the direction of objectivism, risking alienation from the living world. Yet for a multiplicity to emerge there must be a singularity that provisionally, vitally subsumes it.

John Dewey and William James, each in their own way, registered their dissatisfaction with the atomistic, rationalistic approach to philosophy that depends upon scholastic abstraction and objective certainty. Dewey argued that "the most pervasive fallacy of philosophic thinking goes back to neglect of context," and deplored this neglect as "the greatest single disaster which philosophic thought can incur" (*Context and Thought*, p. 206; 212). In the frame I am viewing it (while cognizant of discrepancies between this and Bayne's original sense), phenomenal unity signifies not the organization of things according to some intellectual rubric, however compelling (yet, ultimately, arbitrary) such a rubric may be, but that which emerges as a result of open, processual attending. Dewey urged an understanding of context:

> To see the organism *in* nature, the nervous system in the organism, the brain in the nervous system, the cortex in the brain is the answer to the problems which haunt philosophy. And when thus seen they will be

seen to be *in*, not as marbles are in a box but as events are in history, in a moving, growing, never finished process (*Experience and Nature*, p. 241; emph. in orig.).

Any qualities we might attend to are never to be found "in" the organism *per se*; instead, they are always in the process of emerging as a result of our ceaseless attending to the manifold and dynamic interactions animating them. The active equanimous mind proceeds differently from the absolutist one, as James describes it, noting that "our great difference from the scholastic lies in the way we 'face.' The strength of his system lies in the principles, the origin, the *terminus a quo* of his thought; for us the strength is in the outcome, the upshot, the *terminus ad quem*. Not where it comes from, but what it leads to is to decide" ("Will to Believe," p. 17). To phrase this in terms of the procedure of equanimity: as a path for knowing, it is not a technique whose originating principles determine its courses, but rather it is given meaning by where it unexpectedly ends up.

Dewey's model for knowledge, a kind of endless nesting of Matryoshka dolls, locates us, and whatever we are inquiring into, right in the middle of reality—in the full, moving stream of history-making. Philosophy, for Dewey, amounts to no more than "the conscious inquiry into experience" ("Introduction to Philosophy," p. 211). This tidy definition of philosophical inquiry is supported by his contention that "the value of the notion of experience. . . is that it denotes both the field, the sun and clouds and rain, seeds, and harvest, and the man who labors, who plans, invents, uses, suffers, and enjoys. Experience denotes. . . the world of events and persons; and it denotes that world caught up into experiencing, the career and destiny of mankind. Nature's place in man is no less significant than man's place in nature" ("Experience and Philosophic Method," p. 384). We have experiences precisely because we exist in a continuous transaction with the elements of our world. Experiences themselves cannot be grasped as discrete cognitive episodes since all thought is crucially contextual.

Bringing equanimity into alignment with such a conceptualizing of lived experience reveals precisely why it cannot be anything like Thomas Nagel's famous "view from nowhere," which, by acting as if it is nowhere in particular, masquerades as a "view from everywhere." The view from above that I have described is not an ideal of impartiality or objectivity but rather one of inclusivity and interdependence—*samyak-drishti* (holistic viewing) rather than exclusively *sakaya-drishti* (fragmented viewing). Dewey's rejection of impartiality as a dangerous kind of bias echoes the gist of Nietzsche and Zhuangzi: "One can only see from a certain viewpoint, but this fact does not make all standpoints of equal value. A standpoint which is nowhere in particular and from which things are not seen at a special angle is an absurdity" (*Context and Thought*, p. 216). Dewey allowed for a certain "affection for a standpoint" that is "rich" relative to a "meager" one (ibid.), just as equanimity affords a view from "where it seems best" without ever fastening upon it, never holding it in exclusivity.

There are, as I have suggested, "special angles" that characterize equanimous vision: from above and from the side, for example, with neither having primacy. Characteristic of these angles is their allowance for things to exist in themselves in an integrative way that deprives them of polarization and divisiveness. By remaining comprehensive, equanimous vision sets in motion these angles on reality in such a way that they inspire calm, a sort of confidence and trust in things as they are. Emerson called this simply "knowing that all things go well" ("Self-Reliance," p. 144). It is a rudimentary assurance that stems from knowing that Nature or Reality is—we might say—itself assured. Or, as Emerson puts it in "Uses of Great Men": "The eye repeats every day the first eulogy on things,—'He saw that they were good'" (p. 321). Like Stevens's gesture toward "times of inherent excellence," knowing that all things are already working themselves out means that the only way of seeing which is called for is one whose affinities are supported by a range of vibrant responses and perceptive sensibilities.

Neurobiologically speaking, the brain in such an equanimous state is functioning, as Daniel Siegel describes it, on an "open plane of possibility" (*The Mindful Therapist*, p. 9), that is, an optimal matrix of knowledge configured to encourage and sustain, through multiple attunements and receptivity, the natural flow of life experiences. Reactivity, fixation, habit, and blockages now relax into states of receptivity, integration, spontaneity, and fluidity. Abandoning mechanistic mental activity, along with the egocentric perspective defending it, allows for the emergence of this new paradigm of knowledge, where a holistic attending to ambient reality ensures that we remain sensitive to what is exciting, wondrous. Aurelius expresses it with perfect irony: "You can always become indifferent to song or dance or athletic displays if you resolve the melody into its several notes, and ask yourself of each one in turn, Is it this that I cannot resist? Always remember to go straight for the parts themselves, and by dissecting them achieve your disenchantment" (*Meditations*, 11.2). By anatomizing phenomena, we denature the world, and prevent ourselves from ever seeing it as it really is. And, most fatally, dissection thwarts the process of knowledge by trading inert certainties for intellectual equity. Equanimity sooner recognizes that certainty is inversely proportional to how much we actually know and can come to know. The finality of certainty runs counter to the openness of questions formulated in wonder. Echoing Plato and Aristotle, for whom philosophical thinking starts in wonder (*Theaetetus*, 155c-d; *Metaphysics*, 1.2 982b12-22), Ortega y Gasset affirms that "to be surprised, to wonder, is to begin to understand.... Everything in the world is strange and marvelous to well-open eyes" (*The Revolt of the Masses*, p. 12). Around the same time, Albert Einstein would state something very similar, only this time negatively and in rather sharp-edged terms: the person who fails to encounter the universe with wonder is "as good as dead: his eyes are closed" ("From *Living Philosophies*," p. 6).

Equanimity owes its power of understanding things to "well-open eyes." Part of the integrative power of expansive and ranging eyes is their resistance to habituation. There is some evidence, going back to a famous study of Zen meditators in 1966, suggesting that a phenomenon known as alpha blocking, a marker of the absence of habituation, describes observed EEG (electroencephalogram) recordings of the brain activity of seasoned practitioners. Alpha blocking is an alteration in brain wave activity from alpha to the more desynchronized (i.e., excited) beta condition. Drs. Akira Kasamatsu and Tomio Hirai attached electrodes to the scalps of forty-eight Rinzai and Sōtō sect practitioners and priests, as well as twenty-two control subjects, in order to monitor their EEG patterns during meditation. What interests us is that a later phase of their study included the administering of a series of twenty loud "clicks" at fifteen-second intervals during meditation, where it was discovered that only in the control subjects was there evidence of habituation to the click stimulus. The Zen practitioners, by contrast, exhibited responsiveness to each click, as indicated by the active pattern of their alpha blocking. "Each stimulus is accepted as stimulus itself and treated as such," the researchers reported. "One Zen master described such a state of mind as that of noticing every person one sees on the street but of not looking back with emotional curiosity" (p. 333).

This state of mind, in its perfect responsiveness and sensitivity to the world recalls Zhuangzi's description of "the Consummate Person [who] uses his mind like a mirror, rejecting nothing, welcoming nothing: responding but not storing" (Ziporyn, *Zhuangzi*, p. 54; cf. Graham, *The Inner Chapters*, p. 98). The world is simply "just this," to use the famous Zen expression, and is encountered according to an epistemology of "intuition [that] takes time at its full value. It permits no ossification, as it were, of each moment. Momentariness is therefore characteristic of this philosophy. Each moment is absolute, alive and significant. The frog leaps, the cricket sings, the dew-drop glitters on the lotus leaf, a breeze passes through the pine branches, and the moonlight falls on the murmuring mountain stream" (D. T. Suzuki, *Buddhism in the Life and Thought of Japan*, p. 27). There is nothing to which one can become habituated; everything is happening and to every happening one is responding anew. Zen master Takuan Sōhō (1573-1645) compared such a mind to a hollow gourd floating on water: "The mind of the man who has arrived does not stop at one thing, even for a bit. It is like pushing down the gourd in the water" (*Mysterious Record*, p. 25). Striking at the empty gourd or pushing it under, it just pops up and spins away, never staying in one place no matter what forces act upon it. A Zen capping phrase concisely captures the image of the equanimous mind: "Pushing a gourd on water [*Suijō ni korosu o osu*]" (Hori, *Zen Sand*, p. 240).

A perfectly moving mind, which I have argued is the lynchpin of equanimity as a way of knowing and interacting with the world, is one not stymied by inhibitions, fixations, or habituations. I have been using the idea of a "perfectly" moving mind as a way to illustrate what equanimity is like, cognizant of the fact that, though relatively rare as they may be, there are in fact real world examples of what this looks like. These examples often express ideals of Buddhist and Daoist philosophy. Think of the Zen practitioners in the 1966 study I just mentioned. It turns out that they displayed what psychologists since that time have come to recognize as one of the five major personality domains: Openness to Experience. This domain signifies flexibility and receptivity to the full range of experiential possibilities. Generally, this flexible cognitive stance, as research has shown, enables open people to be creative and to hold value systems and worldviews that tend to be complex and tolerant of difference and contradiction. They process stimuli that others are inclined to ignore as irrelevant or screen out following repeated exposure, a processing phenomenon that psychologists often refer to as latent inhibition (see, e.g., Peterson et al., "Openness and Extroversion"). Decreased latent inhibition among open people is identified with a tendency to have a more permeable consciousness, a sort of porous filter for preconscious information, affording more opportunities to explore information and engage with complex possibilities.

A recent finding by Antinori and colleagues (2017) is fully consistent with this. They examined the phenomenon of binocular rivalry—the perception of two incompatible stimuli presented simultaneously, which usually produces the subjective experience of seeing one image then the other, in a back-and-forth visual suppression—in relation to personality. What they discovered is that open people reported experiencing less switching between rival imagery, meaning they were more prone to combining perceptual information, demonstrating superior divergent thinking skills. The implications of this finding are rather radical: open people may not only think about the world differently compared to their counterparts, but they may *see*, that is, literally perceive, more possibilities in it given their more inclusive and integrative perceptual experiences. They embody more flexible ways of linking information across the perceptual field.

This theme of openness, clearly central to any discussion of equanimity, is here to be understood as pointing in the opposite direction to passive or inert communication with the world.

Receptivity, as we have seen, allows things to grow, to emerge, not as an effort of will but as an unfolding process, a "Negative Capability" as John Keats described it, that is, when we are "capable of being in uncertainties, mysteries, doubts, without any irritable reaching after fact and reason" (*Letters of John Keats*, p. 48). The point here is not to affirm an existence in overwhelming doubt or permanent uncertainty but rather to understand how crucial these capacities to exist in unknowing, open possibility, and wonder are to the very process of thinking. There is, McGilchrist shows, in fact a natural neuropsychological trajectory that captures the progression of thought:

> It begins in wonder, intuition, ambiguity, puzzlement and uncertainty; it progresses through being unpacked, inspected from all angles and wrestled into linearity by the left hemisphere; but its endpoint is to see that the very business of language and linearity must themselves be transcended, and once more left behind. (*The Master and his Emissary*, p. 178)

This movement—from right hemisphere, to left, back to right—defines the working relationship of the hemispheres, one ultimately grounded in the "primacy of broad vigilant attention" and the "primacy of wholeness," both right hemisphere roles (ibid., p. 179). The final work of transcendence here is closest to the aim of equanimity as I am discussing it: a broadly attentive and active engagement with a pristine world that can be grasped as having once been unmarred by the divisions of language and concomitant analysis. This is precisely the world that, as Zen philosophers continually remind us, never needs synthesis since it is perfect in the first place.

In its most rarefied, mystical form, overcoming alienation from the world of perfect wholeness requires nothing less than the dissolution of the ego in order to become aware consciousness through and through. As the Sufi poet Rumi puts it: "Behead yourself! […] Dissolve your whole body into Vision: become seeing, seeing, seeing!" (qtd. in Harding, p. 33). Emerson claimed to have actualized this crystalline, non-interfering view: "Standing on the bare ground—my head bathed by the blithe air and uplifted into infinite space—all mean egotism vanishes. I become a transparent eyeball; I am nothing; I see all; the currents of the Universal Being circulate through me; I am part or particle of God" (*Nature*, p. 6). Emerson's soaring transparent eyeball, unlike Thoreau's down-to-earth "sauntering eye," offers a view from everywhere, the equivalent of a view from nowhere, a decontextualized vantage point. Emerson's view arises from the achievement of negating division from the totality (or God). It will be appreciated that this is not knowledge brought into being through the coming to rest of opposites. In other words, the transcendentalist impulse here heralds an assumption of a kind of ultimate knowledge that in effect has no use for equanimity's power to harmonize division with union. Recalling the epigraph to this section from Coleridge's *Biographia Literaria*: the result of philosophy is the restoration of unity to whatever divisions or paradoxes have presented themselves in the very process of thinking. Similarly, the Romantic poet and philosopher Friedrich von Schlegel (1772-1829), giving expression to the challenge of uniting a totalizing method with its absence, claimed that "it is equally fatal for the mind to have a system and to have none. It will simply have to decide to combine the two" (*Athenaeum Fragments*, p. 247). From a perspective that valorizes order, Schlegel's proposal sounds like chaos, the loss of meaning, rather than a combinatory path toward a mind whose deference to the world mirrors a complex set of transactionally-relating order*s*. Either having a system or not having one forecloses the possibility of seeing these orders as part of the spontaneous array of constellations in which we exist.

Schlegel's use of the word "fatal" (*tödlich*) in this context is telling. As I have urged in this chapter, and indeed in earlier ones, equanimity describes a way the world makes itself available to us to the extent we interact with it harmoniously. The mind and the world enter together into the making of vital experience. So, what would a *fatal* interaction look like? There is a curious story in the *Zhuangzi* that illustrates the dire cost of disequanimity:

> The emperor of the southern sea was called Swoosh. The emperor of the northern sea was called Oblivion. The emperor of the middle sea was called Chaos. Swoosh and Oblivion would sometimes meet in the territory of Chaos, who always attended to them quite well. They decided to repay Chaos for his virtue. "All men have seven holes in them, by means of which they see, hear, eat, and breathe," they said. "But this one alone has

none. Let's drill him some." So each day they drilled another hole. After seven days, Chaos was dead. (Ziporyn, p. 54; cf. Graham, p. 98)

Chaos, who signifies the unordered whole, accommodates the extremities, as denoted by his overseeing a middle space where the polar emperors join. Chaos normally functions without hierarchy—he attends to his neighbors equally—and he represents not confusion and disarray but rather the quality, the "virtue," of non-differentiation, a noncoherent sum of differences. The entity Chaos bears resemblance to philosopher F. S. C. Northrop's "undifferentiated aesthetic continuum," the term he coined to point to the factor in human consciousness that partakes in "the all-embracing, radically empirical continuum of immediacy with all sensing and sensed differentia eliminated" (p. 70). Order is imposed on Chaos by making holes in him, that is, instituting an inside/outside distinction and, with it, discrete channels for exchange with the world. What in effect kills Chaos, what nullifies his uniqueness and all-embracing nature, is the imposition of conventional discriminations predicated on a self/other dichotomy that was previously unknown. The fixed holes are emblematic of the kind of attention which makes each object explicit by placing it under a sort of isolating spotlight. In this way, things are rendered inert, invariable, lifeless.

The floodlight consciousness of equanimity recognizes that, for knowledge and meaning to be generated, momentarily stepping back from the immediacy of experience is necessary. In looking over things, the floodlight never opposes the spotlight, but subsumes it. Since our minds naturally attend to the world in different ways at different times, thereby bringing different worlds into being, at the same time we have the opportunity to see that each world is implicated within every other one. This is a central function of equanimity, that is, grasping the mutual implications of multiple perspectives. What is important to appreciate here is that equanimity never negates the uniqueness of a particular perspective; indeed, a corollary of this radical perspectivism is that the entire field of experience, of knowing, is implicated within each particular object of consciousness. The effect is holographic or, consistent with Daoist and Buddhist philosophies, fully interdependent, where the entire cosmos exists felicitously within each thing to which we could ever attend: "To see a World in a Grain of Sand." Absolute reality (truth beyond dualisms) and relative reality (conventional truth) are in this way coincident, as the verse of the 13th-century Zen Master Shiqi Xinyue captures it: "In an atom of dust, a galaxy of worlds / In a half a second, eighty thousand springs / Going and coming like this, staying like this / No one knows which is the host, which is the guest" (*A Tune Beyond the Clouds*, p. 98).

The simultaneity of a narrow perspective and a broad one affords a kind of "objectivity" understood not as a unified or ultimate, detached point of view but one that is inherently multiple, shifting, inclusive, and therefore most attuned to the flux and flow of Reality itself. In the Vedic tradition, meditating upon Brahman, the ultimate reality through which the universe exists and moves, calls up the inseparability and mutual implication of possible perspectives:

> He who consists of mind, whose body is subtle, whose form is light, whose thoughts are true, whose soul is space, containing all works, containing all desires, containing all odors, containing all tastes, encompassing this whole world . . . this Soul of mine within the heart is smaller than a grain of rice, or a barley-corn, or a mustard-seed, or a grain of millet, or the kernel of a grain of millet. This Soul of mine is greater than the earth, greater than the atmosphere, greater than the sky, greater than these worlds. (*Chandogya Upanishad*, 3.14.2-3)

Yet Eastern philosophy is not alone in offering visions of what thinking and experiencing are like when seemingly antagonistic approaches to and perspectives on the world are integrated.

There are three thinkers I want to look at briefly: William James, Trigant Burrow, and Martin Heidegger, all of whom were concerned with the basic problems of how we attend to the world and with describing the integrative modes of thinking that mediate the mind-world connection.

James is a fallibilist, seeing all truths about existence as, in theory, subject to revision given new experience. Since the relationships between facts and our ideas or beliefs about them are forever malleable, we should in his view be wary of the rationalist tendency to regard any truth as absolute. Knowledge is processual precisely because it originates in "pure experience," or what James called "the instant field of the present," which is itself an ongoing event ("Does 'Consciousness' Exist? p. 23). The present, prior to its verbalization, is paradoxically both unified and inescapably heterogenous, a plenitude whose content is unnamable. In his 1905 essay "The Thing and its Relations," James describes the primordial realm of "pure experience,"

> the name which I gave to the immediate flux of life which furnishes the material to our later reflection with its conceptual categories. Only new-born babes or men in semi-coma from sleep, drugs, illnesses, or blows, may be assumed to have an experience pure in the literal sense of a *that* which is not yet any definite *what*, tho' ready to be all sorts of whats; full both of oneness and of manyness, but in respects that don't appear; changing throughout, yet so confusedly that its phases interpenetrate and no points, either of distinction or of identity, can be caught. (pp. 93-94)

For James, this preconceptual flux of inchoate experience indicates a world knowable at first only by acquaintance. Knowledge by acquaintance is the direct awareness of things, unmediated, as Bertrand Russell puts it, by "any process of inference or any knowledge of truths" (*The Problems of Philosophy*, p. 25), whereas knowledge by description derives from the use or application of concepts. The synthesis of these two very distinct ways of knowing, I wish to suggest, is reflected in equanimity's *Aufhebung*, its process of simultaneously upholding and transcending them in such a way that preserves connection to the liveliness (the "manyness" and confusion) of phenomenal objects and the capacity for reflection belonging to knowing subjects. Equanimity offers access to the "instant field of the present" and to the concepts that allow for describing how the field's "thats" may become particularized "whats." Pathways to the realm of pure experience are possible outside states of altered consciousness or the pre-symbolism of infancy. That said, equanimity does not get caught in the dichotomy between the realm of pre-verbal and concrete feeling and the realm of cognitive abstraction that would end up privileging knowing as some separate intellectual act. Rational thoughts mix with affects, and cognitive contents blend with feelings in their immediacy. A. N. Whitehead expresses this quite beautifully with his observation that "mothers can ponder many things in their hearts that words cannot express" (*Religion in the Making*, p. 67). In this connection, I cannot resist citing the wonderful opening sentence of Iris Murdoch's classic essay "On 'God' and 'Good'": "To do philosophy is to explore one's own temperament, and yet at the same time to attempt to discover the truth" (p. 337).

Doubtless, the pioneer of social psychiatry and group analysis Trigant Burrow (1875-1950) would have agreed that any philosophy, with its aspirations to truth, must attend to the individual's inner life. Burrow goes further, however, insisting that an understanding of how humans experience each other—in groups and in society—is the key not only to their "truth" but their total well-being. How humans think, feel, and behave, he argues, are functions of their relation to the environment, specifically how they relate to it using their attention. There are, he puts forward, two kinds of attention—ditention and cotention—where the former divides us against ourselves and is responsible for pathologies appearing in both individuals and the social body. Ditention is partitive attention, that is, ordinary attention fragmented by the intrusion of biases that are both the cause and symptom of evaluating the symbolic value to us of everything we encounter. D. H. Lawrence, in an insightful review of Burrow's *The Social Basis of Consciousness* (1927), called this type of self-interested attention "image consciousness" (p. 381), and identified it as a token of dysfunction and disharmony. Ditention is that mode of attention, Burrow writes, that looks "from without in" rather than from "within out" as other living things do (*Neurosis of Man*, p. 204). The problem with predominantly looking within from without, Burrow showed, is that it cannot be done without an excess of self-generated images and language whose progressive intrusion distorts what he called biosocial union. We increasingly find ourselves, he submitted, in situations where the irreconcilability of intellect and word, on one side, with emotion and body, on the other, means that a fundamental principle of mutuality in human relations is imperiled. Burrow radically suggested that ditention was the key to explaining disruptions of harmonious intersubjectivity and of the thinking that supports healthy organism-environment attunement.

Burrow reserved the term *cotention* for describing a more direct and total response pattern to the world, one where affect-laden images of others and oneself fade and, concomitantly, an extensive, open attitude emerges, with observation and insight unblemished by fantasies and images associated primarily with self-interest or -reflexivity. As an integrative mode of attending, cotention overlaps with equanimity in terms of how it shifts our ways of relating to the world in the direction of knowledge that more perfectly mirrors the nature of things as they are. It is nothing less than "the primary, natural mode" of humans in which there exists "no compulsion to *like* or *dislike*" (*A Search for Man's Sanity*, p. 562; emph. in orig.). In a letter from 1948 to the British art historian and philosopher Herbert Read, Burrow extolled cotention as "probably the 'kingdom of heaven' and, like the latter, is within us" (ibid., p. 515). As for how to induce cotention, Burrow described the process in a letter to a friend: in a state with closed eyes, hold them still, "in the absence of any point of focus" while maintaining them in "a position of equilibrium." Eventually, the subject becomes aware that the "restless mental habit prompted by emotion" dissolves (ibid., pp. 435-36). In fact, in his first published study on cotention in 1938—in a journal no less prestigious than *Nature*—Burrow found that the respiratory rate of experimental subjects decreased markedly as they transitioned from ditention to cotention. Burrow would later speculate that breathing more slowly and deeply is the physiological correlate of release from the ditentive "hot" (his word) pursuit after "the imaginary mental something man is vainly projecting at every moment." Indeed, ultimately, he would describe cotention—as I have equanimity—as not aimed at anything: in this sense, "cotention is *nothing*," he insists in a letter to a friend shortly before he died (ibid., p. 590). Cotention, like equanimity, is a something that is nothing in the sense that, never reached by causal methods or techniques, it transports you nowhere other than exactly where you are—*in medias res*.

Sometimes it takes a paradoxical figure, in this case the legendary fool Nasrudin, to lay bare just what the dire consequences are for not appreciating the "nothing" that comprises the "all." As a way of introducing Heidegger's take on ways of apprehending the cosmos, let's take a look at this short teaching story collected by Idries Shah:

Nasrudin sometimes took people for trips in his boat. One day a pedagogue hired him to ferry him across a very wide river. As soon as they were afloat, the scholar asked whether it was going to be rough. "Don't ask me nothing about it," said Nasrudin. "Have you never studied grammar?" "No," said the Mulla. "In that case, half of your life has been wasted." The Mulla said nothing. Soon a terrible storm blew up. The Mulla's crazy cockleshell was filling with water. He leaned over toward his companion. "Have you ever learned to swim?" "No," said the pedant. "In that case, schoolmaster, all your life is lost, for we are sinking" (The Exploits of the Incomparable Mulla Nasrudin, p. 18).

In the attitudes of Nasrudin and the scholar, two major modes of consciousness are represented. One is the "prickly" verbal, analytical, rule-bound mode, represented by the pedagogue; the other is the fluidly practical, holistic, and improvisational mode of the fool Nasrudin. Asked to forecast the weather conditions, Nasrudin tellingly deflects the pedant with a double negative, putting before him a grammatical construction whose incorrectness dramatizes the fact that weather conditions, unlike grammar, are never subject to rules or conventions. The weather, as a natural phenomenon, cannot be normed; it obeys no precise constitutive laws about how it is supposed to work from moment to moment. The schoolmaster's reproof that half of Nasrudin's life has been wasted misses the possibility that the non-standard construction has meanings beyond merely its violation of prescriptive grammar: do the two negatives resolve to a positive? Or is the double negative used to emphasize negation? The Mulla's silence, his "nothing" in response to the schoolmaster's criticism, marks the space in which possibilities are radically open, exemplified by the storm's sudden appearance swamping the small boat. Now existence becomes a matter not of words in their tidy, conventional linearity but of excited movement in space as a mode of survival.

The question of how we exist in and through thought was a preeminent concern of the philosopher Martin Heidegger, for whom there are two distinct forms of thinking. One approach to the world is calculative and conventional, relying on the fashioning of our own terms to deal with things, such as pressing verbal realities into grammatical rules. The other approach, reflective and radically open, relies on its closeness to realities as they are actually lived, here and now. Heidegger saw these two modes—calculative thinking (*das rechnende Denken*) and meditative thinking (*das besinnliche Denken*)—as interdependent, though very different. Calculative thinking characterizes, for example, scientific or economic ways of thinking and planning, the modes of thought, Heidegger says, dominant in a technological era like our own. He also calls this kind of thinking under the dominion of technology "one-track thinking" (*What is Called Thinking*, p. 26). Indeed, the ascendancy of calculative thought comes at the expense of meditative thinking, which does not construct a world of objects for our use but rather allows content to emerge within awareness.

Unlike calculative thinking, meditative thinking is not an act of will yet neither is it passive; it exists only in a relation of openness to something, and operates, as Heidegger puts it, "beyond the distinction between activity and passivity" (*Discourse on Thinking*, p. 61). "Meditative thinking," he observes, "demands of us not to cling one-sidedly to a single idea nor to run down a one-track course of ideas. Meditative thinking demands of us that we engage ourselves with what at first sight does not go together at all" (ibid., p. 53). Of this kind of thinking, it is easy to see that Goethe was a master. In its capacity to apprehend things comprehensively, meditative thinking shares with equanimity a readiness to open to the unfamiliar, through "releasing" ourselves to the full attentiveness that the mysteries of nature call into being. Heidegger insists that such an "openness to the mystery" (*Offenheit für das Geheimnis*) requires "persistent, courageous thinking" (ibid., p. 55; 56). This involves nothing less than the daring to transcend what we already know, with a willingness to be surprised, and to engage the surface of objects as merely one dimension of their being. Leaving the familiar behind, it becomes possible to venture into a new, open "region in which everything returns to itself. . .the region of all regions" (ibid., p. 65), where ontological unity in diversity is discoverable. Heidegger defines this mode of thinking, and ultimately the nature of knowledge itself, as "going toward," a single word in ancient Greek borrowed from Heraclitus, the preeminent philosopher of motion (ibid., p. 88).

Thinking is again seen as consonant with vital movement. Yet, for Heidegger, it is a special kind of contemplative motility predicated upon non-willing, and so, without pressure, involves "slowing down our pace" (ibid., p. 60). Whereas, in the mode of calculation, thinking "races from one prospect to the next...never stop[ping], never collect[ing] itself" (ibid., p. 46), the relaxed mode of meditation "leaves us time" (ibid., p. 60) to cultivate an attentive attitude recognized in its serene relation to openness. To describe this radical availability to what is given, in which is found the prospect of letting things be in their full mystery and uncertainty, Heidegger borrowed a term from mystical theology: "releasement" (*Gelassenheit*). Releasement is the sign of all thinking "able to bide its time, to await as does the farmer, whether the seed will come up and ripen" (ibid., p. 47). Attending to seeds emblematizes our releasement from will and so more fully toward things (*Gelassenheit zu den Dingen*). By embodying process rather than final being, seeds, as I have suggested, invite us to abide all becoming for the simple reason that it is unknowable in advance whether or not anything, figuratively speaking, "will come up and ripen." Precisely our non-predetermined intellectual movements toward the world make it possible to see new things and see familiar things anew. With the possibility of shifting our attention in this way comes an openness where the releasement toward things is the indelible mark of equanimous vision. Meditative thinking and calculative thinking have room within this open space to coexist despite their separateness. In the interplay of these two modes, the subject-object duality no longer holds, transcended through "a thinking that is not willing" (ibid., p. 60).

From a Zen perspective, this spacious mental process closely resembles *hishiryō*, or "without-thinking," a term that captures what consciousness is like during meditation when thoughts and images are allowed to appear and disappear naturally, free of the push-and-pull of our ordinary thinking. It can be characterized as a peaceful state beyond thinking and not-thinking, activity and passivity. *Hishiryō* consciousness arises when the mind encounters presence itself (*genjō*), unmediated by the screen of dualistic thought, otherwise busy dividing states of existence and relationality into such conditions as activity and stillness, speech and silence, self and other, and being and non-being. When consciousness in this way operates in sync with the fluctuating totality of what is, it never clings to the mental forms by which reality is conventionally apprehended nor does it grasp them as the sole reality. Self-reflective yet intimately involved with moving things, it sees, instead of isolated objects, the field and flow of phenomena as comprising an extensive, undulating network of vital existence. Here then is another aspect of equanimous knowledge: knowing the world as the middle ground in which such modes of existence as presence and absence, the ordinary and the novel, interfuse.

The interlacing of all things means that different qualities among them are preserved, respected, while at the same time separateness and conceptual opposition crumble. When the twelfth-century Ch'an Master Dahui Zonggao (1089-1163) claimed that "quietude and hustle-and-bustle are *one and the same thing*," he was pointing to a state of meditative awareness in which the duality of "stillness and commotion" is transcended to reveal a world free of, untroubled by, antonymous concepts (Cleary, *Swampland Flowers*, pp. 13-14). It is not only that stillness and commotion are relative and depend upon each other for their definition; it is that they have no defining aspect behind the accidents of change. As they succeed each other, both are part of the ceaseless and often cadenced flow of experience. Stillness may be understood as becoming-commotion, and commotion as becoming-stillness. Renovating the world as movement means that the present condition of all things entails its opposite. To this extent, the equanimous mind opens for the first time to a world of stillness *and* commotion as a "single thusness [*ichi-nyo*]" (ibid., p. 77). A "single thusness" may be appreciated via a flow of vision, a kind of open inspection across multiple perspectives that appeals to the full breadth of experience.

Yet such vision, rooted in equilibrium, also plumbs the shadowy mysteries and indeterminate elements lying beyond the horizons of what is known or immediately perceptible. When experience in this way allows things to exist fully in themselves, they are in a sense reenchanted, through the restorative appreciation of their inexhaustible depth. In the next and final chapter of this section on equanimity and knowledge, we will explore how equanimous knowledge depends upon the content and, especially, the character of our perceptual experiences, as we consider what it is like to know a tree deeply.

CHAPTER 5
NATURALLY EQUANIMOUS
Contemplating a Tree

Ways of Perceiving a Tree

> A fool sees not the same tree that a wise man sees.
> —William Blake, "The Marriage of Heaven and Hell"

> Analyze, weigh and measure a tree as you please, observe and describe its form and functions, its genesis and the laws to which it is subject; still an *acquaintance* with its *essence* never comes about.
> —Abraham Joshua Heschel, *Man is Not Alone*

Knowledge, as I have been suggesting, is performative, a function of ongoing multiplex relationships to the world. According to the humanist geographer Yi-Fu Tuan (1930-2022), "perception is an activity, a reaching out to the world." "Sense organs," he adds, "are minimally operative when they are not actively used. Our tactile sense is very delicate but to tell differences in the texture or hardness of surfaces, it is not sufficient to put a finger on them; the finger has to move over them. It is possible to have eyes and not see, ears and not hear" (*Topophilia*, p. 12). Information about the world depends upon sensory mobility more than it does upon passive sensing, however acute it may be. The German-American phenomenologist and neurologist Erwin Straus summarized it succinctly: "Only a being whose structure affords it the possibility of movement can be a sensing being" (*The Primary World of Senses*, p. 235). We know to the extent that we "move"—perceptually, intellectually, physically, emotionally, spiritually. Coming to know the world is the felicitous result of our ongoing flexibility.

Equanimity appreciates that our registration of the cognizable world, which ultimately constitutes our sense of belonging to it, is, like touch, diachronic and oriented to change. Equanimity shares with touch an experiential fluidity deriving from the correspondence of movement and changing patterns of awareness or sensory stimulation. Touch, as a way of relating to the world, never pulls back from it; rather, access to the world, compared to that of other senses, is unmediated. This led philosopher Brian O'Shaughnessy (1925-2010) to call touch "the most important and most primordial of the senses" since it can "scarcely be distinguished from the having of a body that can act in physical space" ("The Sense of Touch," p. 38). In seeing, we do not, indeed cannot, see our own eyes; instead, we relate to everything as mediated by the visual field of sensations. In touching, however, sense mediation is absent. In this coincidence of means and object—that is, the tactile properties of our own bodies and the self-same tactile properties of other bodies—resides "the source of the pre-eminence of touch" (ibid.). Through touch, we are bodies among other bodies. In place of a "world-view," we may speak, following Walter J. Ong (1912-2003), of "world-as-presence," a concept highlighting the "immediacy and a certain kind of relevance" that equanimity fosters ("World as View and World as Event," p. 646).

In chapter 4's discussion of the necessity of others, I pointed to the deep reciprocity and ease resulting from the process of experiencing the lived world along with others. Others secure the world-as-presence. So too does the active intercommunication of our own senses present an interanimating world in which our bodies and our environments are vitally linked. This is why, as Merleau-Ponty writes, "the lived perspective, that which we actually perceive," is never purely "a geometric or photographic one" ("Cézanne's Doubt," p. 14). Though they may be expedient, such formal, filmic perspectives tend to be cold, distant, abstract. Rather than encountering only static images observed from without or from a fixed place, "vision alone makes us learn that beings that are different, 'exterior,' foreign to one another, are yet absolutely *together,* are 'simultaneity'" ("Eye and Mind," p. 187; emph. in orig.). Disunion, resulting from a detached isolating perspective, and reunion, resulting from a coming together of the disparate, constitute the systole-diastole of total perception.

The phenomenology of touch has then, like fluid vision, a key function in relation to equanimous knowing, namely, its avoidance of a synchronic denial of becoming. Admittedly, my focus to this point has consistently been upon vision, not with the intention of advancing ocularcentrism—as if it needed to be—but rather to move toward thinking about its assimilation with other senses whose motility is also the hallmark of their perceptive range. "What is certain," observes Merleau-Ponty, "is that the perceived is not limited to that which strikes my eyes. When I am sitting at my desk, the space is closed behind me not only in idea but also in reality" (*The Structure of Behavior*, p. 249). For us to make sense of our experience of the world, he is suggesting, sight has to be integrated with other senses. Here, not only does vision forfeit any claim to primacy, but the perceiver, the questioning philosopher herself, abandons the egocentric wish for power over the perceptual world. To relinquish the desire for power is not to need it in the first place, not to have to bear its burden, its limitations. Rather than hold the things of the world "as with forceps, or to immobilize them as under the objective of a microscope," the mission of the genuine thinker is

> to let them be and to witness their continued being, [as] someone who therefore limits himself to giving them the hollow, the free space they ask for in return, the resonance they require, who follows their own movement, who is therefore not a nothingness the full being would come to stop up, but a question consonant with the porous being which it questions and from which it obtains not an answer, but a confirmation of its astonishment. It is necessary to comprehend perception as this interrogative thought which lets the perceived world be rather than posits it, before which the things form and undo themselves in a sort of gliding, beneath the yes and the no. (*The Visible and the Invisible*, pp. 101-2)

This spacious "letting be" of things as they glide below our questioning and provisional answers is at the core of equanimous inquiry. The echoes here with Heidegger's notions of *Gelassenheit* (releasement) and *Lichtung* (the forest clearing in which Being discloses itself) are certainly strong enough to invite comparisons. Above all, there is openness to the presently unsolved or unfinished, the sources of all astonishment.

Resonating with the movement—the becoming—of things opens up the possibility of discovering new knowledges whose fluidity corresponds to the porosity of their subjects. Awareness—and here Merleau-Ponty, for example, brings "the exploratory gaze of true vision" together with the "knowing touch"—depends upon the phenomenal components of movement and time (*Phenomenology of Perception*, p. 315). "The eyes," Noë writes, "direct a flow of perspectives just as the moving hand explores surfaces. Think of a blind person tap-tapping his or her way around a cluttered space, perceiving that space by touch, not all at once, but through time, by skillful probing and movement. This is, or at least ought to be, our paradigm of what perceiving is" (*Action in Perception*, p. 1). And, think of a plant whose flexible bio-attention and intentionality are dispersed in lived time in such a way that "the events of plant development and adaptation do not fill a preexisting temporal axis but form, across their multiple interactions, the inner time consciousness of plant life" (Marder, "Plant Intentionality and the Phenomenological Framework of Plant Intelligence," p. 1369).

As I have noted, from *theorein* to *upeksha*, vision has been embedded in the notion of how humans may acquire and organize knowledge in relation to the world. Sight and vision have a certain primacy for the simple reason that we often depend upon the visible horizon to mark the bounds of what is knowable. Love for and delight in knowing—epistemophilia—motivates the use of senses as they appreciate the range of differing elements with which the world confronts us as a whole. The opening of Aristotle's *Metaphysics* is paradigmatic in this regard:

> All men by nature desire to know. An indication of this is the delight we take in our senses; for even apart from their usefulness they are loved for themselves; and above all others the sense of sight. For not only with a view to action, but even when we are not going to do anything, we prefer seeing (one might say) to everything else. The reason is that this, most of all senses, makes us know and brings to light many differences between things. (1.1 980a22-28)

A crucial part of finding ourselves in a world of cognizable things then is this process of opening to different qualities founded upon the systole-diastole of active mental construction or construal and phenomenal reception. While the historical primacy of vision, as rooted in the concept of *theoria* and dominant from Plato to Descartes, was one of the favorite targets of Heidegger and Bergson, both of whom lamented the neglect of temporality in Western metaphysics since Heraclitus, vision is perhaps less abstractly spectatorial and spatializing than more modern scientific epistemologies. Rather than being strictly aligned with disinterested contemplation and the transfixing gaze, the original Greek concept of *theoria* contained the seeds of what philosopher Hans-Georg Gadamer (1900-2002) called "sacral communion." (Indeed, one sense of the Greek word *theoria* is a religious delegation sent by a city to take part in a festival.) This involves, Gadamer explains, a "true participation" where being receptive means "being totally involved in and carried away by what one sees," thus going some way to explaining "the religious background of the Greek concept of reason" (*Truth and Method*, p. 122).

As in Merleau-Ponty's account of perception, receptive contact with and participation in the sensible world produce a sense of wonder. The thinking that belongs to vision has "in its center a mystery of passivity" ("Eye and Mind," p. 175). As we've seen, the origin of philosophical thinking on Aristotle's account (*Metaphysics*, 1.2 982b12-22) is the wonder emerging when the propensity to know in any final sense is propitiously suspended. To be in a state of wonder means that we equanimously "receive" the world, aware that our premature judgments as well as our conclusions about it only militate against the entertaining of flexible ideas about it. Wonder is the result of a capacity for postponement, one liberated by thought in step with the world it encounters. In this sense, Goethe was perfectly Aristotelian, recorded as he is by Johann Peter Eckermann, at the opening of their conversation on the theory of color published some nineteen years earlier, to have declared: "The highest which man can attain in these matters is astonishment" (18 Feb. 1829; *Conversations with Goethe*, p. 370). The loss of astonishment, as Karl Jaspers (1883-1969) has indicated, amounts to feelings of emptiness, whereby existence appears devitalized, and is, at a minimum, uninspiring, unremarkable. As he put it, any person "who has ceased to be astonished has ceased to question" (*Way to Wisdom*, p. 127), as if their world were without limits to knowing, and thus already known—which is to say, ultimately insipid. This dulled attitude to the world is the cognitive equivalent of the unfortunately popular sentiment of "been there, done that." By contrast, the genuine thinker is the person for whom knowledge about the world and self always has unexpected frontiers, and being aware of at least some of them, she "remains open to the unknowable that is revealed at those limits" (ibid.).

And we are returned once again to the entwinement of wonderment and equanimity. What Rabbi Abraham Joshua Heschel (1907-72) calls "radical amazement" is the precise faculty by which, appreciative of our limits, we "adapt our minds to the world" rather than the world to our concepts, our "memorized knowledge," and our rhetorical questions (*Man is Not Alone*, p. 11; 12). Our humility sustains our amazement. We have seen how equanimity can overcome blindness to the inherent mystery of the world through its sweeping apprehension of the interplay of things, but there is another central aspect of equanimity here that I borrow from Heschel: the fact that "even the minimum of perception is a maximum of enigma" (ibid., p. 14). Radical amazement subtends the total order of things in such a way that, like equanimity, it has "a wider scope than any other act." "While any act of perception or cognition," Heschel continues, "has as its object a selected segment of reality, radical amazement refers to all of reality; not only to what we see, but also to the very act of seeing as well as to our own selves, to the selves that see and are amazed at their ability to see" (ibid., p. 13). To the extent that wonderment and equanimous knowing are coextensive, identity, thoughts, and things may be grasped as unceasingly flowing together when apprehended from a universal perspective.

Part of the meaning of several stories presented in this final chapter on equanimity and knowing is that relatedness to things as common as, say, trees or seeds, brings before us epistemologies that grasp how the marvelous always already imbues the mundane. The eighth-century Ch'an figure known as Layman P'ang (Pangyun), when asked what he does every day, spontaneously generated a famous verse that has echoed through Zen teachings ever since. Its most precise translation is this:

> What I do every day / Is nothing special: / I simply stumble around. / What I do is not thought out, / Where I go is unplanned. / No matter who tries to leave their mark, / The hills and dales are not impressed. / Collecting firewood and carrying water / Are prayers that reach the gods (*The Sayings of Layman P'ang*, p. 15)

P'ang's verse points to the notion that perfectly quotidian, outward actions—like wandering around and collecting wood—can comprise an internal mode of consciousness, one whose origin is unpremeditated and whose unfolding is methodless. As such, no "mark" can be left since both experience and consciousness never go against the world, never make imprints. Instead of leaving behind something, they point to the sacrality already suffusing the mundane. They ultimately comprise gestures of exaltation—prayers with the power to reenchant the world. By doing "nothing special," P'ang effortlessly embodies the inseparability of mind and world. Their separate existences end when it is discovered that they are identical products of the same impromptu processes.

Our first story about a tree involves an iconoclastic Zen figure who, though he adopted the pen name "Crazy Cloud" (Kyōun) and dubbed his hut "Blind Donkey Hermitage," is best known as Ikkyū Sōjun (1394–1481). As an itinerant monk, he spent stretches of his life as a mountain hermit, though popular legend—some of it likely his own creation—places him with some frequency in sake shops and brothels. The story as retold here benefits from the borrowing of Alan Watts's lively dialogue (*Zen and the Beat Way*, p. 71).

The Crooked Tree

Ikkyū once put up a notice, beside a very gnarled, contorted pine tree in front of his house, that read, "I, Ikkyū, will pay 100 yen to anyone who can see this tree straight." Soon people crowded around the tree, lying on the ground, balancing on their heads, craning their necks and gazing at it from multiple angles, and yet no one discovered any way of seeing the tree with a straight trunk. A young boy, however, went to see Ikkyū's friend Rosen, who was a priest of another sect, and asked him, "What about Master Ikkyū's tree?" "Oh," said Rosen, "it is perfectly simple. You go tell him that the answer to seeing the tree straight is to look straight at it." So, the boy returned to Ikkyū, and said, "I claim the award. You see the trunk straight by looking straight at it." And Ikkyū gave the boy a quizzical look, and handed over the handsome sum of 100 yen, saying, "I think you have been talking to Rosen down the street."

If you want to see the world "straight," then getting caught up in technique is a sure way to prevent that from happening. Instead, you must simply look, non-coercively and receptively. Stepping out of loops of re-cognizing and moving from interpretation to an interanimate, equanimous view of reality is to undo the straitjacket of theoretical representations. It is to move toward a distilled, self-evident, contextual, direct knowing of the thing, in the name of rediscovering, as Merleau-Ponty once put it, "a commerce with the world and a presence to the world which is older than intelligence" ("The Film and the New Psychology," p. 52). We recall Goethe's, not to mention Maslow's, insistence that understanding the world as it is results from seeing directly ("straight") and receptively rather than imposing one's assumptions, however shrewd they may be, upon the world.

Scrutinizing a tree with the goal of winning a prize militates against bringing one any closer to its actual existence. Sadly, its essential condition escapes the acquisitive looker. No special techniques of looking can straighten Ikkyū's crooked tree; only their suspension offers the prospect of seeing the tree for what it is—already "perfect" in its deformation. Rosen's advice, to simply look at the tree and not overthink it, safeguards against turning it into a one-dimensional, exploitable object. Just so, Hermann Hesse once observed, quite aptly, that

> If I inspect a forest with the intention of buying it, renting it, cutting it down, going hunting in it, or mortgaging it, then I do not see the forest

but only its relation to my desires, plans, and concerns.... But if I want nothing from it but to gaze, "thoughtlessly," into its green depths, then it becomes a forest, nature, a growing thing; only then is it beautiful. (*My Belief*, p. 37)

The "thoughtless," meditative gaze, as we observed in the previous chapter, is needed to balance the calculative one. The equanimous gaze traverses the middle ground between them. We may now identify another component in our developing description of equanimity: the cognitive flexibility to move between interacting with the world based upon specific needs and desires, more precisely, expectations of their fulfillment, and engaging with it very broadly in a spontaneous way of seeing. The former pays more attention to content, matters of survival and utility, detail, and still-life, whereas the latter attends more to form, growth, pattern, and flux. The former tends to the frozen, the articulated; the latter to the dynamic, the blurry. In the history of painting, the former roughly corresponds to the realism of painters like Gustave Courbet, John Everett Millais, and Jean-François Millet and the latter to the impressionism of Camille Pissarro, Claude Monet, and John Constable (after 1822).

Equanimity valorizes neither mode of interacting with and perceiving the world. It recognizes both as having significance for producing knowledge. Although they make up a binary, the different modes are not mutually exclusive or fixedly oppositional. Bringing them into animated dialogue in the name of understanding means that we may be ready, at one moment, to let one element come into the foreground as the other forms its background, and, at another moment, to allow them to switch places. In this oscillating way, they need each other in order to function sanely. The essence of true knowledge, or, perhaps better, wisdom, I would venture, is this give and take, this interplay. The Chinese philosopher Feng Youlan (1895-1990) once drew attention to the distinguishing of two "diseases" among traditional philosophers. One, he said colorfully, is riding an ass to search for the ass; the other is riding an ass while being unwilling to dismount. The predicament then? "You yourself are the ass. Everything is the ass. Why do you ride on it? If you ride, you cannot cure your disease" (*A Short History of Chinese Philosophy*,

p. 263). The point here is realizing that your inquiry—your search for the ass—will never be satisfied if you cannot realize the mutual entailing of question and answer (the interdependence of rider and ass) or if you cleave to what you take to be *the* answer (never getting off the ass). Being willing to dismount is equivalent to understanding that the blindness of fixity stifles the creation of genuine knowledge.

The novelist D. H. Lawrence (1885-1930) understood this perfectly, and a great deal of his writing, especially his essays, is aimed at dismantling fixities and exploring relativities. It was Lawrence's conviction that the novel affects people so completely that, compared with philosophy, science, or religion, the art form has the greater power to show us how to dismount from orthodox habits of thought and behavior whose very fixity destroys genuine creativity, vital passion, and individual autonomy. The tyranny of absolutes reduces the world to the automatic, the formulaic. He concludes, in one of his most celebrated essays, that "We should ask for no absolutes. Once and for all and for ever, let us have done with the ugly imperialism of any absolute" ("Why the Novel Matters," p. 196). At stake here is nothing less than the expression of a kind of drive toward fluidity, indeterminacy—in short, toward vitality. "There is deep inside one," wrote Lawrence, "a revolt against the fixed thing, fixed society, fixed money, fixed homes, even fixed love" (*Collected Letters*, p. 851). Our sense of being, of identity and knowledge, is experienced as, extrapolated from, movement. Not to be stuck amounts to the freedom to live between extremes. It is also the freedom to question their finality. Boundaries, Heidegger reminds us, are best thought of not as the outer confines where things stop but as the generative horizons from which "something begins its essential unfolding" ("Building Dwelling Thinking," p. 332). Anything between the extreme poles, the absolute limits, is equally up for grabs—cognitively, emotionally, practically. "Things do not begin to live," declares Deleuze, "except in the middle" (*Dialogues*, p. 55).

We inevitably live and think from somewhere in the middle. The interstitial condition of all knowing, as I suggested, is one of the great insights of Daoist philosophy. We have already seen Zhuangzi take aim at the fixed perspectives of the cicada and dove, doing so in order to emphasize the relativity of viewpoints, the notion that there is always another perspective ready to subsume the one you have arrived at or cling to. *Da zhi*, greater knowledge, consists in being forever accommodating to additional perspectives. Consider one of the four parables in the *Zhuangzi* concerning "useless" trees, where here Ziqi comes to a deeper understanding of uselessness:

> Ziqi of Nanbo was travelling in the hills of Shang when he came upon a huge tree. He marveled at it, for the horses from a thousand chariots could have cooled themselves in its shade. "What sort of tree is this?" said Ziqi. "It must be of unusually fine material." Looking up at its branches, he saw that they were too twisted and gnarled to be used for beams or pillars. Looking down at its trunk, he saw that it was too splotched and split to be used for a coffin. It stung and stabbed the tongue when licked and crazed and inebriated the mind for three days when sniffed. Ziqi said, "It turns out to be a worthless tree, and thus it has been able to grow so huge. Ah! This is the worthlessness that the Spirit Man relies on!" (Ziporyn, p. 31; cf. Graham, pp. 73-74)

As in the *Zhuangzi*'s other stories of putatively useless trees, multiple perspectives are presented not for the purpose of choosing among them but rather of underscoring the consequences of not considering all relevant perspectives. The tree can appear alternatively "worthless" and greatly valued: from the perspective of a carpenter, it is no good for beams or coffins; from the perspective of a chariot horse, its cooling shade is welcome. And there is also the perspective of the tree itself where the characteristics that make it unsuitable for use by the woodcutter or builder, or repulsive to the senses, are precisely its protection against the axe. Following Feng Youlan's interpretation, "to be useless is the way to preserve one's life" (*A Short History of Chinese Philosophy*, p. 64). Finally, from the view of the enlightened Spirit Man, it appears that there is nothing to which it is "worth" committing a single perspective. It is useless to affirm a clear distinction between useful and useless. Of course, it may also be momentarily, or expediently, useful to grant, without clinging to, such a distinction. Usefulness emerges relative to perspective only, and the sagacious Spirit Man, in his equanimity, grasps this.

Equanimity is, then, another way of granting the futility of holding onto distinctions. Distinctions, from the point of equanimous knowing, are recognized in the end to be arbitrary, transitory, and merely conventional (however useful they may be). In the *Zhuangzi*, there are many stories concerning the acceptance of the manifold realities and transformative processes (*wuhua*) of the world, free of discriminations and entrenched judgments. In one story, the sage Zilai is asked on his deathbed about his impending transformation: will he become something as seemingly inconsequential as a mouse's liver or an insect's appendage? Zilai, undisturbed, replies that he will go wherever he is sent, abandoning all clinging to human form (Ziporyn, pp. 45-46; cf. Graham, pp. 88-89). Zilai refuses a view of the world that one would have if matters of significance and utility were unduly emphasized, in terms, for instance, that exclude non-human perspectives. The sages of the *Zhuangzi* recognize that applying unitary standards subverts the equanimity that animates *da zhi*. Standards, aiming at differentiation, furnish only the constricted view of the fixed vantage point. Alternatively, the axis or "pivot of the Dao" (*daoshu*) allows for diverse perspectives. Moving smoothly and easefully with the Dao guarantees the uncontrived condition of one's natural knowledge and sensibility. Disrupting the flow of the Dao is compared, in the first of the so-called Outer Chapters, to adding webbing between the toes or acquiring a sixth finger. But, of course, the Dao can never be improved upon nor made grotesque. So then if the webbing or the superfluous digit was not supplemental but, rather, was always present as a part of one's "inborn nature," its removal would also fail as an attempt to enhance "the most perfectly true and unskewed Course" (Ziporyn, p. 58). Any standards we might apply in judging the utility of webbed toes or extra fingers are insufficient since they will inescapably violate the holism intrinsic to any object of our evaluation. "In this," the text reads,

> what is joined is not so because of extra webbing and what is branched is not so because of additions. The long is not excessive and the short is not deficient. The duck's neck may be short, but lengthening it would surely vex him; the swan's neck may be long, but cutting it short would surely sorrow her. What is long in its inborn nature is not to be cut short, and what is short in its inborn nature is not to be lengthened. For there is nothing there that needs to be excised or worried over. (ibid.; cf. Graham, pp. 200-1)

Disequanimity amounts to the refusal to let go of the standards, and the "corrections" based upon them, whose imposition cause vexation and harm. Without equanimity, and the sense of proportionate perspective it brings, any attempts to rectify something, whose supreme essence is in harmony with what is, are in vain. A Confucian philosophical text puts it like this: "Going too far is just like not going far enough. One can compare it to planting a tree upright and then seeking to make its shadow crooked" (Hutton, *Xunzi*, p. 113). As an image, a tree always in harmony with its shadow reminds us of the senselessness of seeing it otherwise.

Denouncing the useless is equally senseless, a point that the *Zhuangzi* makes repeatedly. In the first Inner Chapter, Huizi disparagingly compares Zhuangzi's discourse to a great tree, known as the Stink Tree, whose gnarled trunk and twisted branches make it unsuitable for use as timber. Zhuangzi does not try to directly refute Huizi's claims about the inutility of his (or any) philosophy, but instead simply points out that wild animals exist without worrying about the limitations of what they can and cannot do, though they are skilled in different ways. Zhuangzi goes on to suggest that Huizi worry less about the tree's supposed uselessness, and instead find a suitable place to relax in its shade for, being useless as timber, it will surely never be cut down: "You. . .have this big tree and you worry that it's useless. Why not plant it in our homeland of not-even-anything, the vast wilds of open nowhere? Then you could loaf and wander there, doing lots of nothing there at its side, and take yourself a nap, far-flung and unfettered, there beneath it" (Ziporyn, p. 8; cf. Graham, p. 47). The tree becomes spatialized, as a utopic (literally, no-place) mental reserve in which "lots of nothing" takes place across the open field of wandering. Here a phenomenology of the useless offers the possibility of an equanimity attuned to relativity, presence, and spontaneity. It escapes delimited meaning seen from a remote, singular, fixed viewpoint. In the Daoist account, consciousness radiates like roots from the center out, a pattern that the growth of all living things follows. Its natural course can never be coerced, just as its putative "uselessness" cannot be rectified. Paul Valéry, in one of his aphorisms, expressed the idea quite emphatically: "In making any 'useless' thing, one needs to be godlike. Or else refrain from tackling it" (*Analects*, p. 8).

Modelling an organic kind of thinking, the organizational structure of the root-tree system typically charts connectedness along chronological lines, locating the original source of things and pointing toward the endpoint of those things. While this linear model lacks the full processual, in medias res, sideways quality of an equanimous model, its links to organicism offer a valuable insight. If we have an idea about where something has come from and where it is heading, then the tendency to isolate things and make judgments about them on the basis of their *singular* place in a continuing narrative may be salutarily undercut. Doubtless the tree, whose image has indelibly marked the history of Western thought, significantly gestures toward transcendence, yet other ways of looking at it reveal it to be about immanence. The place of the tree in Western thought has been largely associated with philosophical attempts to discover the true arrangement and ontological structure of the world, for example, with the use of tree diagrams rooted in beliefs about an ordered universe, which, as Nathalie Gontier has shown, can be "traced back to most written cultures" ("Depicting the Tree of Life," p. 536). Trees make the invisible visible, and their figurative use for nearly the last millennium continues to play central roles in conveying different facets of knowledge. The universal prototypal image of the tree has been shown by the noted designer and data visualization scholar Manuel Lima in his rich *The Book of Trees: Visualizing Branches of Knowledge* to be the principal organizing metaphor for contemporary network and information design. In their long history for organizing knowledge, the branching structure of trees has been particularly well suited to depicting conceptual or abstract (e.g., religious and secular) interest in things that can be related, for example, by logic, genealogy, affinity, chronology, or probability. A tree's vertical hierarchical structure symbolically aligns with the calculative in contrast to the horizontality of the roots that aligns with the meditative mode of thinking. Yet, these modes work naturally together. As a wildly "successful model for graphically displaying relationships," the tree "pragmatically expresses the materialization of multiplicity (represented by its succession of boughs, branches, twigs, and leaves) out of unity (its central foundational trunk, which is in turn connected to a common root, source, or origin)" (*The Book of Trees*, pp. 26-27). As difference continually issues from unity, the essence of a tree is discovered in the dynamic balancing act between trunk and branches, trunk and roots. Trees bring before us the coaction of the vertical/analytic and the horizontal/holistic. They structure knowledge, as I will show in a moment, as a movement between the rational-discursive intellect of *vijñāna* and the intuitive understanding of *prajñā*. In this way, they offer an image of equanimous thinking, a kind of vital consciousness engaged with the dynamism of *natura naturans*—nature naturing—where ultimately any sure distinctions between seer and seen collapse in the face of nature's sheer plenitude.

Tree-thinking has played a prominent role in Ch'an/Zen teachings aimed at releasing understanding from its mooring in rigid subject-object distinctions. Trees are seen to embody the suchness of things, to be reminders of the flux of immanent existence untouched by the divisions characteristic of analytic or calculative thinking. The most famous Ch'an example of the tree's escape from analytic meaning is found in the *Wúménguān* (Jp. *Mumonkan*; *The Gateless Barrier*), an early 13th-century text collecting 48 *kōans*, or teaching stories, often in the form of a dialogue between Master and student. Case 37 of the *Wúménguān* presents a monk asking Zhaozhou Congshen (Jp. Joshu Jushin, 778-897) what is the meaning of Bodhidharma's coming from the West. Zhaozhou comments simply, "The cypress tree in the courtyard." Wu-men abbreviates the original story, which has the monk pressing Zhaozhou further:

> "Please don't teach me with reference to outside things." Chao-chou [Zhaozhou] said, "I don't teach you with reference to outside things." The monk said, "What is the meaning of Bodhidharma's coming from the West?" Chao-chou said, "The cypress [oak] tree in the courtyard." (Yamada, *Gateless Gate*, p. 191)

Cleaving to a notion of Ch'an practice as primarily a matter of internal reflection, the monk protests that Zhaozhou, by referring to a mere object, must be somehow leading him astray. Zhaozhou's original response, by answering with reference to the immediate milieu, points to the insight that the meaning of Bodhidharma's coming from elsewhere cannot rest upon contrasting notions of inside and outside, here and there. In this sense, Bodhidharma is nowhere *and* now-here—just look around. The organic truth of Bodhidharma will never emerge by attempting to translate the mutable and conditional into values of unconditional necessity, that is, some final meaning. Zhaozhou's tree is liberated from both all finiteness and all transcendental meaning in which rest from the confusion of the world could possibly be found. Ch'an understanding, like equanimity, moves toward a reverent affirmation of the phenomenal world. What results is a picture of things that respects the conditionality of the living without shifting into a zone of the necessary and abstract.

Regarding Zhaozhou's "cypress tree in the courtyard" (*teizen no hakujushi*), Rinzai Zen Master Kanzan Egen (Jp. Musō Daishi, 1277-1360), founder of the famous Myōshin-ji Temple in Kyoto, remarked without elaboration that "herein lies the cleverness of the bandit" (Hakuin, *Selected Writings*, p. 61). A similar idea is reflected in a Zen capping phrase: "The story of the Cypress Tree has the power to rob you" (Hori, *Zen Sand*, p. 298). Implied here is that the force of Zhaozhou's cypress tree kōan is essentially like that of a thief's terrifying activity (*kiyō*), in this case, the capacity to snatch away the delusions and mental attachments that interfere with true understanding. When the monk comes to Zhaozhou full of ideas about Ch'an, about Bodhidharma and the purpose of his journey, the master's strategy is to divest him of concepts so that the tree in the front garden is seen as anyone might see it. The tree itself is nothing special, yet its place in the process of felicitous, skillful vision is crucial. To see the cypress tree in this unburdened way is to view it with the wisdom-eye (慧眼; *egen*), what is commonly called in the Buddhist tradition the *prajñā*-eye of the enlightened. The eye of *prajñā* bears resemblances to the kinds of vision that we have explored as informing and animating equanimity under various modifiers: intuitive, holistic, participatory, right-hemispheric, B-cognitive, meditative, cotentive, and so on. And, like these different ways of seeing, each with its mutually entailed opposite, *prajñā* must be understood in relation to its unique counterpoint, *vijñāna*.

The monk's rejection of naïve realism as mere *kyō*, or objectification, is the fundamental characteristic of *vijñāna*, the discriminating (that is, discursive and rational) intellect. *Prajñā*, or intuitive wisdom, D. T. Suzuki (1870-1966) tells us, "goes beyond *vijnana*. We make use of *vijnana* in our world of the senses and intellect, which is characterized by dualism in the sense that there is the one who sees and there is the other that is seen—the two standing in contradistinction. In *prajna* this differentiation does not take place; what is seen and the one who sees are identical; the seer is the seen and the seen is the seer" ("Reason and Intuition in Buddhist Philosophy," p. 85). *Vijñāna* divides, analyzes, and its interest is in parts, whereas "*prajna* is content with itself" (ibid.); its concern is with the whole. Their basic differences, however, only point toward their being mutually entailed modes of thinking, like the meditative and calculative. Suzuki summarizes it nicely: "Vijnana cannot work without having prajna behind it; parts are parts of the whole; parts never exist by themselves, for if they did they would not be parts—they would even cease to exist" (ibid.).

Our interest in the holism of *prajñā* derives from its resonance with the movements of consciousness and awareness characteristic of equanimity. Like equanimity as a way of knowing, *prajñā* never attaches itself finally to any part or object since it is a kind of floating consciousness, generating a dynamic, intuitive apprehension of the whole. It cannot be identified with its objects precisely because it is action itself, and therefore it can have "no premeditated methods; it creates them out of itself as they are needed" (ibid., p. 100). As I have emphasized in our discussion of equanimity as an expansive orientation toward the world, the question of a repeatable methodology (or, for that matter, a teleology) is not applicable here, while at the same time equanimity is never incoherent, confused. The equanimity animating *prajñā* is that seamless and synthetic relation to the world coinciding with the total perceptual process itself, something Suzuki once called "pure experience beyond differentiation" (ibid., p. 101). One of the persistent themes of equanimous experience is spelled out very simply in the closing affirmation of a *mondō* (dialogue) between a monk and Baofu Congzan (Pao-fu Ts'ung-chan, Jp. Hofuku Juten, d. 928): "When seeing, there is neither right nor left" (ibid., p. 112). Equanimity, in its even relation to the world, operates in ways not susceptible to singular renderings. To view things from such a universal viewpoint—from that of "being" itself—entails the realization that perspectives bound to "being this" or to "being that" foreclose the spontaneous play of impartial awareness.

Looking at the cypress tree, Zhaozhou immediately understands that any intention ascribed to Bodhidharma cannot go beyond the very act of seeing itself. The abstraction of intentionality finds no place in sheer awareness. Bodhidharma's intention, from the perspective of the unconditioned mind, is just another story that, true or fictitious, has no intrinsic meaning. To presuppose that the first Chinese patriarch's coming from the West has historical significance is no more than the beginning of an attempt to freeze meaning into a concept. But like a living, growing tree, Bodhidharma's "meaning" is something to be experienced or discovered only in the present, where nothing can be said to be lacking and everything is on the move. And so, to know a tree in the courtyard is not a matter of longing or purposiveness but rather of choiceless, bare attention. Only in leaving behind intervening interpretations, moving from calculative to meditative awareness, resides the opportunity to find oneself in the immediacy of relationships with what is present. "Encounters occur," Martin Buber (1878-1965) declares, "only where all means have disintegrated" (*I and Thou*, p. 63). Presence comes into being when the rigor of concepts relaxes to allow particularity to become wholeness, and fantasies rooted in desire of some kind to become appearance.

The *prajñā*-eye is the preeminent "organ" of genuine encounter. Its non-interfering awareness, devoid of purpose, aligns the *prajñā*-eye with the state of emptiness that the German theologian and mystic Meister Eckhart (1260-1327) declares is the proper precondition for identifying with the Godhead. In his famous Sermon 57, he exclaims that "The eye with which I see God is the same with which God sees me: my eye and God's eye are one eye, one seeing, one knowing and one love" (*Complete Mystical Works*, p. 298). This identificatory achievement begins in a state of absolute receptivity, the open, egoless ground on which, according to Eckhart, originates the freedom to ascend: "If a man might and knew how to make a cup completely empty and keep it empty of whatever might fill it, even air, assuredly that cup would lose and forget its own nature, and emptiness would bear it aloft" (ibid., p. 535). Once emptied of conditioned nature, one obtains the possibility of floating, elevating to a total view at once active and passive. Here, without seeking it, is found a dialogical sensibility that appreciates, for example, that the eyes with which the cypress tree is looked at are the same eyes with which the cypress tree looks back. In Eckhart's ascension, an echo may be heard in Emerson's transparent eyeball "uplifted into infinite space." Yet, the *prajñā*-eye is closer to a Thoreauvian *technē* given its avoidance of transcendence in favor of implication and involvement with the lived world. It epitomizes a graceful vision of secure rapport. Alive to rich affinities within the world, the *prajñā*-eye finds unity in diversity, a plenitude in which an epistemology of difference fades into one of semblance and mutuality. Here, I am reminded of Ch'an-master Xuefeng Yicun's (822-908) perspicuous response to a student who was inclined to cast the universe in terms of the perturbing fissure between the subjective (seer) and the objective (seen): "All the universe is this eye" (Suzuki, *Living by Zen*, p. 40). Reciprocality becomes then the ground for a renovated identity (a theme explored in chapter 4). Or, as Goethe describes the intuitive workings of human nature: it "knows itself one with the world and therefore does not experience the objective external world as something alien, that comes toward the inner world of man from without, but recognizes in it the answering counterpart to its own sensations" (qtd. in Worringer, *Abstraction and Empathy*, p. 128).

Equanimity grants us the prospect of seeing Nature in its own Being, not as a means to an end but rather as a dialogic process, not as something subjected to dogma (*shoulds*) but rather as horizons of possibility. Equanimity dissolves any imperative to get one-up on the universe. To encounter what Merleau-Ponty called "the unmotivated upsurge of the world" (*Phenomenology of Perception*, p. xiv), the kind of receptivity that equanimity sets in motion becomes the very element of freedom opening up the world to the fullest range of claims on its meaning. With a latitude of understanding comes wisdom rooted in recognizing the coterminous aspect of Nature and understanding itself. Following the Roman poet Juvenal (c. 55-127): "Nature never says one thing, and philosophy [Wisdom] another" (*Nunquam aliud Natura aliud Sapientia dicit*) (*Satires*, xiv.321, p. 275). Through our continual encounters, the world possesses at any given point the promise of meaning, but only if we equanimously "listen" to its plenitude from a place outside the trap of conditioned attributions of fixed meaning. In this vein, Welsh sinologist A. C. Graham (1919-91) identifies what unites philosophical Daoists, namely, the insight "that while all other things move spontaneously on the course proper to them, man has stunted and maimed his spontaneous aptitude by the habit of distinguishing alternatives, the right and the wrong, benefit and harm, self and others, and reasoning in order to judge between them" (*Chuang-tzu: The Inner Chapters*, p. 6). Of course, it is not only Daoist philosophers who invite an awareness of what living would be like if it were spontaneous, reciprocal, rather than forever occupied with dividing the indivisible. Trees also invite this awareness.

It may be precisely because trees and other plants are rooted in place that they offer us one of the finest opportunities to contemplate our own mental fixities. Drawing inspiration from trees, we may begin to entertain the possibility of an epistemology that accommodates both the solidity of oneness and the fluidity of reciprocal differences. Trees, along with other vegetal life, have since Aristotle enjoyed a kind of liminal position as the universal principle of animation and ensoulment (*psychisme*). Vegetative life, *psuchē trophukē* (the nursing/nourishing/vegetative soul) was, Emanuele Coccia reminds us in his stunning metaphysics of plant-life, never "simply a distinct class of specific forms of life or a taxonomic unity separated from others, but rather a place shared by all living beings, regardless of the distinction between plants, animals, and humans" (*The Life of Plants*, p. 9). In this way, the vegetal contact zone furnishes, according to Aristotle, the principle by "virtue of which all are said to have life" (*De anima* 2.4, 415a25). As the primary site of interanimation and interlocking understandings, the plant world elicits a natural sacramentality, a presence with things as they are and not merely and only how they seem. In response to Emerson's personifying of trees as complaining "imperfect men" in his essay "Nature" (p. 370), the naturalist John Muir (1838-1914) wrote:

> It has been said that trees are imperfect men, and seem to bemoan their imprisonment rooted in the ground. But they never seem so to me. I never saw a discontented tree. They grip the ground as though

they liked it, and though fast rooted they travel about as far as we do. They go wandering forth in all directions with every wind, going and coming like ourselves, traveling with us around the sun two million miles a day, and through space heaven knows how fast and far! (*The Wilderness World*, p. 315)

Trees are content, Muir would have it, because they enjoy the flexibility of being both rooted and mobile. Their capacity to wander, to be moved by the wind or with the planet through space, as intrinsic to their identity as it is for humans, signifies both vitality and the kind of satisfaction that derives from attunement with their total environment. To see trees in this way, like Muir, demands a vision of things constituting each other relationally and in difference. Equanimity nourishes an epistemological structure of relativity where the universality of identity (trees are like us) and the singularity of difference (trees are rooted in the ground; we are not) emerge together. As a mode of knowledge, equanimity encounters identity and difference as a cadence of systole and diastole. And we remember that, by sheer force of conviction and closed-mindedness, we can be, figuratively, as fixed in place as a tree. Trees afford a more complete vision of reality precisely for all their dynamism. As Coccia observes, "If it is from plants that we ought to enquire what the world is, this is because they are the ones who 'play the world' [*font le monde*]" (*The Life of Plants*, p. 8).

Throwing Stones at a Tree

> It is all a Tree: circulation of sap and influences, mutual communication of every minutest leaf with the lowest talon of a root, with every other greatest and minutest portion of the whole.
> —Thomas Carlyle, "The Hero as Poet"

Idries Shah recounts a Sufi story illustrating how trees "play," structuring and fashioning the cognizable world. The story's message resonates with the sentiment of William Blake from a letter of his dated 23 August

1799: "The tree which moves some to tears of joy is in the eyes of others only a green thing that stands in the way. Some see Nature all ridicule and deformity, and some scarce see Nature at all. But to the eyes of the man of imagination, Nature is Imagination itself. As a man is, so he sees" (*The Letters*, p. 62). Here then is the Sufi story:

"Why," a visiting cleric asked Jan Fishan Khan, "do critics and detractors make more noise than those who value the Path?"

"You can answer the question yourself," said the Khan, "if you find the answer to this:

A shouting boy is throwing stones at a tree. People stop and watch him. A wise man passes by and notes that the tree is one which bears delicious fruit. The boy is completely absorbed in his amusement. The onlookers are looking only at what the boy is doing. The wise man is seeing the inwardness of the tree, which will only be manifested for the others in its due season." (The Magic Monastery, p. 115)

In the spirit of an exemplary teaching story, the reader is left with the task of providing the riddle's solution, an interpretation of the Khan's narrative of the tree which, at first blush, appears to have something to do with the value of seeing things in terms of their interiority as opposed to their exteriority. The passing wise man, who we are explicitly told sees the tree's inwardness, is ignored by the onlookers whose attention is focused on the obstreperous boy whose own attention is consumed by targeting the tree. Neither the stopped onlookers nor the boy really see the tree. Specifically, they fail to see it in its timeliness, as the kind of tree whose nature it is to seasonally bear fruit. Yet that season has not yet arrived, something the onlookers realize perhaps but their focus is elsewhere. One angle on the story's diegesis, then, has the boy engaging in an activity that makes sense only if the tree is manifestly bearing fruit and he wants to knock down a few pieces, possibly to eat or to gather to sell. The wise man grasps that this is, however, an inopportune time for throwing stones. The idea here is that seeing deeply is a matter of taking one's time, of letting the nature of things unfold and develop (reminding us of a theme of the Sufi pomegranate story in chapter 2). This marks the crucial difference from those noisy critics the cleric referred to for whom knowledge is merely an instant seized in time and not a path. True knowing, however, is processual; it requires quiet patience, willingness to take the time needed for seeing things from multiple sides and at a suitable distance. To see a tree is to view it quietly through time.

Indeed, to this point, we have mainly relied upon spatial rather than temporal metaphors for aptly describing equanimity—viewing from above, thinking aside, seeing from the middle, and so on. Yet, all along, these felicitous perspectives have depended for their value as ways of knowing upon mobility—variously physical, perceptual, cognitive, emotional. In the Khan's story, only the wise man moves (he "passes by"), suggesting that he is the only one actively building knowledge based upon the ambient array (tree, people, stones) he navigates. Not drawn into the drama he witnesses, the wise man sees what is hidden from the others, having access to knowledge built on temporally extended perception. The wise man alone grasps the place of time/movement in a simultaneously enactive and ecological understanding of the surrounding world. Noë, as we have seen, is one of the chief proponents of enactivism, the theory of consciousness that says mental capacities such as perception and cognition are not solely the functions of brain activities but rather emerge as the result of ongoing interactions between the brain, the mobile body, and the environment. The mind "enacts" its own spatial and temporal world, as in the Machado poem cited above: one lays down a path in walking.

Both enactivist and equanimous ways of knowing are predicated upon open encounters with the world whose navigation is enhanced by the ongoing and dynamic interplay of perception and movement. Coping with the environment hinges on mental flexibility characterized by the collapse of distinctions between action, cognition, and perception. Flexibility ensures continuity with the world in flux. Philosopher Josep Maria Bech sums it up quite well: "Consciousness exists only as long as it is open to the world; therefore, there is neither interiority nor exteriority. There is only one intentional fabric that indissolubly exists, that of consciousness and the world" (*De Husserl a Heidegger*, p. 54; my trans.). Our consciousness is distributed in the vital world that encompasses our movements. Any consideration of the dynamic and enactive fabric of existence owes a great deal to James J. Gibson's (1904-79) pioneering work in ecological psychology. And so, we turn to his perspectivist approach to learn more about the place of embodied cognition in equanimity.

Gibson's early career as a wartime psychologist involved assessing the visual aptitude of candidates for pilot training. As the director of the Aviation Psychology Program of the U.S. Army Air Forces during World War II, he became particularly interested in the effects that flying an aircraft have on visual perception. One of his discoveries was that it is the environment that decides perception, and so meaning is independent of the perceiver. Meaning, as he would eventually formulate it, resides in what the environment "affords" the observer. In other words, the world actively, rather than passively, discloses itself as a field of affordances (a word Gibson coined), such that, paraphrasing Wittgenstein, the world is the totality of possibilities of action, not of things. Perception, Gibson was radically suggesting, can only be studied as an attribute of the complementarity of an organism and its lived milieu. Visualizing a scene occurs in terms of invitations to act: "*affordances* of the environment are what it *offers* the animal, what it *provides* or *furnishes*, either for good or ill" (*The Ecological Approach*, p. 127; emph. in orig.). Gibson's primary concern was with "ambient vison," everyday vision facilitated by moving the head and body (ibid., p. 1; 303). As in the equanimous approach to reality, the senses are treated as active, exploratory organs attuned to dynamic meanings in the environment, which, on the Gibsonian model, are already there. Meaning is discovered in the course of action through the use of ranging attention, what Gibson called generally "an awareness of being in the world" (ibid., p. 284).

Perception emerges, then, as a function of reciprocity, the mutual interchange between the living intentions of organisms and the dynamic affordances of their world. The psyche, as studied by Gibsonian psychologists, cannot be separated from the ecosystem as a whole. Cognition takes place through the mediation of action, movement, where perceptual experience of the world is shaped by those actions that manifold things in the world afford. An affordance "cuts across the dichotomy of subjective-objective. . . . It is equally a fact of the environment as a fact of behavior. It is both physical and psychical, yet neither. An affordance points both ways, to the environment and to the observer" (ibid., p. 123). To illustrate this, consider trees: they afford standing or reclining in their shade, climbing, hanging a swing, supporting a treehouse, hiding behind, nutrition, and so on. Naturally, trees afford different actions to different species. Their ways of directly addressing themselves may result in different dynamic meanings or values. While an oak tree may afford *sitting under* to a human, to sparrows it affords *perching*, to squirrels *climbing*, or to ants *nesting*. Or, as the wonderful Zen capping phrase "One water, four ways of seeing" summarizes a longer Zen verse: "A god looks at water and sees a jewel, a human sees something to drink, a hungry ghost sees blood, a fish sees a place to dwell" (Hori, *Zen Sand*, p. 103). These values, however, are not located beforehand in the minds of the organisms, Gibson argues, but emerge as the dynamic, constitutive properties of the environment itself when it is comprehended in ways that do not artificially separate it from the lives of the organisms who inhabit it and contribute to its ongoing transformation.

The central idea here is that we actively perceive matches between the structure of elements in the environment and our acts (as opposed to responses), our attention (as opposed to triggered impressions), and our achievements (as opposed to reflexes) (ibid., p. 149). While a primary tenet of Gibson's approach to perception is that of direct, unmediated perception, I am interested in moving that approach in the direction of a broader representational account of affordances. In this way, knowledge about the world is *not strictly* a passive, internal, cerebral event. Gibson was reportedly fond of saying, "ask not what's inside your head, but what your head's inside of" (Mace, "James Gibson's Strategy for Perceiving"). Asking what our heads are inside of is one of the primary aspects of equanimous knowledge. We have already explored the centrality of questioning itself to equanimity, which is not a feature of any method but a signal of radical openness to the richly detailed and patterned world we occupy. From the inside, and in the midst, of everything, "perceiving is a registering of certain definite dimensions of invariance in the stimulus flux" (*The Ecological Approach*, p. 249). This process of registering what remains the same about an environment coincides with exploring it from multiple perspectives. To determine features of the surrounding world that may be perceived regardless of perspective depends on our motility—which may be, for example, as basic as normal saccades (fast eye movements) or intentionally pivoting our head. These activities, including body locomotion, spare us the uneconomical business of perceiving all variables individually. At the same time, they allow us the opportunity to grasp that no ecological object is value-free. This is because each possesses "some affordance for benefit or injury to someone" (ibid., p. 140). Like Merleau-Ponty, Gibson holds that cognitive agents do not perceive the world neutrally as possessing merely objective properties like size and shape. Instead, they grasp the world as having value in terms of a range of possibilities for attention and action. Remarkably, we engage things as opportunities for action often at levels below conscious awareness, and it is when affordances collapse or disappear that we then become exquisitely aware of the salience of a thing's objective properties. As Heidegger famously argued in *Being and Time*, only when smooth coping breaks down (say, when a hammer handle breaks when using it) do objective properties of the thing become fully present in perceptual experience.

The implications of this capacity to shift points of view in order to determine the nature of things regardless of perspective are far reaching. Environments, objects, and bodies in the world are not indiscriminate or inherently meaningless configurations onto which significance and purposes are projected. Instead, they come already configured in a range of ways, suiting certain actions and cognitive engagements better than others. This is one reason why an inapt metaphor for comprehending perception is the so-called snapshot conception of visual experience where the eye is conceived as acting like a camera with vision amounting then to a quasi-photographic process. Gibson, however, rightly insists that "the eye is not a camera that forms and delivers an image, nor is the retina simply a keyboard that can be struck by fingers of light" (ibid., p. 61). Indeed, according to the camera model, perception can never be truly equanimous since it is wedded to a mechanistic phenomenology of experience where only centered, uniformly detailed, focused pictures of the world are apprehended in the mind. We have noted already how important peripheral or side vision is to equanimous knowledge. More generally, taking an evenly floating and multi-angled perspective on things means we may learn to see them as making available possibilities—for cognition and action—that are not dependent upon their being exclusive or central points of focus. Possibilities multiply to the degree that thinking is predicated upon movement and intuitive flexibility. With the alternative model for understanding perception, action, and cognition that affordances offer, we can see how the rigid conceptual boundaries separating these categories break down, are traversed. Fluidity of awareness, movement, and thought characterizes, as we have seen, events as seemingly disparate as traditional tea ceremonies (chapter 3) and space-travel (chapter 4). Keeping close to the phenomenology of everyday life, equanimity reminds us that we know the world as much as we live and act in it and continue accumulating experience as we go.

The phenomenology of everyday life involves seeing spontaneously and, less frequently, analytically. Merleau-Ponty observes that "analytical perception, through which we arrive at absolute value of the separate elements, is a belated and rare attitude—that of the scientist who observes or of the philosopher who reflects." The earlier and more common perceptual orientation, he continues, is that concerning "forms, understood very broadly as structure, grouping, or configuration [which] should be considered our spontaneous way of seeing" ("The Film and the New Psychology," p. 49). Spontaneous vision opens up the possibility for appreciating the full range of affordances, from those provided by scopic structural compositions grasped, for example, in aesthetic terms down to the minute individual aspects that capture the attention of scientific analysis. Preserved here is what British critic I. A. Richards (1893-1979) and colleagues once called "free play," the "synaesthetic" organization of vision where attention is not split into competing states of consciousness but rather completed and enriched such that "interest is not canalised in one direction rather than another" (Ogden, Richards, & Wood, *Foundations of Aesthetics*, p. 75; 78). These early critics described the process of aesthetic engagement in terms resonating with the equanimous vision, referring to it as a kind of skillful "detachment" in which "interest becomes ready...to take any direction we choose" (ibid., p. 78). Whether gazing at trees or reading Joyce Kilmer's famous poem about them, the actions that an appreciation of affordances both solicits and creates are based upon a deep reciprocity between perceiving subjects and their objects. What we call thought and reflective awareness are not properties whose boundaries end at the outlines of the human skull but are rather the whole organism's open reply to questions continually posed by the dynamic, often subtle, communicative presences all around us.

The open conditions for such communicative encounters suggest that knowledge does not necessarily involve a neat unfolding toward finality or eventual truth but rather a navigation through a dynamic network of potential meanings. The process of coming to knowledge, as we will see in a moment with reference to Martin Buber's contemplation of a tree, is dialogic and immersive. The archetypal example of coming into being through embeddedness in manifold relationality is the interaction of seed, soil, and clime that bears plant, flower, or fruit and, hence, more seeds. Seeds—and this is one reason I have chosen them as apposite images for understanding equanimity—embody the dynamic relation to the cosmos out of which they appear and through which they proliferate. They are at home in contiguity, contingency, and change, as evidenced by their perennial versatility.

In contrast, the man-made objects of our world structure different kinds of encounters, ones that are reductive and life-draining. Michael Marder, in his philosophical dialogue with Luce Irigaray on the nature of vegetal existence, observes that "In reality, a tree—as any living being—is not only seen by us, as is the case with most of the fabricated objects; it also gives us to see because it lives by itself. I could say that looking at a tree brings me energy, whereas looking at a manufactured object takes energy away from me, notably because the first unceasingly creates the space and the forms of its appearing" (*Through Vegetal Being*, p. 46). "A tree," he continues, "gives us back our potential of vision, brings us back to ourselves with a capacity of seeing and of living, of which we are deprived by most of the familiar objects that surround us" (ibid., p. 47). The fabricated, technical things surrounding us, he suggests, furnish us with an impression of mastery at the cost of dissolving the potency of our senses, canalizing them as merely a means of recognizing use value. Trees, in this reading, offer us a reprieve from our everyday instrumental, purposive relation to things. Yet practical aims, as equanimity frames them, do not exist outside a manifold relation to things in their wholeness and purposelessness. To see no purpose in a tree, as Buber explains, does not imply anything mystical: "The man who gazes without purpose on a tree is no less 'everyday' than the one who looks at a tree to learn which branch would make the best stick. The first way of looking belongs to the constitution of the 'everyday' no less than the second" ("What is Man?" p. 178). With the line between the aesthetic (meditative) and the technical (calculative) blurring, the entirety of ordinary existence may accommodate, and in the process be enlivened by, a kind of sacramentality of the natural event.

The seeming impermeability of the line between the meditative and calculative, however, carries the risk of intellectual bewilderment, triggering what Sartre famously called nausea. Nausea may be understood as the general symptom of a condition in which the distinction between the world as pure event and the world as representation veers toward the categorical. The existentialist hero of the 1938 novel *Nausea*, Antoine Roquentin, is fascinated (L. *fascinum*, "evil spell"), sometimes to the point of abhorrence, by immediate things—a paper scrap, a beer glass, a stone, a tree root—since, as he experiences the unadorned fact of their mute material existence, they defy translation into the abstract products of human consciousness, e.g., words, grammars, categories, concepts. The root of a tree becomes abhorrent at the point when meaning perception fails to provide the context, indeed the total atmosphere, in which such a thing is usually perceived. Roquentin's disgust at a chestnut tree's gnarled, obtrusive root under his park bench represents for him an unsettling encounter with the absurd, a nauseous meeting with the sheer opacity of existence. Unable to justify converting the root into concepts, into generalities of signification, he is confronted with an "existence [that] had suddenly unveiled itself" in all its disorder, "in a frightful, obscene nakedness" (*Nausea*, p. 127). Roquentin finds himself surrounded by a chaotic, pressing field of unnamable objects. Understanding fails:

> Evidently I did not know everything, I had not seen the seeds sprout, or the tree grow. But faced with this great wrinkled paw, neither ignorance nor knowledge was important: the world of explanations and reasons is not the world of existence. A circle is not absurd, it is clearly explained by the rotation of a straight segment around one of its extremities. But neither does a circle exist. This root, on the other hand, existed in such a way that I could not explain it. (ibid., p. 129)

Yet the propensity of things to exceed all conceptualization cannot itself be reduced to a concept. In Roquentin's world, anything whose existence is not, as it were, inside the head stifles the mind's penetrability, defeating reason and meaning. A tree's being transcends the rational methods of human knowledge, and therefore Sartre's hero is forced to conclude that everything that is, including himself, exists in excess or in the way—*de trop*—of consciousness. All is contingent, absurd; and the default reaction to this, on the Sartrean account, is to feel negated, superfluous. Of course, this part of the existentialist conclusion leaves out the crucial component of meaning found precisely in the manifold relations that make existence possible, tolerable. The limits of the absurd and its concomitant angst are clear, and so Sartre has his hero transcend his existential pessimism at the end of the novel. Hearing for a second time the jazz tune "Some of These Days," Roquentin is released from the nauseous presence of things as he had been on the first occasion; only this time, having faced absolute contingency with the veil torn away, he is able to access an immediate freedom of being (verbal *être*). The music has the power to break down distinctions—"like a scythe it has cut through the drab intimacy of the world" (ibid., p. 174)—transforming the meaninglessness of existence into opportunities for human agency and connection and existential pessimism into an understanding that "every project of freedom is an open project" (*Being and Nothingness*, p. 507).

Roquentin's tree root functions as the locus of a thing's raw existence, so excessive that it neutralizes all knowledge (and nonknowledge). Almost paradoxically, what permits knowing for Roquentin is opening to the immateriality of sound, that which cannot be said to be *de trop*, in the sense of *in the way*. Listening to music becomes the primary sign of receptivity to what is. "All perception," Philippe Lacoue-Labarthe tells us, "is at bottom listening. . . . [L]istening is the paradigm (not the metaphor) of perception in general" ("The Echo of the Subject," p. 162). It is perhaps the openness, the equanimity, required in any act of listening that permits redressing the world's inscrutability, rendering the gap between consciousness and its objects bridgeable. To give attention to music involves the simultaneous recognition that we are in the world (sound is all around us) and that we are cleared of purely objectifying thinking. Moving outside the isolated, narrow sphere of subjectivity, we "ek-sist," to borrow Heidegger's terminology, in the sense of being "ec-centric," which is to say non-egocentric. Instead of seeing things from a fixed, self-centered perspective, the possibility of becoming a viewpoint for the whole situation appears. The equanimous attention given to the world does not merely connect us to it but, in the easeful, open attending to what is, our sense of self is extended into the manifold world. A figure like St. Francis of Assisi, who called the trees and birds his brothers, understood this perfectly. Equanimity brings before us the inescapable fact of our dialogic relations to the world, as we will see in the next section concerning Buber's contemplation of a tree.

A question the current chapter poses, then, is how to build knowledge upon relationality. I am reminded of Heidegger's early essay "Why Do I Stay in the Provinces?" where he describes his philosophical work as so intimately bound up with the natural cycles of Swabia, the region where he was born, that he feels compelled to turn down the offer of the chair of philosophy at the University of Berlin in order to stay in Freiburg. In a rather striking passage, he contends that "strictly speaking...[he] never observe[s] the landscape" as some object before a subject. Rather, he experiences

> its hourly changes, day and night, in the great comings and goings of the season. The gravity of the mountains, the hardness of their primeval rock, the slow and deliberate growth of the fir-trees, the brilliant, simple splendor of the meadows in bloom, the rush of the mountain brook in the long autumn night, the stern simplicity of the flatlands covered with snow—all of this moves and flows through and penetrates daily existence up there, and not in forced moments of "aesthetic" immersion or artificial empathy, but only when one's own existence stands in its work. It is the work alone that opens up space for the reality that is

these mountains. The course of the work remains embedded in what happens in the region. (p. 16)

Attunement with the variable movements of the natural world is a register of the capacity to open up the space necessary for the work of thinking. It can never be forced. Openness to self and other, as Heidegger suggests elsewhere (e.g., *Being and Time*), is a way of caring for ourselves in a manner that allows ourselves to be cared for by the natural order. Thinking and living have a fundamentally aesthetic quality. Of course, it was Plato who suggested that we live most harmoniously when the circles of our minds are in tune with the musical spheres of the cosmos. Or, as the American jazz composer Sun Ra (1914-93) put it in his poem "The Neglected Plane of Wisdom": "music is existence" (*The Immeasurable Equation*, p. 250).

Contemplating a Tree

> The tree rustled. It had made music before they were born, and would continue after their deaths, but its song was of the moment.
> —E. M. Forster, *Howards End*

> To those who know them, the trees, like other friends, seem to have their periods of reaching out for sympathetic understanding. How often this outreaching is met with repulse will never be told; for tree friends never reproach us—but wait with calm patience for us to grow into comprehension.
> —Anna Botsford Comstock, *Trees at Leisure*

In his journal for the year 1839, Søren Kierkegaard commented on trees' paradoxical acoustic energy: "The most agreeable, the most refreshing conversation is still that which is carried on by the trees, and irrespective of the fact that all the leaves are chatting away (in defiance of all etiquette) at the same time, this is still far from being disturbing, but as it lulls the outer sense it awakens the inner sense" (*Journal EE*, p. 43). In the trees' noise, opposites coincide: agreeableness with impoliteness, tranquility with stimulation. Trees excite the "inner sense" through this mutual entailment of differences. They invite our participation in their ongoing conversation, not as a mere eavesdropper, but as a full dialogical partner. The conversing trees present a social conception of knowledge based on this "inner sense" where reality cannot be understood as something exclusively objective, entirely external. To abstract an entity from its existence in present relation to others defeats true knowledge. Our embeddedness in the world means that all things—living and nonliving, human and nonhuman—"say" something to us. Receptivity involves a special kind of listening to them, what Buber describes at one point as "looking on" (distinct from scientific "observing"), an equanimous process that occurs "freely" as an "undisturbed await[ing] what will be presented" aided by an "involuntary" letting go ("Dialogue," p. 9). In their address to us, entities are received as realities both within and outside our usual indirect, conceptual ways of knowing.

Buber's alternative understanding of ways in which we know points sharply to the inadequacies of conceptual knowledge in describing human experience in its fullness. For Buber, knowledge issues from participatory and immediate (present) encounters with the world. The exclusive reality of the subject-object (what he terms "I-It") relationship, grounding traditional forms of epistemology, is taken to be derived from a prior, more essential one—what he famously designates the "I-Thou" relation. This kind of relation is marked by the space of encounter "in between" subject and object, which Buber characterizes as inherently mutual, reciprocally active. I-Thou and I-It do not correspond to I-person and I-thing, since both a person and a nonhuman object can be viewed as things, or, in Buber's terms, an It. In its instrumentality, the It is necessary to existence but is never met in reciprocity or mystery. As Buber observes, "Without It a human being cannot live. But whoever lives only with that is not human" (*I and Thou*, p. 85). A tree, then, is not necessarily an It, for in "saying" something, as it did to Kierkegaard, the tree in the process becomes a Thou. Only in this I-Thou relationship with a tree does the existence of such a nonhuman entity assume its true being as something more than the passive object of thought categories or the inert instruments of a will to use. The I-Thou relationship preserves the particularity of the other, its independence from purpose, at the same time it appreciates the other's existence as deeply reciprocal and relational. Any Thou is a sensed presence in the here-and-now, rather than a specifiable content or substance. Encountering a Thou is analogous to listening to music—or contemplating a tree.

With the opening declaration "I contemplate a tree [*Ich betrachte einen Baum*]," Buber, in the space of a page and a half of *I and Thou*, offers a rich, poetic meditation on what it means to have a genuine encounter that does not "divide the indivisible" (p. 59). After laying out various ways he can know a tree—appreciating it as image, understanding it as movement, assigning it to a species, applying the laws of physics and numerical measurement to it—he concludes that "throughout all of this the tree remains my object" (p. 58). "But," he then declares, "it can also happen,"

> if will and grace are joined, that as I contemplate the tree I am drawn into a relation, and the tree ceases to be an It. The power of exclusiveness has seized me. This does not require me to forego any of the modes of contemplation.
>
> There is nothing that I must not see in order to see, and there is no knowledge that I must forget. Rather is everything, picture and movement, species and instance, law and number included and inseparably fused.
>
> Whatever belongs to the tree is included: its form and its mechanics, its colors and its chemistry, its conversation with the elements and its conversation with the stars—all this in its entirety.
>
> The tree is no impression, no play of my imagination, no aspect of a mood [*Stimmungswert*]; it confronts me bodily and has to deal with me as I must deal with it—only differently.
>
> One should not try to dilute the meaning of the relation: relation is reciprocity. (ibid.)

Here, the scientific method, the long-established model of I-It ways of knowing, is not discarded but folded into a more capacious and flexible awareness. In the transition of its status from It to Thou, the tree is known in its wholeness, with its internal and external qualities all understood in "conversation with [*Unterredung mit*]" the universe. And as a complete Thou, the tree resists reduction to a mental image or idea, a fantasy, or sentimental value. A tree and its elements belong now to the wider world of relationality rather than solely to the world of private experience. Relating to a tree in this open and reciprocal way means seeing it without specific purpose, seeing it in terms of the kind of respect that I discussed in chapter 1 as underpinning equanimity.

In its expansive epistemological approach to natural things, equanimity appreciates that there is no requirement to abandon instrumental relations, rather only that an objectifying attitude not be allowed to exhaust the range of possible relations with the natural. Plants, Buber admits, present a special problem to our usual ways of thinking since, given their sessility, they seemingly "lack spontaneity." Our habits of thought, he suggests, make it difficult to recognize our full dialogic participation in being. The chief obstacle to owning our reciprocity with plants and trees is attributable, he says, to our not normally imagining them as "replying [*erwidern*]" or "reacting [*reagieren*]" to our actions (ibid., p. 173). Buber is, however, ultimately untroubled by a tree's apparent quiescence:

> We find here not the deed of posture of an individual being but a reciprocity of being itself—a reciprocity that has nothing except being. The living wholeness and unity of a tree that denies itself to the eye, no matter how keen, of anyone who merely investigates, while it is manifest to those who say You, is present when they are present: they grant the tree the opportunity to manifest it, and now the tree that has being manifests it. (ibid.)

Being appears through sheer presence, not restricted to the broad involvement of the I encountering the Thou, though clearly enhanced by it. Buber underscores what is most important in relationality: "What matters in this sphere is that we should do justice with an open mind to the actuality that opens up before us" (ibid.). Compared to manufactured things, which tend to impose upon us certain ways of looking at them mainly according to their use or what experiences they offer, the animate world is more conducive to opening up rich fields of possible dialogue and association. Any apparent I-Thou/I-It dichotomy is never neatly divisible, though many critics of Buber have taken it to be so. Doing justice, inspired by equanimity, to things means that the sphere of the open mind is where *Thou*s and *It*s may alternate. This in-between sphere, once it is recognized as the vital space where the usually separated worlds of fact and imagination, analysis and synthesis, rational closure and emotional opening intermingle and unceasingly give way to one another, coincides with life as it is actually lived.

For Buber, the in-between is where genuine encounters occur, where the existential realm of reciprocity is affirmed. Buber recognized that those moments in which the Thou becomes my unbounded world are never permanent and that they oscillate with other more prosaic states. What we know is built without a precise or single cognitive map, moment to moment, and without rules. The unrehearsed shifting of our multiplex relationships to the world—full of *Thou*s, *It*s, *Thou*s that were once *It*s, and *It*s that were once *Thou*s—provides the thresholds for novel encounters, new openings where meaning cannot be exhausted. This spirit of openness locates me always in the midst of others such that to perceive means to radically participate in a world, the rules for which can never be decided in advance. The inertia of the I is dissolved: "Life is not lived by my playing the enigmatic game on a board by myself, but by my being placed in the presence of a being with whom I have agreed on no rules for the game and with whom no rules can be agreed on" ("What is Man?" p. 166).

The next section closes this chapter with a reflection on equanimity's global function to provide consciousness at a given moment with an object other than itself. By examining the extraordinary story of a famous, nearly 600-year-old tree—one that lives, and was almost killed, in the city where I reside—the serious, "enigmatic game" in which plants and humans play without (in the double sense of "in absence of" and "outside of") rules is brought into relief.

Attempting to Murder a Tree

> Trees are sanctuaries. Whoever knows how to speak to them, whoever knows how to listen to them, can learn the truth. They do not preach learning and precepts, they preach, undeterred by particulars, the ancient law of life.
>
> —Hermann Hesse, *Wandering*

> Toward a vegetal wisdom: I would abjure all my terrors for the smile of a tree.
> —E. M. Cioran, *All Gall is Divided*

> A tree does not question nature.
> —Georges Bataille, *Guilty*

In what unfolds like a whodunit, complete with a detective pursuing clues leading to the perpetrator of the crime, the story of Treaty Oak in Austin, Texas, is remarkable in ways that undo the security of the subject-object split, and go beyond how a tree is equanimously figured from perspectives such as Gibson's theory of affordances or Buber's I-Thou economy. The ecological invitations of this magnificent tree illustrate how living objects and forms express not only apparent causal relations and pragmatic affordances but also tertiary qualities or atmospheric (and, perhaps, utopian) ones, which permeate the total environment in which they are perceived. The tree's story suggests most fully what it means to be against nature: "to be against (opposed to) is also to be against (close up, in proximity to) or, in other words, up against" (Dollimore, *Sexual Dissidence*, p. 229). This is the "case" of Treaty Oak:

The victim: Treaty Oak is centuries older than the city in whose downtown area it resides. Local indigenous tribes such as the Tonkawa and the Comanche believed in the tree's sacredness, it being the sole survivor of 14 live oak (or evergreen oak; Quercus fusiformis) trees revered as the Council Oaks, the site of both war councils and dances and the making of peace agreements and formal treaties. In the shade of the Council Oaks, religious ceremonies are said to have been performed. Folklore associated with the tree includes tea-brewing rituals where its acorns and leaves provided ingredients for potions ensuring a lover's faithfulness or, with a tribe at war, the safe return of warriors. An historically unverified legend holds that, under the tree, the empresario and early colonist of the territory Stephen F. Austin signed the first boundary-line agreement between indigenous peoples and the Anglos in 1824. In 1861, after he was removed as Texas governor, Sam Houston is said to have found solace under the tree as he pondered his future. In the 1920s, with urban developers eager for more land, the tree was marked to be cut down until women's organizations across the state took up the cause to save the tree with letter writing campaigns and public speeches. These efforts garnered a designation by the American Forestry Association as a historic tree, and, in 1927, it was inducted into that organization's Hall of Fame as the most perfect specimen of a tree in North America. That same year, the literary magazine The Poets' Scroll *had published "The Treaty Oak Edition" full of poetry aimed at supporting efforts to preserve the tree. Local fundraising efforts led in 1937 to the creation of a city park where the tree currently resides as its legal owner. As the city expanded around it, the tree remained popular as the site of picnics, weddings, and other important personal events including the marriage proposal made by Austin's first city forester, John Giedraitis, the person at the center of efforts to prevent the tree's demise in 1989.*

The crime: On March 2, 1989, the Treaty Oak was the final stop on a local tree conference tour led by Giedraitis. It was noticed then that there was a band of about three to four feet of dead grass around the base of the tree. At first it was speculated that a city employee carelessly applied a chemical grass edger during routine maintenance. Since these chemicals rarely damage trees, no further thought was given to the issue. Then, on June 1, a woman who works nearby the tree called the city forester's office after noticing some brown leaves. The initial diagnosis was oak wilt, an infectious fungal tree disease that had destroyed more than 10,000 local oaks over the previous two decades. Further investigation, however, discovered leaf symptoms more typical of chemical damage than disease. The city then enlisted the assistance of the State Department of Agriculture and Texas A&M University. Soil and tissue samples collected revealed that Velpar, an herbicide (hexazinone) made by the DuPont Corporation in LaPorte, Texas, was present in what was apparently a massive dosage. With the toxin identified, the city arborist was faced with the first recorded intentional poisoning of an historic tree.

The reaction: *The mystery of who could have done this, and why, made the tree world famous, with television, newspapers, and magazines from* People *to* National Geographic *covering the story. Thousands of people began to show up, leaving chicken soup, Maalox and Tums, and money, and get-well cards were received from all over the world. Religious and spiritual groups appeared, from Evangelicals to Buddhist monks, white witches, and New Agers with crystals, all trying to connect to the tree's spirit or entreat a higher power to offer a healing intervention. In August, a group of psychics gathered to perform a transference of energy in order to release the tree's negative energy into the universe. Texas billionaire H. Ross Perot offered a blank check to cover expenses incurred in the effort to save the tree. Now funded, the Treaty Oak Task Force, a group of 22 experts from around the country, was quickly assembled. Shortly after, DuPont offered a $10,000 reward for information leading to the vandal's arrest, and the Texas Forestry Association added another $1,000.*

The investigation: With specialists working to save the deteriorating tree, a case file marked "criminal mischief" showed up on the desk of Sergeant John Jones, who, after over a decade as an undercover street cop, had just joined the detective unit of the Austin Police Department. With this case one of his first as a detective, there being no suspects and the victim a tree, Jones initially thought he could just file it away. Given the incredible interest in the strange case, however, Jones was fast on the investigation, working according to his personal motto, "You have to be one with the crime." He started diligently researching botany and the chemistry of herbicides. He earned the mocking nicknames "Johnny Appleseed" and "Johnny Acorn" among his detective peers. Following what evidence he had about Velpar, where it is sold, how much it cost, and if it could be stolen, Jones started with a general suspect profile—a disgruntled city employee. Examining purchase records revealed, however, that the city does not use Velpar. The case now having gathered global media coverage, Jones started fielding calls from around the world. Among the barrage of tips, one stood out, from a local woman who had information she believed would crack the case open. The woman was acquainted with a man named Paul Stedman Cullen, with whom she carpooled to a city methadone clinic. The woman reported that Cullen often referred to his unreciprocated love for his methadone counselor, and his desire to find an anti-love spell to assuage his wounded heart. She knew that Cullen had turned to books on witchcraft to find such a spell, and he was alleged to have said that, by killing the largest thing close by, it would also do away with his love. Another possible motive was discovered: Cullen harbored anger toward the state for assigning him to plant and attend to trees while he was imprisoned for a prior crime. The poison appeared to be spread in the shape of a moon. This led many to believe Cullen had indeed performed an occult ritual. Jones knew, however, that without evidence directly linking Cullen to the crime or an outright admission of guilt, he could not make an arrest. Drawing upon his undercover police experience, Jones wired up his informant and got enough evidence to support a search warrant of Cullen's home, where incriminating books on magic were discovered, at the same time as dirt samples from the bed of his impounded truck, found later to be positive for Velpar, were collected. On June 29, 1989, officers of the Austin Police Department arrested Cullen.

The trial: Because of his prior conviction for a burglary offense, Cullen faced the possibility of life in prison. A jury found him guilty of criminal mischief, and he was sentenced to 9 years in prison and fined $1000. Cullen maintained his innocence throughout the trial. After an appeal, Cullen's conviction was affirmed on June 24, 1992.

Today: The city spent a quarter of a million dollars in the attempt to save the tree, of which about 35% now survives (Figure 1). The tree continues to grow, and in 1997 it produced its first crop of acorns since the poisoning. The acorns were collected and germinated, and, by 1999, all "Baby Treaty Oaks" found homes in Texas and other states. Giedraitis made this statement in 1989 at an urban forestry conference, when the tree's future was uncertain:

> Its poisoning begs us to consider not only the reality of its desperate plight but also the larger truths it represents. Just as many cultures have held the tree to be a symbol of knowledge and life, we today are being asked to believe in the tree once again; to believe that billions of new trees will give us Global ReLeaf. But tree planting is also a symbol of a larger truth. While there are many symbolic and practical reasons for

tree planting, perhaps the best is that it reminds us that we are part of the world. ("Treating the Treaty Oak," p. 163)

Fig. 1. Treaty Oak, Austin, Texas, U.S.A (Author photo)

This case provides an exquisite illustration of the manifold ways of literally and figuratively looking at, or generally relating to, a tree. (I count around 50 different ways the tree was and is part of interactions with its total environment.) Any understanding of Treaty Oak must exceed the categories and dualisms that figure it over time: living entity/place, It/Thou, objectivity/subjectivity, sacred/profane, rationality/magic, reality/symbol, matter/spirit, nature/civilization, science/religion, and so on. Never merely the object of discursive thought, the tree exceeds explanation according to the oppositional terms of any binary. To describe the tree as neither an It nor a Thou, but rather as an It-Thou would be to say that it is mutually constituted, perhaps in such a way that the oscillation between It and Thou is so rapid as to appear simultaneous. Even for Cullen the convicted poisoner, Treaty Oak was "simultaneously" It and Thou, an object so woven into his subjectivity that he felt *it* had to die so, in the process, *he* could become unburdened by frustrated love.

While life may be lived in both objectivist and subjectivist modes, neither mode alone can account fully for phenomena whose socio-cultural historical meaning, like that of Treaty Oak, is so richly multi-layered, multi-directional. To perceive the tree at any moment is in fact to understand, borrowing from Merleau-Ponty, that its "Gestalt arises from polymorphism, [and] this situates us entirely outside of the philosophy of the subject and the object" (*The Visible and the Invisible*, p. 207). All reality-engendering stances in the world issue from recognizing the momentarily intertwined, mutually participatory nature of subjectivity and objectivity, that is, intersubjectivity. Knowledge in this case is built upon an unfolding, non-teleological, intersubjective understanding of objectivity and subjectivity. Treaty Oak is, then, the occasion for recognizing that we live nowhere other than in a field of proliferating meanings that arise because of connections, associations, reflections, and never only in a world of bare physical objects and events. "Every tree," Thoreau wrote, "sends forth its fibres in search of the Wild" ("Walking," p. 260).

Knowledge and equanimity meet in the space where an emergent, holistic understanding of reality eclipses a fixed essentialist one. As intensely focused on the tree as Giedraitis was in his efforts to save it, he never lost sight of relational, as opposed to purely cognitive or simply emotional, ways of knowing and being. In 1989, he saw "larger truths" involved in the story of the tree. And, looking back on the tree with the perspective of more than 30 years, Giedraitis reflected that "it survives because it follows the rules of nature, and it's good…it just gives and gives and gives, it never takes anything back again" (Gopal et al., "The Bizarre Story"). These claims should not be dismissed as romanticism or as idealism. The tree persists because, in a sense, it does not question itself, which is also to say, nature. It acts without motive; it just gives because it gives; that is its nature. It does not think, as humans do—indeed, as they must if they want to solve crimes, for example—by means of considering reasons and interrogating (their) existence. It is not calculating, deliberating. It is reminiscent of the rose in Angelus Silesius's

(1624-77) couplet: "The rose does have no why; it blossoms without reason, / Forgetful of itself, oblivious to our vision" (*The Cherubinic Wanderer*, p. 54). Heidegger would reflect on Silesius's distich in his 1955-56 lecture course *The Principle of Reason*, pointing to its ethical relevance, namely, its significance for how to live and to be: "What is unsaid in the fragment—and everything depends on this—instead says that humans, in the concealed grounds of their essential being, first truly are when in their own way they are like the rose—without why" (*Principle of Reason*, p. 38). This "without why" (a trope of medieval mysticism) points to the possibility of freedom found in releasement (*Gelassenheit*), a *letting things be* that bears resemblance to Daoist, Zen, and Sufi ways of relating to things, that is, through an equanimity that neutralizes treatment of them as charged instruments for the ego's own desire-driven, narrow ends. As Rumi indicates, "the eye goes blind when it only wants to see *why*" (*Essential Rumi*, p. 107; emph. in orig.).

This state of being "without why" opens passages to greater connectedness and an easeful openness to and graceful fluidity with things that appreciates perceptual motility according to Blake's maxim: "As the Eye, Such the Object" (*Complete Writings*, p. 456). An eye alive with awareness encounters objects that are released from being reified in a polarizing structure where, obligatorily, they are to be explained. Treaty Oak, like Silesius's rose, blooms without concern. It blooms not because it wants to attract admirers or because it wishes to make seeds and reproduce. If the tree or rose were only an object to our thinking, then the latter desires may make sense. But, for tree and rose, their existence as things in the world displaces the subject whose knowledges, whose *why*s, attempt to pin it down. For a thinker like the philosopher of science Gaston Bachelard (1884-1962), the human imagination is implicated in the very materiality of experience, and so affective, poetic ways of engaging the world have the power to dislodge the more usual intellectual, disembodied ones. "As for nature," Bachelard observes, "we begin by loving it without knowing it, without really seeing it, by actualizing in things a love that has its basis elsewhere. Then we search for its details because we love it as a whole *without knowing why*" (*Water and Dreams*, p. 115; emph. mine). It is true that we grasp entities before details, we engage with multi-sensorial syntheses before individual sensory aspects, and affective meanings before intellectual understanding. Equanimity is the form of coming to know the world that accommodates the space for knowledge to unfold smoothly, undisturbed by missing *why*s and the compulsion to generate and answer them.

There are then chiefly two ways, in the context of equanimous knowledge, that an unsettling of the subject presumed to know may proceed. The first lines up with the practices of Thoreau and the advice of the Zen poet Matsuo Bashō (1644-94): "go to the bamboo if you want to learn about the bamboo. . . leave your subjective preoccupation with yourself" (*The Narrow Road*, p. 33). Bashō was clear that, by approaching the plant world from a narrow human perspective, "you impose yourself on the object and do not learn" (ibid.). Equanimity is precisely that which prevents us from getting in our own way while on the endless path of building knowledge. Aware of the inevitability of interpretative "why" questions, equanimity puts before us the often neglected empirical "what" that every moment presents. The second, more radical, way the knowledgeable subject is decentered involves what French philosopher and geographer Augustin Berque recently called "thinking the ambient." The idea here is that, consistent with linguistic traits of Japanese (and other Asian languages), since verbs do not require subjects, the subject can then be implied as part of the total "scene," or Jp. *bamen* (場面), a word whose elements signify "facing (*men* 面) the place (*ba* 場)." In other words, a field of dynamic relations is opened up where a person's very existence is implied by the objects themselves. The windbell's chime, for example, engenders a set of synesthetic relationships without requiring, but only implying, a subject. As Berque summarizes the concept, "Subjecthood here is not concentrated into an 'I,' it is diffused into the whole *bamen*. . . . [It] is nothing else than being that particular set of circumstances: an ambience" ("Thinking the Ambient," pp. 17-18).

The encapsulated (and often self-defended) subject is replaced by "an ambient," an entity present atmospherically as a function of the things around it which call it into existence. If reality can be figured according to ambienthood, as opposed to subjecthood, then any bit of knowledge about, any image of, nature amounts to a reflection of an active relationship *with* nature. "Subjectivity," Jacques Maritain (1882-1973) observes, "awakens to itself only by simultaneously awakening to things" (*Creative Intuition*, p. 218). Facing nature in a non-oppositional way allows for the development of a hermeneutics that operates from the inside (of everything). Anything that we can claim to know presents itself then as one particular aspect of nature's atmospheric dynamics, of which we are always in the middle. And, as we will see in the last two chapters, equanimous subjectivity itself can have therefore no unitary or prescribed model, its vitality deriving precisely from its multiple and dynamic relations with the total ambiance—just like a tree. In *On Liberty*, John Stuart Mill (1806-73) captured this at the same time he revealed the core of his thought: "Human nature is not a machine to be built after a model, and set to do exactly the work prescribed for it, but a tree which requires to grow and develop itself on all sides, according to the tendency of the inward forces which make it a living thing" (p. 58).

As this chapter has elaborated, equanimity underpins a phenomenology attuned to apparent and shifting affordances, sensitive also to what philosopher Tonino Griffero, in his recent work, has discussed in terms of "the tertiary," that is, the affective and atmospheric qualities that suffuse the total milieu in which things are perceived (*Places, Affordances, Atmospheres*, p. 101). While philosophers, from Plato (*Republic* 596a-b) to Bertrand Russell (*The Problems of Philosophy*, p. 7), have referenced tables as the perfectly handy example of how to figure reality, I have chosen a tree—perhaps in the spirit of the recent so-called plant turn in philosophy, yet more basically so—because I believe trees (and seeds) offer an especially felicitous model for the relational understanding that is equanimity. In the end, trees are better teachers for how to know the world than any bookish insights may offer—those in this book not excepted. My perspective is shared, according to a Zen verse, by the birds who inhabit trees: "The old pine is talking prajñā-wisdom, / The hidden bird is playing with true suchness" (Hori, *Zen Sand*, p. 394). It is also shared by the monk and mystic Bernard of Clairvaux (1090-1153), who, in a famous letter addressed to Henry Murdac around 1130, was persuading him to leave his promising academic career to come to Clairvaux. Bernard spoke from the place of his own earned wisdom with these striking words: "Believe my experience: you will find more in forests than in books [*aliquid amplius invenies in silvis quam in libris*]. The trees and the rocks will teach you what you can never learn from any master [*Ligna et lapides docebunt te, quod a magistris audire non possis*] (*Epistola* 106.2; cf. Underhill, p. 128).

Leaving the study table or desk for the forest trees offers the occasion for a more complete understanding of the role played by equanimity in the formation of our sense of reality and, as we will see in the following chapters, in our sense of identity and its mysterious possibilities. In one of Wittgenstein's remarks on Frazer's magisterial *The Golden Bough* (1906-15), he proposed, prior to eventually omitting it from his text, that "the depth of magic should be preserved," since, looking back at his own earlier works, "when [he] began talking about the 'world' (and not about this tree or table), what else," he asks himself, "did I want but to keep something higher spellbound in my words?" (*Philosophical Occasions*, pp. 116-17). In the spirit of "something higher," I let then the Polish poet Zbigniew Herbert's (1924-98) meditation on a table be my segue to thinking more about equanimity's role in reenchanting the dynamic self:

> At table you should sit calmly and not daydream. Let us recall what an effort it took for the stormy ocean tides to arrange themselves in quiet rings. A moment of inattention and everything might wash away. It is also forbidden to rub the table legs, as they are very sensitive. Everything at the table must be done coolly and matter-of-factly. You can't sit down here with things not completely thought through. For daydreaming we have been given other objects made of wood: the forest, the bed. ("Careful with the Table," *The Collected Poems*, p. 216)

III.
EQUANIMITY AND IDENTITY

CHAPTER 6
SUBJECTS OF EQUANIMITY
In Motion

> It is, therefore, a source of great virtue for the practiced mind to learn, bit by bit, first to change about in visible and transitory things, so that afterwards it may be able to leave them behind altogether. The person who finds his homeland sweet is a tender beginner; he to whom every soil is as his native one is already strong; but he is perfect to whom the entire world is as a foreign land. The tender soul has fixed his love on one spot in the world; the strong man has extended his love to all places; the perfect man has extinguished his.
> —Hugh of St. Victor, *Didascalicon*

> He who is fettered has a fettered mind,
> He who has a dynamic mind does dynamic things.
> —*Shinsan zengoshū*, Verse 14.75

> Philosophy is really homesickness, *the urge to be at home everywhere in the world.*
> —Novalis, *The Universal Brouillon: Materials for an Encyclopaedia*

The above epigraphs signal my critical direction in the next two chapters, that is, toward considering links between equanimity, as a mobile attitude toward the world, and the formation of subjectivity. Because equanimity as a way of cognition is untethered to fixed notions, it has the potential to frame identities whose freedom can be figured in multiple ways. This chapter, along with the next, considers then the different subject positions that may emerge under forms of awareness that value flexibility, interrelatedness, and spontaneity. It reflects upon who we are when we inhabit the world equanimously.

The ontological corollary of the operations of equanimous knowledge, examined in the previous chapters, is that identity appears as unfinished, unrepeatable, contingent, and, for all that, totally assured, authentic. Equanimity discloses what is relevant for identity as precisely that which cannot be reached by causal methods or techniques. Equanimity encompasses the field in which all things are allowed to appear with equal urgency and non-hierarchical respect (recall: *re + specere*, to look back at, to look again). Here, in this space of unforced, even, and deferential awareness, the limits of subjecthood are opened up to, transformed into, a kind of ambienthood (as I suggested at the end of the last chapter). Purely personal concerns dissolve when the distinction between personhood and the lived world is recognized to be provisional. The more completely integrated into one's ambient field of experience one is, the more a balance emerges between the valuing and the losing of one's person. This balance between value and loss, I suggest, stands for an especially adaptive, if rare, harmonizing where encounters between subjects and the world turn on the never finished work of "interrogating our experience precisely in order to know how it opens us to what is not ourselves" (Merleau-Ponty, *The Visible and Invisible*, p. 159).

Equanimity, in short, undoes self-preoccupation. It fundamentally challenges the tendency to navel gaze. The self, undeniably, has the power to attract a degree of attention that narrows and obfuscates the fields through which all selves, all objects, move and interact. Lacking the equilibrium that enables us to take in the flowing world as it is, without parts of it arrested by desires and aversions, we remain separable, indeed isolated, from it, whether that world be internal or external. In this sense, disequanimity leads to identity in exile, to narcissistic enclosure. However, as we have seen in the preceding chapters, equanimous knowing entails holism, proximity, mimesis. As an epistemology, equanimity emphasizes neither what is external as objects of knowledge nor the subjects internal to the solitary knower herself, but instead the interstitial site, the ambient field, where the events of knowing come to pass. Only equanimity as a way of knowing appreciates the full range of relationships that from moment to moment make up this site. Here, in this fluid contact zone, one of the global functions of equanimity, I suggested, is to provide consciousness at any given moment with an object other than itself.

In the *Zhuangzi*, this immersion into one's shifting field of experience is the ongoing process by which we "hide the world in the world, so there is nowhere for anything to escape to" (Ziporyn, p. 43; cf. Graham, p. 86). This rather gnomic expression points to a radically situated sense of being in the world where the ongoing realizing of the way things actually are (*dao*) coincides with absolute interdependence and mutual sustenance of self and world. There is nowhere to stand *outside* the world—this much is obvious—nor is there, as I have argued, anywhere to stand with a sense of finality *in* the world since everything is moving, shifting, flowing. And so there always appear more individual perspectives from which to explore the changing cosmos. It is precisely equanimity that helps us to realize that the more we attach value to any piece of the total field, to any single perspective, the more we are vulnerable to its loss, its "escape." As the path to valuing the whole field of events as such, equanimity shows us that we are never actually without (as both adverb and preposition: lacking and outside of) the whole, for there is simply nowhere for it to go. Whatever seemingly escapes or hides never really disappears.

This chapter and the next describe the kinds of subjectivity capable of hiding the world in the world, the identities whose formation would not be possible without the soft focus, which we call equanimity, allowing the world to be mirrored as it is. Winding through the chapters' charting of subjectivity are eight modes of existence whose essential signature is equanimity—from roaming, floating, being in the middle, and generating in this chapter, then to hunting, being at play, without borders, and "with belly" (Jp. *Hara no aru hito*, the person with center) in the next. These different subject positions will be approached descriptively rather than prescriptively, since each opens access to a range of possibilities inherent in lived circumstances. My intent is to create a sort of typology of dynamic ways of being colored by equanimity, in order to think about how identities arise in the process of yielding in various ways to the unfolding of the present moment. With this intent in mind, there really can be no possibility of exhausting the subjectivities that equanimity sets in motion. As in previous chapters, the overarching aim here is to observe how Eastern and Western philosophies and psychologies may contribute together to a fuller understanding of equanimity as both concept and (non)praxis.

Equanimity, it will be seen, brings us before a sense of being, of identity, which is experienced in and extrapolated from movement. There can be nothing like an identity that preexists movement through the world, no place where identities can be located or fixed, since identity emerges in and through such movement in the world. Equanimity, in this sense, means existing in concert with the mobile world. The first section, borrowing its title from that of the first Inner Chapter of the *Zhuangzi*, looks at the terms related to ways of traveling and sauntering by which we may understand the first figure of equanimous existence: the wanderer.

Free and Easy Rambling

> Who acknowledge space—moving
> Know as many dimensions
> As they have muscles
>
> —Louis Zukofsky, *"A"*

> I have always been drawn by windblown clouds into dreams of a lifetime of wandering.
>
> —Matsuo Bashō, *Narrow Road to the Interior*

> Neither the small who laugh at the large nor the large who pity the small have yet found the true ease of far and unfettered wandering.
>
> —Wang Fuzhi (1619-92), commentary on the *Zhuangzi*

The making of the self, like the making of self-knowledge, may be described as a Quixotean enterprise, one that involves travel, the changing of places and thus the multiplying of perspectives. Previous chapters revealed the critical place of movement in the formation of equanimous knowledge. It is precisely our capacity to wander that offers us the freedom to wonder. More space is found for cultivating identities poised for probing and questioning as opposed to receding into listless indifference. Equanimity puts into motion a subject who is ready to entertain the world on its own terms and not merely conform to it. To put brakes on the world through fixed standards or discriminations creates nothing but the illusion of a fixed cosmos. The literary critic Georges Van Den Abbeele observes that "to call an existing order (whether epistemological, aesthetic, or political) into question by placing oneself 'outside' that order, by taking a 'critical distance' from it, is implicitly to invoke the metaphor of thought as travel" (*Travel as Metaphor*, p. xiii). This capacity for momentary critical distance on the part of the thinker/traveler means embracing the freedom and ease necessary to navigate broad complex fields. The equanimous rambler, the very figure of flexibility, is, then, the first ontological "profile" I will describe.

Among the 114 sayings attributed to Jesus in the extraordinary *Gospel of Thomas*, the best known of the Nag Hammadi manuscripts (a collection buried circa 370 CE, and found accidentally by an Egyptian farmer in 1945), is a simple, compact exhortation: "be passersby" (Meyer, *Gospel of Thomas*, p. 41). To be a passerby signifies, at one level, always moving past the mundane temptations whose satisfaction impedes the soul's journey toward salvation. And to be a soul means, in its essence, to travel. The philosopher Gabriel Marcel (1889-1973) expressed this idea perfectly: "It is precisely the soul that is the traveller; it is of the soul and of the soul alone that we can say with supreme truth that 'being' necessarily means 'being on the way' (*en route*)" (*Homo Viator*, p. 11). Marcel's aperçu resonates with the fundamental scriptural notion of the Christian as both pilgrim and stranger, a transitory traveler on the way, however indirectly, to the Kingdom of God. Indeed, early Christian theologians such as Clement of Alexandria (ca. 150-ca. 215) and Basil the Great (330-379) interpreted the mythic travels of the hero Odysseus as a reflection of the Christian's ideal journey through terrestrial life. The Christian traveler (*peregrinus*) is here one who pursues her proper course unsusceptible to the perilous

Siren calls of the temporal world and of false doctrine, ferried on a ship (the Church) and anchored by a mast (the Cross). Thomas Aquinas (1225-74), in his *Summa Theologica*, went as far as to describe Christ himself as a robust traveler (*viator*) during his earthly life due to his corporeal incarnation, a trait shared with all human beings. Consistent with this, the 14th-century Cistercian poet Guillaume de Deguileville mapped Christ's redemptive action explicitly in terms of a pilgrimage in the final part of his religious trilogy, *Le Pèlerinage Jhesucrist* (ca. 1358). As the supreme model for Christian identity and spiritual conduct, Christ in the figure of a traveler brings before us an image of the mobility essential for negotiating the perils of worldly living. Movement signifies the antithesis of sin, as metaphorized in many Old and New Testament verses (e.g., Proverbs 29:6; Psalms 9:15; Psalms 124:7; Ecclesiastes 7:26; 2 Timothy 2:26), where being ensnared in a net or trapped in a pit is a primary analogy for arrested states of iniquity. Escape from sin depends then upon mobility: idle hands, it has been said, are the devil's workshop (a maxim likely linked to Jerome's [ca. 345–420] advice to "engage in some occupation, so that the devil may always find you busy" [*Letters*, p. 417]).

Exponents of Stoic philosophy also placed a premium upon motion as the hallmark of virtuous character. The Roman philosopher Seneca (4 BCE–65 CE) found in the traveler Odysseus one of the most compelling exemplars of tranquility (*tranquillitas*), characters who maintain their balance by "being unbeaten by labors and being scorners of pleasure and victors over every kind of fear" ("On the Constancy of the Wise Person," p. 150). The wisdom of equanimity reveals itself not in moments of stasis but of vital action. The renowned Stoic teacher Epictetus (ca. 55-135) once put forward Socrates as a kind of Stoic sage whose style of living he compared to skillfully playing a game with a ball:

> [Socrates] was like one playing with a ball. What then was the ball that he played with? Life, imprisonment, exile, taking poison, being deprived of his wife, leaving his children orphans. These were the things he played with, but none the less he played and tossed the ball with balance. So we ought to play the game, so to speak, with

all possible care and skill, but treat the ball itself as indifferent. (*Discourses*, II.5, p. 80)

After being condemned to death, Socrates would leave his wife, children, and friends in order not to compromise his moral duty to accept the law despite its unjustness. All else—his family, his friends, what he had endured—was "indifferent," not because the philosopher was unfeeling, but because one thing, on the Stoic account, mattered far more—separating what is under one's control from what is not, and fully accepting the latter. Equanimity helps us gracefully play the games in which we find ourselves since so-called indifferents, those things that in themselves neither contribute to nor detract from a satisfactory life, are more easily recognized. We are better able to "toss the ball with balance" since we grasp that, although it is everyone's focus, the ball serves merely as the means to some end (a win, loss, or draw), which will be determined by how skillfully the ball is played. The Stoic, summoning her equanimity, accepts any outcome in the knowledge that she has acted skillfully given the circumstances. Compare the tennis player who enters Centre Court at Wimbledon by passing under two stirring lines from Rudyard Kipling's poem "If—" inscribed in capital letters above the tunnel leading from the locker room: "If you can meet with Triumph and Disaster, and treat those two imposters just the same" (*100 Poems*, p. 137). Equanimity susses out the elements of the "game" or situation we find ourselves in, suspending final identification with or interpretation of results since the possibility exists to meet them at any moment even-handedly. This prospect of imperturbability is the crucial "if" upon which equanimous identity hangs.

Ramblers, roamers, wanderers, and other drifters are known for their refusal of telos. Their vitality is a matter of traversal, being somewhere in the middle, on the way, in process. As flexible characters embracing uncertainty, they pretend to no final knowledge. Not only that, but according to the *Dao de jing*, "able travelers leave no ruts or tracks along the way" (p. 119). To be a nomad whose trail no one can follow supposes a subject who, by going with the shifting world rather than against it, is ill suited for producing ruts of received ideas or the tracks of divisive judgments. "Drifting," observes Jean-François Lyotard, "is in itself the end of all critique" (*Driftworks*, p. 13). The fixity of a critical vision of things gives way to a diverse, expanding, and momentarily satisfying field of impressions and appearances. As I will argue in a future work on ethics, equanimity cannot be pressed into the service of countering ideologies or narratives, no matter how morally compelling it may be to do so. Once equanimity is deployed polemically, it forfeits its constitutive range and flexibility. We could say that it no longer properly is equanimity since it has succumbed to a binary way of thinking that disguises a hierarchical one. Narrowing of vision, as we have seen in the previous section on knowledge, categorically defeats equanimity. Equanimity does not constitute ideal objects because it never puts them at the constant disposition of a fixed penetrative gaze. The motility of the equanimous subject guards against callous indifference in favor of the serenity of detachment. "True nomads," travel writer Bruce Chatwin (1940-89) declares, "watch the passing of civilisations with equanimity" ("Letter to Tom Maschler," p. 83).

Perhaps the greatest draws of travel and wandering are the changing panoramas of the self and the world that they afford. The landscapes through which we move and that forever move around us variously furnish wonder, knowledge (about self and world), and an acute sense of possibility. An Arabic saying captures the favorable dimensions of transit: *fil harakeh barakah* (In movement, there is a blessing). While seeking novelty for self-enrichment or a mere antidote to boredom is certainly part of the attraction to travel, its more profound motives circulate around forming and assuming new identities. The identities performed through wandering are ineluctably produced *en route*. Not focused on final destinations, they remain open to unforeseen and ephemeral encounters with what is external and internal. In the *Liezi*, there is a striking dialogue concerning motivations for traveling and their relation to aspects of equanimous identity:

Before this Lieh-tzu liked travel.

Hu-tzu asked him: What is it you like so much about travel?

[Lieh-tzu replied:] The joy of travel is that the things which amuse you never remain the same. Other men travel to contemplate the sights, I travel to contemplate the way things change. There is travel and travel, and I have still to meet someone who can tell the difference!

[Hu-tzu responded:] Is not your travel really the same as other men's? Would you insist there is really a difference? Anything at all that we see, we always see changing. You are amused that other things never remain the same, but do not know that you yourself never remain the same. You busy yourself with outward travel and do not know how to busy yourself with inward contemplation. By outward travel we seek what we lack in things outside us, while by inward contemplation we find sufficiency in ourselves. The latter is the perfect, the former an imperfect kind of travelling.

From this time Lieh-tzu never went out anymore, thinking that he did not understand travel.

Hu-tzu told him: How perfect is travel! In perfect travel we do not know where we are going, in perfect contemplation we do not know what we are looking at. To travel over all things without exception, contemplate all things without exception, this is what I call travel and contemplation. That is why I say: How perfect is travel! (The Book of Lieh-tzu, pp. 81-82)

Lieh-tzu loves travel precisely for its encounters with form rather than content. He imagines that his own displacement mirrors the perpetual transitioning of things. With his attention to flux, he represents the antithesis of the typical sight-seer or contemporary tourist whose interest is guided by presumptions about what is immediately consumable as something picturesque or foreign. The tourist is concerned with ends; Lieh-tzu with means. Unlike a tourist seeking unspoiled beauty or a packaged experience of "history," Lieh-tzu is the kind of traveler always ready, as Iain Chambers puts it, "to abandon the fixed geometry of sites and roots for the unstable calculations of transit" itself ("Leaky Habitats," p. 244). That was until Hu-tzu reminded him that his encounters with exterior form have an ineluctable partiality about them. Lieh-tzu's paramount interest in changing appearances apparently entails a disregard for interiority, an inattention to internal plenitude. In Hu-tzu's account, travel's perfection involves the aimlessness and suspension of knowing necessary for opening without exception to all outer and inner states. Equanimity emerges at the intersection of travel with no destination and contemplation without preconception (e.g., Jp. *shoshin*, beginner's mind).

It seems that Lieh-tzu's abandonment of his mobile identity may have been a bit hasty. One thing that is true of travel is that the "outer" journey of physical and spatial mobility often functions as a reflection of the "interior" journey of the soul, the mind or consciousness. This is because movement, like vision, requires distance, the space over and through which identity shifts. In his foreword to the writings of the legendary explorer and travel writer Freya Stark (1893-1993), Lawrence Durrell observes that "A great traveler (in distinction to a merely good one) is a kind of introspective; as she covers the ground outwardly, so she advances toward fresh interpretations of herself inwardly" (*The Journey's Echo*, p. xi). In this sense, Goethe was evidently a "great traveler." "Nothing," he writes in his *Italian Journey* (1816), "is comparable to the new life that a reflective person experiences when he observes a new country. Though I am still always myself, I believe I have been changed to the very marrow of my bones" (p. 27). The mobile and the contemplative flow together in equanimous existence such that who we are while wandering is always in process, never finished, and therefore inexhaustible. Travel's perfection, referring back to Hu-tzu, depends upon it being a way (*dao*), a methodless method that eschews objects in favor of an open range of novel encounters with them. The author Henry Miller's (1891-1980) take on the meaning of wandering sums this up well: "One's destination is never a place but rather a new way of looking at things. Which is to say that there are no limits to vision" (*Big Sur and the Oranges of Hieronymus Bosch*, p. 30).

Identity is then less something that may be intentionally fashioned or completed than something that may be allowed simply to flow with no final destination. Certainly, what permits us to act in a given moment is the firm belief in the closure of the self, its boundedness and completeness rather than its open and fractional nature. Yet wandering subjectivity brings before us the possibility of acting in the subjunctive mode (or mood), *as if we had* a unitary identity while recognizing that subjectivity is precarious, founded as it is in the transit space between the familiar and the unfamiliar. The equanimity fostered by movement accommodates this space where divergent perspectives meet. It tolerates the paradoxes inherent in wandering where, for example, experiences of unfamiliarity concentrate as well as broaden the mind. A related paradox touches directly on identity: understanding the familiar or Same may be enhanced to the extent that we attain distance on it. This means that the Same is most fully recognized on condition that it be an Other, an idea echoed in poet Arthur Rimbaud's (1854-91) famous ungrammatical pronouncement, "Je est un autre" (I is someone else) (*Complete Works*, p. 370). Identity is preeminently a question of space; its process is one of spatialization, or ambience, as I suggested at the end of the previous chapter. "The paradox of identity," declares philosopher Jacques Rancière, "is that you must travel to disclose it" ("Discovering New Worlds," p. 31). Identity, in this sense, always appears "*over* there." It possesses distantiation as well as that hovering quality we have discussed as central to the meanings of equanimity. A text no less significant than the oldest treatise on Islamic mysticism (Sufism), ʿAlī al-Hujwīrī's eleventh-century *Kashf al-mahjūb*, describes the dervish as "a place over which something is passing, not a wayfarer following his own free will" (p. 29). Travel, as opposed to the sessile condition, involves a certain humility (L. *humilis* "low, lowly," from *humus* "ground"). Its "ground" is deference to the array of perspectives opened up in the act of wandering. Walt Whitman's "Song of the Open Road" expresses this quite felicitously: "O Public Road . . . / You express me better than I can express myself / You shall be more to me than my poem" (*Leaves of Grass*, p. 92).

In Tibetan, one word for *person* is *'gro ba* ("go-er," "wanderer or migrator"). Only such an entity, one who inveterately "goes," can appreciate what Buddhists call the "suchness" (Skt. *tathātā*; T. *de bzhin nyid/de kho na nyid*) of the world, or the way things themselves go or transpire. To reflect the suchness of reality means being able to move freely, unhampered or blinkered by rigidified conceptual systems. In the *Sansuigkō* (Mountains and Waters Sutra), Dōgen describes this liberation as the strategic employment of different conceptual frameworks without ever becoming fixated on or stuck in any of them. Indeed, Dōgen draws upon the teaching of Master Fuyo

Dokai (1043-1118) who uses the image of "constant walking" as the key to liberation (p. 217). So, the word *'gro ba* is significant because, in the Buddhist tradition, to construe the shifting, interdependent experiential world from multiple perspectives requires movement, that is, being in sync with the way things themselves "go" together. The consummate *'gro ba* was the Buddha, whose followers described him as the *tathāgata*, the rare person so completely enlightened that he *goes in thusness* (*tathā-gata*)—he continually walks the suchness (*tathātā*) of what is.

To be a thus-goer is directly and without exception to encounter the phenomenal, concrete world in such a way that this nonconceptual world is not confused with the ideas and signs conventionally used to pin it down. Such a subject keeps moving—unrestricted by distinctions and judgments (e.g., good/bad) or conventional dualities (e.g., past/future, permanent/impermanent). She artlessly moves through a naturally unfolding world prior to its dizzying encoding. In the *Saptaśatikā Prajñāpāramitā Sūtra*, the Buddha's dialogue with the bodhisattva Mañjuśrī illustrates the terms in which such an identity may be recognized:

> The Buddha: How then, Manjusri, should the Tathagata be seen, revered and honoured?
> Manjusri: Through the mode of Suchness (*tathatā*) do I see the Tathagata, through the mode of nondiscrimination, in the manner of nonobservance. I see Him through the aspect of nonproduction, through the aspect of nonexistence. But Suchness does not attain (enlightenment) — thus do I see the Tathagata. Suchness does not become or cease to become — thus do I see the Tathagata. Suchness does not stand at any point or spot—thus do I see the Tathagata. Suchness is not past, future or present — thus do I see the Tathagata. Suchness is not brought about by duality or nonduality — thus do I see the Tathagata. Suchness is neither defiled nor purified — thus do I see the Tathagata. Suchness is neither produced nor stopped — thus do I see the Tathagata. In this way the Tathagata is seen, revered and honoured. (*The Perfection of Wisdom in 700 Lines*, p. 80)

Outside of supreme Buddhahood, how does one embody a suchness that "does not stand at any point or spot"? An example may be a select group of the Buddha's followers, monks who, dispersed throughout the land to teach, wander forest areas in observance of precepts regulating ascetic practices (Pali *dhutaṅga*; Thai *thudong*). The subjectivity of so-called *thudong* monks blurs the distinction between existence and nonexistence, sufficiency and lack. In their extended treks, these solitary wanderers often "never knew where [they] would spend the night, where the next meal would come from, or what difficulties [they] would encounter" (Tiyavanich, *Forest Recollections*, p. 143). Despite, or precisely because of, the precarity of their lives, *thudong* monks have access to a poised subjectivity unburdened by attachments. A text known as the Rhinoceros Sutra (*Khaggavisāṇa-sutta*), found in the early Buddhist collection *Sutta Nipāta*, offers an apt image for the forest monk: "As a deer in the wilds, unfettered, goes for forage wherever it wants: The observant person, valuing freedom, wanders alone like a rhinoceros" (pp. 40-41).

Equanimity is not recognized for producing certain kinds of subjects; rather, it is that, in specific kinds of subjectivity, elements of equanimity are most manifestly apparent. One version of the rambler who reveals aspects of equanimity "through the aspect of nonproduction" is the 19th-century literary figure of the *flâneur*, the solitary, idle, and anonymous observer of urban life. This bourgeois male character found a homely domain in the crowded public streets and arcades of cities like Paris and Berlin. The gender division of labor and the separation of the private and public spheres at the time meant not only that the *flâneuse* would remain largely invisible but that her reduced access to the resource of mobility, considered both as a social value and material practice, had limited effects on the production—and reproduction—of knowledge. The *flâneur* was that privileged identity whose idleness and aimlessness, while marking a protest against the division of labor through wasteful forms of mobility, allowed for the discovery of both pleasure in and knowledge of the diverse stimuli of the urban landscape. Walter Benjamin described the *flâneur*, in his role as metropolitan observer, as variously a dreamer, an artist, a spy, a detective, a sandwich-man, and, in his sheer spontaneity and ability to read traces, a hunter (a figure we will discuss in chapter 7). Each of these embodiments of *flânerie* are capable, Benjamin suggested, of producing knowledge for the precise reason that movement through the cityscape means "there is always something more to see" (*Arcades Project*, p. 806). In his abiding position relative to "something more to see," the *flâneur* possesses an equanimous power: he can act freely and apparently without purpose while maintaining a meditative wonder and a limitless capacity to absorb the mysteries of his surroundings. In this sense, Benjamin aptly dubbed him "the priest of the genius loci" ("The Return of the *Flâneur*," p. 264).

The *flâneur*'s openness and concern with the sheer act of perception allow for the avoidance of settled interpretations in favor of what Simone Stirner, in her essay on Benjamin's theory of reading, astutely describes as "a form of experience, an attitude of nonteleological attentiveness toward the world." "Reading like a flâneur," she continues, "entails surrendering oneself to what a text, an object, or a site might bring to us" ("A Technique of Closeness," p. 283). It epitomizes, Stirner writes, "an opening of the self toward being moved and affected by something yet unknown" (ibid.). The world becomes, for the urban wanderer, an expansive horizon of possibilities whose unfolding must depend upon a dialectic of intensity (acute attention) and flexibility (alert receptivity). Benjamin famously remarked that the *flâneur* "makes 'studies'" (*Arcades*, p. 453), and we may see his broad erudition as never complete since it turns to affairs whose breadth and depth are unfathomable, transitory. One of François de Curel's (1854-1928) characters rhetorically poses the problem of the knowable and unknowable in *L'amour brode* (1893) as the problem of *flânerie* itself: "La connaissance du coeur humain, n'est-ce pas l'érudition des flâneurs?" [knowledge of the human heart, isn't this the erudition of flâneurs?] (p. 56). For the *flâneur* being and reading are synonymous. Wandering the city, as the founder of the Germanic tradition of *Spazieren/flânerie* Franz Hessel (1880-1941) recognized, becomes the occasion for encountering an environment in which "the street, and human faces, displays, window dressings, café terraces, trains, cars, and trees become letters that yield the words, sentences, and pages of a book that is always new. To correctly play the flaneur, you can't have anything too particular in mind" (*Walking in Berlin*, p. 133). One cannot read to the end of the "book" of the world for there is always another page to be both composed and read. The *flâneur* continues to read it out anyway. In this sense, the *flâneur* never occupies the position of any subject presumed to know who may be imparting something to those who do not know. We can begin again to appreciate just how ultimately non-didactic the equanimous subject truly is. Equanimity is the ground for an art of seeing and relating not founded on the "power-knowledge" nexus.

Flânerie amounts to the attentive tolerance of paradox. Its aim, the late literary critic Christopher Butler observes, is "to derive 'l'éternel du transitoire' ('the eternal from the transitory') and to see the 'poétique dans l'historique' ('the poetic in the historic')" (*Early Modernism*, p. 133). The eternal and the poetic are not achievable, let alone intelligible, without the transitory and the historical. The genuine *flâneur* subsumes everything with his roving, dispersed attention. While this orientation "equally regards everything as a sign, his eclectic, open attitude does not collapse into a mitigation of his attention. Instead, it resists this contemporary tendency in favor of an acute sharpening of his overall sense of attentiveness" (Gleber, *The Art of Taking a Walk*, p. 27). Lacking a formal methodology, the *flâneur* goes out to encounter, above all, a world of multiplying possibilities. Synchronic spatial sensibilities oscillate with those of diachrony, where, for the *flâneur* who moves at his own pace, vistas or horizons of experience are not reducible to static structures. For the equanimous subject of *flânerie*, there are only unfolding horizons. Here, the connection to Edmund Husserl's phenomenology is revealing: "Everywhere, apprehension includes in itself, by the mediation of a 'sense,' empty horizons of 'possible perceptions'; thus I can, at any given time, enter into a system of possible and, if I follow them up, actual, perceptual nexuses" (*Studies in the Phenomenology of Constitution*, p. 42). As things are taken up in perception, experience emerges as a harmonious flow, becoming the seeding ground for the appearance of further possibilities. It is equanimity that most fully lends continuity to the experience of the world. To be equanimous means encountering one thing, then another and another—this is how time enters experience—while paying attention to each thing in even measure—this is how space comes into being.

The continuity of the world necessarily remains elusive to the fixating observer primarily concerned with teleology and reducing reality to abstract concepts. Ferdinand Bloch in his *Types du boulevard* (1880) strikingly compared the Parisian ambulator to "an explorer, always ready to set off again, or, better like some marvelous alchemist of life" (cited in Cohen, *Profane Illumination*, p. 84). The poetics of rambling resides precisely in renewable encounters with a world that retains its enchantment. Through their holistic consciousness and participating identity, wanderers have a capacity to (re)enchant the world, one that is less a function of will than inhabiting an equanimous relationship with things that constitute the context of self-realization. Honoré Balzac, in *The Physiology of Marriage* (1829), insists that "to stroll is. . . the gastronomy of the eye. . . [It] is to enjoy, it is to assume a mindset, it is to admire the sublime pictures of unhappiness, of love, of joy, of graceful or grotesque portraits; it is to plunge one's vision to the depths of a thousand existences" (p. 29). The sublimity of engaging the world in this way hinges on an evenly hovering attention, with its expansive regard for the universal, one that is coextensive with its immediate power to dive deep into particulars. For the equanimous subject, strolling becomes the occasion for identity to unfold itself in the space between differences and contradictions, dispersion and particularity. The city walker is one type of traveler untroubled by difference since she commands an interdisciplinarity based upon open attention. The poet Charles Simic observes that "We call 'street wise' someone who knows how to look, listen, and interpret the teeming life around him. To walk down a busy city block is a critical act. Literature, aesthetics, and psychology all come into play" along with, I might add, myriad other disciplines (*The Monster*, p. 72). Such omnivalent—and omnivident—critical acts shift from block to block, their interpretative axes becoming features of the randomness inherent in the fluctuating environs of any journey. The peripatetic philosopher recognizes that her thought cannot take place from a fixed point but only along what Gibson calls "paths of observation," stretching itineraries of movement (*Ecological Approach*, p. 197). Thought, or the critical act, stays alive if it is kept from settling.

"The history of mankind," Franz Kafka mused, "is the instant between two strides taken by a traveler" (*The Blue Octavo Notebooks*, p. 16). In an important sense, without travel, without roaming, there can be no such thing as history. For something to "take place" it must in an important sense realize itself before it inevitably changes place. Before considering in the next section a complementary modality of equanimous existence—floating—I want to emphasize how crucial walking can be to inhabiting the world in receptive, participatory, and ultimately poised ways. In his paean to walking, Shiv Visvanathan depicts the activity as "a great equalizer and democracies' greatest act... Walking is the act of the body exploring itself as it traces the world." Involving, he reflects, "exploration, discovery, conversation, companionship, meditation, reflection, prayer...[It] is the beginning of civics and citizenship... Walking invites the sensorium, the collective repertoire of the senses... curiosity begins with walking and so does science. In walking you not only converse with the world but question it" ("In Praise of Walking," n. p.). Moving through the world in this salutary way unlocks aspects of identity: those that connect us through inquiry, immersion, deference, and dialogue. Augustine of Hippo (354-430) is said to have distilled the virtue of walking to a simple phrase (originally Diogenes's) in response to one of Zeno's paradoxes: *Solvitur ambulando* (It is solved by walking). Solving in this sense means productively framing the problem itself in terms of a fundamental and necessary wandering. "A philosophical problem," Wittgenstein declares, "has the form: 'I don't know my way about'" (*Philosophical Investigations*, I, 123).

Ukiyo Existence

> The clever man wears himself out, the wise man worries. But the man of no ability has nothing he seeks. He eats his fill and wanders idly about. Drifting like an unmoored boat, emptily and idly he floats along.
> —Zhuangzi, "Lie Yukou"

> I am a floating being with whom geniuses form spaces.
> —Peter Sloterdijk, *Bubbles*

> He lies down in moonlight and sleeps on the clouds.
> —*Shinsan zengoshū*, 4.193

Prior to the peaceful and prosperous Edo period (1603-1867) in Japan, a Buddhist term captured the relentless civil war and social turmoil that marked the Sengoku period (1467-1615). The term was *ukiyo* (憂き世; this sorrowful/miserable world), the site of ceaseless rebirth into a brief, uncertain life of suffering. By homophonous and rather ironic analogy, *ukiyo* assumed during the Edo period a lighter connotation: 浮き世 (this transient/floating world). This fleeting, floating world now signaled something of the emerging pleasure-seeking and decadence of urban life, where *ukiyo* corresponded to the entertainments of kabuki theater, sumo wrestling, geisha artists, and courtesans of the legal red-light districts (*yūkaku*). Woodblock prints known as *ukiyo-e* (floating world pictures), emerging in the late seventeenth century, celebrated scenes and figures of this beguiling buoyant world, and they remain one of the most popular and widely known forms of Japanese art. *Ukiyo* describes an imponderous realm, unbound by worry concerning the unknowable future or by the past and its depressing reach into the present. Asai Ryōi (c. 1612-91) devotes the first chapter of his *Ukiyo monogatari* (浮世物語, *Tales of the Floating World* [1666]) to defining *ukiyo*, distinguishing it from the earlier Buddhist samsaric appreciation:

> So we talk about the "world of sadness." So some say, but I think *ukiyo* means something else. Living in this world, we see good and bad everywhere, and it is all interesting. An inch ahead, all is darkness, and worrying about the future, which is no more important than a gourd shell, only makes us ill. Putting everything else aside, we can turn to the moon, the snow, flowers and red maple leaves, sing songs, and drink sake, drifting through life and amusing ourselves. The fact that there is no money in the house does not distress us. This not being caught up in anything, like a gourd floating in water, is called the floating world. Those who have experienced it felt it was "just like floating." (p. 25)

Ukiyo clearly amounts to more than the narrow pursuit of hedonism or amusement for amusement's sake. It involves possessing the psychological space for appreciating the mosaic of present experience, the "good and bad everywhere." In the Zen motif of the imperturbable floating gourd (discussed in chapter 4) resides *ukiyo*'s existential center: the equanimous subject is never overwhelmed because she dances upon the surface no matter which way she is pushed. *Ukiyo* represents nothing less than an open attitude toward life, taken up by subjects who are immune to getting entangled in the negative or the positive, the past or the future. The salutary effects of *ukiyo*, however, do not derive from some impervious neutrality or resignation (*akirame*) but rather from a lightness and ease of being in which existence is discoverable as enchanting.

Ukiyo stages an art of living, an exquisitely responsive relation to whatever presents itself in the moment. It allows for savoring that ataraxic space between attention being pulled retrospectively or aimed prospectively. As an instance of adaptation to the flow of things, immune to the imposition of will, *ukiyo* reminds us of how easily harmony may be undermined by analyzing and choosing. Inhabiting *ukiyo*, subjects relinquish choice and thus method, going with the immediate reality instead. In the *Zhuangzi*, Confucius learns the central message of *ukiyo* after observing a man miraculously staying afloat under a tremendous waterfall:

> Confucius was viewing the Lu waterfall, which plummets several hundred feet, whitening the waters for forty miles around, impassable to fishes and turtles. And yet he saw an old man swimming there in the torrent. Thinking the man had attempted suicide due to some suffering in his life, Confucius sent his disciples to run along the bank and try to pull him out. But the old man emerged several hundred paces downstream, walking along the bank singing, his hair streaming down his back. Confucius hurried after him and said, "I thought you were a ghost, but now I see you are a man! Do you have a course that allows you to tread upon the waters?" "No, I have no course," said the old man. [. . .] "I enter into the navels of the whirlpools and emerge with the surging eddies. I just follow the course of the water itself, without making any private one of my own. This is how I tread the waters." (Ziporyn, p. 80; cf. Graham, p. 136)

Confucius's attempts at interpreting the swimmer's subjectivity—first as suicidal, then as otherworldly—fail since such categories and valuations fix, or pin down, a subject who is naturally spontaneous and entirely unself-conscious. Swimming embodies the *ukiyo* condition of *arugamama* (things as they are), an existence beyond any conventional differentiation of self-other, existence-nonexistence. It is to embody a state where flowing patterns, figured here by crossfading whirlpools and eddies, make up a transitory world into which the subject is vitally and thoroughly integrated. The swimmer cannot drown since he perfectly harmonizes with the *dao* of the water itself. This attunement to things as they are in their changing relations with us sustains the light, care-free nature of *ukiyo*. As a Japanese *tanka* (short poem) renders this state: "I am floating and sinking among the waves indistinguishable from the mandarin duck or the sea gull" (Nakamura, *Ways of Thinking*, p. 555).

In the famous first lines of chapter 34 of the *Dao de jing*, subjectivity itself emerges as a process of *dao*, a ceaseless surrendering of the certainties of teleological existence to the unpremeditated and radically open: "Way-making (dao) is an easy-flowing stream / Which can run in any direction" (p. 130). The word for "flow(ing)" is *fan*, which also, significantly, means "float" or "drift." The dynamic world of way-making excludes appeal to purpose or design. To navigate the streaming world becomes then a matter of relinquishing a self that exerts itself to accomplish things. In this shifted subjectivity, the very spontaneity (自然 *zìrán*, to be so-of-itself) of all actions are experienced as what the contemplative Daoist tradition refers to as non-action (*wu wei*), that is, unforced action. Effortlessness is another way to describe floating where the lightness of *ukiyo* is a function of discovering the freedom in letting go of the ego's demands for mastery. When Liezi was under his master's tutelage—so the story goes—he initially stopped himself from thinking in terms of right and wrong, then, after greater realization, he accepted the concepts but also understood that he could not distinguish between them. Eventually Liezi reached the stage where he accepted the radical uncertainty of the very origin of right and wrong, and so by not finding their origin internally or externally, all his thoughts and words became utterly spontaneous. At this point, he describes himself as starting to float:

> Only then, when I had come to the end of everything inside me and outside me, my eyes became like my ears, my ears like my nose, my nose like my mouth; everything was the same. My mind concentrated and my body relaxed, bones and flesh fused completely, I did not notice what my body leaned against and my feet trod, I drifted with the wind

East or West, like a leaf from a tree or a dry husk, and never knew whether it was the wind that rode me or I that rode the wind. (*The Book of Lieh-tzu*, pp. 36-37)

When all distinctions are transcended, a state of absolute equanimity may be reached where a new kind of freedom and lightness of being is found in surrendering to the interconnectedness of all things. This notion of discovering liberty, symbolized by drifting here and there, in the (inter)dependence of things, runs counter to our usual notion of freedom that glamorizes independence. The more independent we take ourselves to be, Liezi is demonstrating, the more mired we are in fixed mental structures (Jp. *hakarai*) and so the less capable we are of letting go of self-focused mentalities (Jp. *gashu*; Skt. *ātmagrāha*).

The person who is open to the interdependence of all things and fully attunes to transience begins to feel weightless. It has been said that when the philosopher D. T. Suzuki was asked what it is like to experience *satori*—apprehending the true nature of reality—he replied, "It's like everyday experience—but about two inches off the ground" (Watts, "The Doctrine of Emptiness," p. 156; cf. *The Way of Zen*, p. 22). With the realization that there is no isolatable agency that controls the stream of experience, you begin to float. A fine illustration of this is found in a collection of biographies of various Zen masters, where Tōzan Sōkaku Rōshi of Empuku-ji recounts that, as an attendant to Sōhan Genhō (Shōun; 1848-1922), he once accompanied him to Kyoto Station when Shōun was embarking on a lecture tour. Tōzan secured first-class tickets, but his master was nowhere to be found. A station attendant had mistakenly escorted Shōun to the third-class car. Eventually Tōzan found Rōshi seated in a small corner seat. "Rōshi, the first-class car is this way," explained Tōzan. "Oh, is that so?" replied Shōun, untroubled by any inconvenience. As they made their way to the first-class car, Tōzan described the Rōshi's exiting figure as "floating without a care" (Kishida, *Hōmyaku gendai zen sho retsudan*, p. 318). To have what we might call an *ukiyo* sensibility is a hallmark of equanimous existence, and its wisdom is tied to poise, movement, and perspicacity. In Aldous Huxley's novel *Island* (1962), Susila recalls the foundational advice she was given as a young girl: "You've got to learn to do everything lightly. Think lightly, act lightly, feel lightly. Yes, feel lightly, even though you're feeling deeply. Just let things happen and lightly cope with them" (p. 243). Equanimity never equates to passivity; it is to feel deeply, as the immediate occasion requires. All the while being like "moving clouds, flowing water" (*kōun ryūsui*), not stopping in anything whatsoever, equanimity handles the currents of existence completely at ease and without obstruction (*jizai muge*).

In the Western tradition, levitation has a special history in relation to a kind of pure and unimpeded identity. Tied to saintliness, levitation was taken to be a clear sign of sacred subjectivity. The early Christian and medieval anti-pagan tradition, beginning with a no less authoritative figure than Augustine of Hippo, attempted to distinguish among divine miracles, natural wonders, and human marvels. Augustine used the example of a floating pagan idol—suspended by lodestone—in order to emphasize the error of confusing human artifice with holy miracle (*Concerning the City of God against the Pagans*, 21.7.977-78). In the medieval anti-Muslim tradition, Muhammad's sacred identity was impugned by the claim that his tomb floated, but again only by magnetic artifice (e.g., Embrico of Mainz's *Vita Mahumeti*, pp. 487-88; Walter of Compiegne's *Otia de Machomete*, p. 327). The miracle of levitation, as evidence of legitimate divinity, was reserved for Christian saints' lives. Examples in the hagiographic literature are plentiful, among which some are especially memorable: praying Mary levitates in Hildebert of Lavardin's (ca. 1056-1133) *Vita Beatae Mariae Aegyptiacae* (*Patrologia Latina* 171: 1327D); Mary of Loreto is associated with a floating house; and other famous levitating saints include Francis of Assisi (ca. 1181-1226), Teresa of Ávila (1515-82), Joseph of Cupertino (1603–63), and Pio of Pietrelcina (1887-1968). These miracles are remarkable for what they suggest about the intimate connection between elevated awareness, transcendence of self or ego, and the peculiar quality of weightlessness. Liberatory and visionary states are those in which identity appears so radically revisable that it may inhabit even something as fantastic as microgravity with ease.

The trajectory of increasing awareness and receptivity is one directed toward the feeling of weightlessness. In a passage tracing an episode of intense mystical absorption, naturalist and author Annie Dillard describes a process of peaking identification with her natural surroundings, as she walks home "faster and faster," feeling herself becoming "weightless," until finally declaring, "I am light. I am prayer." At this apex of receptivity, she "floats" among other spectators at the bay's edge, where she has a vision of Christ's baptism by John, sensing that each drop of water on the former's body contains, like a hologram, a complete world in itself (*Holy the Firm*, pp. 64-65). The consolation she would find in this vision of fluidity, buoyancy, and light derives from an attitude of utter security (L. *se* + *cura*, without care, concern), allowing for freely contemplating our place in the inscrutable universe. Another American naturalist, Thoreau, found that he too could ponder the universe best from the effortless place of floating. In an early journal entry, he writes: "If one would reflect, let him embark on some placid stream, and float with the current" (*Journal*, 3 November 1837, vol. 7, p. 8). The next year, Thoreau recorded, in a remarkable passage, an experience that apparently was readily available to him:

> If with closed ears and eyes I consult consciousness for a moment, immediately are all walls and barriers dissipated, earth rolls from under me, and I float, by the impetus derived from the earth and the system, a subjective, heavily laden thought, in the midst of an unknown and infinite sea, or else heave and swell like a vast ocean of thought, without rock or headland, where are all riddles solved, all straight lines making there their two ends to meet, eternity and space gambolling familiarly through my depths. I am from the beginning, knowing no end, no aim. No sun illumines me, for I dissolve all lesser lights in my own intenser and steadier light. I am a restful kernel in the magazine of the universe. (*Journal*, 13 August 1838, vol. 7, pp. 53-54)

The imagery here is striking. Unanchored by the senses, consciousness, which here is to say subjectivity, floats and flows in absolute expansiveness. Who (or what) Thoreau is, in this meditative moment, is a function of internal and external landscapes vitally integrating and interanimating. The determinant effect is mimetic, where, as he says in a letter of 21 July, 1841, his identity is nothing but "nature looking into nature" (*Familiar Letters*, p. 42). Water, mind, and the universe become mutually reflective. He would find in such reciprocity the peace of equanimous vision: "water, indeed, reflects heaven because my mind does; such is its own serenity, its transparency" (*Journal*, 31 August 1851, vol. 8, p. 437). As the mind floats without aim, without attachment, it enjoys the freedom necessary for integrating the universal and the particular. Thoreau becomes pure potentiality, one seed, harbored in a universal storehouse, whose fate it is to illumine the floating world: "The oldest nature is elastic. I just felt myself raised upon the swell of the eternal ocean, which came rolling this way to land" (*Journal*, 1850, vol. 8, p. 18).

Middle Beings

> Life is a bridge. Cross over it, but build no house on it.
> —Indian proverb

In the first chapter, I pointed to an interesting word in the Buddhist tradition often translated as equanimity: *tatramajjhattatā*, whose literal meaning is "(being) there in the middle." The present section considers the significance of this middle position for what it tells us about subjects in the midst. Being forever somewhere in the midst of everything describes existence unhampered by dualistic ideations, which, in the Zen tradition, is referred to as "leaving no trace" (Jp. *mosshōseki*). One cannot leave a trace when there is no side to adhere to (as over against another side) or, finally, when self and world are perfectly, fluidly concurrent. In the words of Ch'an Master Shitou Xiqian (Jp. Sekito Kisen, 700-90), "a sage has no self, yet there is nothing that is not himself" (Cleary, *Book of Serenity*, p. 391). The sage possesses no separate, private self since her only condition is one of ongoing reciprocation with the changing world. This conception of dynamic selfhood is, as we have seen at various points, hardly confined to Eastern philosophies. The Czech author

Karel Čapek (1890-1938) summed up the composure entailed in affinity with the world: "*Similia similibus*: we apprehend the world through what we are ourselves, and in apprehending the world we discover ourselves. Thank God, now we are home again; we are of the same stuff as that plurality of the world; we are at home in that spaciousness and infinity, and we can respond to those numerous voices" ("Afterword," *Three Novels*, p. 319). Through this experience of mimesis, an intimate immensity is discovered, situating identity and at the same time dialogically opening it up.

One thinker whose general method involved a dialogic approach to the always-existing possibilities of reciprocity between private and universal worlds is the sociologist Georg Simmel (1858-1918). In his last work, *The View of Life* (1918), he advances, through a series of aphorisms, a view of human life and, with it, human freedom that situates them in a middle position. "I locate myself," he declares, "in the concept of life as though in the center," between the ego and idea, subject and object, person and cosmos ("Journal Aphorisms," p. 163). With this middle position "granted to us," he says, "we are neither the masters nor the slaves of existence, and precisely on that account we are free" (ibid.). A crucial element of the sublime freedom of equanimous existence lies precisely in the recognition that only from the middle does genuine possibility arise. It is here, Simmel suggests, that our genuine humanity may be found:

> Man as middle-being. Man can exist only in a middle region between spiritual constriction and spiritual breadth, with neither too little nor too much knowing. That is why an old person finds it so difficult—even impossible—to live any longer: he knows too much. Illusion is a middle ground between knowing and not-knowing, an as-if for the practical. Indeed, even error is a similar middle ground, utterly different from not-knowing-at-all. However, to know that one could know more than he knows—that is something characteristically human. Man's doubt is what makes him human. ("Journal Aphorisms," p. 166)

Avoiding dogma, equanimity embraces, without reducing itself to, fiction or "illusion." It spans the broad middle ground of possibility. This is the territory of the "as-if" that the philosopher Hans Vaihinger (1852-1933) saw as affording expedient "transit-points" for thinking and being (*The Philosophy of 'As if'*, p. 155). Knowing too much and, conversely, knowing nothing are states of disequanimity since both place the subject beyond the field of doubt and error. In order to have doubt, one has to know just enough, while knowing too much removes all doubt. Equanimous identity, accentuating the provisional, finds space for doubting such that error can be tolerated.

In the Daoist ontology, the so-called Genuine Human Being or Consummate Person relates to the world in a state of open suspense: "trembling, like ice that is about to melt; unassuming, like a piece of wood not yet carved; vacant, like a valley; formless, like troubled waters" (Okakura, *The Book of Tea*, pp. 27-28). Being in doubt is one way to signify this expectant state of receptivity and pure process. Not suspiciousness or diffidence, the adaptive kind of doubt inhabiting equanimity figures identity as something *as yet* to be created. Just as equanimity is by its nature always ongoing, unfinished, so the subject is forever a work in progress. For Emerson, the pluralist and philosopher of process, it was insincerity rather than doubt that made most sense as an attitude for middle being. "I am," he writes, "always insincere, as always knowing there are other moods" ("Nominalist and Realist," p. 401). And, so, whatever distinguishes us is no more than a pose at a given moment, a stage in a natural process of change:

> We fancy men as individuals; so are pumpkins; but every pumpkin in the field goes through every point of pumpkin history. The rabid democrat, as soon as he is senator and rich man, has ripened beyond possibility of sincere radicalism, and unless he can resist the sun, he must be conservative the remainder of his days" (ibid., p. 400)

What looks like the antipodal change from radical to conservative derives only from a rich process, an inevitable unfolding, so Emerson seems to be suggesting. Yet if it is the *dao* of human nature to change, then who we are at any moment is merely one characterological destination, such as conservative contraction, that then serves as a possible point of origin for a new quality, always part of an open, dynamic process.

Perhaps nowhere is this phenomenon of subjective transformation more clearly illustrated than in the story of Ebenezer Scrooge of

Dickens's *A Christmas Carol* (1843). Scrooge's narrow acquisitive drive has destroyed any capacity for equanimous vision. The extent of his contraction and isolation is profound: "a squeezing, wrenching, grasping, scraping, clutching, covetous, old sinner!... self-contained and solitary as an oyster" (p. 10). Scrooge, possessing "little of what we call fancy [imagination] about him" (p. 16), receives an education by the three spirits in the power of expanded vision. The Ghost of Christmas Past, for instance, recalls him to the time when, as a schoolboy, he was deeply and joyously moved by romance and adventure tales such as *The Arabian Nights* and *Robinson Crusoe*. Each Ghost guides Scrooge further toward a rounded out view of the world, where being in the midst of scenes of the past, present, and future offers alternative visions of his place in the cosmos. His transforming wisdom is rooted in awareness of the interdependence of persons that transcends those of the cold, objectifying mercantile world. Scrooge ultimately learns less about goodness or kindness than about the fundamental capacity to imagine the range of human relations as comprising more than merely reified, alienated ones. In short, he receives an education not in ethics but in equanimous imagination, the basis for open-heartedness and -mindedness. Scrooge signals his transformation by whooping that he feels "as light as a feather" (p. 78). Having gained a sense of the buoyancy of the middle, humility emerges choicelessly, naturally, on its own. It rests upon a kind of newly recognized internal poise, and is unforced by exercises of deliberation or will. Indeed, as Colin Wilson perfectly summarized it, "It is not [Scrooge's] will that is the trouble; it is the way that he has allowed his imagination to go dead" (*New Pathways*, p. 221).

Scrooge recovers a subjectivity from which he was estranged rather than one he had lost altogether. The arc of his life culminated in a disavowal of his place in the middle. He reached that point where he could no longer even imagine it. Part of the function of the famous Hindu expression *tat tvam asi* (that's how you are) is precisely to remind one that identity is inescapably intermediate— you are nothing (or nowhere) other than (in) the middle of Everything (*brahman*). It is, crucially, an identity provided with the ongoing space for potential self-renewal. When existence receptively inhabits the rhythms of life, spontaneity replaces fixity, and whatever has moved to the extremes is tempered. The first lines of the dharma transmission verse by the 22nd Indian Patriarch Manorhita record this state of being: "The heart flows with the cycles of the ten-thousand things, / These cycles are truly mysterious. / Follow the flow and know, / The True Nature is without joy or sorrow" (Daoyuan, *Records of the Transmission of the Lamp*, vol. 1, p. 127). This verse captures the essence of equanimous being—one may, of course, experience joy or sorrow in a given moment but, alive to the vital flow of total reality, there can be no getting stuck in, or identifying with, either state. Before reflecting in the next section on the nature of generative existence, I offer an observation of Simmel's that resonates through the present book:

> Among the great categorical distinctions that divide people into two principal groups is the question of whether one is immobile [*starr*] or vital. Fichte's identification of inertia [*Trägheit*] as the radical evil of humans lies entirely within this sense: for fixity [*Starrheit*] seems more and more to me the decisive negation of our life-value. ("Journal Aphorisms," p. 167)

Generative Being

> What is the work of works for man if not to establish, in and by each one of us, an absolutely original center in which the universe reflects itself in a unique and inimitable way?
> —Teilhard de Chardin, *The Phenomenon of Man*

Simmel's proposal that fixity is the negation of vitality implies that the richness of our "life-value" lies in the inexhaustibility of its possibilities. These possibilities multiply the more supplely life-value reflects the changing universe in its mystery and novelty. To achieve the "absolutely original center" that Teilhard identifies as the principal work of human identity involves finding that momentary point of balance in relation to whatever the universe presents. This subjective fulcrum is utterly originative in the sense that it renews itself through every encounter with the cosmos. It embodies that state of equipoise between value and loss, the interanimating products of an equanimous orientation. Dainin Katagiri describes the originative axis as "Life at the pivot of nothingness [that] is nothing but motion and process" (*Each Moment is the Universe*, p. 80). To be at the pivot is to move seamlessly and ceaselessly, where dynamism abolishes the gap between subject and object, self and world. This is not a question of merger, of mystical union to the point of identity loss, but one of actively and flexibly integrating what is typically figured as separate. Consider the traditional Japanese house whose basic architecture integrates opposed existential categories such as structure and flow, interior and exterior. Such a house presents multiple options, with portable folding screens (*byōbu*) and sliding partitions (*fusuma*) functioning as room dividers, along with sliding exterior wall panels (*shōji*) serving as doors or windows. Several rooms, for instance, can be transformed into one with the removal or opening of partitions, just as *shōji* can be thrown back partly or completely to open up the entire house to the garden. In marked contrast to stationary walls, the built-in provisional nature of the Japanese house allows for ongoing combinations of the bounded and the boundless. Traditional Japanese houses, as *loci* of possible events, afford and reflect the generative subjectivity of their inhabitants.

Equanimity allows for tuning into the total field of possibilities, or affordances, that both implicitly and explicitly shape present experience. For the subjects inhabiting them, the different atmospheres of Japanese and Western houses offer distinctive horizons of potential attunement. Some buildings or rooms feel more—or less—comfortable, pleasurable, or inviting than others based precisely on the judgements that form immediately as intuitive readings of spatial ambiances. Emotive and perceptual impressions of a particular space or an entire landscape arise before their conscious deduction from details. That is, intellectual understanding and comprehension of details occur subsequently to the grasping of ambiance. Experiences of atmosphere are pre-reflective. The existential implications of this are profound: the essence of experience is immediate, embodied, emotive, and largely choiceless. As Dewey points out, the holistic intensity of atmospheres does not survive cognitive penetrability:

> The total overwhelming impression comes first, perhaps in a seizure by a sudden glory of the landscape, or by the effect upon us of entrance into a cathedral when dim light, incense, stained glass and majestic proportions fuse in one indistinguishable whole. We say with truth that a painting strikes us. There is an impact that precedes all definite recognition of what it is about. (*Art as Experience*, p. 50)

Being subject to the authority of atmosphere or ambiance takes us out of the insulated sphere of our interiority. In one of the most famous passages of Rainer Maria Rilke's *The Notebooks of Malte Laurids Brigge* (1910), the involuted protagonist recognizes the traces of domestic life that a demolished house has left on the party wall shared with the adjoining buildings on each side (pp. 46-48). Fragmentary wall traces—peeling wallpaper, remnants of plumbing and gas light piping—create a total ambiance, evoking an affectively-charged range of sights and odors. They serve for the young man as crucial signs by which he regenerates and clarifies essential aspects of his autobiography. The awakening of atmospheric feelings becomes the occasion for the renovation of subjectivity.

In the case of Rilke's architectural imagery or the Japanese house, what emerges through equanimity is a kind of syncing up of the subject and the external that begins from the outside. Contact with the exterior world alternately undoes and reinforces subjectivity, and the acceptance of this fluctuating state of affairs places identity in a state of perpetual becoming or generation. Indeed, philosopher-psychoanalyst Julia Kristeva conceives of the subject as forever *en procès*, an expression that translates doubly as "in process" and "on trial" ("The Subject in Process," p. 142). Such a processual subject, rather than "representing a reality posed in advance," is instead richly "experimenting" through "immersion" in the signs and social realities conditioning her existence (ibid.). Generativity is naturally inherent, the product of our embeddedness in the dynamic universe, as the Greek philosopher-historian Plutarch (c. 45-120 CE) once observed:

No one stays still, or is a single person, but we become many, with matter whirling and sliding round a single image and a shared mould.... Each of us is compounded of hundreds of different factors which arise in the course of our experience, a heterogeneous collection combined in a haphazard way." (*On the E at Delphi* 392B, in Sorabji, *Emotion*, p. 248; 393B, *Moralia*, p. 247)

In Plutarch's affirmation of the multiplex, motile subject lies a latent assurance. That is, through a balance of the unitary and the fragmentary, the existent and the random, the continuous and the cyclical, we are axiologically at one. The biological truth of this, as the sociologist and theologian Andrew Greeley (1928-2013) sees it, relates to the way each of us already exists, in the most fundamentally vital way, "at one with the hydrogen-nitrogen-oxygen cycles, the processes of growth and decay, day and night, autumn and spring, sleep and waking, death and rebirth. In the ecstatic interlude, we are taken possession of by that which we already possess" (*Ecstasy*, p. 66). For Greeley, the "ecstatic interlude" hinges on making broader contact with "The Way Things Are," that is, allowing subjectivity to be inaugurated by the fully ordinary (ibid., p. 45). In this episode of acute awareness, the most trenchant moments of equanimity emerge.

The perfectly ordinary aspects of identity are precisely those which are most readily overlooked, discounted, or misapprehended. As I described it in the last chapter, equanimity, as a mode of apprehending, encounters identity and difference as a rhythm of systole (the striking or novel) and diastole (the tuned-out or familiar). Affirming one phase of the pole at the expense of the other results in a partial view, while insensibility to the tension that continually exists between them denies change or generativity. Generative being becomes then a matter of the equipoise inherent in relations to self and world as they unfurl in the present. On its way to equanimity, generative being abandons the ego's partiality and suspends its projections in favor of scopic awareness and acceptance. The course of such transformation is captured in a fine seed story, an apparently Chinese folktale retold by Dulce Rodrigues and titled "The Cracked Pot":

An elderly Chinese woman had two large pots, each hung on the ends of a pole which she carried across her neck. One of the pots had a crack in it while the other pot was perfect and always delivered a full portion of water. At the end of the long walks from the stream to the house, the cracked pot arrived only half full. For a full two years this went on daily, with the woman bringing home only one and a half pots of water. Of course, the perfect pot was proud of its accomplishments. But the poor cracked pot was ashamed of its own imperfection, and miserable that it could only do half of what it had been made to do. After two years of what it perceived to be bitter failure, it spoke to the woman one day by the stream. "I am ashamed of myself, because this crack in my side causes water to leak out all the way back to your house." The old woman smiled, "Did you notice that there are flowers on your side of the path, but not on the other pot's side? That's because I have always known about your flaw, so I planted flower seeds on your side of the path, and every day while we walk back, you water them. For two years I have been able to pick these beautiful flowers to decorate the table. Without you being just the way you are, there would not be this beauty to grace the house."

With the two large pots connected at the ends of a pole, it is implied from the outset that any difference between them is not truly dichotomous but rather continuous. Yet the cracked pot, regarding itself in the debasing mirror of shame, cannot escape a singular viewpoint tied to its absolute difference from the other pot, its delivery of only half as much water. Ultimately, the cracked pot's narrow view of utility will be replaced by an equanimous vision of the generative power of its leak, its putative defect. The old woman's smile, itself significantly a crack or opening, marks the turning point in the tale: self-focus may now give way to field awareness, psychological rigidity to flexibility, false consciousness to insight, and judgement to acceptance. The notion of imperfection generating beauty requires a mental attitude tolerant of contradiction where either-or is displaced by both-and vision. This new kind of creative seeing is above all a new kind of subjectivity, one resting upon the joyful liberty that comes from transcending the false self.

The cracked pot misrecognized its own identity by failing to see the environment in which it is embedded and, with that, all the ways it shapes and is shaped by that milieu. The old woman recalled the pot to a state of equanimous being, a sort of field existence. Without equanimity, the risk is always that we misrecognize ourselves—and others. In the absence of a flexible, processual view of experience, a rich understanding of the larger picture is unfortunately forfeited, and, along with it, the capacity to locate and appreciate the particulars within that frame. Diagnostic labels, in mental health for example, regularly militate against situating particular features of identity more broadly in terms of how a total life develops or flows. The real utility of labels must reside in their being starting rather than ending points. Through them—the particularized—we may join, and even multiply, the field of subjectivities but instead what often occurs is fixation at the point of the label. Once isolated from the field, all things are subject to exclusive, often partisan, judgments. In the story of the cracked pot, we see how such circumscription may dissolve with flexible identificatory relations across opposed qualities, such as flaws and beauty, deficiency and surplus. Only equanimity ensures unimpeded access to the complexity of foci beyond ego-generated dualities, as in the Zen saying, "Dispense with the small mind called 'me,' and lo! A billion worlds, no obstructions" (Tsuchiya, *Zenrin Segoshū*, p. 216). The path for regenerating identity necessarily goes through the multiple.

There is a transformative moment in the life of Ram Dass (1931-2019) that has suggestive parallels to the story of the cracked pot. In 1967, Ram Dass, author of the wildly popular *Be Here Now* (1971), was encouraged by his Hindu guru Neem Karoli Baba to leave India and return to the United States in order to teach. Faced with his guru's straightforward message to "Love people and feed them," Ram Dass balked, protesting that his spiritual imperfection and impurities disqualified him from such a humane mission. His guru then stood up, and began circling Ram Dass slowly and thoughtfully, regarding him from all angles. After he sat down again, Neem Karoli Baba looked him deeply in the eyes, and concluded simply, "I see no imperfections" (see Ram Dass, *Polishing the Mirror*, pp. xxv-vi; Kornfield, *No Time*, p. 99). Imperfection, as in the story of the pot, is nothing more than a function of partiality, a result of focusing on the particular rather than the whole. Perhaps this is the essential meaning of the love that Ram Dass, upon his return to the U.S., would teach to millions for the next five decades—that is, to subsume everything to love necessitates seeing universally, totally, from all sides, with equanimity. Anything less than this imperils spiritual generativity of the vital kind that returns the person to a state of wholeness and perfection from which they have never actually departed.

In other words, perfection is always there to be seen but only from perspectives that fully appreciate generativity. Here then is one of the truths of generative being from the point of view of equanimity: natural processes, such as maturation, only *appear* to produce in the subject an identity or character that was not there before. As Rabindranath Tagore suggests, living processes are not in the business of turning the unfinished into the finished:

> A young friend of mine comes to me this morning to inform me that it is his birthday and that he has just reached his nineteenth year. The distance between my age and his is great, and yet when I look at him it is not the incompleteness of his life which strikes me, but something which is complete in his youth. And in this differs the thing which grows, from the thing which is being made. A building in its unfinished stage is only too evidently unfinished. But in life's growth every stage has its perfection, the flower as well as the fruit. (*Thought Relics*, p. 98)

To appreciate how a flower grows, from a seed, from the inside out, as opposed to a building constructed from the outside in, is to recognize the perfection characteristic of each moment in the process of metamorphosis. We grant an organism its completeness, its perfection, only when we ourselves first possess what Gordon Allport called the "primary virtue" of adopting "an impartial and objective attitude toward oneself." In his 1937 textbook launching the science of personality, Allport insisted that "if any trait of personality is intrinsically desirable, it is the disposition and ability to see oneself in perspective" (*Personality*, p. 422). This capacity to see oneself equanimously is precisely analogous to how we may view others in the world by gaining perspective from multiple sides, with spaciousness, like Neem Karoli Baba revolving around Ram

Dass. One thoughtful proponent of seeing oneself from manifold angles is the psychoanalyst Michael Eigen. He identifies one of the key functions of psychotherapy as the cultivation of what he terms "a more democratic psyche," that is, an open and flexible mind able to entertain multiple viewpoints. He contrasts the democratic psyche to one of "tyranny" of the kind a person with rage or hatred would possess. The hope, he writes, is that "one learns to walk around oneself, akin to walking around a sculpture and seeing it from different points of view" (*Eigen in Seoul*, p. 12).

When the self becomes in such a way panoramically visible, it enters a state of being where imperatives of reactivity, along with defensive or aggressive egoic investments, may be surrendered. The observer is no longer only external to the observed. As the temporary object of a non-coercive or non-constraining panopticism, subjectivity becomes pure response-ability. All pretense fades. Generativity emerges here, as reflected by the Hindu term *moksha* (liberation) in its rudimentary meaning, through experiences of deliverance from the blockages created by epistemological division and ontological estrangement. Interestingly, Emerson thought that the people most able to see and express reality as it is, "from within," he indicated, rather than from without, are "the lowly and the simple" ("The Oversoul," p. 246; 247). As Emerson saw it, the unsophisticated person, who "dwells in the hour that is now," possesses an "energy" of union and contact that "comes to whomsoever will put off what is foreign and proud; it comes as insight; it comes as serenity" (ibid., p. 247). Emerson's point was not to encourage a romanticizing of the pastoral but to carefully consider the value of deferential relationships with the world. Such multiple relationships, in their respectful attention to everything, suspend distinctions. In this serene situation, openness and impartiality replace defensiveness and discrimination. Subjectivity, consistent with Kobori (Nanrei) Sōhaku's (1918-92) metaphoric definition of the workings of Zen, is allowed to "return to the basic simplicity of the undyed fabric" (Austin, *Zen and the Brain*, p. 61). This unpretentious state embodies calm potentiality.

Images of subjective simplicity and equanimity are pivotal to the Zen tradition with its philosophy of the transcendence of all dualities through present-centered awareness. Of the many memorable images employed in both Daoist and Zen traditions, perhaps the one that points most clearly to the state without discrimination or attachment is "the True Person without any title." This enigmatic expression, among Ch'an Master Linji's (Jp. Rinzai; d. 866) best known, is usually translated as "True Man (or Person) with no rank" (Ch. *wuwei zhenren*; Jp. *mu-i no shinnin*) (*The Zen Teachings of Master Lin-chi*, p. 13). Borrowed from Zhuangzi, this image represents the person *free from any obstacles* (Jp. *muge*), the subject whose generativity is never blocked. Linji's teacher, Huangbo Xiyun (d. 850), referred to this as cultivating a state of non-dependence, in which there is "nothing on which to lay hold, nothing on which to rely, nothing in which to abide" (*The Zen Teaching of Huang-po*, p. 38). Generativity is equivalent to being unhindered by attachment to the binaries conventionally used to split up the world into neat categories. The True Person with no rank, whom "they can never bind or fetter," occupies the space between and prior to consensus (binary) reality and absolute (empty) reality (*The Zen Teachings of Master Lin-chi*, p. 49). In Linji's famous expression, we encounter, according to the philosopher Masao Abe (1915-2006), the living concretization of the "Ultimate seer" in the here and now prior to any duality of past and future, seer and seen. Here, the finite and the infinite (Emptiness) coalesce ("True Person and Compassion," p. 74).

So, in less mystical language, what kind of ideal subject is the "True Person with no rank," this "Ultimate seer" who integrates the finite with the infinite? There are, I think, two deeply interrelating features to emphasize. The first corresponds to the reiterated description of such a subject as "doing nothing" or having nothing to do since her existence is "simple, direct, with nothing mixed in" (*The Zen Teachings of Master Lin-chi*, p. 24; 69). This doing nothing is of a special kind. It is not apathy or dormancy but the ongoing generativity, even spontaneity, that issues from realizing, however momentarily, complete ease and freedom without hindrance (Jp. *jizai muge*). Wonderfully encapsulated in the Zen phrase "when the mind is at ease [*buji*], one bed is wide enough" is the notion of allowing for the sheer breadth of the perfectly composed mind (Kusumoto, *Zengo Nyūmon*, p. 285). The second feature, then, is the state of *buji* itself, the tranquility that comes with achieving equilibrium, often expressed as the peace of having returned to a perspective unblemished by striving and grasping. There is a story in the *Śūraṅgama Sūtra* (vol. 4, pp. 101-4), to which Linji briefly refers, about a young man named Yajñadatta who looks in a mirror one morning and, to his horror, cannot see his face. He rashly concludes that he must be missing his head, and so, thinking he must be some kind of spirit or ghost, he runs all over town in order to recover his head. In the *sūtra* commentary, Yajñadatta's plight is used to illustrate the actions of a deluded mind. In Linji's reading, however, what is crucial is the fact that when Yajñadatta "had put a stop to his seeking mind, he found he was perfectly all right" (*The Zen Teachings of Master Lin-chi*, p. 27). Likewise, the True Person with no rank enjoys the serenity of the perfection she already possesses, without ever lapsing into inert passivity. "To live in complete inward and therefore outward tranquility," Jiddu Krishnamurti (1895-1986) observes, "does not mean that we shall vegetate or stagnate. On the contrary, we shall become dynamic, vital, full of energy" (*Freedom from the Known*, p. 61).

In the next chapter, I offer four more profiles of the dynamic and vital subjects of equanimous existence. By sustaining postures of equilibrium, they are immune to the agitation the world so often produces.

CHAPTER 7
SUBJECTS OF EQUANIMITY
With the Possible

> If I am not for myself, who will be? And if I am only for myself, what am I? And if not now, when?
> —Hillel, *Pirke Avot*, I:14

Continuing to consider equanimity as a mode of vibrant being, this chapter looks at four dynamic figures or flexible types—the "priest without borders," the "person with belly," the hunter, and the playful person (*homo ludens*). They have been enduring objects of philosophical speculation and felicitous meditation in both Eastern and Western traditions. Each has been seen in its own way as embodying dimensions of the fluid and processual character of lived experience. Together, they exemplify the balancing and coordination that issue from harmony with the interdependent workings of the contexts in which they emerge. They refigure the apparently determinative factuality of this world as being comprised of nothing other than starting points from which the truest potential for resonating with it may be realized. They are figures of the possible. And, finally, they point to more ways equanimity dissolves the excesses or extremes of dogmatism, certainty, and finality. No single subject position outlined in this or the previous chapter can possibly exhaust the manifold nature of equanimity as it may be lived. Nonetheless, each is remarkable for the clues it offers for how to embody the existential space necessary for appreciating that, as Ortega y Gasset neatly observed, "Life is many-sided.... Every moment and every place opens different roads to us...life is a permanent crossroads, a constant perplexity" (*Man and People*, p. 45). How to manage this ambit of incredible possibility demands a continual flexibility of being, the willingness to experiment at any time with subjectivity, with our place in the world. The equanimous subject is clearly recognizable in those moments of detachment from the determinative and equally the strictly utilitarian and familiar.

The Priest without Borders

> The Great Way is without difficulty, just avoid picking and choosing.
> —Shibayama Zenkei, *Zenrin kushū*

The *Aṭṭhakavagga* ("Chapter of Eights"), a small collection of *suttas* within the earliest stratum of the Pāli Canon of Theravāda Buddhism, contains some striking verses inaugurating a novel kind of identity:

> Wrong-minded people do voice opinions
> as do truth-minded people too.
> When an opinion is stated, the sage is not drawn in—
> there's nothing arid about the sage.
> Nowhere does a lucid one
> hold contrived views about is or is not.
> How could he succumb to them,
> having let go of illusions and conceit? He's uninvolved.
> He does not take up or discard any view—
> he has shaken them all off, right here.
> Dropping one, you clutch the next—
> urged ahead by self-concern
> you reject and adopt opinions
> as a monkey lets go of a branch and seizes another.
> The priest without borders
> doesn't seize on what he's known or beheld.
> Not passionate, not dispassionate,
> he doesn't posit anything as 'ultimate.'
> He lets go of one position without taking another—
> he's not defined by what he knows.
> Nor does he join a dissenting faction—
> he assumes no view at all.
> He's not lured into the blind alleys

of is and is not, this world and the next—
for he lacks those commitments
that make people ponder and seize hold of teachings.
(*Sutta-Nipāta*, 780, 786, 787, 791, 795, 800, 801; cf. Norman,
pp. 104-7; trans. Batchelor, "Greek Buddha," pp. 202-3)

This passage from an early Buddhist text emphasizes the liberation marking an existence that cannot be considered "arid" or barren at the same time that it seizes upon nothing. To be a "priest without borders" apparently involves evading all binaries, slipping past epistemological lures, and escaping existential *culs-de-sac*. Enjoyment of total flexibility is the priest's hallowed privilege. She can be any- and everywhere, with no boundaries, no insides or outsides, formed by convention, precisely because her ego is not compulsively swinging, as in the image of the clutching monkey, from one illusion to the next. In my reading of the verses, then, to assume "no view at all" may be understood as assuming *no single or fixed view*. That is, no views are adopted simply from the expediency of self-interest or the weight of opinion or convention. What emerges is the crucial difference between letting go of views themselves and letting go of attachment to views, a difference I take to be definitive for equanimity. Equanimity here is closest to the attitude of skepticism, which, for our immediate purposes, is less a theoretical (e.g., epistemological) posture than a way of being-in-the-world of the sort prescribed in the Greek and Hellenistic worlds as a way or path of well-being (*eudaimonia*).

Indeed, the Buddhist scholar and teacher Stephen Batchelor sees the attitude expressed in this passage as one of "skepticism" (*After Buddhism*, p. 22), and links it elsewhere specifically to Pyrrhonian skepticism (see "Greek Buddha," pp. 202-3). The resonances of certain strands and layers of Buddhist thought with Pyrrhonism are indeed striking, with both seeing tranquility or inner peace (*ataraxia*) as an ongoing process involving the active suspension of judgment and letting go of any attachment to entrenched viewpoints. As in equanimity where the place of telos is always called into question, in *ataraxia* final judgment is suspended as part of a flexible and vital process. Sextus Empiricus, who probably wrote his *Outlines of Pyrrhonism* during the 2nd or 3rd centuries CE, observed that *ataraxia* follows fortuitously (*tuchikôs*) the suspension of judgment (*epoché*) just as a shadow follows the body (I 28-29; p. 11). *Tuchikôs* here suggests holding to no precondition, there being no method, rule, or intentionality. Shadows follow a moving body in the sun naturally, with immediacy, effortlessly. A skeptic is one whose nondogmatic attitude is a manifestation of genuine open-mindedness and ongoing, flexible inquiry. When now we use the term *skeptic* to refer to a negative doubter, we lose sight of its etymology in the ancient Greek term *skeptikos*, which literally means a person who looks or examines (verbal forms: *skopein, skeptesthai*). As I suggested in chapter 4, the intertwining of perception and movement means that we figure out how the world is by actively exploring how it appears. In our abiding experiences of the world, we discover in open inquiry the possibility of moving across manifold readings, among multiple meanings. Equanimity and skeptical looking share this propensity to meander, what the philosopher Pascal Massie astutely calls skepticism's "wandering motive" ("Philosophy and *Ataraxia*," p. 228). To find oneself in a place one was not necessarily seeking offers the very possibility of *ataraxia*: "Whereas a traveler organizes her journey *in order* to reach a pre-established destination, the full-fledged Skeptic is an explorer who has found that it is possible to continue the search, to pursue the journey, and simultaneously to experience *ataraxia*" (ibid., p. 229; emph. in orig.).

It would be beyond the scope of this chapter to adjudicate the rich debates concerning the parallels, differences, and lines of influence between early Buddhist philosophical skepticism and ancient Greek philosophy (see, e.g., most recently, Hanner, *Buddhism and Scepticism*). I will, however, reapproach the meaning of a skeptical life in a later treatment of ethics, and explore some of its moral rewards. Certainly, the *Sutta-Nipāta*'s description of the "priest without borders" makes some of these benefits clear. By "releasing the knot of grasping" (*Sutta-Nipāta*, 794; Norman, p. 106), sages avoid any drama inevitably generated by conflicts of opinion and dissent rooted in dogma. Their position is not one of absolute indifference but of uninvolvement to the extent that their minds are never grasping, their egos never wholly invested. They may be said to possess an unpremeditated relation to all things without morbid self-absorption. They entertain the psychological space to step aside from dogmatic assertions of any kind. "Priests without borders" embody an equanimity that issues from recognizing that, because doctrines and opinions invariably invite equal and opposing arguments, attachment to them only fuels conflict or suffering.

States of equanimity and *ataraxia* may be ruined with intentionality. For the appearance of even-minded, flexible, and peaceful states of subjectivity, strands of Zen and Daoist thinking agree that its conditions include letting them happen as a result of not adhering to the notion that there are prerequisites to their emergence. In the case of the Pyrrhonist, this means that desired tranquility only comes unforced or indirectly in the pursuit of truth, as the skeptic, true to her name, ceaselessly just looks and examines. Through this open-ended process, which never rises to the level of a method, she finds refuge from the conditions that ordinarily lead to investment in doctrine or fixed views of any kind, such as egoic pitfalls and the seductions of polemic. From one perspective, this process of investigating with suspended judgment is daunting, cutting as it does against the grain of our usual habits of mind. From another perspective, when it is realized that suspending judgment is essentially a function of ongoing inquiry, then the process may be acknowledged to be natural and hardly inscrutable. As Martha Nussbaum observes, "the orientation to *ataraxia* is not a belief or a value commitment. It has the status of a natural inclination. Naturally, without belief or teaching, we move to free ourselves from burdens and disturbances. . . .not intensely or with any committed attachment, but because that's just the way we go" (*The Therapy of Desire*, p. 305). What is natural here is a kind of unforced self-care that, avoiding dogmatic commitments, is vitally responsive to impingements and turmoil as they appear. Having divested herself of "contrived views about is or is not," the priest without borders discovers the ataractic freedom of a non-oppositional relation to simply what is. Nussbaum summarizes it well: "So *ataraxia* is not like the other ends we go for, with the help of belief; it is just there for us as things flow along" (ibid., p. 306).

So, when striving and seizing dissolve, the "priest without borders" finds herself in a subject position characterized by intellectual and emotional reserve: "Not passionate, not dispassionate, [s]he doesn't posit anything as 'ultimate.'" This ideal personhood, I suggest, enjoys a rich psychological latitude allowing for the unfolding of creativity of any kind. It is telling that, to illustrate the skeptical process, Sextus used the example of an artist, Apelles, who was endeavoring to depict the foaming at a horse's mouth. Having grown so frustrated with his efforts to achieve the desired effect, the story goes, he threw the sponge he had been using to wipe paint off his brush. Once it struck the painting's surface, the sponge inadvertently produced the very effect he had been struggling so hard to achieve (*Outlines of Scepticism*, pp. 10-11). Although Sextus does not say, it is plausible that Apelles relished a moment of *ataraxia* upon first seeing the transformed composition. Perhaps he grasped that, once creative production progresses contingently rather than deliberately, relief may be found through suspending (as opposed to completely negating) questions of intentionality, rationality, and decision-making. The point is not that this sense of inner peace only happens randomly or unpredictably, but that intentionality, pushing and striving intensely, are sure to prevent it. Throwing a sponge, in the absence of a particular goal, reminds us that sometimes what is most striking or profound about an artwork is distinctly the work of chance itself, as in the compositions of Marcel Duchamp, Jean Arp, André Breton, Jackson Pollock, and John Cage.

Equanimity does not involve or depend upon final suspension of judgment in all circumstances. Suspending judgment is part of the open-ended and ruleless process of equanimity, not its telos. Equanimity is thus like an intermission affording opportunities for considering the manifold sides of an issue at hand, whether internal (e.g., ideas and urges) or external, in one's immediate world. And, in the course of contemplating multiple sides, it may be determined how fully they can be affirmed or opposed at the moment. Opportunities for a kind of intellectual playfulness arise. With supple awareness, rather than emphatic commitment and myopic attachment, a positionless position emerges from which the value, or lack of such, in all positions may be glimpsed. This process often leads to an unbounded relaxation of judgment, to repose and deference rather than tense fixation on one side over against others. The "priest without borders" deploys a skepticism resembling that of the Daoist sage who employs both *ming*, meaning something like "acuity" or open awareness which is opposed to "small knowing" (*xiao zhi*), and *lun* or sorting. As the second Inner Chapter of the *Zhuangzi*, entitled *Qiwulun* or "The Sorting that Evens Things Out," describes it, the sage sifts reality but does not appraise or judge. She evenly parses the interdependent things of the world with a detached, though lively, and uncommitted, though discerning, attitude. The sage recognizes all the while that the more synoptically one investigates things, the more holistically they appear. A. C. Graham describes the dynamic process of *lun*:

> In common usage *lun* tended to imply grading in terms of relative value, but Chuang-tzu's kind...cover[s] all common-sense thinking about objective facts in order to arrive at a coherent picture of the conditions before responding. What Chuang-tzu does forbid is thinking about what I or others ought to do about the situation, instead of simply answering with the spontaneous act or spontaneous approval or disapproval. The sage, we are told, "assesses" actions but does not argue over them, "sorts" physical events but does not assess them, and as for what is outside the cosmos. . .he "locates" it but does not include it in the sorting. (*Disputers of the Tao*, p. 189; see Graham, *Chuang-tzu*, p. 57; cf. Ziporyn, *Zhuangzi*, p. 16)

Suspending the judgments that generate dogmatism and any conflicts it potentially stirs up, *lun* calls to mind the process of aporetic skepticism. In what I have been outlining, I do not wish to equate the Pyrrhonian skeptic with the Daoist sage, or, for that matter, either figure with the Buddhist "priest without borders," since it can be argued that a true skeptic would never assert the existence of a "greater knowledge" (*da zhi*) and is satisfied living a life in accordance with how things appear *before* inquiry. That said, it is clear that, across these traditions, the kinds of subjects who do embody equanimity are precisely those who consistently divest themselves of dogmatic judgments at the same time that their ataractic attitude never prevents them from acting in harmony with what Daoism refers to as the "Way [that] has never had borders" (Graham, *Chuang-tzu*, p. 57; cf. Ziporyn, p. 16).

A few further comments then about "the priest without borders [who] doesn't seize on what he's known or beheld" and who is never "lured into the blind alleys of is and is not." The *Zhuangzi*, in my reading, clarifies what this equanimous approach to experience is based upon. Making use of awareness (*ming*) of the plurality of perspectives, the sage lightly occupies a place of supreme flexibility where potential conflicts—"that's it/that's not it" (*shi/fei*) or "right/wrong"—dissolve as oppositionality fades into mutual entailment. The *Zhuangzi* names this flexible site *daoshu*, the axis, hinge, or pivot of *dao* (Ziporyn, p. 12; cf. Graham, p. 53), where, "when this axis finds its place in the center, it responds to all the endless things it confronts, thwarted by none" (Ziporyn, p. 12). As the intimate point upon which things turn or oscillate, *daoshu* allows for an unqualified mobility favoring no single position and transcending none. In short, *daoshu* is the vantage point that allows for swinging between the possibilities inherent in one's situation. Through *ming*, constantly adjusting to the world, the sage reaches the state where nothing obstructs the calm evenness and the attunement to things that contextualize her existence. The equanimous sage traverses everything and finds herself nowhere other than in the center of all things.

It is tempting to construct a sort of pantheon of characters within the Daoist tradition who model different aspects of equanimous existence. In the *Zhuangzi*, the figures with the strongest family resemblance to "priests without borders" are called the "The Genuine Human Beings [who] breathed from their heels" (Ziporyn, p. 40). These beings are the ones in whom the *dao* circulates spontaneously, and whose entire comportment is animated by its virtue (*de*). They effortlessly move through the world as it is in all its interdependent relations with them. In their frictionless "sliding along," as the text puts it, they recall the ramblers and floaters we have already considered:

> The Genuine Human Beings of old seemed to do whatever was called for but were not partisan to any one course. They appeared to be in want but accepted no assistance. Taking part in all things, they were solitary but never rigid. Spreading out everywhere, they were empty but never insubstantial. Cheerful, they seemed to be enjoying themselves. Impelled along, they did what they could not help doing. They let everything gather within them but still it manifested outwardly to the

world as their own countenance. They gave it all away, but still it rested securely within them as their own Virtuosity. [...] They took Virtuosity as a sliding along. [...] Their understanding was a temporary expedient, arising only when the situation made it unavoidable. Their Virtuosity was a sliding along, like strolling with other able-legged people through the village, so to speak. And yet others thought they had worked hard to get there. (Ziporyn, pp. 41-42; cf. Graham, p. 85)

The liberation from dogmatism characteristic of "priests without borders" and the give-and-take with the world distinguishing "Genuine Human Beings" are brilliantly summarized in a Zen capping verse: "To produce sound, the bell cracks itself; / To produce light, the candle consumes itself" (Hori, *Zen Sand*, p. 456). Bells and candles, it is suggested, realize their natures most completely when they reach the limits of their own existence. In other words, there can be *nothing more* for them to produce; by simply acting in accordance with their natures, they avoid all exorbitance. Their fitting self-expenditure serves as a model for having nothing (left) to invest in activities giving rise to and supporting the excesses of dogmatism—resistance to change, intolerance of contradiction, ego-driven denial, and discounting the present as intrinsically unimportant.

The Person with Belly

> If one divides people into ranks, the lowest is he who values his head. But those who regard the belly as the most important part and so have built the stronghold where the Divine can grow—these are the people of the highest rank.
> —Okada Torajiro, "Sayings"

> Every investigation which is guided by principles of Nature fixes its ultimate aim entirely on gratifying the stomach.
> —Athenaeus, *The Deipnosophists* VII.11

> [Sages] exert their efforts on behalf of the abdomen rather than the eye.
> —*Dao de jing*, ch. 12

A little below the navel is an area, according to some Daoist texts (e.g., *The Yellow Court Classic* [*Huang T'ing Jing*] and the *Baopuzi*), called the *dantian* (Jp. *tanden*), where the physical center of gravity and the seat of one's vitality (Ch. *qi*; Jp. *ki*) are said to reside. *Dantian*, often used interchangeably with the Japanese term *hara* (腹) referring to the whole belly region, symbolizes the point of equilibrium where no extremes dominate. Presently, I will focus on *hara* as the axis of an equanimous existence represented by what we might call a corporeal *daoshu* at the center of the body. The *hara no aru hito* (person with belly or center) is a figure for whom *hara* comprises the essence of the total character. As we will see, this center is both physical and psychological, where *hara* indicates the overall comportment and disposition of the person. The idea of *hara* proposes that fundamental features of the self, located in the belly, allow one to act skillfully in the world—with composure, balance, and openness. *Hara* marks, according to Karlfried Dürckheim (1899-1988), nothing less than "creative liberation from the small I," that is, the equanimous dissolution of entrenched ways of being that otherwise rely on orienting oneself only by what one can pin down (*Hara*, p. 151; cf. 159). In short, *hara* offers a reference point for considering what is possible for human subjecthood. However, before we describe the fuller relevance of *hara* for exemplifying certain dimensions of equanimous subjectivity, let's take a look at the range of the word's meaning as reflected in Japanese idioms.

Semantically, *hara* offers a rich field for describing specific ways of being in the world. To be called *hara no hito* (a person of *hara*) is a compliment, signaling one's integrity, poise, calm, and flexibility. Such a person may also exemplify courage, determination, and consistency of spirit. The practice of self-development is known as *hara-zukuri* (making-*hara*). In the person described as having accomplished his or her belly (*hara no suwatta hito*) is the implication of having reached some higher state of self-improvement. And so, persons who have finished their belly (*hara no dekita hito*), or have become "someone with a big *hara*" (*hara no ōkii hito*), are recognized as notably broad-minded, humane, and generous. Such people are recognized for their mature wisdom. In this context, there appears the person in whom "the belly sits or is sedate" (*hara ga suwatte iru*), whose composure and stability become the attitudinal ground for unflappability and impartiality. In connection with these latter two idiomatic expressions is another that captures the role of *hara* in equanimous subjectivity: *seidaku awase nomu*, literally, "to swallow the pure and the impure together." Expressing the "inner elasticity" that Dürckheim identifies as a preeminent mark of the person of *hara* (ibid., p. 50), swallowing the pure with the impure is an act of consummate acceptance and non-discrimination. A relaxed attitude toward experiences of any kind, it welcomes them without having to categorize them such that then there is nothing to avoid. *Hara*, a multifaceted metonym for subjectivity, points always in the direction of imperturbability and an inclusive deftness with respect to whatever presents itself. *Hara* relieves the pressure to make sense of everything since it represents that center of gravity around which everything smoothly circulates without unwieldiness.

The capacious-minded person of the belly (*hara no hirio hito*), a magnanimous relative of the *hara no aru hito*, likewise exemplifies unconditional calm, a centered serenity resistant to the sharp extremes of external vicissitudes. The antithetical kind of person, described as lacking a belly or center (*hara no nai hito*) or having only a small or narrow belly (*hara no chiisai [semai] hito*), does not necessarily exhibit any physiological difference from persons with a cultivated belly but their character and psychological disposition are radically different. So, to be in any sense a person who has not finished his or her belly (*hara no dekite inai hito*) signifies a deficit of balance due to a loss of center. Without an internal axis, people lacking a belly are recognizable as acting unevenly, engaging the world from the limited perspective of their chronically evaluative egos and often externalizing negative emotions such as anxiety and irritation. Managing their emotions and relations proves to be very difficult, and they may often appear defensive or impulsive. When offended, a person's belly is said to rise (*hara ga tatsu*), indicating an unsettled, excitable state, a propensity to anger. And once offended, a person may find revenge through an act of *haraise* (soothing the belly). For the *hara no nai hito*, the problem is one of maladaptive psychological motility—in short, disequanimity. In a state of discomposure, they may act erratically, or, at the other extreme, they appear "one-tracked and rigid, mentally or emotionally fixed" (ibid., p. 51).

For all subjects, *hara* furnishes the most telling clues to their hidden character. Idiomatic expressions such as *hara wo saguru* (to investigate the belly) and *hara ga yomu* (to read the belly of another) convey the idea that, without a sense of the other's *hara*, intention and attitude remain inscrutable. Corresponding to the figuration of the heart as emotional center in Western culture, conventional language around the belly expresses the imbrication of the corporeal and the psychic. *Hara* signifies across multiple registers of selfhood—the moral, psychological, and social. So, when a person is marked as a *haraguroi hito* (black-stomached person), this denotes that their ill-intentions or deviousness may threaten the social contract. It is likewise with the scheming person, the *hara ni ichimotsu aru hito* (a person with an ulterior motive or hidden intention in his belly). Other expressions signifying the notion that hara reveals the characterological core of the social subject include *kare wa hara no naka wa shojiki na hito desu* (he is an honest person in *hara*, i.e., "at heart") and, indicating duplicity, *kare no kuchi to hara to wa chigau* (his mouth and his hara are different, i.e., "he says one thing but means another"). That hara functions as the cardinal repository of subjective meaning is reflected in its status as the natural source of resolution. Representative phrases like *hara de iku* (to go with the belly), meaning to act determinedly or courageously, and *hara wo kimeru* (to decide one's belly), meaning to make up one's mind, suggest the discrepancy between the activity of *hara* and tendencies to abulia. And, lastly, *hara* embodies a relay point in the sphere of intersubjective communication. One especially flexible term for this is *haragei* (belly-art), which refers to, among other things as we'll see, intuitive and tacit forms of mutual disclosure and resonance. In this vein, *hara wo awaseru* (to join one's belly with another) expresses either colluding with another or, more commonly, having deep rapport with another. Indeed, the art of conversing takes place belly-to-belly instead of *tête-à-tête*, bypassing the ego with its signature bias and impulsiveness. Thus, *hara wo waru* (to split or open one's belly) means dropping all pretense, conversing frankly or, as the Western idiom has it, speaking heart-to-heart. It is no wonder then that trusted friends are designated *fukushin* (the center of the stomach). *Hara* thus represents that center point through which our resonant relations to all other beings—and, as we will see, things and events—are equanimously mediated.

When one connects either privately or socially with *hara*, the latent, genuine content of the self, what is referred to as *honne* (本音; true intention or feeling) emerges. Inner nature becomes scrutable. At the same time, *hara* orients itself toward *tatemae* (建前; social façade), the term often employed as the antipode of *honne*. *Tatemae* reflects attunement to the intricate field of social roles and attendant conventions governing what counts as appropriate expressions of inner states. Formal situations, like those in some work settings, may call for the dissociation of *honne* and *tatemae*, where the former is utterly masked by the social face. *Hara*, however, bridges the apparent polarity of the private sphere and the civil self, allowing for *honne* and *tatemae* to alternate relative to given social contexts. *Hara* serves as a suspension point of reorientation, enhancing the flexibility and extending the range of one's perspectives toward oneself, others, and the world. It grants a sort of spiritual breathing space where a moment of equipoise makes it possible both to receptively experience and intentionally act in the world. We can understand then why, as Dürckheim describes it, a "man with center...has a quality of breadth" keeping the subject equanimously oriented (ibid., p. 49). Spaciously accommodating the interior *honne*-world and the exterior *tatemae*-world, *hara* spans the dichotomy of the phenomenal body (the body as the place of being, i.e., awareness and experience) and the objective body (the body as tool or object for others). Both the phenomenal and the objective body, well theorized in contemporary phenomenology, properly belong to natural existence. Apprehended then from the even vantage point of *hara*, they are not grasped as figures on a ground but as ground itself, sites of possible balance and stability. Notably, in the German language, the objective body (*Körper*) is etymologically linked to the "dead body" (L. *corpus*, the root of Eng. *corpse*), while the phenomenal body (*Leib*, from Middle High German *līp* and Old Teutonic *lîba-*) is etymologically associated with life (*Leben*) and lived experience (*Erlebnis*). To the person with belly, the forces of life and death, vitality and inertia, form the warp and woof through which "a firm anchorage... acts like a plummet by means of which such a man will always automatically swing back into his right centre of gravity even though for a time he may fall out of it" (ibid., p. 70).

This ongoing process of swinging and settling is a constitutive element of the equanimous subject, enabling a smoothness of attitude toward others and the world. *Hara* thus describes easeful modes of being-in-the-world, frictionless ways (*dao*) for subjects and the world to come into relation with each other. As an attitude of unflappability and readiness for whatever presents itself, *hara* finds its essence detached from the forced certitude of a centralized ego dependent upon preconception and fixed ideas. *Hara* decenters the egoic subject who now enjoys an elastic relation to all things. Less something that one actually "has" than the spaciousness in which one finds oneself—a mode of *being* as opposed to *having* in Erich Fromm's classic terms—*hara* embodies a "life [that] because of its deeply mysterious flexibility swings around an axis which is firm" (ibid., p. 88). In this way, activities of ordinary life freely circulate precisely because the center of *hara* continually sanctions them. Along the same lines, mastery of a so-called *dō* art, such as the tea ceremony, calligraphy, flower arrangement, swordsmanship, or archery, is traditionally recognized as a mode of *haragei* (belly-art), expressing the conditions under which attitudes of unconditional poise achieve their most complete expression. To act from *hara* involves an experience of reality recognizable primarily for its quality of fluidity, the rhythm of admitting and flowing out as happens in breathing.

Through the vitality of *hara*, in place of ego there is only interchange, an affirmation of both independence and relationality between self and the world. Dürckheim, echoing Nietzsche, summarized this vibrant state as "man's Yes to his bi-polar wholeness" (ibid., p. 81), and depicted it as follows: the person of *hara* "gives himself to the world without losing himself in it, abides there awhile without being swallowed by it, withdraws himself without thereby cutting himself off from it and remains alone without ever hardening himself" (ibid., p. 82). Vestiges of the partialized ego/I, with its tendency toward fixity, fade into something like the receptivity and independent creativity of the whole person, a positive instantiation of the psychoanalytic total-subject—the *Gesamt-Ich*, as Freud called it—comprising the subject in all its aspects, objective as well as subjective, individual as well as social, somatic as well as psychic (see Loewald, *Sublimation*, p. 17). From the Zen perspective, to be a "total-subject" conveys a deep sense of satisfaction issuing from a special state of wisdom, the preeminent sign of which is nothing other than cheerfully drumming one's own belly (e.g., Cleary, *Tune beyond the Clouds*, p. 46; 78).

Haragei represents the special wisdom of the body. It reminds us that no fixity, for example, no single body schema, will be adequate to lively existence. In order to move around in the physical world, the body cannot be reducible simply to a factual entity—a Cartesian *res extensa*—for the reason that competence and mastery depend upon shifting configurations of the body, as in dancing where our center of gravity is constantly displaced as we move. Another aspect of this active decentering is the idea that a particular part cannot be taken as the definitive or permanent axis of the whole. This general notion is reflected in Jewish tradition, expressed in both the Torah and the Talmud, where the direct counting and measurement of living bodies is prohibited. The idea, according to commentary on Midrash Rabba, is that counting persons (e.g., census-taking) separates them from the collective, potentially interfering with the beneficent process of heavenly judgment which applies to the whole community (*klal*) rather than to the individual. In its flexible relation to part and whole, *haragei* describes modalities of existence most colorfully illustrated, as we will see, in the choreographies of European marionette theater and Japanese Nō theater.

In his famous essay of 1810 on the marionette theater, the German Romantic poet and dramatist Heinrich von Kleist (1777-1811) explored themes related to art and artifice, movement, and the role of self-consciousness as they shape particular modes of being. In the course of a dialogue with the essay's unnamed narrator, a celebrated dancer expresses his admiration for a local performance of dancing puppets by provocatively suggesting that their movements are superior to those of humans. The dancer explains that unself-consciousness on the part of the inanimate objects is the source of their graceful actions, putting them supremely in sync with nature. When the puppeteer's art, he argues, discovers "the soul"—the physical center of gravity—in the puppet's pendular movements, the constraining forces of the material world, such as inertia, fade away. One can therefore, in the dancer's view, rightly speak of the puppet's absolute eloquence, its unfallen grace, the signs of which are its lightness, symmetry, flexibility, and instantaneity of stopping and starting that no human body is able to match. Unencumbered by self-consciousness, puppets possess a centering equanimity:

> And the advantage such a puppet would have over a living dancer?
> The advantage? First a negative gain... specifically this: that such a figure would never be affected. For affectation appears, as you know, when the soul (vis motrix) locates itself at any point other than the center of gravity of the movement. Because the puppeteer absolutely controls the wire or string, he controls and has power over no other point than this one: therefore, all the other limbs are what they should be—dead, pure pendulums following the simple law of gravity, an outstanding quality that we look for in vain in most dancers. ("On the Marionette Theatre," p. 24)

Haragei is inextricably related to the smooth function of the *vis motrix* (the force of motion). Interestingly, "motion" was in fact the 16th-century English term for a puppet show, and sometimes indicated the puppet itself. With the movement of wires, the center of gravity constantly shifts, and different appendages come "alive" as others become quiescent. From the marionette's *hara* the true art of puppetry symbolically issues. "Only where the tension of the whole is held in a true balance," writes Dürckheim, "is it properly alive" (*Hara*, p. 80). Animating puppets, the dancer concludes, is less a Pygmalion intervention than an act of sheer grace (Ger. *Grazie*) that "appears to best advantage in that human bodily structure that has no consciousness at all—or has infinite consciousness—that is, in the mechanical puppet, or in the God" ("On the Marionette Theatre," p. 26). Puppet or God: in either direction lies what the narrator deems a pure "state of innocence," achievable only, Kleist tells us, by eating for the second time from the Tree of Knowledge (ibid.).

In another form of theater whose mastery requires nothing less than a perfection of movement—the Nō theater of medieval Japan—we find a related focus on cultivating an equanimous subjectivity uninterrupted by self-consciousness or intentionality. Taking its name from the word *nō* ("talent" or "skill"), this form of theater relies purely upon the visual presence and movements of its performers to suggest the essence of a story well known to its audience. The codified performative elements of Nō theater reflect a language of movement systematized over centuries and drawn from a variety of preexisting ritual performances. In the *katazuke*, the secret choreography manuals that are passed down generation by generation through the Nō families, a methodology of motion is revealed where the rigors of training are viewed from the metaphysical perspective of managing *ki* (cosmic energy). In this context, *ki* is neither purely self-generated nor reactive energy but rather involves the "hidden spiritual goal" of perfecting external or visible movement only in total harmony or opposed balance with the internal movements "generated by the spirit" (Umewaka, "Inner World of the Nō," p. 32; 34).

Here, a new kind of dynamically aware person emerges, one whose *haragei* manifests as "the inner and the outer exist[ing] not against but for each other" (*Hara*, p. 83). In Nō performance, external gestures and postures seamlessly and continuously flow from internal movements or from absoluteness centeredness. The internal world of the performer dramatizes, as the contemporary Nō artist Naohiko Umewaka describes it, a "perfect harmony between the immanent and the phenomenological worlds." "Attaining consummate balance," he continues, "between the world within and the visible world, the static and dynamic, is a quintessential quality for mastery in the Nō theatre, and the constant flow between spiritual and physical control is the assurance of a superior performance on the stage" ("Inner World of the Nō," p. 34). The complementarity of inner and outer worlds becomes accessible and communicable, recalling the precise disposition of *haragei* where there is no abandonment of or resistance to the inner emotional-intellectual and to the outer life pattern. *Haragei* makes coordinated experience possible, where a center of gravity anchors any temporary shifts to the periphery. In the Umewaka family *katazuke* manual (*Ōnarai Konarai Hisho*) written by the author's highly accomplished grandfather Umewaka Manzaburō XII, a characteristic instruction beautifully illustrates this modulating of internal and external motion: "When you are moving in a very energetic manner, you should be in a state of absolute inner calm; when performing very slow movements, even sitting or standing, the movement within should be especially dynamic and active" (ibid., pp. 34-35). The Nō performer shares with the Kleistian mechanical puppet a dynamism that does not depend upon the mind of an actor thinking outside his role but instead upon the coordinated modulation of elements (body parts, affectivities).

Both the marionette and the Nō actor embody, then, a dialectical balance of the dynamic and the static. In the marionette, this relation of the vital and the inert or inanimate is said to be articulated through a fluent center of gravity, and, in the Nō performer, through a rhythmical flow of *ki*. In such ways, an incredible breadth of existence is granted to both theatrical figures, and this is quite likely what contributes to the flourishing of these age-old theatrical genres to this day. With the true person with belly, marionette/puppeteer and the Nō drama performers share an existential equanimity absolutely unimpeded by the will or unblemished by desire. It was the Daoists who most strikingly articulated a vision of subjectivity free from intentionality. For them, to act or live in accordance with the Dao is comparable to the movements of inanimate objects, and so they were fond of mechanical metaphors for existence such as that found in the *Liezi* and the 6th-century *Book of the Golden Hall Master* where a Chinese king interacts with a life-size automaton (see Needham, *History of Scientific Thought*, pp. 53-54). This condition of unhindered existence—as I have suggested, one of the essential hallmarks of equanimity—is celebrated in the *Liezi* using the simile of the machinic:

> The Book of the Yellow Emperor says:
> "The highest man at rest is as though dead, in movement is like a machine. He knows neither why he is at rest nor why he is not, why he is in movement nor why he is not. He neither changes his feelings and expression because ordinary people are watching, nor fails to change them because ordinary people are not watching. He comes alone and

goes alone, comes out alone and goes in alone; what can obstruct him?" (*The Book of Lieh-tzu*, p. 130)

Like the *hara no aru hito*, the marionette, or the Nō performer, persons living in accordance with the Dao can never be described as getting in their own way. They act fluidly, freely, in no way pinned down by mind-manufactured dualisms. Their inherent balance and effortless equanimity find expression in an identity that naturally eludes the pitfalls of striving: "There is no shame more shameful than having many desires, / There is no joy more joyous than non-seeking" (Hori, *Zen Sand*, p. 431).

As we will see in the next section, the hunter is also a figure for whom fixation on and striving toward the goal (in this case, the taking of an animal) counterintuitively yield to the inherently joyful process of discovering an identity the authenticity of which is proportional to its being grounded in keen awareness. The alert hunter is one whose clear vision never gets caught in partializing polarities. Here is Blake: "This life's dim Windows of the Soul / Distorts the Heavens from Pole to Pole / And leads you to Believe a Lie / When you see with, not thro', the Eye" ("The Everlasting Gospel," *Complete Writings*, p. 753).

The Alert Hunter

> The text is a forest in which the reader is hunter.
> —Walter Benjamin, *The Arcades Project*

> He enters the forest, but does not disturb the grass; He enters the water, but does not cause waves.
> —Shibayama Zenkei, *Zenrin kushū*, verse 280

My primary concern in this section is to consider what it is like for the hunter who sees and engages with the world in rather distinctive ways. Commonly, when we think of hunting, we picture immediately, if not exclusively, the act of killing and the death of an animal. On this view, the hunter's focus appears to be killing, pure and simple. I will propose instead an understanding of the hunter and hunting in terms of the equanimous relations to the world they open and set in motion. How may the hunter be understood as an identity committed not to taking up a view *of* the world but views *in* it? In all its dynamic relationality, equanimity on the part of the hunter has no purpose beyond dwelling in a series of contacts with realities whose sheer immediacy and universality thwart tendencies toward objectifying and reifying. To consider, as I will, the possible non-moral values of hunting is decidedly not to defend or justify it but rather to point to dimensions of it often elided when phenomenologies of hunting are situated utterly within an ethics centered on animal rights or welfare perspectives. While undeniably a social practice whose meaning is historically conditioned, hunting, for more than 90% of human history, has been simultaneously a matter of subsistence and a powerful means, socially as well as cognitively, of taking up mobile views of and approaches to the world while being wholly immersed in it. Historically, hunting was a grounding element of subjectivity since it placed Paleolithic humans in deep relation to natural surroundings in which, as the ecological philosopher Max Oelschlaeger suggestively puts it, they "could never be lost": "Given the reality of flux in all human society, this link to the natural throws people into closer intellectual and emotional recognition of the one constant in their lives, the terrain with its enduring natural community" (*The Idea of Wilderness*, p. 13). Indeed, part of the modern hunter's sense of being always at home derives from this awareness rooted in a kind of intimacy with the world.

In what follows I will be situating the subject of hunting in the context of what is called the fair chase ethic of the traditional hunt. In a traditional hunt, prey must be capable of eluding the hunter, that is, there is a reasonable chance for the animal of surviving the hunt since pursuit takes place in its natural habitat. The fair chase ethic codifies this possibility. It involves hunters striving to equalize the field by foregoing more efficient means (e.g., the use of dogs, electronic tracking, baiting, spotlighting, all-terrain vehicles or helicopters, excessive weaponry) in favor of less efficient ones (e.g., hunting only in open seasons). These efforts to neutralize technological advantage are supposed to ensure that the prey, as philosopher John Pauley writes, has full access to "its full range of capacities...in continuity with its world." As a result, fair chase and the traditional hunt, Pauley continues, depend upon the hunter being "made vividly aware of these capacities," and thus acutely "aware of the independent reality of animals" ("The Value of Hunting," p. 238). As we will see, this consciousness of *in*dependence is, for the equanimous hunter, folded into a more capacious awareness of *inter*dependence rooted in something like what Henri Bergson called simply "attention to life," which in his view depends upon sensorimotor equilibrium guaranteeing nothing less than our mental freedom (*Matter and Memory*, pp. 225-27). Ortega y Gasset, whose phenomenological approach to hunting will organize my own, termed the free equanimity of the hunter "universal attention" and, further, "alertness." It is precisely the cultivation of this attitude of alertness, according to Ortega, that constitutes the real process of hunting and precludes it from devolving into mere sadism.

In his *Meditations on Hunting* (1942), Ortega acknowledges the "essential inequality" between human predator and animal prey at the same time that he emphasizes that sportive hunting cannot be understood apart from the ethical code that maintains some semblance of balance in the hunter-hunted binary (p. 48). As he puts it rather eloquently:

> Hunting involves a complete code of ethics of the most distinguished design; the hunter who accepts the sporting code of ethics keeps his commandments in the greatest solitude, with no witnesses or audience other than the sharp peaks of the mountain, the roaming cloud, the stern oak, the trembling juniper, and the passing animal. (ibid., p. 31)

There is a sense here in which the natural environment conditions the very possibility of ethical commitment. The fluid quality of the hunter's attention, as we will see, is rooted in vital habits of alertness and acuity that connect to, and allow the hunter to participate in, the totality. For Ortega, this is the crucial point at which "existing becomes a poetic task," where one is nowhere other than in the present, "free from desire and nostalgia" (ibid., p. 24; 26), unburdened by the future and the past. This deep, equanimous presence, he suggests, is ruined in a hunt without fair chase. Fair chase allows for the emergence of existence as the dynamic interchange between persons and surroundings. This existential condition depends upon the kind of knowledge Ortega famously termed *razón vital* (reason from the point of view of life), a knowledge of how to act and what to pay attention to in the midst of life given to us as "empty," something to be filled with vital tasks (ibid., p. 23). A hunt without fair chase does not require this sort of attitude toward life, and thus, Ortega puts it clearly, is not a hunt at all: "if man did not do this he would not only destroy animals, he would also destroy, coincidentally, the very act of hunting which fascinates him" (ibid., pp. 50-1).

Ortega is far from the only one to suggest that the operations of hunting themselves, as opposed to the end (the death of quarry), are for participants hunting's deepest motivation. Erich Fromm, commenting on the sheer joy of enactment and the experience of skills in hunting, points out that people who reduce its various pleasures to those of killing miss something crucial: "The interpretation of the pleasure in hunting as pleasure in killing, rather than in skill, is indicative of the person of our time for whom the only thing that counts is the *result* of an effort, in this case killing, rather than the process itself" (*The Anatomy of Human Destructiveness*, p. 158; emph. in orig.). The hunter is rewarded by hunting as an end in itself, the supreme virtue of which appears to be, for Ortega, the practice of an engagement with the world he calls alertness. This alertness, just as I have argued with respect to equanimity as a way of seeing or encountering the world, is non-instrumental.

In a fascinating essay on hunting and tragic wisdom, James Tantillo argues that there must always be an inherent ambivalence in the venatic act (e.g., the mix of pleasure and pain, reflected in regret, having killed the animal), such that elation on the part of the hunter can never be unadulterated. There can be in hunting, he argues, a "tragic pensiveness" reflecting what Hans Gadamer claims for the spectator responding to a tragedy (*Truth and Method*, p. 127). Tantillo's most radical (and insightful) claim, however, is that hunting—"a comprehensive project for some individuals"—may be compared to the aesthetic response, and is itself "a highly aesthetic activity" ("Sport Hunting, *Eudaimonia*, and Tragic Wisdom," p.

105; cf. Inglis, "Meditations on Sport," pp. 91-94). As others might respond to music, art, or literature, the hunter responds to the natural world with an engagement of sensory and cognitive capacities that are valued purely for their own sake. And so, as Ortega frames it, hunting via its return to and interaction with nature comprises "a form of happiness" (*Meditations*, p. 120), that is, an end in itself, and precisely the sort of thing capable of being valuable independently of its being a means to something else. The putative end—that is, the death of the game animal—is never what interests the hunter: "What interests him," Ortega contends, "is everything he has to do to achieve that death—that is, the hunt" (ibid., p. 96). Or, as he aphoristically puts it, "one does not hunt in order to kill; on the contrary, one kills in order to have hunted" (ibid., pp. 96-97).

Like game players who go for the gaming experience itself rather than some end toward which it works, fair chase hunters *choose* to follow rules or codes precisely and solely because they desire the hunt experience itself. The sociological literature on modern hunting is virtually univocal on this point: a "successful" modern hunt is not determined by the taking of an animal since it is nonessential to the total experience. In Ortega's words, once "freed of its obligatory nature, hunting is elevated to the rank of sport" (ibid., p. 29), in other words, an activity inseparable from an "effort made completely freely" (ibid., p. 32). Hunters freely accept certain impediments to their venatic practices, with the process of the hunt becoming a form of enjoyment per se. "A sport," Ortega writes, "is the effort which is carried out for the pleasure that it gives in itself and not for the transitory result that the effort brings forth" (ibid., p. 96). Heard here (and in Fromm's and Tantillo's analyses) are echoes of John Rawls's Aristotelian Principle, according to which "other things equal, human beings enjoy the exercise of their realized capacities (their innate or trained abilities), and this enjoyment increases the more the capacity is realized, or the greater its complexity" (*A Theory of Justice*, p. 414). On this view, tic-tac-toe will always be less satisfying than chess. The more skill required and the greater complexity of the game, the greater the consciousness of the special value of ends in themselves. By offering a reprieve from instrumentality, hunting may bring together mental and physical actions whose intrinsic value permit "something like a vacation from the human condition" (*Meditations*, p. 111). If there is anything utopic about hunting, it may be along the lines of Ortega's sense that it temporarily recovers an aspect of humanity otherwise squelched by what he calls "the enormous discomfort and all-embracing disquiet of history" (ibid., p. 121).

Perhaps it is unsurprising then that Ortega saw deep connections between hunting and Plato's ideal *polis* in the *Republic*, placing hunting in relation to the philosophical enterprise itself. We recall that the construction of the imaginary city (*polis*) is for Socrates in the *Republic* a form of "play" and a "game" (*paidia*). Indeed, Ortega would find in Plato in particular—where the significance of attention is deemed the preeminent philosophical attitude, metaphorically represented by the act of hunting (e.g., *Republic* 432b)—a premium placed on the multiperspectivism and the musical-like shifting of "keys and moods" (Ardley, "The Role of Play in the Philosophy of Plato," p. 236) that finds its most powerful expression in sportsmanship. For Ortega, the sporting life is synonymous with the authentically philosophical life, an idea he derives from Plato's definition of philosophy, *he episteme ton eleutheron* (*Sophist* 253c), which Ortega elsewhere translates *más exacta* (he says) as "the science of sportsmen" (*la ciencia de los deportistas*) (*Historical Reason*, p. 25; *What is Philosophy?*, p. 93). The science of existence here is precisely knowledge of how to act, of how to pay attention in the face of shifting circumstantial demands. This calls for expansiveness of vision and an equanimous attitude of adaptable judgment. Ortega applies the Socratic formula of *Apology* 23b to the hunter's mental attitude and orientation: "The hunter knows he does not know what is going to happen" (*Meditations*, p. 130). Because all events are processual and at the outset undecided, the elements of the hunt themselves relate attention to the indeterminacy of what may come to be. In short, it exemplifies the playful and open Zen beginner's mind (Jp. *shoshin*) in action. Like Johan Huizinga (in *Homo Ludens* [1938]), Ortega often quotes *Laws* VII.803b-c with its metaphor of life as an open game: in Plato's phrase, "Let us play as good plays as we can," yet also "we must be sometimes serious, which is not agreeable, but necessary." As we will explore in the chapter's final section, there is no genuine play separate from equanimity, an active balancing of the serious and the ludic defying all fixations.

To see in hunting a metaphor for philosophizing helps us approach the heart of the association of the alert hunter with equanimous subjectivity. For Ortega, the projects of both philosophy and hunting involve the sportive pursuit, from multiple perspectives, of objects that have become "problems" to be understood. That for Plato the quest for knowledge could be generally compared to a hunt, means for Ortega that both require a singular alertness or perceptual elasticity in order to avoid dogmatism and superficiality. The meditating philosopher is like the hunter in the field, ready for a truth to leap, as it were, into sight anytime from any point. And, crucially, both hunters and philosophers value their exploratory practices in themselves more than any outcomes. "Like the hunter in the absolute *outside* of the countryside," writes Ortega, "the philosopher is the alert man in the absolute *inside* of ideas, which are also an unconquerable and dangerous jungle. As problematic a task as hunting, meditation always runs the risk of returning empty-handed" (*Meditations*, p. 132; emph. in orig.). The Scottish philosopher David Hume (1711-76)—to whom, curiously, Ortega never refers—is in perfect agreement. Hume, too, draws an analogy between hunting and the pursuit of knowledge. In the section of *A Treatise of Human Nature* entitled "Of curiosity, or the love of truth," Hume sees profound similarities between the two activities: the minute possibility of success in either means the processes themselves are rendered valuable:

> ... there cannot be two passions more nearly resembling each other, than those of hunting and philosophy, whatever disproportion may at first sight appear betwixt them. 'Tis evident, that the pleasure of hunting consists in the action of the mind and body; the motion, the attention, the difficulty, and the uncertainty. (*A Treatise*, p. 288)

Rewarded as challenging processes, hunting and philosophical curiosity are always more than simply quests with an end goal. Hunting, Hume argues, is enjoyable and valuable for its own sake, even though the hunter, however disappointed, might return home without a catch; similarly, curiosity demands the joy of pursuing knowledge. Though hard-won, knowledge and quarry would be devalued if the full process of their acquisition were skipped. As Hume sums it up, "the same person, who over-looks a ten times greater profit in any other subject, is pleas'd to bring home half a dozen woodcocks or plovers, after having employ'd several hours in hunting after them" (ibid., pp. 288-89). Agreeing with Hume's insight, the philosopher Walter Brand points out that "Duck or geese make a good meal, but it would be easier to buy one than to hunt for one. Why are we proud of our small catch when we can purchase a large fish at the market?" ("Hume's Account of Curiosity and Motivation," p. 94). If one were solely after the feast, eating market-bought fish would be just as satisfying, but this is hardly the case. Similarly, as curious beings, what is more satisfying to us is "not so much what we have come to understand, but the time and labor invested for the sake of understanding" (ibid., p. 95). Hunters, in their equanimity, must always be ready to fail in the search, as they understand that ultimately this search *is* the hunting.

Ortega's philosophy of hunting, gesturing toward Plato's *Symposium* with its passion for "the interlocking of things… synthesis" (*Meditations on Quixote*, p. 89), finds in the projects of both the meditator and the hunter a sensibility by which every object now becomes a problem to be sportively pursued from multiple viewpoints. In one sense, hunters and thinkers express equanimity by displaying the deference that perspectivism often demands. In this context, it is interesting to note that a 14th-century text concerning the sportive diversions of aristocratic life by Gace de la Buigne cautions hunters against making any definitive statements or proposals concerning the stags they have seen without first qualifying them with expressions such as "I think" and "perhaps" (Thiébaux, "The Mediaeval Chase," p. 267). This stance of deference characterizes a dimension of equanimity called into being by encounters with the conditional and uncertain. Without romanticizing them, the operations of hunting naturally rely upon a keenness of receptivity and equanimous attention. It becomes clear then why the Platonic metaphor of the quest for knowledge as a hunt is for Ortega a powerful emblem for the kind of perceptual elasticity required of persons for whom the whole field or world becomes vibrant as a dynamic, interdependent network. "The hunter's soul," he observes, "leaps out, spreads out over the hunting ground like a net, anchored here and there with the fingernails of his attention" (*Meditations*, p. 78). Ortega summarizes this open attentional skill as "alert thought," opposing it to "inertial thinking" where the mind, under the influence of accepted ideas and preconceived concepts, proceeds "vaguely and mechanically in the same direction" (ibid., pp. 57-58). The inertial mind does not deviate, operating on auto-pilot. Alert thinking, however, is fluid, equanimous, "always ready to rectify its trajectory, to break its direction, attentive to the reality outside of it" (ibid., p. 58). To be an alert hunter, insists Ortega, amounts to being "the only man who truly thinks," who, in refusing inertial thought, is forever "ready to accept that the solution [to problems] might spring from the least foreseeable spot on the great rotundity of the horizon" (ibid., p. 132). Relying upon "a universal attention, which does not inscribe itself on any point and tries to be on all points" (ibid., p. 130), the hunter moves through a world whose structures and processes are there to be discovered rather than imposed upon it.

Hunting involves a set of skills that may contribute to the formation of an equanimous subject whose immersion in and awareness of the contingency of existence produce profound moments of connection and attunement. Again, a defense of hunting is not undertaken here; rather, it is clear to me that to overlook aspects of hunting that bear upon ways of perceiving and attending to the world would be to ignore singular ways the world may be inhabited, engaged with. Consider the way hunter-gatherers' intimate and ongoing relationships to the world—what social anthropologist Tim Ingold frames as an ontology of dwelling—point toward an understanding of self and nature that does not admit binaristic thinking. Through these dynamic, immersive relationships, the separateness of human culture and the natural environment crumbles. One engages with the phenomenal world *before* formulating or determining it:

> And so one gets to know the forest, and the plants and animals that dwell therein, in just the same way that one becomes familiar with other people, by spending time with them, investing in one's relations with them the same qualities of care, feeling and attention. This explains why hunters and gatherers consider time devoted to forays in the forest

to be well spent, even if it yields little or nothing by way of useful return (Ingold, *The Perception of the Environment*, p. 47).

Ortega too reminds us that, in hunting, one is not a mere spectator of nature but a participant in it, unburdened by any teleology and untroubled by any lack of return. The meanings and connections forged in nature both produce and are produced by a profound identity shift that occurs by which "our most spontaneous, evident, and comfortable being" is (re)encountered (*Meditations*, p. 118). Indeed, when he qualifies this renewed personhood by noting that "our life seems to lose weight" (ibid.), we are pointed to the equanimous subject who floats that I described in chapter 6. In Ortega's view, the principal emblematic foil to the philosophically transformative attention of hunting is the serial sight-seeing typical of the tense tourist. Tourists, bearing some passing resemblance to hunters, traverse open spaces, aiming their cameras, shooting pictures, capturing experiences to take back home, and "hunting down" souvenirs. Yet the tourist, for whom the world is reducible to a series of trackable spectacles, pays attention to things only paratactically by multiplying fixed points of attention, hurrying in relatively short spans of time from one to the next. The archetypal tourist, keeping to her agenda, is rarely spontaneous. Ortega's hunter, by contrast, is relaxed, open, unhampered by "must-sees." Whereas the tourist rarely has time to wait, the hunter's attention dilates, always situated in the in-between, literally, the milieu. The hunter attends to the surrounding world with a quiet awareness, which, as Ortega emphasizes, "does not consist in riveting itself on the presumed but consists precisely in not presuming anything and in avoiding inattentiveness" (ibid., p. 130).

Through the equanimity of universal attention or fluid alertness, the world of the hunter comes singularly alive. Ortega calls this "being within the countryside":

> Only when we see it through the drama that unfolds in the hunt can we absorb its particular richness. Articulated in that action which is a minor zoological tragedy, wind, light, temperature, ground contour, minerals, vegetation, all play a part; they are not simply there, as they are for the tourist or the botanist, but rather they function, they act. (ibid., p. 124)

Hunting provides access to one way that the natural world may be opened to vital awareness, in the process becoming more charged with significance. "When one is hunting," Ortega declares, "the air has another, more exquisite feel as it glides over the skin or enters the lungs, the rocks acquire a more expressive physiognomy, and the vegetation becomes loaded with meaning" (ibid., p. 123). Ortega's lyricism notwithstanding, the potential for new relations to the non-human world appears to be related to the enhanced presence and perception of the meditative subject. When flexible relations replace inertial ones, the hunter has access to the phenomenal world in novel ways. Pauley points out that "the motivation to hunt is often grounded in an urge to immerse the self into a world unmediated by thought" ("The Value of Hunting," p. 240). In the immediacy of experience, attitudes toward the natural world shift in the direction of the contemplative. Richard Nelson, who lived on and off for decades with the Koyukon of Alaska, a North American hunting group, compared venery to "walking meditation" ("Life Ways of the Hunter," p. 89). Insofar as the practice of hunting involves what the social anthropologist Adrian Franklin has described as a deep "sensual and proximate relation to nature," it entails a complex sensuous integration through "the loss of specific sensual control in favour of multi-sensual reaction or intuitive sensing" ("Neo-Darwinian Leisures, the Body and Nature," p. 57; 69). As focal sensory control fades, as the abiding space between prospection and retrospection is more keenly occupied, the landscape becomes less something to be looked at, to get hold of, than moved through and experienced corporeally from within. The sheer dynamism of the landscape, as philosopher Edward Casey shrewdly observes, "is found in its encouragement of motion in its midst, its 'e-motive' (and often explicitly emotional) thrust" ("How to Get from Space to Place," p. 23).

Ortega declared reason "the greatest enemy of hunting" (*Meditations*, p. 69) in part because it stifles the hunter's most significant asset, the capacity to remain alert in such a way that abstraction and the over-intellectualizing of life do not interfere with the flow of immediate, interdependent experiencing. Ortega's overarching philosophical project is in many ways the effort to reacquaint us with the e-motive dimensions of existence, what moves us to exist. In what I have outlined here, it has not been necessary to agree completely with Ortega's views on hunting (or condone hunting at all) in order to grasp something fundamental about the kind of subjectivity it conditions. The reward of alertness he describes is nothing other than one kind of existential authenticity that grants the sustaining of a sense of equanimity toward and wonder about being in the middle of a world that otherwise and too often denies the choices guaranteeing the fullest sense of freedom. The hunter, in common with the other figures we have examined, invites us to mark the futility of reducing the flow of life to a narrow utilitarian account. With this, we turn to playing, the archetypal form of the nonutilitarian, and to the subjects who embody the equanimous attitudes it sets in motion.

Homo Ludens

> A human being [*der Mensch*] only plays when he is in the fullest sense of the word a human being, and he is only a full human being [*ganz Mensch*] when he plays.
> —Friedrich Schiller, *Letter XV* (*Ästhetische Briefe*)

> A human being plays, where he celebrates existence. [*Der Mensch spielt, wo er das Dasein feiert.*]
> —Eugen Fink, "Maske und Kothurn," in *Epiloge zur Dichtung*

Considerations of the hunter have planted some seeds for a discussion of the final exemplary figure of equanimous existence—the person at play or, more suggestively, the playful person. A compelling link between hunting and playing has already emerged, one that was crucial for Ortega, namely, the phenomenology of a certain activity for its own sake, regardless of its achieving specific ends. Sport hunting thus raises the issue of play in this sense: it stands outside the aims of obligatory labor, occupying a realm where, Ortega claims, we are no longer estranged from happiness. Instead of feeling as if we were "losing time," "another kind of life" may be imagined, one "successful in itself" and thus infinitely richer (*Meditations*, p. 25). Playing, like hunting, involves us in a potential, liberatory attitude toward life at the same time that it refashions identity. The philosopher of sport Klaus Meier summed it up in precise terms Ortega doubtless would have fully endorsed: "play is the impulse for, the gate to, and the exercise, instantiation, and essence of freedom" ("An Affair of Flutes," p. 32). This path to liberty resonates with the openness of equanimity, as we will see. My comments on playing, then, will be less concerned with the manifold *activities* of play than with the existential *attitudes* it motivates. Two guiding questions present themselves: What are the affinities between playfulness and equanimity? Who are we when we are playful?

Playfulness situates us in relation to a vibrant and animated world. It continually presents and responds to invitations to what is possible. For children, who can be marvelously inventive with toys or ordinary utilitarian objects such as chairs and blankets, the world is full of enticements to playful encounters. A Zen capping phrase celebrates the value of such a felicitous world: "Play with it and even broken tile is gold" (Hori, *Zen Sand*, p. 297). When we are playful, the world is endowed with a lightness and ease with which we then harmonize through increased open attentiveness. The richness of immediate experience becomes the animated field in which possibilities are welcomed, realized, risked. Play engenders equanimity, providing opportunities for the lightminded and lighthearted deference that becomes the basis of any commitment, however transitory, to one or more of the multifarious outcomes in the world. In play, as in equanimity, we accept the ontological parity of things. For as long as we may play, a singular focus on the seriousness of things and outcomes dissolves. The ultimate privilege of worldviews, otherwise comfortably resting upon partialized focus and evidence, begins to crumble. Crucially, A. N. Whitehead once called upon philosophers to transcend such narrow selectivity in the name of holding opposites, such as the tragic and the lighthearted aspects of existence, in a single impartial intuition. "Philosophy," he declared, "may not neglect the multifariousness of things—the fairies dance, and Christ is nailed to the cross" (*Process and Reality*,

p. 338). Playing, no less than philosophizing, offers a spacious enough context in which oscillations between movement and fixity are not only tolerated but acknowledged as the very processes of transformation allowing us to become what we are not yet. Lightness of identity, the floating existence I described earlier, is not granted by spotlighting the fairies' jubilant dance in some effort to avoid the lugubrious vision of the crucifixion. In equanimity, the burden of questioning *why* things are one way as opposed to another, *why* there is something rather than nothing, is lifted, and we are free to turn toward the gratuitous and resplendent presentations of any and every thing. Play leaves behind *why*s, in the process awakening and refashioning our perceptions of *what* is. It adjusts to fluid reality with a flexible attitude of "free entertainment," in George Santayana's phrase (*The Realm of Spirit*, p. 18).

This state of free entertainment emerges as a result of detaching from absorption in practical activities so that novel and uncalculated interests may flourish. The playful person is free to cultivate attitudes of spontaneity and ease while requirements to value ends over means and functionality over beauty slacken. Utilitarian aspirations fade, allowing for attention to the present plenitude as an end in itself. Play is fundamentally a manner of comportment, a flow of attitudinal stances where temporary suspension of the concerns of ordinary or everyday life leads to diminished consciousness of a separate ego through responsive openness and ongoing attunement. In play, we respect that it has a life of its own, proceeding in manifold directions, often nonlinearly, with stops and starts, zigzags, and forward and backward motions. The will to play is a leap into the recursive, self-organized, and unpredictable. "Play," Huizinga famously observed, "only becomes possible, thinkable, and understandable when an influx of mind breaks down the absolute determinism of the cosmos" (*Homo Ludens*, p. 3). Ludic interaction with the world brings us to that juncture where everything is less delineated, determined, and closed off. The inherent ambiguity of things is no longer strictly a source of anxiety or defensiveness, but rather the origin of wonderment, opportunities to traverse new lines of possibility. This feature of play's inherent openness marks, as Miguel Sicart implies, a shift in identity: "to be playful is to add ambiguity to the world and to play with that ambiguity" (*Play Matters*, p. 28). Playful subjects then do more than tolerate ambiguity; they craft a world whose plasticity offers new and unforeseen freedoms. Order and coherence are actively balanced with complexity and the unarticulated. The play of equanimity here allows us to do precisely what we normally do not—remake the world in order to embrace its undecidability, its unanticipated possibilities. A new cadence of life emerges involving the dynamic balancing of the serious and the ludic, defying all fixations.

Ludic interactions with people, things, and spaces are always delicate balancings between the private, our internal world of desires and fears, and the public, the pressing external world of obstinacies and limits. The point, of course, is not to determine, and then stay still at, some precise point of balance or equilibrium—which is impossible anyway—but to enjoy, through play, alternative modes of awareness and identity as they appear and disappear. In this way, the interpenetration of inner and outer experience cannot be isolated from a process of becoming. Playfulness is that liberatory disposition whose dynamism multiplies, like equanimity, views of the mystery of the world and the objects belonging to it. Playfulness immerses us joyfully in the polysemy of existence. Indeed, we recognize art at its most playful when it is most ambiguous, inexhaustible, and least purposeful—from the polyglot, hermetic punning of Joyce's *Finnegans Wake* (1939) to the vibrant, ludic Neo-Pop imagery of Takashi Murakami to the ironic, whimsical "Tropical Space Projects" of Salvadorian installation artist Simón Vega. The realm of art, like that of play, offers a reprieve from the limits of ponderous everyday realities. It moves us to vantage points where engagement with context or form offers alternative modes of existence not constrained by singular meaning or content. "We experience in beauty and art," Georg Simmel observed, "a lightness and freedom of *play* in contrast to a reality of existence exhausted in concrete particulars. . . . For play means that the functions normally bearing life's content and imprint of reality we now exercise without this fulfillment, purely formally" ("Kant and Modern Aesthetics," p. 116; emph. in orig.).

Perhaps no artwork better exemplifies this lightness and play of the formal than Robert Delauney's (1885-1941) *Simultaneous Windows* series (1912), a group of twenty-two paintings from the artist's self-styled "constructive" phase (Figure 2). Here, Delaunay overlaid and contrasted translucent complementary colors to create a synthetic, harmonic composition. Moving beyond painting's traditional function as a sort of static window onto an imaginary world, he turned instead to the pictorial surface itself as a site for registering the dynamic process of seeing. The name of the series references the French scientist Michel-Eugène Chevreul's (1786-1889) principle of color harmony explaining how the play of divergent hues may be perceived at once. The perception of color through light, the way light structures vision, and the motion of simultaneous color contrasts were the main subjects of exploration in *Windows*. Defining what he would call Simultaneism, a new aesthetic of simultaneous contrast, is Delaunay's notion that "without visual perception there is no light, no movement," as he wrote in 1912. "This movement," he continued, "is provided by relationships of *uneven measures*, by color contrasts, which constitute *Reality*" ("Light," p. 156; emph. in orig.). *Windows* puts viewers in sync with the movement and play of perceptible things, reminding us of the value of motion for equanimous approaches to the world. Attention here is strong to the extent that it is prevented from settling. In Delaunay's account, art has the power to furnish us with nothing less than the "the idea of the living movement of the world, and its movement is simultaneity" (ibid., p. 157). Harmonic vision, as Delaunay conceived it, amounts to a flexible taking part in what is perceived. It thereby brings into play a celebration of the intrinsic openness of interpretative processes, the space at the heart of the lusory attitude. Art, like play, depends upon participatory responses that ultimately generate new identificatory possibilities. "As he reacts to the play of stimuli and his own response to the artist's patterning, the individual addressee," Umberto Eco asserts, "supplies his own existential credentials, the sense conditioning that is purely his own" (*The Open Work*, p. 3). Art ceaselessly calls up new meanings when focus on the end result, in the form of some discrete product of knowledge, is suspended. Playfulness preserves wonder. As playfulness displaces the finality of knowledge and identity, art becomes one vital arena in which interaction with the world represents a form of continual engagement by the equanimous self in the making.

In lieu of purposiveness and the drive to closure, the play attitude welcomes the undecided, the open. It abides in processes embracing uncertainty. Indeterminacy contributes to forming the subject position of the player, the person for whom doubt often remains until the very end. Hinging upon the denouement, games like cards and chess are mutually curtailed when the outcome is no longer unpredictable. Up to that point, players are poised for the unexpected, and it is their imaginative responsiveness to what may unfold that led the child psychoanalyst D. W. Winnicott (1896-1971) to declare that playing is "always a creative experience... a basic form of living" (*Playing and Reality*, p. 50). Equating the lusory attitude with living itself—a theme I will take up in a bit—carries with it the radical corollary that humans are most themselves when at play. This may be so since playfulness is animated by impulses born of curiosity and the desire to know. "To play," Eugen Fink suggests, "is to take an explanatory attitude toward being at all times" ("The Ontology of Play," p. 155). This attentive situating of ourselves in playful relations to being serves to keep us going, offsetting the impenetrable gloominess that qualifies how we relate to the world at times.

So, the opposite of play is not work but depression, to paraphrase the eminent theorist of play Brian Sutton-Smith (see *The Ambiguity of Play*, p. 198). Play allows for the space to keep up a lively attitude of investigation. At its foundation, play is no more than continual questioning and answering. It resists stagnation as a kind of call and response ensues, bringing about an especially vibrant engagement with the world. Indeed, the sociologist Henning Eichberg frames play as both "a bodily-practical way to *answer* the world" and "primarily... a way of *asking* the world. Through practical engagement, play puts questions and tries to find or create patterns based on them. In this respect, play deepens the relation of the human being to the world—to the environment, to others, to oneself" ("Play against Alienation?" p. 217; emph. in orig.). The questions play poses always remain more important than any answers. Playfulness engages both a way of understanding and a riddle. In its easeful curiosity and equanimity, the playful attitude engages us with the not-yet-known. The richness of our relationship to the world reflects the degree to which questioning itself remains open, flexible, unforced. Revelations of meaning and pattern become provisional relays on the way to posing one more question—in other words, to playing some more.

Always in the process of emerging in the intervening spaces between sense and nonsense, repetition and novelty, and the visible and the invisible, play invites the subject to hold identity and meaning lightly. It thwarts dogmatisms of any sort. Belonging in and to the intermediary, playfulness involves, then, an oscillating, often fragile, search for both reality and fantasy. The variable pleasures of the ludic are found here, in the continual interplay and balancing of appreciable polarities: e.g., presence/absence, actuality/ideality, revelation/concealment, form/flux, and tension/release. Playfulness, as a mode of equanimous subjectivity, neither clings to coherence nor collapses in chaos. It embraces the dynamic interval between order and disorder, as reflected in the distinctive imagery of a Zen capping phrase: "Playing ball on running water" (Hori, *Zen Sand*, p. 231). Moving across a range of possibilities, playfulness promotes a litheness of being. In this fluid engagement with the world emerges the essence of the equanimous subject for whom the full context of a given situation may be disclosed. Central to playfulness, then, is what Susanna Millar, in her classic *The Psychology of Play* (1968), aptly calls "an attitude of throwing off constraint" (p. 21). The logic of calculation and resolution is too strict for play.

Playfulness freely sets up dispositions of purposelessness. And so, the ludic must entail, in French linguist Émile Benveniste's (1902-76) famous idiom, "forgetting the useful" [*oubli de l'utile*] ("Le jeu comme structure," p. 166). Free from the constraint of utilitarian considerations and unguided by ulterior motives, players discover a reprieve from instrumentality, entering a realm of "the sovereignly useless," to use George Steiner's fabulous phrase (*Has Truth a Future?*, p. 16). They are free now to cultivate encounters with the spontaneous, the possible, and the aleatory. Activities are now desirable as ends in themselves rather than as means to some further end. What is thus so unsettling about cheating at games is not necessarily victimization at the hands of the cheater but rather the recognition that the dishonest act alters the relation of means to end in such a precalculated way that it holds the end fixed. The game loses its status as play, as something whose inherent nature is to be gratuitous. To summarize this suggestively: playing, like equanimity, is recognized as a context for existence when reasons for inhabiting it are natural or intrinsic to existence itself.

In place of the content of ultimate meaning, then, there is only the context of free, autonomous movement. To the extent we look for a singular purpose to existence, we renounce the full confluence of living and playing. Part of the suspense—the intricate back-and-forth—of playing is that, while one can be wholly engaged in it, play itself is structurally nonserious. This notion aptly led the philosopher Randolph Feezell to describe playing as a mode of "serious nonseriousness" (passim, *Sport, Play, and Ethical Reflection*). Gadamer, who equates playing with pure movement, suggests that the autotelic nature of play guarantees a degree of freedom and ease for the subject:

> Play clearly represents an order in which the to-and-fro motion of play follows of itself. It is part of play that the movement is not only without goal or purpose but also without effort. It happens, as it were, by itself. The ease of play—which naturally does not mean that there is any real absence of effort but refers phenomenologically only to the absence of strain—is experienced subjectively as relaxation. The structure of play absorbs the player into itself, and thus frees him from the burden of taking the initiative, which constitutes the actual strain of existence. (*Truth and Method*, p. 105)

Playful subjects, folded into the nonserious structure of play, experience relaxation in the giving of themselves (or their egos) over to absolutely autogenic, incessant movement. Gadamer understands play in terms of a radical fading of self-consciousness that reflects harmony with the dynamic forces of nature. "Inasmuch as nature," Gadamer comments, "is without purpose and intention, just as it is without exertion, it is a constantly self-renewing play" (ibid.). Precisely because "the mode of being of play is so close to the mobile form of nature" (ibid.), it permits a state of equanimity that cannot be located within any method. Not something fixed or prescribed, playfulness, like equanimity, is lived completely within the "continuous series of transactions" between subjects and their environments (Dewey, *Unmodern Philosophy*, p. 235). Every unfolding transaction clears a brief space for recognizing that interrelation can exist without any intentionality and truth without any method.

The centrality of the ludic attitude to existence has often been remarked upon, from Sartre's ontology to Derrida's anti-nostalgic deconstruction to Roger Callois's broad agreement with philosopher Karl Groos's (1861-1946) pioneering work on play to Fink's reflection on our nature as time-bound creatures:

> The desire to play is fundamentally the desire to be. (*Being and Nothingness*, p. 581)
>
> Being must be conceived as presence or absence on the basis of the possibility of play and not the other way around. ("Structure, Sign and Play," p. 292)
>
> All the sensations or emotions that man can experience, all his movements and thoughts, give rise to games. (*Man, Play and Games*, p. 164)
>
> Play = an essential basic phenomenon of human existence—we play because we are temporally transient. ("Notes on 'The World-Significance of Play,'" p. 285)

Across the extensive overlap of playing and existing, spaces for metamorphosis and self-renewal, carried within the attitude of playfulness, open up. Playfulness is, then, a model for grasping how novelty emerges spontaneously, naturally, within the rhythms of living. It perennially holds out the possibility of interpreting the world itself as *at play*, which is never about seeing the freedoms latent in the world as purely arbitrary or denying the sometimes cruel causality among the things of it. Playfulness, like equanimity, is simply a way of *relating to* the world as it richly unfolds on its terms at the same time that we participate in it, openly and with deference. Through playfulness, the world is perceived in its variable pleasurableness, where pleasure may involve unadulterated fun or cross at times into unease and conflict. Play encompasses a hedonic field spanning the enjoyable to the distressing. So, framing playful existence within traditional views that identify it strictly with leisure activity, amusement, or escape from serious living is reductive. The range of playful existence reminds us of the tragic wisdom informing hunting as a flexible perspective on and in the world. At the heart of playfulness, tragic wisdom arises from the realization that, considered as a whole, all things—with their singular beauty and horror—comprise what Nietzsche in *The Birth of Tragedy* (1872) calls "an artful game [*ein künstlerisches Spiel*] which the will plays with itself for its own infinite fullness of pleasure" (*Der Geburt der Tragödie*, p. 152; trans. mine). "Fullness of pleasure" becomes accessible only through an equanimous vision that allows us to grasp the total process of the world's movement as a delicate balancing of forces constantly at variance.

Adjusting so as to be in sync with the perceived variance of inner and outer worlds is, as I have suggested, the essence of equanimity. As a flexible disposition, equanimity is not to be understood as some kind of non-reactive state promoting a bland or affectively neutral vision of things or events. Rather, it is a lively mode of relating to the changing world that necessarily entails multiple ways of being in the world. Like playfulness, it never unlocks in an instant some unitary or totalizing understanding of the cosmos but becomes the ontological marker of our intrinsic capacity for fluent receptivity and freedom. In a marginal note to his groundbreaking essay on "The World-Significance of Play," Fink observes that "The essential world-significance of play does not lie in its possible character of being a model for a universal understanding of the world... it lies in the position of cosmic openness that the playing human being is" ("Notes on 'The World-Significance of Play,'" p. 291). Playful existence cannot be separated from this position of receptivity. Indeed, Fink was fond of referring, by way of a genealogy starting with Heraclitus's Fragment 52 ("A [whole human] life-time is [nothing but] a child playing, playing checkers"), to Nietzsche's speech by Zarathustra "On the Three Metamorphoses": "The child is innocence and forgetting, a new beginning, a game, a self-propelled wheel, a first movement, a sacred 'Yes' [*ein heiliges Ja-sagen*]. For the game of creation, my brothers, a sacred 'Yes' is needed" (*Thus Spoke Zarathustra*, p. 27). *Ja-sagen* (yes-saying), a form of radical acceptance, becomes the very condition for the kind of deep similitude between subjects and their world that underpins what I discussed in Chapter 3 as the symbolic and metaphorical figuring of the cosmos in some philosophical strains of Romanticism. In the cosmicity of play—the game of creation—reside possibilities for attunement and synchrony, ways of relating and resembling animated by equanimity (again, L. *aequus*, "equal" + *animus*, "mind"). Nietzsche's Heraclitan intuition points to a singular determination and conception of subjectivity through play's openness: "Exposed to the all-embracing play of the world, the soul itself becomes cosmic and becomes similar to the world" (Fink, *Nietzsche's Philosophy*, p. 95).

Through a kind of benevolent expansion of perspective, being at play offers us *the* world, and through play *a* world becomes momentarily ours. Playfulness, in its purposeless equanimity, orients us in the grand cosmic game of which we are inescapably players. Understanding cosmology apart from playfulness is implausible in Hinduism where the ceaseless play (Skt. *līlā*) of Brahman is taken to pervade and constitute all of existence. Play thus defies singular structure or method. When something has "play," it has freedom or room for movement. And so, existence is conceived and determined through play when it is recognized that, as a positive dimension of freedom, play's "yes" to the world is not about changing the world as it is but adding something to it, introducing new experiences that arise, as philosopher of games Bernard Suits (1925-2007) insists, primarily "serendipitously" ("Tricky Triad," p. 2). This raises the question of whether there are any situations intrinsically immune to the fortuitous experiences of playfulness. Some appear at least allergic to playfulness (e.g., courtrooms and operating rooms), yet it is striking how the wide range of circumstances that can give rise to the attitude of playfulness includes ones not as a rule associated with it—consider warfare and life in a prisoner-of-war or concentration camp, brutal situations that I will take up momentarily.

At the other end of the civil spectrum lies Utopia, a site of ideality where play and games are seemingly superfluous since there is no need to find alternatives to labor, which is nonexistent. Yet, as Suits points out, with all instrumental needs satisfied, utopian existence becomes organized precisely around "a state of affairs where people are engaged only in those activities which they value intrinsically"

(*The Grasshopper*, p. 167), and thus "the only thing left to do would be to play games, so that game playing turns out to be the whole of the ideal of existence" (ibid., p. 172). In an instrumentalized world, however, where seriousness must prevail, games never rise above being "trifling fillers of the interstices in our lives." But in forms of utopic living, games do much more; they offer vital "clues to the future," such that their "serious cultivation now is perhaps our only salvation" (ibid., p. 176). This is a fascinating claim. Suits does not identify what these clues are or what salvation might look like, but literature and film often do. I think of brilliant war films like *Grand Illusion* (1937; dir. Jean Renoir), which figures war as just another scene of play, or *Forbidden Games* (1952; dir. René Clément) and *Grave of the Fireflies* (1988; dir. Isao Takahata), whose child protagonists naturally discover the intrinsic power of games to restore sense, even beauty and grace, to circumstances that otherwise utterly deny it. Play embodies attitudes of serious nonseriousness that are, I would argue, among the most human and salvific responses gesturing to anything like a future in the direst circumstances. Games, despite their powerlessness to stave off the realities of loss and death, allow us some of the most profound opportunities for coming to terms with them, to counterbalance them just long enough and just in time. Indeed, one of the less remarked upon features of playfulness as an attitude is its power to relieve fears associated with the threat of loss and death.

Two popular texts—one film and one novel—have relieved any doubt for me that the opposite of playfulness is not seriousness but rather depression, the loss of hope. One is the critically polarizing 1997 film *Life is Beautiful* (*La vita è bella*; dir. Roberto Benigni), and the other is Romain Gary's 1956 novel *The Roots of Heaven* (*Les racines du ciel*), which became a John Huston film in 1958 with the same title. Moments in each text point to how playfulness ensures a crucial continuity to the world in the face of its traumatic disruption. Prior to the upheavals of trauma, certain models of the world as it is and how it might be comprise what is called the "assumptive world," C. Murray Parkes's pioneering term for the set of beliefs shaped by experience that we bring to a changing world. Radical alterations in the life space—captivity in a concentration camp (*Life is Beautiful*) and a prisoner-of-war camp (*The Roots of Heaven*)—typically result in significant restructurings of persons' assumptive worlds. Yet for the characters of these fictions something else—or, we might say, something more—takes place. Key elements of their assumptive worlds—the comic and the civil—are now creatively fitted to a life space invested with play, meaning, and equilibrium. Playfulness, as these fictions present it, serves as an adaptive orientation in a world that is incalculably cruel.

In *Life is Beautiful*, when the Jewish Guido (Benigni) and his five-year-old son Giosuè (Giorgio Cantarini) are seized by the SS and sent to a concentration camp, it becomes Guido's fervent mission to make life there as bearable as possible for his son. Guido invents a game world in which father and son are in competition with the other camp inmates. The winner, who receives the prize of a military tank, is the person who earns the most points for tasks, crafted for his son, related to tranquility and resilience: e.g., staying still longest in the barracks, not crying for his mother, and not asking for lollipops. Guido carries on this playful fiction right until the very end when, in the chaos of shutting down the camp as Allied forces approach, he tells his son to stay in a mailbox until everybody has left, the final task in the game before the promised tank is his. Guido, attempting to find his wife who is somewhere in the camp, is apprehended by a German soldier. Ordered by an officer to be executed, Guido, while being led off to his death, passes by Giosuè for the last time and winks, reassuring his son that the game is still in motion. This is what games can do: they smooth out tragic vicissitudes by providing a momentary and flexible ideal. They support, as I put it in chapter 4 in a different context, the possibility of a softer, smoother world. Playfulness is then never an antidote to cruelty but a co-existing reality that may make it survivable. Guido's game, lacking the power to negate or deny the reality of life in the camp, works rather from within, functioning as one more lens through which to see a world that is brutally structured to deny any perspectives contrary to existence without freedom. Guido's game rescripts the binary of cruelty's required roles of perpetrator and victim by restoring agency, and along with it a crucial sense of freedom, to the supremely vulnerable—children and the child-like.

One of the elements that makes this film particularly challenging, even troubling, for some viewers is coming to terms with Guido's assumptive world, that is, maintaining the view, which the film promotes, that he is a holy fool who, like a child, naturally sees life as enchanted, full of possibilities drawing on illusion. How, some critics of the film legitimately ask, is fantasy, let alone humor, even plausible in the face of atrocities like the Shoah? Are they merely forms of denial or are they grave efforts, however imperfect, to give meaning to the unfathomable? Within the film's diegetic world, Guido consistently embodies a holy-foolish innocence, his natural and humble defense against realizing the true horror of his total situation, which, as the film shows, the other adult inmates clearly recognize. Guido's assumptive world, for better and for worse, is a barrier to understanding, as at one point when he solemnly chides Giosuè for refusing to take a "shower" with the other children. What Guido cannot or does not want to believe about the world becomes the precise point of departure for play. Guido's heroic efforts to find within the space of the concentration camp all that is needed for an elaborate game signify a wish to shelter his son in the armor of illusions and—crucially, I think—to preserve his own irrepressible assumptive world.

It is Nietzsche who speaks more compellingly than any modern writer of the buoyant, exuberant human drive to keep afloat life-enriching illusion. To maintain an aesthetic distance above the anguishes and indignities of everyday life preserves our freedom, even in the harshest realities like those of the Holocaust. A well-known passage in *The Gay Science* speaks to the equanimity of folly, to the liberatory value of foolishness:

> As an aesthetic phenomenon existence is still *bearable* for us, and art furnishes us with eyes and hands and above all the good conscience to be *able* to turn ourselves into such a phenomenon. . . . We must occasionally find pleasure in our folly, or we cannot continue to find pleasure in our wisdom. Precisely because we are at bottom grave and serious human beings—really, more weights than human beings—nothing does us as much good as a *fool's cap*: we need it in relation to ourselves—we need all exuberant, floating, dancing, mocking, childish,

and blissful art lest we lose the *freedom above things* that our ideal demands of us. (pp. 163-64; emph. in orig.)

Playfulness, along with the comical, offers multiple opportunities to float above, to keep moving, dancing, and pretending, not in the name of avoiding the cruelties of existence but of crafting an endurable world or of reenchanting it. Humor, as philosopher Nicolai Hartmann states, is "the genuine benefactor of humankind," where the beneficence of comedy derives from an ethos of "receptivity" and "simple broad-mindedness" (*Aesthetics*, p. 466) that serves to "elevate" us above the ugliness of the world (ibid., p. 483).

In the embedded narrative that is Gary's *Les racines du ciel* appears a vignette about World War II POWs who find a playful way to preserve their assumptive world. Robert, a prisoner in a German camp, responds to his fellow prisoners' decaying morale by creating an imaginary woman whom all must respect and in whose presence all should behave. Dismissed initially as ludicrous, the idea is quickly accepted by his comrades in Block K, who come to see that "if there wasn't some convention of dignity left to sustain us, if we didn't cling to some fiction, to some myth, there would be nothing left but to let ourselves go, submit to anything, including the Nazis, to give in and to betray" (*Roots*, p. 170). The men begin to gather flowers for "Mademoiselle" and to make speeches aimed to impress her with their witticism. Robert explains the often comical performance of remaining decorous in front of an invisible woman in terms of what he calls the "as if": "You'll try and behave in front of her as if you were men. I say 'as if'—it's the only thing that matters" (ibid.). The German commandant, whose suspicions are aroused by Block K's striking change in morale, demands that Robert hand over the imaginary woman living in the barracks. Understanding that it is all a game on the part of the prisoners, the commandant makes clear his repugnance for playfulness by declaring that he does not believe "in the omnipotence of the human spirit. . . . in the noble conventions or in the myth of dignity. . . . in the primacy of the spiritual" (ibid., p. 171). Faced with the grim deadline of surrendering the woman, Robert appears "jubilant. . .thoroughly happy" (ibid.) in his defiance, the price for which is 30 days of solitary confinement and beatings.

When Robert returns to his comrades, they notice not only his emaciated and bruised body but his buoyant attitude, his capacity to make light of his trials by preserving a fantasy life. Social laughter, like fantasy, Bergson pointed out, remedies something unnatural for human beings in any conditions. He described this unnaturalness as an "inelasticity of character, of mind and even of body" (*Laughter*, p. 19). To remain fluid is the preeminent creative response to an untenable world, to a fascistically rigid one. We survive the world as it is to the extent we play with and in it. Within it.

Fig. 2. Robert Delaunay, *Windows*, Paris, 1912

FUTURE DIRECTIONS

> The eyesight has another eyesight, and the hearing another hearing, and the voice another voice.
> —Walt Whitman, "Assurances"
>
> An adjustable horizon cannot be narrow.
> —Karl Kraus, *Dicta and Contradicta*

One way to put it is like this: equanimity amounts to a series of positionless positions realizable as natural, conscious, and dynamic relationships to the moving world that fit themselves to situations as they appear and disappear. Intentionality, serving the stability of patterned, rule-governed features of personality and behavior, is ill suited to a shifting world that constantly approaches and withdraws. No sooner is equanimity admitted in a single instance than the world again impinges itself—positively, negatively, or neutrally—and so delicate balancing and rebalancing acts may begin again, without the imperative to do so. In its mutable responsiveness to the world, equanimity is like playing with a kaleidoscope where order collapses into an exciting new one with each turn. Approaching the cognizable world equanimously without giving priority to process over form and change over stasis is not possible. Nevertheless, genuine attunement to the changeful world means moments will arise when equanimous rebalancing becomes temporarily suspended or paused, when, for example, it gets subordinated in the immediacy of urgent situations such as standing against injustice or contesting abuses of power.

This is one reason why it has seemed to me misguided to promote equanimity as some kind of tonic to heal the ills of persons and societies whose too-frequent lack of kindness, care, humility, and respect is nevertheless indisputable. If equanimity produces anything of what humanity needs, it does so only as by-products of its methodless method. Unlike the other three *brahmavihāras* (sublime attitudes)—compassion, loving-kindness, and sympathetic joy—equanimity is not intrinsically a pro-social function of the evolution of attachment. In contrast to the others, it is not a social mentality aimed at, to paraphrase psychologist Paul Gilbert, organizing competencies motivated by securing specific types of social relatedness (see *Human Nature and Suffering*). As a non-teleological attitude toward the world, it simply consists in the smooth taking up of one perspective on the way to taking up more. Its fundamental activity is thus that of ongoing and quiet questioning, the primary means through which the world presents its possibilities. Questioning is not the same thing as suspending judgment, and, against the grain of much contemporary writing on equanimity, it is clear that the suspension of judgment is simply one possible dimension of the open-ended and ruleless process of equanimity, not its primary condition, certainly not its telos. If equanimity did not offer reprieve from instrumentality, it would hardly be as compelling an attitude as it is and historically has been. Indeed, to focus on instrumentalizing equanimity deprives it of its richness as a multifaceted approach to the world.

The reader has likely noticed my predilection for the word "salutary" when describing aspects of equanimity. Doesn't the use of this word somehow militate against my basic position that equanimity is without end purpose, that it is relieved of aim? I have wanted to preserve something of the word's archaic sense—health-giving. Equanimity, a dynamic process whose very mobility is an index of health (Old English *hœlp*, "wholeness"), serves as one vital seed of psychological freedom. So, in the background of my genealogy of equanimity as an idea has been its hallowed place in Buddhist visions of the processes of awakening: its association with *samādhi*, the last of the eight elements of the Noble Eightfold Path; its status as the final of the four *brahmavihāras*; its rank as the last of the seven factors of enlightenment or awakening; its status as the fourth and ultimate *jhāna* (meditative absorption, where here happiness and discontent are replaced by total equanimity); its place as the last of the ten *pāramitās* (Pali: *pāramī*; perfections) in the Theravāda tradition; and its supreme function as offering protection from the eight worldly winds (praise and blame, gain and loss, pleasure and pain, fame and disgrace). The awakened mind possesses a broad state of awareness, and is like an undivided context for the experience of things. In the "The Parable of the Plants" of the *Lotus Sūtra*, it is compared to falling rain:

> The rain falls everywhere,
> Coming from all sides,
> Flowing everywhere without limit,
> Reaching over the face of the earth.
>
> Into the hidden recesses of the mountains, streams, and steep valleys,
> Where plants and trees grow, and medicinal herbs,
> Big trees and small,
> A hundred grains, rice seedlings, sugar cane, and grapevines.
>
> All are moistened by the rain
> And abundantly enriched.
> The dry ground is soaked,
> And both herbs and trees flourish.
>
> By that same water that
> Comes from that cloud,
> Plants, trees, thickets, and forest,
> According to their need, receive moisture.
>
> Roots, stems, branches, and leaves
> Blossoms and fruit in brilliant color,
> One rain goes to all,
> And all becomes bright and shiny.
> (*The Lotus Sutra*, pp. 162-63)

Never reducible to a state of stillness, equanimity has the conditions of vibrancy and range that are said to mark an awakened mind. As an image of how consciousness operates generatively, it is like falling rain—it "goes to all." Equanimity is normally circumstance independent, expressed in whatever context one occupies, without the goal of *freedom from*. There is a Zen expression, once popular on New

Years greeting cards in Japan, that neatly encapsulates the unifying perspective of equanimity: "a thousand miles, the same breeze." Across the great expanse of what we can be aware of, the same wind moves. Equanimity is the winding current of consciousness between what the esoteric philosopher Franklin Merrell-Wolff (1887-1985) calls the perspectives of the "point-I" and the "Space-I" (*Pathways through to Space*, pp. 217-18). Whereas the former is consciousness striving to separate pleasure from unpleasure and is thus restrictive in scope, the latter represents consciousness working within a broad and finally limitless field in ways that create continuity through non-striving. While equanimity seems more compatible with the integrating Space-I, it also crucially depends on the differentiating point-I. Only in the frictionless functioning of both perspectives does equanimity emerge.

Equanimity involves, then, the dialogic play of perspectives, the function of (at least) two fundamental ways of seeing the world. This book has considered some of the key terms with which thinkers from different philosophical traditions have framed the interactive perspectivism that underpins equanimity. Parallel formulations describing the play and mutual entailment of perspectives extend beyond the current book and multiply across disciplinary fields: art and art history (e. g., Paul Klee, Anton Ehrenzweig, José Argüelles), psychology and psychoanalysis (Heinz Werner, E. Graham Howe, Marion Milner, Michael Balint), philosophy (Henri Bergson, A. N. Whitehead, Iris Murdoch), marine biology (Edward Ricketts), and Egyptology (René Schwaller de Lubicz). In addition, there are integrative thinkers, such as Edward de Bono, Colin Wilson, and Herbert A. Simon, who have speculated on the dynamic interaction between perspectival positions involved in creativity and deliberation, intuition and problem-solving. This skeletal sketch indicates the genealogies remaining to be mapped out in terms of their relevance to how equanimity may inform perceiving, thinking, valuing, and acting.

In a future volume on equanimity and its relation to ethics and to states of adversity, I will explore the deep relations between equanimous ways of approaching the world and our capacities to negotiate it. There I will be interested, for example, in the question of how mobile perspectives interact with elements in the lived field, where it can be acknowledged that, while ethical life and adversities have their qualities, they never define realms that exist outside of the perspectives in which they may be discovered. Equanimity, in its fluid attentions and provisional appraisals, never decontextualizes the objects of awareness, reifies them, or considers them independent of all that exists. What emerges are important implications for treating the forms that equanimity gives to ethical life as based less on moral self-cultivation than on inquiring of ourselves and communities what sort of life we might sensibly desire to live in the full range of situations we find ourselves. To understand the roles of equanimity in shaping ethical sensibilities and responses to adverse situational factors it will be helpful to consider equanimity in relation to the traditions of virtue theory and virtue ethics, where the former tradition, according to the useful distinction made by philosophers Roger Crisp (1996) and Julia Driver (1996), encompasses inquiries concerning the virtues in general, while the latter, narrower in scope, consists primarily in the promotion of the virtues.

My sense is that softening the compelling critiques of virtue ethics, particularly as rooted in the situationism of social psychology, allows for spacious exploration of the roles that equanimous awareness plays in mediating less deliberative relations to virtuous action. What equanimity might offer to virtue theory emerges in part from its conceptual debt to features of quietism, as found, for example, in Epicureanism and Pyrrhonism, the Neo-Confucianism of Chéng Hào (1032-85), or the internalized spirituality of Miguel de Molinos (1628-96). (The place of quietism in equanimity, as I will recover it, is neither symptomatic nor encouraging of political quietism.) The ethical intensity of equanimity may summarily be said to be inversely proportional to what Maslow plainly called "bad behavior": "There's a kind of not quite Socratic notion to which I would subscribe and which I think I could document fairly well without going as far as Socrates, to say that bad behavior, evil behavior, is impossible to anyone who knows all the facts that are involved" (*Abraham H. Maslow: A Memorial Volume*, p. 41). Certainly, if it requires knowing all the facts, then equanimity asks too much of us. However, the point is that the more details one knows, the more sides of any situation that are taken into account, the less propensity to corruption and inhumanity there will be. Equanimity can never strictly be an antidote to bad behavior; rather, through promoting a kind of perspicacious trust in the world's varying affordances, it leaves us unblemished, just as Ch'an Master Baizhang Huaihai (720-814) declared in response to a student's question concerning the true meaning of right perception (*zhengjian*): "It means beholding all sorts of forms, but without being stained by them, because no thoughts of love or aversion arise in the mind" (*Zen Teaching of Instantaneous Awakening*, p. 35).

Equanimity allows for the arrival and disappearance of desire and dread through flexible relations to a full range of sensible forms. Its immunity to emotional inertia ensures that thought formations never set into the rigor mortis of received concepts and formulaic plots. Undoubtedly, Thomas Hobbes (1588-1679) was right when he proclaimed that "there is no such thing as perpetuall Tranquillity of mind, while we live here; because Life itself is but Motion, and can never be without Desire, nor without Feare, no more than without Sense" (*Leviathan*, p. 46). Equanimity joins with tranquility not at the point of stillness or sedateness but of total harmony with what is—that is, the multiple and the processual. Wallace Stevens, in offering "Thirteen Ways of Looking at a Blackbird," reveals the implicit unity—as opposed to oneness—in separate visions: "I was of three minds, / Like the tree / In which there are three blackbirds" (*The Collected Poems*, p. 92). One observer/contemplator, one tree, containing three birds, generating three apprehensions (or six, counting the tree's). To approach the world in such a way that the phenomenological intricacy of and affinities among things may be experienced in their dynamism runs counter to the way ordinary language works to differentiate realities, to settle and reduce their meanings, as if finished with them. Day-to-day language only weakly tempts us to appreciate the many-sidedness (Goethe's *Vielseitigkeit*) of things. No wonder, then, Rilke was so leery of everyday words, and, like Stevens in his later poetry, just wanted things themselves to sing (e. g., the former's poetics of the *Dinggedicht* [thing-poem] and the latter's poetry aptly described as "the resonance, reverberation, or echo of the song of things" [Mahoney, "Like a New Knowledge of Reality," p. 235]). Here is Rilke, from his early *In Celebration of Myself* (*Mir zur Feier*, 1899):

> I am so afraid of people's words.
> Everything they pronounce is so clear:
> this is a hand, and that is a house,
> and beginning is here, and the end over there.
> Their meaning frightens, their mockery-play
> and their claims to know what's coming, what was;
> no mountain thrills them now; their estates
> and their gardens abut directly on God.
> I warn; I ward them off. Stay back.
> It's a wonder to me to hear things sing.
> You touch them, and they stultify.
> You are the very destroyer of things. (*Selected Poems*, p. 7)

Certainty about the world we encounter is no more than a function (and fiction) of approaching it from sclerosed and predisposed points of view. As Rilke admonishes, such certitude is acquired at the insufferable cost of being sentenced to a deadened world. In place of the drive to certainty there must be trust, as I suggested—trust that if things are left alone, approached with openness, they may sing or spring up impromptu.

Disequanimity, in its partiality of vision and its inflexibility, ruins the possibility of connecting to the immanence of the vital. It ignores—is ignorant of—the plenitude whose inexhaustibility announces itself immediately, pre-reflectively. Valuing the multifaceted nature of things, equanimity joins with the effects of the poetic image, bringing out what escapes categorizing not only through its mystery but through its unmediated ordinariness. It is precisely equanimity that points to the inherently fugitive, putting before us what resides beyond the linguistic divisions—this is a hand, that is a house—that dampen the wonder of hearing things sing. There is no forcing things to sing. This may be the heart of equanimity: the recognition that, as Bakhtin put it when he was describing the catharsis of Dostoyevsky's novels, "Nothing conclusive has yet taken place in the world, the ultimate word of the world and about the world has not yet been spoken, the world is open and free, everything is still in the future and will always be in the future" (*Problems of Dostoevsky's Poetics*, p. 166). And so, with no ending to be projected or conclusion to be anticipated, the query prevails over the answer.

There is no final question.

REFERENCES

Abbott, E. A. (1992). *Flatland: A romance of many dimensions.* New York: Dover Publications.

Abe Masao (1985). True Person and compassion: D. T. Suzuki's appreciation of Lin-chi and Chao-chu. In W. R. La Fleur (Ed.), *Zen and western thought* (pp. 69-80). Honolulu, HI: University of Hawaii Press.

Adler, A. (1944). Disintegration and restoration of optic recognition in visual agnosia: Analysis of a case. *Archives of Neurology & Psychiatry, 51*(3), 243-59.

Alberti, L. B. (1966). *On Painting* (Trans. J. R. Spencer). New Haven, CT: Yale University Press.

Alexander, C. (1979). *The timeless way of building.* New York: Oxford University Press.

Al-Hujwiri, A. bin 'U. al-J. (1911). *The Kashf al-mahjúb: The oldest Persian treatise on Súfiism* (Trans. R. A. Nicholson). Leyden: A. J. Brill.

Allport, G. W. (1937). *Personality: A psychological interpretation.* New York: Henry Holt & Co.

American Psychiatric Association. (1980). *Diagnostic and statistical manual of mental disorders* (3rd ed.). Washington, DC: Author.

Aṅguttara Nikāya. (1999). *Numerical Discourses of the Buddha: An Anthology of Suttas from the Aṅguttara Nikāya* (Trans. N. Thera & B. Bodhi). Walnut Creek, CA: AltaMira Press.

Antinori, A., Carter, O. L., & Smillie, L. D. (2017). Seeing it both ways: Openness to experience and binocular rivalry suppression. *Journal of Research in Personality, 68,* 15-22.

Appleton, G. (Ed.) (1988). *The Oxford book of prayer.* Oxford: Oxford University Press.

Ardley, G. (1967). The role of play in the philosophy of Plato. *Philosophy, 42*(161), 226-44.

Arendt, H. (1963/1968). The conquest of space and the stature of man. In *Between past and future: Eight exercises in political thought* (pp. 265-80). New York: Penguin Books.

Asai Ryōi. (1984). *Tales of the floating world: The Ukiyo monogatari of Asai Ryōi* (Trans. D. L. Barber) [Unpublished master's thesis]. The Ohio State University.

Asaṅga. (2018). *A compendium of the Mahayana: Asaṅga's Mahāyānasaṃgraha and its Indian and Tibetan commentaries* (Trans. K. Brunnhölzl). 3 vols. Boulder, CO: Snow Lion.

Augustine of Hippo. (1972). *Concerning the city of God against the pagans* (Trans. H. Bettenson). Baltimore, MD: Penguin.

Austin, J. H. (1998). *Zen and the brain: Toward an understanding of meditation and consciousness*. Cambridge, MA: MIT Press.

Bachelard, G. (1983). *Water and dreams: An essay on the imagination of matter* (Trans. E. R. Farrell). Dallas, TX: Dallas Institute Publications.

Bakhtin, M. M. (1981). *The dialogic imagination: Four essays* (Trans. C. Emerson & M. Holquist; Ed. M. Holquist). Austin, TX: University of Texas Press.

Bakhtin, M. M. (1984). *Problems of Dostoevsky's poetics* (Ed. & Trans. C. Emerson). Minneapolis, MN: University of Minnesota Press.

Bakhtin, M. M. (1986). Toward a methodology for the human sciences (Trans. V. W. McGee). In C. Emerson & M. Holquist (Eds.), *Speech genres and other late essays* (pp. 159-72). Austin, TX: University of Texas Press.

Bakhtin, M. M. (1993). *Toward a philosophy of the act* (Trans. V. Liapunov; Ed. V. Liapuniv & M. Holquist). Austin, TX: University of Texas Press.

Baldwin, T. (1786). *Airopaidia: containing the narrative of a balloon excursion from Chester, the eighth of September, 1785, taken from minutes made during the voyage: hints on the improvement of balloons ... to which is subjoined mensuration of heights by the barometer, made plain; with extensive tables. The whole serving as an introduction to aërial navigation: With a copious index*. Chester, UK: J. Fletcher.

Balzac, H. (1915). *The physiology of marriage*. In vol. 36 of *The works of Honoré de Balzac*. New York: McKinlay, Stone, & MacKenzie.

Barfield, O. (1977). Participation and isolation: A fresh light on present discontents. In *The rediscovery of meaning and other essays* (pp. 210-16). Middletown, CT: Wesleyan University Press.

Bashō Matsuo. (1966). *The narrow road to the deep north and other travel sketches* (Trans. N. Yuasa). Harmondsworth, UK: Penguin.

Bataille, G. (2011). *Guilty* (Trans. S. Kendall). Albany, NY: State University of New York Press.
Batchelor, S. (2015). *After Buddhism: Rethinking the dharma for a secular age.* New Haven, CT: Yale University Press.
Batchelor, S. (2016). Greek Buddha: Pyrrho's encounter with early Buddhism in central Asia. *Contemporary Buddhism, 17*(1), 195-215.
Bayne, T. (2010). *The unity of consciousness.* Oxford: Oxford University Press.
Bayne, T., & Chalmers, D. J. (2003). What is the unity of consciousness? In A. Cleeremans (Ed.), *The unity of consciousness: Binding, integration, dissociation* (pp. 23-58). Oxford: Oxford University Press.
Bech, J. M. (2001). *De Husserl a Heidegger: La transformación del pensamiento fenomenológi.* Barcelona: Ediciones Universidad de Barcelona.
Beckett, S. (1957). *Murphy.* New York: Grove Press.
Beisser, A. R. (1970). The paradoxical theory of change. In J. Fagan & I. L. Shepherd (Eds.), *Gestalt therapy now: Theory, techniques, applications* (pp. 77-80). New York: Harper & Row.
Benjamin, W. (1999). Surrealism: The last snapshot of the European intelligentsia (Trans. E. Jephcott). In M. W. Jennings, H. Eiland, & G. Smith (Eds.), *Selected writings, 1927-1934* (pp. 207-21). Cambridge, MA: Belknap Press of Harvard University Press.
Benjamin, W. (1999). *The Arcades project* (Trans. H. Eiland & K. McLaughlin). Cambridge, MA: Harvard University Press.
Benjamin, W. (1999). The return of the flâneur (Trans. R. Livingstone). In M. W. Jennings, H. Eiland, & G. Smith (Eds.), *Selected writings, 1927-1934* (pp. 262-67). Cambridge, MA: Belknap Press of Harvard University Press.
Benveniste, É. (1947). Le jeu comme structure. *Deucalion, 2,* 161-167.
Berger, J. (1972). *Ways of seeing.* New York: Penguin.
Bergson, H. (1911). *Laughter: An essay on the meaning of the comic* (Trans. C. Brereton & F. Rothwell. London: Macmillan.
Bergson, H. (1911). *Matter and memory* (Trans. N. M. Paul & W. S. Palmer). London: George Allen & Unwin.
Bergson, H. (1960). *Creative evolution* (Trans. A. Mitchell). London: Macmillan & Co.
Berland, J. (2009). *North of empire: Essays on the cultural technologies of space.* Durham, NC: Duke University Press.

Bernard of Clairvaux. (1957-98). Epistola 106.2. In J. Leclercq & H. M. Rochais (Eds.), *Epistolae I, Corpus epistolarum 1-180*, vol. 7 of *Sancti Bernardi Opera* (p. 266). Rome: Editiones Cistercienses.

Berque, A. (2017). Thinking the ambient: On the possibility of Shizengaku (Naturing Science). In J. B. Callicott, & J. McRae (Eds.), *Japanese environmental philosophy* (pp. 13-28). Oxford: Oxford University Press.

Berthier, F. (2000). *Reading Zen in rocks: The Japanese dry landscape* (Trans. G. Parkes). Chicago, IL: University of Chicago Press.

Bevis, W. (1988). *Mind of winter: Wallace Stevens, meditation, and literature*. Pittsburgh, PA: University of Pittsburgh Press.

Birukoff, P. (1911). *The life of Tolstoy*. London: Cassell and Company.

Blake, W. (1906). *The letters of William Blake* (Ed. A. G. B. Russell). New York: Charles Scribner's Sons.

Blake, W. (1966). *Complete writings with variant readings* (Ed. G. Keynes). Oxford: Oxford University Press.

Blyth, R. H. (1981). *Haiku, Vol. 1: Eastern culture*. Tokyo, Japan: Hokuseido Press.

Bohm, D. (1980). *Wholeness and the implicate order*. London: Routledge & Kegan Paul.

Bohm, D. (1988). *On creativity* (Ed. L. Nichol). New York: Routledge.

Bollnow, O. F. (2011). *Human space* (Ed. J. Kohlmaier & Trans. C. Shuttleworth). London: Hyphen Press.

Bourke-White, M. (1963). *Portrait of myself*. New York: Simon & Schuster.

Brady, H. (2018, April 19). This tea master is preserving an ancient art for future generations. *National Geographic*. Retrieved from https://www.nationalgeographic.com/news/2018/04/japanese-tea-ceremony-master-matcha-culture/.

Brand, D. (1991). *The spectator and the city in nineteenth-century American literature*. Cambridge: Cambridge University Press.

Brand, W. (2009). Hume's account of curiosity and motivation. *Journal of Value Inquiry, 43*(1), 83-96.

Bruner, J. S., & Goodman, C. C. (1947). Value and need as organizing factors in perception. *Journal of Abnormal and Social Psychology, 42*, 33-44.

Buber, M. (1965). Dialogue (Trans. R. G. Smith). In *Between man and man* (pp. 1-39). New York: Collier Books.

Buber, M. (1965). What is man? (Trans. R. G. Smith). In *Between man and man* (pp. 118-205). New York: Collier Books.

Buber, M. (1970). *I and thou* (Trans. W. Kaufman). New York: Simon & Schuster.

Buddhaghosa. (1976). *The path of purification (Visuddhimagga)* (Trans. B. Ñāṇamoli). Boulder, CO: Shambhala.

Burrow, T. (1938). Kymograph studies of physiological (respiratory) concomitants in two types of attentional adaptation. *Nature, 142*(3586), 156.

Burrow, T. (1953). The neurosis of man. In W. E. Galt (Ed.), *Science and man's behavior: The contribution of phylobiology* (pp. 119-536). New York: Philosophical Library.

Burrow, T. (1958). *A search for man's sanity: The selected letters of Trigant Burrow*. New York: Oxford University Press.

Butler, C. (1994). *Early modernism: Literature, music and painting in Europe, 1900–1916*. Oxford: Oxford University Press.

Caillois, R. (2001). *Man, play and games* (Trans. M. Barash). Urbana, IL: University of Illinois Press.

Čapek, K. (1990). Afterword. In *Three novels: Hordubal, Meteor, An ordinary life* (Trans. M. & R. Weatherall) (pp. 316-19). North Haven, CT: Catbird Press.

Casey, E. S. (1996). How to get from space to place in a fairly short stretch of time: Phenomenological prolegomena. In S. Feld & K. H. Basso (Eds.), *Senses of place* (pp. 13-52). Santa Fe, NM: School of American Research Press.

Cavell, S. (1979). *The claim of reason: Wittgenstein, skepticism, morality, and tragedy*. Oxford: Oxford University Press.

Chah, A. (1985). *A still forest pool: The insight meditation of Achaan Chah* (Ed. J. Kornfield & P. Breiter). Wheaton, IL: Quest Books.

Chambers, I. (1994). Leaky habitats and broken grammar. In G. Robertson, M. Mash, L. Tickner, J. Bird, B. Curtis & T. Putnam (Eds.), *Travellers' tales: Narratives of home and displacement* (pp. 243-47). New York: Routledge.

Chatwin, B. (1996). Letter to Tom Maschler. In J. Borm & M. Graves (Eds.), *The anatomy of restlessness: Selected writing, 1969-1989* (pp. 75-84). New York: Viking.

Cleary, J. C. (Ed. & Trans.) (1990). *A tune beyond the clouds: Zen teachings from old China*. Berkeley, CA: Asian Humanities Press.

Cleary, J. C. (Trans.) (2006). *Swampland flowers: The letters and lectures of Zen Master Ta Hui*. Boulder, CO: Shambhala Publications.

Cleary, T. (Trans.) (2010). *Book of serenity*. Hudson, NY: Lindisfarne Press.

Coccia, E. (2019). *The life of plants: A metaphysics of mixture* (Trans. D. J. Montanari). Cambridge, UK: Polity Press.

Cohen, M. (1995). *Profane illumination: Walter Benjamin and the Paris of surrealist revolution*. Berkeley: University of California Press.
Coleridge, S. T. (1895). *Letters of Samuel Taylor Coleridge*. 2 vols. (Ed. E. H. Coleridge). Boston: Houghton Mifflin and Company.
Conrad, J. (1919). *Chance: A tale in two parts*. New York: Doubleday, Page, and Co.
Cosgrove, D. (2001). *Apollo's eye: A cartographic genealogy of the Earth in the Western imagination*. Baltimore: Johns Hopkins University Press.
Crisp, R. (1996). Modern moral philosophy and the virtues. In R. Crisp (Ed.), *How should one live? Essays on the virtues* (pp. 1-18). Oxford: Oxford University Press.
Dao de jing: A philosophical translation (Trans. R. T. Ames & D. L. Hall). (2003). New York: Ballantine Books.
Daoyuan. (2015). *The Buddhas and Indian patriarchs*. Vol. 1 of *Records of the Transmission of the Lamp* (Trans. R. S. Whitfield). Munich: Books on Demand Verlag.
De Certeau, M. (1984). *The practice of everyday life* (Trans. S. Rendall). Berkeley, CA: University of California Press.
De Curel, F. (1893). *L'amour brode: Pièce en trois actes*. Paris: Tresses et Stock.
Delaunay, R. (2001). Light. In M. A. Caws (Ed.), *Manifesto: A century of isms* (pp. 156-59). Lincoln, NE: University of Nebraska Press.
Deleuze, G. (1990). *The logic of sense* (Trans. M. Lester & Ed. C. V. Boundas). New York: Columbia University Press.
Deleuze, G., & Guattari, F. (1987). *A thousand plateaus: Capitalism and schizophrenia* (Trans. B. Massumi). Minneapolis, MN: University of Minnesota Press.
Deleuze, G., & Parnet, C. (1987). *Dialogues* (Trans. H. Tomlinson & B. Habberjam). New York: Columbia University Press.
Derrida, J. (1978). Structure, sign and play in the discourses of the human sciences. In *Writing and difference* (Trans. A. Bass) (pp. 278-93). Chicago, IL: University of Chicago Press.
Desbordes, G., Gard, T., Hoge, E. A., Hölzel, B. K., Kerr, C., Lazar, S. W., Olendzki, A., & Vago, D. R. (2015). Moving beyond mindfulness: Defining equanimity as an outcome measure in meditation and contemplative research. *Mindfulness, 6*(2), 356-372.
Dewey, J. (1929). *Experience and nature*. Chicago, IL: Open Court Publishing.
Dewey, J. (1931). *Context and thought*. Berkeley, CA: University of California Press.

Dewey, J. (1969–1972). Introduction to philosophy, Syllabus of course 5. In vol. 3 of J. A. Boydston (Ed.), *The early works: 1892–1898* (pp. 211-35). Carbondale, IL: Southern Illinois University Press.
Dewey, J. (1981–1991). Appendix 2: Experience and philosophic method. In vol. 1 of J. A. Boydston (Ed.), *The later works, 1925–1953* (pp. 365-91). Carbondale, IL: Southern Illinois University Press.
Dewey, J. (1987). Art as Experience. In vol. 10 of J. A. Boydston (Ed.), *The later works, 1925–1953* (pp. 1-352). Carbondale, IL: Southern Illinois University Press.
Dewey, J. (1989). *Experience and education*. Carbondale, IL: Southern Illinois University Press.
Dewey, J. (2012). *Unmodern philosophy and modern philosophy* (Ed. P. Deen). Carbondale, IL: Southern Illinois University Press.
Dickens, C. (2006). *A Christmas carol and other Christmas books* (Ed. R. Douglas-Fairhurst). Oxford: Oxford University Press.
Dickinson, E. (1961). *Final harvest: Emily Dickinson's poems*. Boston: Little, Brown, and Co.
Dillard, A. (1977). *Holy the firm*. New York: Harper & Row.
Dōgen. (1982). *Shōbōgenzō: Zen essays of Dōgen* (Trans. T. Cleary). Honolulu: University of Hawaii Press.
Dōgen. (2007). *Sansuigkō*. In Vol. 1 of *Shōbōgenzō: The true dharma-eye treasury* (Trans. G. W. Nishijima & C. Cross) (pp. 217-27). Berkeley, CA: Numata Center for Buddhist Translation and Research.
Dollimore, J. (1991). *Sexual dissidence: Augustine to Wilde, Freud to Foucault*. Oxford: Oxford University Press.
Driver, J. (1996). The virtues and human nature. In R. Crisp (Ed.), *How should one live? Essays on the virtues* (pp. 111-29). Oxford: Oxford University Press.
Durrell, L. (1988). Foreword. In *The journey's echo: Selections from Freya Stark* (pp. xi-xii). New York: Ecco Press.
Eckermann, J. P. (1875). *Conversations of Goethe* (Trans. J. Oxenford). London: George Bell & Sons.
Eco, U. (1989). *The open work* (Trans. A. Cancogni). Cambridge, MA: Harvard University Press.
Eichberg, H. (2018). Play against alienation? In W. Russell, E. Ryle, & M. Maclean (Eds.), *The philosophy of play as life* (pp. 211-26). New York: Routledge.
Eigen, M. (1993). Omniscience. In A. Phillips (Ed.), *The electrified tightrope* (pp. 243-57). Northvale, NJ: Jason Aronson.

Eigen, M. (2021). *Eigen in Seoul, volume three: Pain and beauty, terror and wonder*. New York: Routledge.

Einstein, A. (1990). From Living Philosophies (1931). In C. Fadiman (Ed.), *Living philosophies: The reflections of some eminent men and women of our time* (pp. 3-6). New York: Doubleday.

Embrico of Mainz. (1935). *Vita Mahumeti* (Ed. F. Hubner), *Historische Vierteljahrschrift 29*, 441-90.

Emerson, R. W. (1957). *Selections from Ralph Waldo Emerson: An organic anthology* (Ed. S. E. Whicher). Boston, MA: Houghton Mifflin Company.

Emerson, R. W. (1975). *The journals and miscellaneous notebooks of Ralph Waldo Emerson: 1848-1851* (Ed. W. H. Gilman). Cambridge, MA: Harvard University Press.

Emerson, R. W. (1992). Experience. In B. Atkinson (Ed.), *The selected writings of Ralph Waldo Emerson* (pp. 307-26). New York: Modern Library.

Emerson, R. W. (1992). Intellect. In B. Atkinson (Ed.), *The selected writings of Ralph Waldo Emerson* (pp. 263-73). New York: Modern Library.

Emerson, R. W. (1992). Nature. In B. Atkinson (Ed.), *The selected writings of Ralph Waldo Emerson* (pp. 3-39). New York: Modern Library.

Emerson, R. W. (1992). Nature. In B. Atkinson (Ed.), *The selected writings of Ralph Waldo Emerson* (pp. 364-77). New York: Modern Library.

Emerson, R. W. (1992). Nominalist and realist. In B. Atkinson (Ed.), *The selected writings of Ralph Waldo Emerson* (pp. 390-401). New York: Modern Library.

Emerson, R. W. (1992). Self-reliance. In B. Atkinson (Ed.), *The selected writings of Ralph Waldo Emerson* (pp. 132-53). New York: Modern Library.

Emerson, R. W. (1992). The over-soul. In B. Atkinson (Ed.), *The selected writings of Ralph Waldo Emerson* (pp. 236-51). New York: Modern Library.

Emerson, R. W. (2014). Uses of great men. In J. S. Cramer (Ed.), *The Portable Emerson* (pp. 318-34). New York: Penguin Books.

Epictetus. (1916). *The discourses* (Trans. P. E. Matheson). Oxford: Clarendon Press.

Feezell, R. (2004). *Sport, play, and ethical reflection*. Urbana, IL: University of Illinois Press.

Feldman, C., & Kuyken, W. (2019). *Mindfulness: Ancient wisdom meets modern psychology*. New York: Guilford Press.

Feng, Y. (1950). *A short history of Chinese philosophy* (Trans. D. Bodde). New York: The Macmillan Company.

Feng, Y. (1953). *The period of classical learning.* Vol. 2 of *A history of Chinese philosophy* (Trans. D. Bodde). Princeton, NJ: Princeton University Press.

Fink, E. (1974). The ontology of play. *Philosophy Today, 18*(2), 147-61.

Fink. E. (2003). *Nietzsche's philosophy* (Trans. G. Richter). New York: Continuum.

Fink, E. (2016). Notes on "The world-significance of play." In *Play as symbol of the world and other writings* (Trans. I. A. Moore & C. Turner) (pp. 283-92). Bloomington, IN: Indiana University Press.

Fink, E. (2016). The world-significance of play. In *Play as symbol of the world and other writings* (Trans. I. A. Moore & C. Turner) (pp. 234-48). Bloomington, IN: Indiana University Press.

Flaubert, G. (1980). *The letters of Gustave Flaubert: 1830-1857* (Trans. F. Steegmuller). Cambridge, MA: Harvard University Press.

Foster, N., & Shoemaker, J. (Eds.) (1996). *The roaring stream: A new Zen reader.* Hopewell, NJ: The Ecco Press.

Franklin, A. (2001). Neo-Darwinian leisures, the body, and nature: Hunting and angling in modernity. *Body and Society, 7*(4), 57-76.

Friedmann, G. (1970). *La puissance et la sagesse.* Paris: Gallimard.

Fromm, E. (1973). *The anatomy of human destructiveness.* New York: Henry Holt & Co.

Gadamer, H.-G. (2004). *Truth and method* (Trans. J. Weinsheimer & D. G. Marshall). New York: Continuum.

Gallup, G. (2002). *The 2001 Gallup poll: Public opinion.* Lanham, MD: Rowman & Littlefield.

Gary, R. (1958). *The roots of heaven* (Trans. J. Griffin). New York: Pocket Books.

Gaster, M. (1921). Roumanian tales. Killing of the old men. *Folk-Lore: A Quarterly Review of Myth, Tradition, Institution, and Custom, 32*(3), 213-15.

Gibson, J. J. (1986). *The ecological approach to visual perception.* New York: Psychology Press.

Giedraitis, J. (1990). Treating Treaty Oak. In P. D. Rodbell (Ed.), *Making our cities safe for trees: Proceedings of the fourth urban forestry conference, St. Louis, Missouri, October 15-19, 1989* (pp. 159-63). Washington, D. C.: American Forestry Association.

Gilbert, P. (1989). *Human nature and suffering.* Hove, UK: Lawrence Erlbaum Associates.

Gleber, A. (1999). *The art of taking a walk: Flanerie, literature, and film in Weimar culture.* Princeton, NJ: Princeton University Press.

Goethe, J. W. von (1964). *Selected verse* (Ed. & Trans. D. Luke). New York: Viking Penguin.

Goethe, J. W. von (1971). Cautions for the observer. In R. Matthaei (Ed.) & H. Aach (Ed. & Trans.), *Goethe's color theory* (pp. 57-64). New York: Van Nostrand Reinhold.

Goethe, J. W. von (1982). Maximen und Reflexion. In *Werke* (Hamburger Ausgabe), vol. 12. Munich: deutscher Taschenbuch Verlag.

Goethe, J. W. von (1982). "Vorwort," *Zur Farbenlehre. Didaktischer Teil* (1808). In *Werke* (Hamburger Ausgabe) vol. 13. Munich: deutscher Taschenbuch Verlag.

Goethe, J. W. von. (1985-99). *Sämtliche Werke. Frankfurter Ausgabe* (Ed. F. Apel, H. Birus et al.). 40 vols. Frankfurt a.M.: Deutscher Klassiker Verlag.

Goethe, J. W. von (1992). *Italian journey: 1786–1788*. London: Penguin Classics.

Goethe, J. W. von (1994). Significant help given by an ingenious turn of phrase. In D. Miller (Ed. & Trans.), *Scientific studies. Goethe: The collected works*, vol. 12 (pp. 39-41). Princeton: Princeton University Press.

Goethe, J. W. von (1994). *Scientific studies*. Vol. 12 of D. Miller (Ed. & Trans.), *Goethe: The collected works*. Princeton, NJ: Princeton University Press.

Goethe, J. W. von (2013). *Briefe, 1821-1832*. Vol. 4 of K. R. Mandelkow (Ed.), *Briefe* (Hamburger Ausgabe). Munich: C. H. Beck.

Gontier, N. (2011). Depicting the tree of life: The philosophical and historical roots of evolutionary tree diagrams. *Evolution: Education and Outreach, 4*(3), 515-38.

Gopal, T., Robibero, P., & Yim, D. (2020). The bizarre story of a man who tried to murder a 600-year-old tree. *CNN*. Retrieved from: https://www.cnn.com/2020/08/30/us/treaty-oak-gbs-great-big-story-trnd/index.html.

Graham, A. C. (1989). *Disputers of the tao: Philosophical argument in ancient China*. La Salle, IL: Open Court.

Graham, A. C. (Trans.) (2001). *Chuang-tzu: The inner chapters*. Indianapolis, IN: Hackett Publishing Company.

Graves, R. (1967). *Poetic craft and principle*. London: Cassell.

Greeley, A. (1974). *Ecstasy: A way of knowing*. Englewood Cliffs, N.J.: Prentice-Hall.

Griffero, T. (2020). *Places, affordances, atmospheres: A pathic aesthetics*. New York: Routledge.

Hadash, Y., Segev, N., Tanay, G., Goldstein, P., & Bernstein, A. (2016). The decoupling model of equanimity: Theory, measurement, and test in a mindfulness intervention. *Mindfulness, 7*(5), 1214-26.

Hadot, P. (2009). *The present alone is our happiness: Conversations with Jeannie Carlier and Arnold I. Davidson* (Trans. M. Djaballah). Stanford, CA: Stanford University Press.

Hafiz. (2006). *I heard God laughing: Poems of hope and joy* (Trans. D. Ladinsky). New York: Penguin Books.

Hakuin. (1971). *Selected writings* (Trans. P. B. Yampolsky). New York: Columbia University Press.

Hanner, O. (Ed.) (2020). *Buddhism and scepticism: Historical, philosophical, and comparative perspectives.* Bochum/Freiburg, Germany: projekt verlag.

Harberd, N. (2006). *Seed to seed: The secret life of plants.* New York: Bloomsbury Publishing.

Harding, D. E. (2014). *On having no head: Zen and the rediscovery of the obvious.* London: The Shollond Trust.

Hartmann, N. (2014). *Aesthetics* (Trans. E. Kelly). Berlin: De Gruyter.

Hegel, G. W. F. (1949). *The phenomenology of mind* (Trans. J. B. Baillie). London: George Allen & Unwin.

Hegel, G. W. F. (1970). *Hegel's philosophy of nature* (Ed. & Trans. M. J. Petry). 3 vols. New York: Humanities Press, 1970.

Heidegger, M. (1962). *Being and time* (Trans. J. Macquarrie & E. Robinson). New York: Harper & Row.

Heidegger, M. (1966). *Discourse on thinking* (Trans. J. M. Anderson & E. H. Freund). New York: Harper & Row.

Heidegger, M. (1968). *What is called thinking?* (Trans. F. D. Wieck & J. G. Gray). New York: Harper & Row.

Heidegger, M. (1977). Building dwelling thinking (Trans. A. Hofstadter). In D. F. Krell (Ed.), *Basic writings* (pp. 319-39). New York: Harper & Row.

Heidegger, M. (1977). Science and reflection (Trans. W. Lovitt). In *The question concerning technology and other essays* (pp. 155-82). New York: Garland.

Heidegger, M. (1991). *The principle of reason* (Trans R. Lilly). Bloomington, IN: Indiana University Press.

Heidegger, M. (2003). Why Do I Stay in the Provinces? (Trans. T. J. Sheehan). In M. Strasser (Ed.), *Philosophical and political writings* (pp. 16-18). New York: Continuum.

Herbert, Z. (2007). *The collected poems: 1956-1998* (Ed. & Trans. A. Valles). New York: HarperCollins Publishers.

Heschel, A. J. (1951). *Man is not alone: A philosophy of religion.* New York: Farrar, Straus and Giroux.

Hesse, H. (1972). *Wandering: Notes and sketches* (Trans. J. Wright). New York: Farrar, Straus and Giroux.

Hesse, H. (1974). *My belief: Essays on life and art* (Ed. T. Ziolkowski & Trans. D. Lindley). New York: Farrar, Straus and Giroux.

Hesse, H. (1974). *Reflections* (Trans. R. Manheim). New York: Farrar, Straus and Giroux.

Hessel, F. (2017). *Walking in Berlin: A flaneur in the capital.* Cambridge, MA: MIT Press.

Hildebert of Lavardin (1854). *Vita Beatae Mariae Aegyptiacae.* In J.-P. Migne (Ed.), *Patrologia Latina* 171: 1321-1340.

Hirota, D. (ed.). (1995). *Wind in the pines: Classic writings of the Way of Tea as a Buddhist path.* Kyoto: Asian Humanities Press.

Hobbes, T. (1991). *Leviathan* (Ed. R. Tuck). Cambridge, UK: Cambridge University Press.

Hoff, H., & Pötzl, O. (1939/1988). Time acceleration in brain disease. In J. W. Brown (Ed.), *Agnosia and apraxia: Selected papers of Liepmann, Lange and Pötzl.* Hillsdale, NJ: Lawrence Erlbaum.

Hofmannsthal, H. von (1952). From the "book of friends." In *Selected prose* (Trans. M. Hottinger & T. & J. Stern) (pp. 349-74). New York: Pantheon Books.

Holdrege, C. (2013). *Thinking like a plant: A living science for life.* Great Barrington, MA: Lindisfarne Books.

Hongzhi, Z. (1991). *Cultivating the empty field: The silent illumination of Zen Master Hongzhi* (Trans. T. D. Leighton). New York: Tuttle.

Hori, V. S. (2003). *Zen sand: The book of capping phrases for koan practice.* Honolulu, HA: University of Hawai'i Press.

Huang Po. (1958). *The Zen teaching of Huang Po: On the transmission of mind* (Trans. J. Blofeld). New York: Grove Press.

Hui Hai. (2015). *Zen teaching of instantaneous awakening* (Trans. J. Blofeld). Totnes, UK: Buddhist Publishing Group.

Huizinga, J. (1950). *Homo ludens: A study of the play-impulse in culture.* New York: Roy Publishers.

Hume, D. (2007). *A treatise of human nature: A critical edition* (Ed. D. F. Norton & M. J. Norton). Oxford: Clarendon Press.

Hurst, H. (1899). *Oxford topography: An essay.* Oxford: Clarendon Press.

Husserl, E. (1989). *Studies in the phenomenology of constitution*. Bk. 2 of *Ideas pertaining to a pure phenomenology and to a phenomenological philosophy* (Trans. R. Rojcewicz & A. Schuwer). Dordrecht: Kluwer Academic.
Hutton, E. L. (Trans.) (2014). *Xunzi: The complete text*. Princeton, NJ: Princeton University Press.
Huxley, A. (1974). *The art of seeing*. London: Chatto & Windus.
Huxley, A. (2009). *Island: A novel*. New York: HarperCollins.
Iguchi Kaisen (2020). *Rikyū's hundred verses in Japanese and English* (Trans. G. Mittwer). Kyoto: Tankosha Publishing.
Ikkyū Sōjun. (1989). *Crow with no mouth* (Trans. S. Berg). Port Townsend, WA: Copper Canyon Press.
Inglis, D. (2004). Meditations on sport: On the trail of Ortega y Gasset's philosophy of sportive existence. *Journal of the Philosophy of Sport, 31*(1), 78-96.
Ingold, T. (2000). *The perception of the environment: Essays on livelihood, dwelling and skill*. New York: Routledge.
Irigaray, L. (2002). *Between east and west: From singularity to community* (Trans. S. Pluháček). New York: Columbia University Press.
Irigaray, L., & Marder, M. (2016). *Through vegetal being: Two philosophical perspectives*. New York: Columbia University Press.
Jacobson, E. (1934). *You must relax: A practical method of reducing the strains of modern living*. New York: McGraw-Hill.
James, W. (1897). *Will to believe and other essays in popular philosophy*. New York: Longmans Green and Co.
James, W. (1911/1996). *Some problems in philosophy: A beginning of an introduction to philosophy*. Lincoln, NE: University of Nebraska Press.
James, W. (1912). Does "consciousness" exist? In *Essays in radical empiricism* (pp. 1-38). New York: Longmans, Green and Company.
James, W. (1912). On a certain blindness in human beings. In *On some of life's ideals* (pp. 3-46). New York: Henry Holt and Company.
James, W. (1912). The thing and its relations. In *Essays in radical empiricism* (pp. 92-122). New York: Longmans, Green and Company.
Jaspers, K. (1954). *The way to wisdom: An introduction to philosophy* (Trans. R. Manheim). New Haven, CT: Yale University Press.
Jenks, C. (1995). Watching your step: The history and practice of the flâneur. In C. Jenks (Ed.), *Visual culture* (pp. 142-60). New York: Routledge.
Jerome. (1933). *Select letters* (Trans. F. A. Wright). New York: G. P. Putnam's Sons.

Jonas, H. (1954). The nobility of sight: A study in the phenomenology of the senses. *Philosophy and Phenomenological Research, 14*(4), 507-19.

Jullien, F. (2004). *A treatise on efficacy: Between Western and Chinese thinking* (Trans. J. Lloyd). Honolulu: University of Hawai'i Press.

Juneau, C., Shankland, R., Knäuper, B. & Dambrun, M. (2021) Mindfulness and equanimity moderate approach/avoidance motor responses. *Cognition and Emotion, 35*(6), 1085-1098.

Juvenal. (1974). *The sixteen satires* (Trans. P. Green). New York: Penguin.

Kafka, F. (1991). *The blue octavo notebooks* (Trans. E. Kaiser & E. Wilkins). Cambridge, MA: Exact Exchange.

Kant, I. (1991). *The metaphysics of morals* (Trans. M. Gregor). Cambridge: Cambridge University Press.

Kasamatsu, A., & Hirai, T. (1966). An electroencephalographic study on the Zen meditation (Zazen). *Psychiatry and Clinical Neurosciences, 20*(4), 315-36.

Katagiri, D. (2007). *Each moment is the universe: Zen and the way of being time* (Ed. A. Martin). Boston, MA: Shambhala Publications.

Kato, S. (1971). *Form, style, tradition: Reflections on Japanese art and society* (Trans. J. Bester). Berkeley, CA: University of California Press.

Katz, L. (1970). Matisse, Picasso, and Gertrude Stein. In *Four Americans in Paris: The collections of Gertrude Stein and her family* (pp. 51-64). New York: The Museum of Modern Art.

Keats, J. (1925). *Letters of John Keats to his family and friends* (Ed. S. Colvin). London: Macmillan and Company.

Kierkegaard, S. (2008). *Journal EE.* In vol. 2 of K. B. Söderquist & B. H. Kirmmse (Eds.), *Kierkegaard's journals and notebooks* (Trans. G. Pattison) (pp. 3-65). 6 vols. Princeton, NJ: Princeton University Press.

Kipling, R. (2013). *100 poems: Old and new* (Ed. T. Pinney). Cambridge: Cambridge University Press.

Kirsch, A. M. (1891). Cytology of cellular biology. *The Microscope, 11*(3), 65-70.

Kishida Kembu. (1973). *Hōmyaku gendai zen sho retsudan* [Pulse of the law: Modern Zen biographies]. Kyoto: Chugai Nipponsha.

Koestler, A. (1964). *The act of creation.* New York: Macmillan Company.

Kornfield, J. (2017). *No time like the present: Finding freedom, love, and joy right where you are.* New York: Atria Books.

Krishnamurti, J. (1969). *Freedom from the known.* New York: Harper and Row.

Kristeva, J. (1998). The subject in process. In P. ffrench & R.-F. Lack (Eds.), *The Tel Quel reader* (pp. 133-78). New York: Routledge.

Kusumoto Bunyu. (1982). *Zengo Nyūmon: An introduction to Zen words and phrases*. Tokyo: Daihōrin-kaku Co. Ltd.

Lacoue-Labarthe, P. (1998). The echo of the subject. In *Typography: mimesis, philosophy, politics* (Trans. C. Fynsk). Stanford: Stanford University Press.

Lawrence, D. H. (1936). Review of The social basis of consciousness. In E. D. MacDonald (Ed.), *Phoenix: The posthumous papers of D. H. Lawrence* (pp. 377-82). London: William Heinemann.

Lawrence, D. H. (1962). *Collected letters of D. H. Lawrence* (Ed. H. T. Moore). New York: Viking.

Lawrence, D. H. (1983). Why the novel matters. In B. Steele (Ed.), *Study of Thomas Hardy and other essays* (pp. 193-98). Cambridge: Cambridge University Press.

Lewis, C. S. (1960). *The four loves*. New York: Harcourt, Brace, & World.

Lewis, M. (2016). *The undoing project: A friendship that changed our minds*. New York: W. W. Norton.

Lieh-tzu. (1990). *The book of Lieh-tzu: A classic of the Tao* (Trans. A. C. Graham). New York: Columbia University Press.

Lima, M. (2014). *The book of trees: Visualizing the branches of knowledge*. New York: Princeton Architectural Press.

Lin-chi. (1993). *The Zen teachings of Master Lin-chi: A translation of the Lin-chi Lu* (Trans. B. Watson). Boston, MA: Shambhala.

Loewald, H. W. (1988). *Sublimation: Inquiries into theoretical psychoanalysis*. New Haven, CT: Yale University Press.

Lucian of Samosata (1905). The way to write history. In vol. 2 of *The works of Lucian of Samosata* (Trans. H. W. Fowler & F. G. Fowler) (pp. 109-36). 4 vols. Oxford: Clarendon Press.

Lyotard, J.-F. (1984). *Driftworks* (Ed. R. McKeon). New York: Semiotext(e).

Lyotard, J.-F. (1991). *The inhuman: Reflections on time* (Trans. G. Bennington & R. Bowlby). Stanford, CA: Stanford University Press.

Mace, W. (1977). James Gibson's strategy for perceiving: Ask not what's inside your head, but what your head's inside of. In R. Shaw & J. Bransford (Eds.), *Perceiving, acting and knowing: Toward an ecological psychology* (pp. 43-66). Mahwah, NJ: Lawrence Erlbaum.

Mahoney, B. (2012). Like a new knowledge of reality: Stevens' poetry at the end of the mind. *Wallace Stevens Journal*, 36(2), 225-41.

Mansell, C. M., Dakhloul, M. & Ismail, F. (2018). A view from above: Balloon mapping Bourj Al Shamali. In *This is not an atlas: A global collection of counter-cartographies* (Ed. Kollectiv Orangotango+) (pp. 54-56). Bielefeld, Germany: Transcript Verlag.

Marcel, G. (1951). *Homo viator: Introduction to a metaphysic of hope* (Trans. E. Craufurd). Chicago, IL: Henry Regnery Co.

Marder, M. (2012). Plant intentionality and the phenomenological framework of plant intelligence. *Plant Signaling & Behavior, 7*(11), 1365-72.

Marder, M. (2013). Plant intelligence and attention. *Plant Signaling & Behavior, 8*(5), e23902.

Marder, M. (2013). *Plant-Thinking: A philosophy of vegetal life.* New York: Columbia University Press.

Maritain, J. (1953). *Creative intuition in art and poetry.* Princeton, NJ: Princeton University Press.

Maslow, A. H. (1966). *The psychology of science: A reconnaissance.* New York: Harper & Row.

Maslow, A. H. (1979). *The journals of A. H. Maslow.* (Ed. R. J. Lowry). 2 vols. Monterey, CA: Brooks/Cole Publishing.

Maslow, A. H. (1999). *Toward a psychology of being* (3rd Ed.). New York: John Wiley & Sons.

Maslow, B. G. (Ed.) (1972). *Abraham H. Maslow: A memorial volume.* Monterey, CA: Brooks/Cole Publishing.

Massie, P. (2013). Philosophy and ataraxia in Sextus Empiricus. *PEITHO / Examina Antiqua, 1*(4), 211-34.

McCullough, D. (2015). *The Wright brothers.* New York: Simon & Schuster.

McGilchrist, I. (2019). *The master and his emissary: The divided brain and the making of the Western world.* New Haven, CT: Yale University Press.

Meier, K. V. (1980) An affair of flutes: An appreciation of play. *Journal of the Philosophy of Sport, 7*(1), 24-45.

Meister Eckhart. (2009). *The complete mystical works of Meister Eckhart* (Ed. & Trans. M. O'C. Walshe; Rev. B. McGinn). New York: Herder & Herder.

Merleau-Ponty, M. (1962). *The phenomenology of perception* (Trans. C. Smith). London: Routledge.

Merleau-Ponty, M. (1963). *The structure of behavior* (Trans. A. L. Fisher). Boston, MA: Beacon.

Merleau-Ponty, M. (1964). Cézanne's doubt. In *Sense and non-sense* (Trans. H. L. Dreyfus & P. A. Dreyfus) (pp. 9-25). Evanston, IL: Northwestern University Press.

Merleau-Ponty, M. (1964). Eye and mind (Trans. C. Dallery). In *The primacy of perception and other essays on phenomenological psychology, the*

philosophy of art, history and politics (Ed. J. M. Edie) (pp. 159-90). Evanston, IL: Northwestern University Press.
Merleau-Ponty, M. (1964). The film and the new psychology. In *Sense and non-sense* (Trans. H. L. Dreyfus & P. A. Dreyfus) (pp. 48-59). Evanston, IL: Northwestern University Press.
Merleau-Ponty, M. (1964). The primacy of perception and its philosophical consequences (Trans. J. M. Edie). In *The primacy of perception and other essays on phenomenological psychology, the philosophy of art, history and politics* (Ed. J. M. Edie) (pp. 12-42). Evanston, IL: Northwestern University Press.
Merleau-Ponty, M. (1968). *The visible and the invisible* (Ed. C. Lefort; Trans. A. Lingis). Evanston, IL: Northwestern University Press.
Merrell-Wolff, F. (1973). *Pathways through to space: A personal record of transformation in consciousness*. New York: Julian Press.
Meyer, M. (Tr.) (1992). *The Gospel of Thomas: The hidden sayings of Jesus*. New York: Harper.
Mill, J. S. (2015). *On liberty, Utilitarianism, and other essays* (Ed. M. Philp & F. Rosen). Oxford: Oxford University Press.
Millar, S. (1968). *The psychology of play*. New York: Penguin.
Miller, E. P. (2002). *The vegetative soul: From philosophy of nature to subjectivity in the feminine*. Albany, NY: State University of New York Press.
Miller, H. (1957). *Big Sur and the oranges of Hieronymus Bosch*. New York: New Directions Books.
Moholy-Nagy, L. (1932). *The new vision: From material to architecture*. New York: Brewer, Warren and Putnam, Inc.
Moholy-Nagy, L. (1947). *Vision in motion*. Chicago, IL: Paul Theobald.
Monod, J. (1971). *Chance and necessity: Essay on the natural philosophy of modern biology*. New York: Alfred A. Knopf.
Morrison, T. (2007). The bird is in your hands. In *Nobel lectures from the literature laureates, 1986 to 2006* (pp. 182-90). New York: New Press.
Muir, J. (1954). *The wilderness world of John Muir: A selection from his collected work* (Ed. E. W. Teale). Boston, MA: Houghton Mifflin.
Murdoch, I. (1999). On "God" and "Good."' In P. Conradi (Ed.), *Existentialists and mystics: Writings on philosophy and literature* (pp. 337-62). New York: Penguin Books.
Nagel, T. (1986). *The view from nowhere*. Oxford: Oxford University Press.
Nakamura, H. (1964). *Ways of thinking of Eastern peoples: India, China, Tibet, Japan* (Trans. P. P. Wiener). Honolulu, HI: East-West Center Press.

Nealon, J. T. (2016). *Plant theory: Biopower and vegetable life*. Stanford, CA: Stanford University Press.

Needham, J. (1956). *History of scientific thought*. Vol. 2 of *Science and civilization in China*. Cambridge: Cambridge University Press.

Nehamas, A. (1985). *Nietzsche: Life as literature*. Cambridge, MA: Harvard University Press.

Nelson, R. (1994). Life ways of the hunter. In J. White (Ed.), *Talking on the water: Conversations about nature and creativity* (pp. 79-97). San Francisco, CA: Sierra Club Books.

Nhat Hanh, T. (1987). *The miracle of mindfulness: An introduction to the practice of meditation* (Trans. M. Ho). Boston, MA: Beacon Press.

Nietzsche, F. (1966). *Thus spoke Zarathustra: A book for all and none* (Trans. W. Kaufmann). New York: Viking.

Nietzsche, F. (1967). *On the genealogy of morals* (Trans. W. Kaufmann & R. J. Hollingdale). New York: Random House.

Nietzsche, F. (1974). *The gay science, with a prelude in rhymes and an appendix of songs* (Trans. W. Kaufmann). New York: Random House.

Nietzsche, F. (1980). *Nachgelassene Fragmente, 1880-1882*. Vol. 9 of *Sämtliche Werke: Kritische Studienausgabe* (Ed. G. Colli & M. Montinari). 15 vols. Munich: de Gruyter.

Nietzsche, F. (1982). *Daybreak: Thoughts on the prejudices of morality* (Trans. R. J. Hollingdale). Cambridge: Cambridge University Press.

Nietzsche, F. (1982). Nietzsche contra Wagner: Out of the files of a psychologist. In W. Kaufmann (Ed. & Trans.), *The portable Nietzsche* (pp. 661-83). New York: Viking Penguin.

Nietzsche, F. (1986). *Human, all too human: A book for free spirits* (Trans. R. J. Hollingdale). Cambridge: Cambridge University Press.

Nietzsche, F. (1988). *Die Geburt der Tragödie*. In vol. 1 of G. Colli & M. Montinari (Eds.), *Sämtliche Werke: Kritische Studienausgabe* (pp. 11-156). Munich: Deutscher Taschenbuch Verlag.

Noë, A. (2004). *Action in perception*. Cambridge, MA: MIT Press.

Noë, A. (2008). Précis of Action in Perception. *Philosophy and Phenomenological Research, 76*(3), 660-65.

Norman, K. R. (Trans.). (2001). *The Group of Discourses (Sutta-nipāta)*. 2nd Ed. Oxford, UK: Pali Text Society.

Northrop, F. S. C. (1964). The undifferentiated aesthetic continuum. *Philosophy East and West, 14*(1), 67-71.

Nussbaum, M. C. (1994). *The therapy of desire: Theory and practice in Hellenistic ethics*. Princeton, NJ: Princeton University Press.

Oelschlaeger, M. (1991). *The idea of wilderness: From prehistory to the age of ecology*. New Haven, CT: Yale University Press.

Ogden, C. K., Richards, I. A., & Wood, J. (1925). *Foundations of aesthetics* (2nd Ed.). New York: International Publishers.

Okakura Kakuzō. (1956). *The book of tea*. Rutland, VT: Charles E. Tuttle.

Ong, W. J. (1969). World as view and world as event. *American Anthropologist, 71*(4), 634-47.

Ortega y Gasset, J. (1932). In search of Goethe from within: Letter to a German (Trans. W. Trask). In W. Phillips & P. Rahv (Eds.), *The New Partisan reader, 1945-1953: An anthology* (pp. 289-313). New York: Harcourt, Brace and Company.

Ortega y Gasset, J. (1942/1985). *Meditations on hunting* (Trans. H. B. Wescott). New York: Charles Scribner's Sons.

Ortega y Gasset, J. (1948). *The dehumanization of art and notes on the novel* (Trans. H. Weyl). Princeton, NJ: Princeton University Press.

Ortega y Gasset, J. (1957). *Man and people* (Trans. W. R. Trask). New York: W. W. Norton and Co.

Ortega y Gasset, J. (1957). *The revolt of the masses* (Trans. T. Carey). New York: W. W. Norton and Co.

Ortega y Gasset, J. (1960). *What is philosophy?* (Trans. M. Adams). New York: W. W. Norton and Co.

Ortega y Gasset, J. (1961). *Meditations on Quixote* (Trans. E. Rugg & D. Marín). New York: W. W. Norton and Co.

Ortega y Gasset, J. (1984). *Historical reason* (Trans. P. W. Silver). New York: W. W. Norton and Co.

O'Shaughnessy, B. (1989). The sense of touch. *Australasian Journal of Philosophy, 67*(1), 37-58.

Pang, Y. (2011). *The Sayings of Layman P'ang: A Zen classic of China* (Trans. J. Green). Boston, MA: Shambhala.

Parkes, C. M. (1971). Psychosocial transitions: A field for study. *Social Science & Medicine, 5*(2), 101-15.

Pascal, B. (1995). *Pensées and other writings* (Trans. H. Levi). Oxford: Oxford University Press.

Pauley, J. A. (2003). The value of hunting. *The Journal of Value Inquiry, 37*, 233-44.

Peterson, J. B., Smith, K. W., & Carson, S. (2002). Openness and extraversion are associated with reduced latent inhibition: Replication and commentary. *Personality and Individual Differences, 33*, 1137-47.

Plutarch. (1936). *The E at Delphi*. In vol. 5 of *Moralia* (Trans. F. C. Babbitt) (pp. 194-253). Cambridge, MA: Harvard University Press.

Quine, W. V. (1961). Two dogmas of empiricism. In W. V. Quine, *From a logical point of view: Nine logico-philosophical essays* (pp. 20-46). Cambridge, MA: Harvard University Press.

Ram Dass. (2013). *Polishing the mirror: How to live from your spiritual heart*. Boulder, CO: Sounds True.

Rancière, J. (1994). Discovering new worlds: Politics of travel and metaphors of space. In G. Robertson, M. Mash, L. Tickner, J. Bird, B. Curtis & T. Putnam (Eds.), *Travellers' Tales: Narratives of home and displacement* (pp. 27-35). New York: Routledge.

Ratcliffe, M. (2010). The phenomenology of mood and the meaning of life. In P. Goldie (Ed.), *The Oxford handbook of philosophy of emotion* (pp. 349-71). Oxford: Oxford University Press.

Rawls, J. (1971). *A theory of justice*. Cambridge, MA: Harvard University Press.

Renan, E. (1948). *Oeuvres complètes*. 10 vols. Paris: Calmann-Lévy.

Rilke, R. M. (1949). *The notebooks of Malte Laurids Brigge* (Trans. M. D. Herter Norton). New York: W. W. Norton & Company.

Rilke, R. M. (2011). *Selected poems with parallel German text* (Ed. R. Vilain; Trans. S. Ranson & M. Sutherland). Oxford: Oxford University Press.

Rimbaud, A. (2005). *Complete works, selected letters: A bilingual edition* (Trans. W. Fowlie). Chicago: University of Chicago Press.

Robinson, A. (2002). *The man who deciphered Linear B: The story of Michael Ventris*. London: Thames & Hudson.

Rodrigues, D. (2020). The cracked pot. Retrieved from: http://www.barry4kids.net/LER/UK/ler_contos_cantaro_rachado_uk.html

Rumi. (1997). *The essential Rumi* (Trans. C. Barks). Edison, NJ: Castle Books.

Russell, B. (1998). *The problems of philosophy*. 2nd Ed. Oxford: Oxford University Press.

Santayana, G. (1940). *The realm of spirit: Book fourth of* Realms of Being. London: Constable and Company.

Sartre, J.-P. (1964). *Nausea* (Trans. L. Alexander). New York: New Directions.

Sartre, J.-P. (1994). *Being and nothingness* (Trans. H. E. Barnes). New York: Gramercy Books.

Sasaki Joshu. (1974). *Buddha is the center of gravity* (Trans. F. Akino). San Cristobal, NM: Lama Foundation.

Schlegel, F. (2003). Athenaeum fragments. In J. M. Bernstein (Ed.), *Classical and romantic German aesthetics* (pp. 246-60). Cambridge: Cambridge University Press.

Schopenhauer, A. (1969). *The world as will and representation* (Trans. E. F. J. Payne). New York: Dover.

Schrödinger, E. (1992). *What is life? with Mind and matter and Autobiographical sketches*. Cambridge: Cambridge University Press.

Seneca, L. A. (2014). On the constancy of the wise person (Trans. J. Ker). In *Hardship and happiness* (pp. 141-74). Chicago, IL: University of Chicago Press.

Sertillanges, A. (1950). *Recollection* (Trans. Dominican Nuns of Corpus Christi Monastery). New York: McMullen Books.

Severinus, P. (1571). *Idea medicinae philosophicae, fundamenta continens totius doctrinae Paracelsinae, Hippocraticae et Galienicae*. Basel: Ex officina Sixti Henricpetri.

Sextus Empiricus. (2000). *Outlines of scepticism* (Ed. J. Annas & J. Barnes). Cambridge: Cambridge University Press.

Shah, I. (1970). Pomegranates. In *The dermis probe* (pp. 92-93). London: Jonathan Cape.

Shah, I. (1972). *The exploits of the incomparable Mulla Nasrudin*. New York: E. P. Dutton.

Shah, I. (1972). *The magic monastery: Analogical and action philosophy in the Middle East and central Asia*. New York: E. P. Dutton.

Shah, I. (2015). *Caravan of dreams*. London: ISF Publishing.

Shotter, J. (2005). Goethe and the refiguring of intellectual inquiry: From 'aboutness'-thinking to 'withness'-thinking in everyday life. *Janus Head, 8*(1), 132-58.

Shōyō Roku: Gendai-go yaku (Book of Serenity: A contemporary translation) (2003). (Trans. Harada Hiromichi). Tokyo: Daizō Shuppan.

Sicart, M. (2014). *Play matters*. Cambridge, MA: MIT Press.

Siegel, D. J. (2010). *The mindful therapist: A clinician's guide to mindsight and neural integration*. New York: W. W. Norton.

Silesius, A. (1986). *The cherubinic wanderer* (Trans. M. Shrady). New York: Paulist Press.

Simic, C. (2008). *The monster loves his labyrinth: Notebooks*. Keene, NY: Ausable Press.

Simmel, G. (2010). Journal aphorisms, with an introduction (Trans. J. A. Y. Andrews). In *The view of life: Four metaphysical essays* (pp. 155-88). Chicago, IL: University of Chicago Press.

Simmel, G. (2020). Kant and modern aesthetics. In A. Harrington (Ed.), *Essays on art and aesthetics* (pp. 108-20). Chicago, IL: University of Chicago Press.

Skinner, C. M. (1911). *Myths and legends of flowers, trees, fruits, and plants in all ages and in all climes*. Philadelphia: J. B. Lippincott Company.

Sorabji, R. (2000). *Emotion and peace of mind: From stoic agitation to Christian temptation*. Oxford: Oxford University Press.

Stein, G. (1898). Cultivated motor automatism: A study of character in its relation to attention. *Psychological Review, 5*(3), 295-306.

Steiner, G. (1978). *Has truth a future?* London: British Broadcasting Corporation.

Steiner, R. (1947). *Paths to knowledge of higher worlds* (Trans. D. S. Osmond). London: Anthroposophic Publishing Company.

Steiner, R. (2006). *The philosophy of freedom: The basis for a modern world conception* (Trans. M. Wilson). London: Rudolf Steiner Press.

Steiner, R. (2008). *Goethe's theory of knowledge: An outline of the epistemology of his worldview* (Trans. P. Clemm). Great Barrington, MA: Steiner Books.

Stendhal. (1992). *Mémoires d'un touriste*. In V. Del Litto (ed.), *Voyages en France*. Paris: Gallimard.

Stevens, W. (1954). *The collected poems of Wallace Stevens*. New York: Alfred A. Knopf.

Stirner, S. (2019). A technique of closeness, an art of straying: Reading with Walter Benjamin. *New Literary History, 50*(2), 271-91.

Straus, E. W. (1963). *The primary world of senses: A vindication of sensory experience* (Trans. J. Needleman). New York: The Free Press of Glencoe.

Straus, E. W. (1966). The forms of spatiality. In E. Eng (Trans.), *Phenomenological psychology: The selected papers of Erwin W. Straus* (pp. 3-37). New York: Basic Books.

Suits, B. (1978). *The grasshopper: Games, life and utopia*. Toronto: University of Toronto Press.

Suits, B. (1988). Tricky triad: Games, play and sport. *Journal of the Philosophy of Sport, 15*, 1-9.

Sun Ra. (2005). *The immeasurable equation: The collected poetry and prose* (Ed. J. L. Wolf & H. Geerken). Norderstedt: Waitawhile Press.

Sutton-Smith, B. (1997). *The ambiguity of play*. Cambridge, MA: Harvard University Press.

Suzuki, D. T. (1937). *Buddhism in the life and thought of Japan*. London: Buddhist Lodge.

Suzuki, D. T. (1955). Reason and intuition in Buddhist philosophy. In C. Humphreys (Ed.), *Studies in Zen* (pp. 85-128). New York: Philosophical Library.

Suzuki, D. T. (1972). *Living by Zen: A synthesis of the historical and practical aspects of Zen Buddhism*. York Beach, ME: Samuel Weiser.

Tagore, R. (1921). *Thought relics*. New York: Macmillan Company.

Takuan Sōhō. (2012). The marvelous record of immovable wisdom. In *The unfettered mind: Writings from a Zen master to a master swordsman* (Trans. W. S. Wilson) (pp. 1-38). Boston, MA: Shambhala.

Tantillo, J. A. (2001). Sport hunting, eudaimonia, and tragic wisdom. *Philosophy in the Contemporary World, 8*(2), 101-12.

Tashi Tsering, G. (2005). *The four noble truths* (Ed. G. Mcdougall). Somerville, MA: Wisdom Publications.

The book of Leih-tzu: A classic of Tao (Trans. A. C. Graham). (1990). New York: Columbia University Press.

The connected discourses of the Buddha: A new translation of the Saṃyutta Nikāya (Trans. B. Bodhi). (2000). Somerville, MA: Wisdom Publications.

The lotus sutra: A contemporary translation of a Buddhist classic (Trans. G. Reeves). (2008). Boston: Wisdom Publications.

The perfection of wisdom in 700 lines. (1993). Perfect wisdom: The short prajñāpāramitā texts (Trans. E. Conze) (pp. 79-107). Totnes, UK: Buddhist Publishing Group.

The Shurangama Sutra (Trans. Buddhist Text Translation Society). (2002). 8 vols. Burlingame, CA: Buddhist Text Translation Society.

Thiébaux, M. (1967). The mediaeval chase. *Speculum, 42*(2), 260-74.

Thoreau, H. D. (1895). *Familiar letters of Henry David Thoreau* (Ed. F. B. Sanborn). Boston, MA: Houghton Mifflin.

Thoreau, H. D. (1906). *The Journal of Henry David Thoreau* (Ed. B. Torrey). 14 vols. Boston, MA: Houghton Mifflin.

Thoreau, H. D. (2013). Walking. In J. S. Cramer (Ed.), *Essays* (pp. 243-80). New Haven, CT: Yale University Press.

Tien, A. Y. (1991). Distribution of hallucinations in the population. *Social Psychiatry and Psychiatric Epidemiology, 26*(6), 287-92.

Tiyavanich, K. (1997). *Forest recollections: Wandering monks in twentieth-century Thailand*. Honolulu: University of Hawai'i Press.

Trewavas, A. (2003). Aspects of plant intelligence. *Annals of Botany, 92*(1), 1-20.

Tsuchiya Etsudō. (Ed.) (2002). *Zenrin segoshū* [Zen Sangha Vernacular Phrase Collection]. Kyoto: Kichūdō.

Tuan, Y. (1974). *Topophilia: A study of environmental perception, attitudes and values*. New York: Columbia University Press.

Uchiyama Kōshō. (2004). *Opening the hand of thought: Foundations of Zen Buddhist practice* (Ed. & Trans. Tom Wright, Jisho Warner, & Shohaku Okumuro). Somerville, MA: Wisdom Publications.

Ueda, M. (1967). *Literary and art theories in Japan*. Cleveland, OH: The Press of Western Reserve University.

Umewaka Naohiko. (1994). The inner world of the Nō. *Contemporary Theatre Review, 1*(2), 29-38.

Underhill, E. (2010). *The making of a mystic: New and selected letters of Evelyn Underhill* (Ed. C. Poston) Urbana, IL: University of Illinois Press.

Vaihinger, H. (1924). *The philosophy of 'as if': A system of the theoretical, practical and religious fictions of mankind* (Trans. C. K. Ogden). London: Routledge & Kegan Paul.

Valéry, P. (1970). *Analects* (Trans. S. Gilbert). Vol. 14 of *Collected works of Paul Valéry*. Princeton, NJ: Princeton University Press.

Vasubandhu. (1975). *Abhidharmakośabhāṣyam of Vasubandhu* (Ed. P. Pradhan). Tibetan Sanskrit Works 8. Patna: K. P. Jayaswal Research Institute.

Visvanathan, S. (2014, April 23). In praise of walking. *The Times of India*. Retrieved from http://www.thehindu.com/opinion/op-ed/in-praise-ofwalking/article5938019.ece.

von Kleist, H. (1972). On the marionette theatre (Trans. T. G. Neumiller). *The Drama Review, 16*(3), 22-26.

Walpole, H. (1971). *The Yale edition of Horace Walpole's correspondence* (Ed. W. S. Lewis). 48 vols. New Haven: Yale University Press.

Walter of Compiegne. (1956). *Otia de Machomete* (Ed. R. B. C. Huygens), *Sacris Erudiri, 8*, 287-328.

Ward, A. F., Duke, K., Gneezy, A., & Bos, M. W. (2017). Brain drain: the mere presence of one's own smartphone reduces available cognitive capacity. *Journal of the Association for Consumer Research, 2*(2), 140-54.

Watts, A. W. (1951). *The wisdom of insecurity*. New York: Vintage Books.

Watts, A. W. (1957). *The way of Zen*. New York: Vintage Books.

Watts, A. W. (1971). *Psychotherapy East and West*. London: Jonathan Cape.

Watts, A. W. (1997). *Zen and the beat way*. Boston: Tuttle Publishing.

Watts, A. W. (2003). Zen. In M. Watts (Ed.), *Become what you are: Expanded edition* (pp. 57-63). Boston, MA: Shambhala.

Watts, A. W. (2017). The doctrine of emptiness. In *Out of your mind: Tricksters, interdependence, and the cosmic game of hide-and-seek* (pp. 152-58). Boulder, CO: Sounds True.

Wegner, D. M., Schneider, D. J., Carter, S. R., & White, T. L. (1987). Paradoxical effects of thought suppression. *Journal of personality and social psychology, 53*(1), 5-13.

Weschler, L. (2008). *Seeing is forgetting the name of the thing one sees: Over thirty years of conversations with Robert Irwin.* Berkeley, CA: University of California Press.

Wezler, A. (1984). On the Quadruple Division of the Yogaśāstra, the Caturvyūhatva of the Cikitsaśāstra and the "Four Noble Truths" of the Buddha. *Indologica Taurinensia, 12*, 290-337.

White, F. (1987). *The overview effect: Space exploration and human evolution.* Boston, MA: Houghton Mifflin.

White, F. (17 June 2007). Interview. *The Space Show*. Retrieved from https://www.thespaceshow.com/show/16-jun-2017/broadcast-2930-frank-white.

White, F. (2014). *The overview effect: Space exploration and human evolution.* 3rd Ed. Reston, VA: American Institute of Aeronautics and Astronautics.

Whitehead, A. N. (1926). *Religion in the making.* New York: Macmillan.

Whitehead, A. N. (1938). *Modes of thought.* New York: Macmillan.

Whitehead, A. N. (1978). *Process and reality: An essay in cosmology* (Eds. D. R. Griffin & D. W. Sherburne). New York: Free Press.

Whitman, W. (1993). *Leaves of grass: The "death-bed" edition.* New York: Modern Library.

Wilhelm, R. (Trans.) (1989). *I Ching or Book of Changes.* London: Penguin.

Wilson, C. (1969). *Poetry and mysticism.* San Francisco, CA: City Lights Books.

Wilson, C. (1972). *New pathways in psychology: Maslow and the post-Freudian revolution.* New York: The New American Library.

Wilson, C. (2005). *G. I. Gurdjieff: The war against sleep.* London: Aeon Books.

Wilson, C. (2013). *The philosopher's stone.* Richmond, VA: Valancourt Books.

Winnicott, D. W. (1971). *Playing and reality.* London: Tavistock Publications.

Wittgenstein, L. (1958). *Philosophical investigations* (2nd Ed.) (Trans. G. E. M. Anscombe). Oxford, UK: Blackwell Publishers.

Wittgenstein, L. (1993). *Philosophical occasions, 1912-1951* (Ed. J. C. Klagge & A. Nordmann). Indianapolis, IN: Hackett Publishing.

Wood, F. (1997). *The delights and dilemmas of hunting: The hunting versus anti-hunting debate.* Lanham, MD: University Press of America.

Worringer, W. (1953). *Abstraction and empathy: A contribution to the psychology of style* (Trans. M. Bullock). New York: International Universities Press.

Xinyue, S. (1990). *A tune beyond the clouds: Zen teachings from old China* (Trans. J. C. Cleary). Berkeley, CA: Asian Humanities Press.

Yaden, D. B., Iwry, J., Slack, K. J., Eichstaedt, J. C., Zhao, Y., Vaillant, G. E., & Newberg, A. B. (2016). The overview effect: Awe and self-transcendent experience in space flight. *Psychology of Consciousness: Theory, Research, and Practice, 3*(1), 1-11.

Yamada, K. (1979). *Gateless gate: Newly translated with commentary.* Los Angeles, CA: Center Publications.

Zalewska, A. (2015). Expressing the essence of the way of tea: Tanka poems used by tea masters. *Analecta Nipponica, 5,* 43-56.

Zhuangzi. (2013). *The complete works of Zhuangzi* (Trans. B. Watson). New York: Columbia University Press.

Zihl, J., & Heywood, C. A. (2015). The contribution of LM to the neuroscience of movement vision. *Frontiers in Integrative Neuroscience, 9,* 1-13. doi: 10.3389/fnint.2015.00006

Zihl, J., Von Cramon, D., & Mai, N. (1983). Selective disturbance of movement vision after bilateral brain damage. *Brain, 106*(2), 313-40.

Ziporyn, B. (Ed. & Trans.). (2009). *Zhuangzi: The essential writings, with selections from traditional commentaries.* Indianapolis, IN: Hackett Publishing Company.

MIMESIS GROUP
www.mimesis-group.com

MIMESIS INTERNATIONAL
www.mimesisinternational.com
info@mimesisinternational.com

MIMESIS EDIZIONI
www.mimesisedizioni.it
mimesis@mimesisedizioni.it

ÉDITIONS MIMÉSIS
www.editionsmimesis.fr
info@editionsmimesis.fr

MIMESIS COMMUNICATION
www.mim-c.net

MIMESIS EU
www.mim-eu.com

Printed by
Rotomail Italia S.p.A.
June 2025

www.ingramcontent.com/pod-product-compliance
Lightning Source LLC
Chambersburg PA
CBHW021149230426
43667CB00006B/314